Race and American Political Development

Race has been present at every critical moment in American political development, shaping political institutions, political discourse, public policy, and its denizens' political identities. But because of the nature of race—its evolving and dynamic status as a structure of inequality, a political organizing principle, an ideology, and a system of power—we must study the politics of race historically, institutionally, and discursively.

Covering more than three hundred years of American political history from the founding to the contemporary moment, the contributors in this volume make this extended argument. Together, they provide an understanding of American politics that challenges our conventional disciplinary tools of studying politics and our conservative political moment's dominant narrative of racial progress. This volume, the first to collect essays on the role of race in American political history and development, resituates race in American politics as an issue for sustained and broadened critical attention.

Joseph Lowndes is Assistant Professor of Political Science at the University of Oregon. He is author of *From the New Deal to the New Right: Race and the Southern Origins of Modern Conservatism*.

Julie Novkov is Associate Professor of Political Science and Women's Studies at the University of Albany, SUNY. She is the author of *Constituting Workers, Protecting Women* and *Racial Union*, and a co-editor with Bárbara Sutton and Sandra Morgen of *Security Disarmed*.

Dorian T. Warren is Assistant Professor in the Department of Political Science and the School of International and Public Affairs at Columbia University. He is also a Faculty Affiliate at the Institute for Research in African-American Studies and a Faculty Fellow at the Institute for Social and Economic Research and Policy.

Race and American Political Development

Edited by
Joseph Lowndes, Julie Novkov,
and Dorian T. Warren

Routledge
Taylor & Francis Group
NEW YORK AND LONDON

First published 2008
by Routledge
270 Madison Ave, New York, NY 10016

Simultaneously published in the UK
by Routledge
2 Park Square, Milton Park, Abingdon, Oxon OX14 4RN

Routledge is an imprint of the Taylor & Francis Group, an informa business

Typeset in Galliard by
Keystroke, 28 High Street, Tettenhall, Wolverhampton
Printed and bound in the United States of America on acid-free paper by
Edwards Brothers, Inc.

Library of Congress Cataloging in Publication Data
Race and American political development / edited by Joseph Lowndes, Julie Novkov, and Dorian
Warren.
p. cm.
Includes bibliographical references and index.
ISBN 978–0–415–96151–6 (hardback : alk. paper)—ISBN 978–0–415–96153–0 (pbk. : alk.
paper) 1. United States—Race relations—Political aspects. 2. United States—Politics and
government. I. Lowndes, Joseph, 1966– II. Novkov, Julie, 1966– III. Warren, Dorian, 1976–
E185.61.R18 2008
305.896073—dc22
2007045388

ISBN10: 0–415–96151–3 (hbk)
ISBN 10: 0–415–96153–X (pbk)

ISBN13: 978–0–415–96151–6 (hbk)
ISBN 13: 978–0–415–96153–0 (pbk)

Contents

Illustrations

Figures

Table

Contributors

Pamela Brandwein is Associate Professor of Political Science at the University of Michigan. She is the author of the award-winning book, *Reconstructing Reconstruction: The Supreme Court and the Production of Historical Truth* (Duke University Press, 1999). She is currently working on a new book, *The Supreme Court, State Action, and Civil Rights: Rethinking the Judicial Settlement of Reconstruction* (Cambridge University Press, forthcoming), which challenges conventional wisdom about the Supreme Court's settlement of the great debates involving race and rights opened by the Civil War. A piece of this project appeared recently in *Law & Society Review* 41:2 (2007).

Kevin Bruyneel is Associate Professor of Politics in the History & Society Division of Babson College. His main research interests are in the areas of race and ethnicity politics in the United States, indigenous people's politics, settler nationalism, postcolonial theory, and American political development. He is the author of *The Third Space of Sovereignty: The Postcolonial Politics of U.S.–Indigenous Relations* (University of Minnesota Press, Indigenous Americas Series, 2007), which utilizes a postcolonial theoretical framework to examine U.S.–Indigenous relations from the Civil War era to the contemporary era. In the book, Bruyneel shows how this time period is marked by the articulation of modern American colonial rule over indigenous people and by the efforts of indigenous political actors and tribes to resist and transcend the boundaries of colonial rule in the fight to secure and cultivate meaningful sovereignty.

Paul Frymer is Associate Professor of Politics at UC Santa Cruz. He is the author of *Uneasy Alliances: Race and Party Competition in America* and *Black and Blue: African Americans, the Labor Movement, and the Decline of the Democratic Party*.

Kimberley S. Johnson is Assistant Professor of Political Science at Barnard College, Columbia University. She is the author of *Governing the American State: Congress and the New Federalism, 1877–1929* (Princeton University Press, 2006). Her current research project examines southern politics in the pre-Civil Rights Era.

Desmond S. King holds the Andrew W. Mellon Chair of American Government at the University of Oxford and is a Fellow of Nuffield College. His research on American political development includes *Separate and Unequal: African Americans and the U.S. Federal Government* (2007, new edn), *Making Americans: Immigration, Race and the Origins of the Diverse Democracy* (2000), *The Liberty of Strangers: Making the American Nation* (2005), and collaborative work with Rogers M. Smith on the racial orders framework.

Robert C. Lieberman is Professor of Political Science and Public Affairs at Columbia University. He is the author of *Shifting the Color Line: Race and the American Welfare State* and *Shaping Race Policy: The United States in Comparative Perspective.*

Joseph Lowndes is Assistant Professor of Political Science at the University of Oregon. His research interests include institutions, language and identity, and U.S. racial politics. His book, *From the New Deal to the New Right: Race and the Southern Origins of Modern Conservatism* (Yale 2008), analyzes the long-term development of the discourse and practices that linked southern segregationists to economic conservatives in the rise of the modern Republican Party. He teaches courses on American political culture, racial politics, and the presidency.

Daniel Martinez-HoSang is Assistant Professor of Ethnic Studies and Political Science at the University of Oregon. His current book project, *Racial Propositions: Genteel Apartheid in Postwar California* is under contract with the University of California Press. It examines the rise of colorblind ideology in California through a study of racialized statewide ballot initiatives from 1946 to 2003. He teaches courses in racial politics, history, and theory.

Jeffrey Meiser is currently a Ph.D. student in political science at Johns Hopkins University. He holds degrees from Seattle University and the University of California, Santa Barbara. His main research interests lie at the nexus between American political development and international relations. He is currently working on a book manuscript with Richard Young about the institutionalization and collapse of the American republic, 1787–1861.

Sidney M. Milkis is the White Burkett Miller Professor of the Department of Politics and Assistant Director for Academic Programs at the Miller of Public Affairs at the University of Virginia. His books include: *The President and the Parties: The Transformation of the American Party System Since the New Deal* (1993); *Political Parties and Constitutional Government: Remaking American Democracy* (1999); *Presidential Greatness* (2000), coauthored with Marc Landy; and *The American Presidency: Origins and Development, 1776–2007* (2007), 5th edn, coauthored with Michael Nelson; and *American Government: Balancing Democracy and Rights* (2008), 2nd edn, coauthored with Marc Landy. He is the co-editor, with Jerome Mileur, of three volumes on twentieth-century political reform: *Progressivism and the New Democracy* (1999); *The New Deal and the Triumph of Liberalism* (2002); and *The Great Society and the High Tide of Liberalism* (2005). His articles on American government and political history have appeared in *Perspectives on Politics, Political Science Quarterly, Studies in American Political Development, PS: Political Science and Politics,* the *Journal of Policy History, Antitrust Law Journal* and several edited volumes. In addition to teaching graduate and undergraduate students, he regularly gives public lectures on American politics and participates in programs that teach the political history of the United States to international scholars and high school teachers.

Naomi Murakawa is Assistant Professor of Political Science at the University of Washington and a visiting scholar with the Robert Wood Johnson Health Policy Research Program at the University of California, Berkeley. She is broadly interested in racial politics, American political development, and crime policy and the carceral state, and she is currently completing a book manuscript provisionally titled *Electing to Punish: Race and the U.S. Carceral State*.

Julie Novkov is Associate Professor of Political Science and Women's Studies at the University at Albany, SUNY. She is the author of *Constituting Workers, Protecting Women* and *Racial Union: Law, Intimacy, and the White State in Alabama 1865–1954* (both with the University of Michigan Press), and a co-editor with Bárbara Sutton and Sandra Morgen of *Security Disarmed: Critical Perspectives on Gender, Race, and Militarization,* as well as several articles and book chapters addressing the intersections of law, history, U.S. political development, and subordinated identity.

Rogers M. Smith is the Christopher H. Browne Distinguished Professor of Political Science at the University of Pennsylvania. He teaches American constitutional law and American political thought, with special interests in issues of citizenship and racial, gender, and class inequalities. He has published over 100 essays in academic journals, edited volumes and public interest publications, including the *American Political Science Review,* the *Western Political Quarterly, Studies in American Political Development, Daedalus, Social Research, Yale Law Journal,* the *American Prospect,* the *Nation,* and others. He is author or co-author of five books: *Stories of Peoplehood: The Politics and Morals of Political Memberships* (Cambridge University Press, 2003); *The Unsteady March: The Rise and Decline of Racial Equality in America* (with Philip A. Klinkner, 1999); *Civic Ideals: Conflicting Visions of Citizenship in U.S. History* (1997); *Citizenship without Consent: The Illegal Alien in the American Polity* (with Peter H. Schuck, 1985); and *Liberalism and American Constitutional Law* (1985, rev. edn, 1990).

Kathleen Sullivan is Associate Professor of Political Science at Ohio University. She is the author of *Constitutional Context: Women and Rights Discourse in Nineteenth-Century America*, published by Johns Hopkins University Press. Her current research projects address the role of governance in American political development and the role of sex and race in the development of political authority under the police power.

Nancy D. Wadsworth is Assistant Professor of Political Science at the University of Denver, where she studies cultural and historical aspects of American politics. Her current research focuses on the intersection of race and religion in American political culture. She is revising a book project entitled *Ambivalent Miracles: Evangelical Racial Reconciliation Efforts in American Political Culture*. With Professor Robin Jacobson of the University of Puget Sound, she is editing a volume about the intersections of race and religion. She also serves in the Religion and Social Change concentration of DU's Joint Committee with the Iliff School of Theology.

Dorian T. Warren is Assistant Professor in the Department of Political Science and the School of International and Public Affairs at Columbia University. He is also a Faculty Affiliate at the Institute for Research in African-American Studies and a Faculty Fellow at the Institute for Social and Economic Research and Policy. Warren specializes in the study of inequality and American politics, focusing on the political organization of marginalized groups. His research and teaching interests include race and ethnic politics, labor politics, urban politics, American political development, and social science methodology.

Richard Young is Associate Professor of History and Political Science at Seattle University. He did graduate work in American history at Northwestern and Edinburgh Universities before receiving his doctorate in political science from Stanford. He has published in the areas of American race relations and politics and is currently writing a book with Jeffrey Meiser whose working title is *The Anglo-American Republic: 1787–1860*.

Acknowledgments

While this volume has been a collaborative effort among the chapter authors, the collaboration that has produced it extends beyond its pages. It had its inception at a conference on race and U.S. political development held at the University of Oregon on May 18, 2006, where many of the initial chapter drafts were presented. The conference was sponsored and supported by the Department of Political Science and the College of Arts and Sciences at the University of Oregon and the Miller Center for Public Affairs at the University of Virginia. In particular, we thank Gerry Berk and Sidney Milkis for enthusiastically supporting our vision for the conference and ultimately this volume. We are also grateful for the cosponsorship of the Center on Diversity and Community, the Program in Ethnic Studies, the Oregon Humanities Center, the Wayne Morse Center for Law and Politics, and the Center for the Study of Women in Society at the University of Oregon. We also thank the staffs at the EMU and the Jordan Schnitzer Museum of Art for their support and assistance.

Several other scholars presented work at the conference that has critically influenced our own thinking on these questions, and the conference as a whole helped the chapter authors to refine their visions. We therefore thank participants Neal Allen, Robert Bateman, Laura Evans, Edmund Fong, Shamira Gelbman, Matthew Gritter, Victoria Hattam, Ron Hayduk, Matthew Holden, Robin Jacobson, Daniel Lipson, Daniel Mulcare, Joel Olson, Patrick Roberts, Nikhil Singh, Scott Spitzer, and Vesla Weaver. Many of these folks have terrific projects recently out or forthcoming relating to race and political development, and we encourage readers to pursue these works as well as to read this volume.

We have had outstanding support from graduate students at the University of Oregon and Columbia University. Courtney Smith, Sean Parson, and Jennifer Hehnke provided crucial assistance and support with the conference in Eugene. And Quinn Mulroy of Columbia University has been an outstanding assistant editor for the volume.

We also thank Michael Kerns at Routledge for his enthusiastic support for the volume through every stage of the process.

1 Race and American political development

*Joseph Lowndes, Julie Novkov, and
Dorian T. Warren*

Race is present at every critical moment in political development in the
United States, shaping political institutions, political discourse, public policy
and its denizens' political identities. But because of the nature of race—its
evolving and dynamic status as a structure of inequality, a political organizing
principle, an ideology, and a system of power—historical, institutional and
discursive modes of analysis are necessary to study it adequately. Covering more
than three hundred years of American political history, the chapters in this
volume make this sustained argument. Together, they provide an understanding of American politics that challenges our conventional disciplinary tools
for studying politics. Just as important, they challenge the complacency of the
belief—common to political scientists and the American public—that the
United States has steadily moved toward racial equality and inclusion over
the course of its history.

The generations who came of age in the United States since about 1980
have learned a standard liberal history of race. This story, written in black and
white terms, reads as follows: the Revolution and founding together were a
novel moment of visionary political transformation that promised the recognition of freedom and equality. While the founders tragically chose to allow
slavery to persist, they did so to ensure national unity, with many mistakenly
believing that slavery was already on a path toward rapid extinction. Yet slavery
continued and expanded, and the inevitable result was a fratricidal Civil War.
After the war Congress rearticulated the ideals of freedom and equality,
collectively writing these ideals into the Constitution in the Thirteenth,
Fourteenth, and Fifteenth Amendments. This normative vision remained
unfulfilled as southern racists retrenched, and Jim Crow was the result. Nearly
a century later, this narrative has it, the United States Supreme Court finally
recognized the fundamental wrongs of segregation and began to dismantle
it in the *Brown v. Board of Education* decision in 1954. Soon afterward, African
Americans mobilized to demand justice through the civil rights movement.
The federal government responded by finally ending the American state's
longstanding practice of enforcing and institutionalizing racism. The court
decisions and national legislation of the 1960s reversed the flow of nearly two
hundred years of history, bringing American institutions into line with the

"true" American ideals. The subsequent history of racial politics, the story has it, has been marked with legitimate disagreements over the extent to which the state should still see and attend to race.

The widespread acceptance of this reassuring story of progress, invoked with different emphases along most of the conventional political spectrum, helps to explain why those engaged in contemporary struggles over, and the study of, race should reconsider the history of the relationship between race and politics. Race and racialization, or the processes through which racial categories are constructed and imbued with meaning, have defined, delimited, and shaped interactions between cultural beliefs and expressions, individual and collective actions, and governmental policies and practices. Likewise, governmental actions in the U.S.—local, state, and national—have profoundly shaped race and its political significance over time. Thus instead of presenting a triumphalist narrative of progression toward a racially egalitarian society, the authors in this volume make clear that commitments to race and racial hierarchy have also moved in the opposite direction, often producing new forms of exclusion and stratification.

The authors herein understand race as a social construction, but in particular they assume or argue that political interactions have contributed to defining racial categories and determining what meaning race has, taking the concept beyond a psychological sleight-of-hand that allows individuals to classify others by physical characteristics. Rather, these chapters tell how struggles over racial categories and the meaning of these categories have shaped allocations of power and privilege over time. And they show that a dream of a race-free polity ignores how deeply and thoroughly the warp of American politics is interwoven with the woof of race. A central goal of this volume then is to reinterpret what Du Bois called the "problem of the color line" and Myrdal the "American dilemma": how to understand the legacies and constantly transforming manifestations of racial hierarchies as expressed in American politics.

The chapters critique conventional political and historical approaches, but in doing so, generate alternative analyses of race and political development and how to study them. In the remainder of this chapter, we discuss the role of race in the study of American political development, and provide an overview of the book. The next section provides a brief synopsis of the role of race in American political history from what we argue is a racialized political development framework, noting how the chapters in the volume support this history and framework. We then situate this approach within the discipline of political science. Here we argue that an American political development (APD) approach to the study of racial politics expands the range of questions we ask, while centering race within APD fundamentally alters our common understandings of American politics. The last two sections outline the chapters in this volume, suggesting a future and expansive research agenda that those focusing on race and political development can pursue, and briefly discussing how the contributors integrate race and APD in their analyses.

Racialized political development

Rethinking the history of race and politics in the U.S. as these chapters do involves dislodging race from a static, defined scheme of categorization. These chapters focus explicitly on processes of racialization and racialized political development, or how the ideological and material elements of race are produced, negotiated and altered in and through politics. How race has structured and been structured by political institutions, political discourse and public policy has varied. And this focus emphasizes some moments in American political history that have received little sustained attention while not attending as deeply to other moments that are usually seen as transformational. Nonetheless, race has been present on the North American continent and salient in structuring politics and conquest from the arrival of the first English and Spanish colonists in the seventeenth century. The colonists and their governments across the Atlantic distinguished themselves from indigenous American nations, and black chattel slavery arrived in what would become the United States in 1619, less than fifteen years after the founding of the first successful English colony in Jamestown. The first encounters with Native Americans and the establishment of black slavery almost at the outset of European history in North America pointed toward a path that would lead to racial domination and subordination in multiple institutional, cultural, political, and social settings. While historians following Barbara Fields (1982) have highlighted the ideological nature of race in the establishment of this path, the racialized political development frame we endorse focuses the analysis on race's political nature.

The colonial experience highlights the continuity of race's salience over almost five hundred years. However, the early history of racialization also demonstrates the contingency of race as a framework for domination and subordination. In Virginia and elsewhere, colonial authorities debated how to handle slavery and whether it would pass from generation to generation (Wallenstein 2002). Native Americans participated in armed conflicts between European nations as allies and signed treaties with Europeans, but also suffered mass killings and the expropriation of their land. Whiteness as a collective description of English, Dutch, French, Scots, and German settlers, and their descendants developed through these groups' encounters with each other in the political and social context of the colonies, and through their encounters with Native Americans and blacks imported as slaves and descended from slaves (Allen 1997). Indeed, as Edmund Morgan demonstrated, American ideals of freedom and the codification of slavery were co-constitutive, each developing in reference to and in opposition to the other (Morgan 1973).

By the time of the Revolution, racial categories with political significance had emerged. While some still understood themselves primarily as Seneca or Muskogee, Dutch or English, Asante or Dahomey; racial identity was pivotal in defining how these groups related to the political structures that would ground the states and the nation. Likewise, the emerging political entities shaped their institutions around race, particularly with respect to chattel slavery. As the Revolution approached, slavery and blackness became increasingly intertwined until slaves were exclusively understood to be black, although some whites obsessively taxonomized shades of blackness and degrees of descent (Stanton 1960). The Revolutionary era saw the formalization of the white American institutions of the states. While the Revolution did sweep away European colonial dominance in the United States, it maintained the structure of race and racial hierarchy by leaving the organization of most racial institutions to the new sovereign entities of the states. The new classes of nonwhites fought on both sides in the Revolution, but those who took the American side saw few of the fruits of the universal freedom, fundamental equality, and individual autonomy invoked in the Declaration of Independence (Nash 2006).

Some political actors sought to extend the revolutionary ethos to challenge slavery and to extend more political rights to free blacks, but this moment was fleeting (Klinkner and Smith 1999). The design of the Constitution attended carefully to race and actively cemented racial hierarchy into the governing structure of the nation. Core questions over slavery and expansion into "Indian" territory shaped the national structure for governance. Compromises sought to accommodate fundamentally different viewpoints about slavery, and disagreements over slavery strongly marked the new nation's endorsement for a robust version of federalism (Finkelman 2001; Graber 2006). These competing visions also drove a careful balancing of regional power in the national legislature and executive branch, defining politics at the outset as being in part about whether a political actor was from a slaveholding or non-slaveholding political entity. The text of the constitution itself raised the issue of slavery repeatedly, particularly in defining the limited powers of the legislature and committing the national government to acknowledgement and protection of slavery as an institution (Bell 1989; Finkelman 2001).

As Richard Young and Jeffrey Meiser explain in chapter 2, the early Republic and the struggles between Federalists and their opponents coincided with the implementation of the founders' vision of geographic expansion. The newly redesigned nation moved swiftly to acquire territory and organize it into political subdivisions, placing the territory on the path for full political integration and settlement by whites, and in the south, their slaves. The national government pushed Native Americans out of ancestral lands through treaty and conquest, clearing the path for the liberal and optimistic development of the contract state that Alexis de Tocqueville visited and Young and Meiser analyze. As the memories of revolution faded, race became increasingly important as a dividing line among Americans and as a contentious factor in politics in the 1820s and 1830s. The states maintained their sovereignty and transformed conceptions of civic membership by linking white male equality and empowerment to suffrage. Those eligible to participate in selecting executive leadership increasingly turned to Indian fighters, and the first major congressional compromises rearticulated the foundational commitment to protect slavery. While some political actors in the north and south considered abolishing slavery, and others attempted to homogenize the Republic with schemes of black colonization beyond American borders, in collective terms national political actors sought to quell conflict through strategic balancing of state-based representation in Congress. As Kathleen Sullivan describes in chapter 3, federalism increasingly developed to mediate or resolve tensions between slaveholding political entities and societies like Charleston, South Carolina, and those that had rejected slavery, like the maritime and mercantile north. The precedence of slavery politics over ideological commitments about states' rights versus national authority became increasingly clear in conflicts over fugitive slaves. In the 1842 case of *Prigg v. Pennsylvania*, pro-slavery and states' rights champion Roger Taney passionately argued for the dominance of national power over Pennsylvania's autonomous capacity to regulate fact-finding and punish the illegitimate seizure of free blacks.

Almost simultaneously, national institutional debates over whether the United States should seek continental hegemony were resolved in favor of promoting expansion. This took place either through straightforward ideological commitment and political will, as in the persistent prosecution of war against the Seminoles and the national choice to engage the Mexican American War, or through the incapacity of national institutions to check expansion, as in the Supreme Court's failed efforts to protect individual property rights for Cherokees against aggressive ouster by the Georgia legislature. Further, even to the extent that national institutional actors questioned the allocation of rights for people of color or hesitantly suggested enforcement, they mostly hewed to increasingly harsh and hierarchic conceptions of race with significant political consequences. The Supreme Court thus denied full sovereignty to the Cherokees, framing Native Americans as domestic dependents and allowing rampant treaty violations, and saw Africans as full persons with meaningful rights only under circumstances when the state was utterly absent.[1] The interactions among the branches of government over highly charged racial issues also had long-term institutional effects, ranging from shaping the congressional power to regulate commerce to building a heavily militarized state to encouraging but bounding the capacity of the federal courts to resolve seemingly intractable conflicts. Meanwhile, the republic's racial identity became more congealed in the Jacksonian era. Emergent democratic visions necessitated the theft of indigenous land for poor white settlers, and the American working class was forged as a producerist identity that projected the qualities of laziness, spontaneity, and sexual license onto blacks (Rawick 1972; Roediger 1991).

As struggles over slavery and empire permeated politics, Skowronek's (1982) "state of courts and parties" increasingly found its institutional actors classified within the political system based on their racialized political commitments. Parties had to take positions on slavery and, as sectional tensions mounted, explain and defend their vision of what a white state should mean for all of its denizens. The executive branch over the years sought to pacify tensions over slavery through conquest and expansion. Congress crafted compromises that balanced and rebalanced power between slave and free states. And the Supreme Court finally attempted to resolve the conflict by embracing an institutionally and legally unassailable vision of property rights in human beings for slaveholders in its *Dred Scott* decision. But neither constitutional design, nor aggressive territorial expansion, nor crafted compromises, nor judicial fiat could preserve union and peace, and ultimately the slaveocracy sought separation from the emerging white capitalist state in the north (see Graber 2006).

The bloody Civil War briefly opened space for ground-up revolutionary transformation, as slaves freed through military conquest, proclamation, and their own agency demanded land reform and political power (DuBois 1935). The reconstitution of the nation took place through structural and institutional reform on the national level and in individual states and localities in the south. These reforms had radical potential both for dismantling racial and labor hierarchies and for enhancing the national state's capacity to formulate and implement policy. But as Reconstruction waned in the face of a violent insurgency and national institutions stepped back from attempting to reconfigure the national state racially, resurgent conservative southern interests pressed for the restoration of political and economic autonomy.[2] The victory of white supremacy required intensive struggle at the national level as well as political and paramilitary organization on the part of conservative Democrats in the south, and ultimately crushed nascent elements of cross-racial, class-based, agrarian and labor coalitions seeking political and economic reform on the ground in the conquered southern states. As Pamela Brandwein describes in chapter 6, the hoped-for revolution was stillborn, and gave way to a different type of transformation.

The Jim Crow order that prevailed in the early twentieth century was neither inevitable nor clearly predictable from the standpoint of observers in the 1870s and early 1880s (e.g. Woodward 1974; Brandwein 1999). Nonetheless, incremental changes in state and national elections and major decisions on the part of all branches of the national government allowed the south free rein over what was defined as the domestic and local problem of race. Although sweeping reforms were written into the constitution and remained a tantalizing, contingent possibility for some years afterward, the promises were not fulfilled. By the turn of the century, the nation and states had negotiated a compact allowing for the constitutionalized and legalized Jim Crow regime in the south, the more informal articulation of citizenship conditioned through racial status in the north, and the emergence of complex, multiracial social and labor hierarchies in the west.[3] These diverse racial regimes held in common a loose national conception of white citizenship as normative and a commitment to largely state-based articulation and maintenance of racial hierarchy. As Kevin Bruyneel explains in chapter 5, national political actors, however, confronted race directly through efforts to assimilate conquered Mexican territory, the transition from crabbed notions of sovereignty to active assimilation for Native Americans, developing dilemmas over immigration and Asian labor particularly, and the emergence of turn-of-century imperialism through overseas conquest. While the Spanish American War was written into the annals of American history as heroic (and quick) conquest and extension of the American spirit, the much longer and bloodier campaign to crush the Filipino resistance that had sought freedom in the wake of conflict between old colonialist Spain and new imperialist America was largely forgotten (Ngai 2004).

The unspoken agreement to leave the day-to-day management of "race relations," a phrase popularized by Alabaman child labor activist Edgar Murphy, to the states, while allowing the national government to set the broad boundaries for access to American citizenship characterized the early twentieth century. Resistance to the supremacist order existed and developed legal, political, and scientific sophistication during the Progressive Era. Nonetheless, serious challengers to the Jim Crow order struggled as racialized hierarchies become more rigid, less nuanced, and more violent (Feldman 1999; Novkov 2008). Simultaneously, national policymakers essentially closed down non-white immigration in the 1920s and supported the development of a grudging citizenship in name only for blacks, Mexican immigrants and their descendants, Asian immigrants and their descendants, and residents who had emigrated from the U.S.'s client states. Likewise, the gift of citizenship to individual Native Americans in the Progressive Era entailed an implied reciprocal giving up of sovereignty on the part of the tribes (see Bruyneel 2007). Progressive Era activists' penchant for pragmatic, scientific, liberal reforms designed to support and enhance democracy often incorporated strongly normative and racialized conceptions of the ideal democratic citizen, with tragic implications for the public policies directed at racialized minorities and other unreformable or undesirable citizens.

The Jim Crow order, while repressive and powerful, saw significant development not just in national capacity with the rise of the New Deal, but also in how national and state policymakers understood and addressed race in the Progressive Era. Progressive reforms sought to raise the standard of living of immigrants and to shape immigrants and their offspring into more fully assimilated American citizens, but in this process they actively struggled over which ethnic and national origins could be rendered politically and socially white (see Jacobson 1998; Guterl 2001; Hattam 2007). Other advocates for the scientific management of the state drew up measures and administrative regulations employing eugenic theories, seeking to contain the contamination of racial inferiority through obsessive racial registration, stricter and better enforced anti-miscegenation laws, and new "hygienic" regulations of marriage (Pascoe 1996; Yamin 2005; Novkov 2008). By the 1930s, however, African-American resistance was growing throughout the south in a variety of locations, and southern states began to face increasing external scrutiny and criticism. And Paul Frymer shows in chapter 8 that the New Deal era saw increased engagement and struggle between NAACP elites and white labor leaders. In chapter 7, Kim Johnson explains how these changes generated incentives for moderate reform of the Jim Crow order to ensure its long-term viability.

Yet despite growing political mobilization and advocacy for inclusion into New Deal social programs (Hamilton and Hamilton 1997), race again shaped a major turning point in U.S. political development as black Americans were excluded explicitly and implicitly from Depression-era expansions of the American welfare state, with long-term implications for the viability of national social welfare policy (Lieberman 1998; Brown 1999; Williams 2003).

The civil rights movement, fostered both by black experiences in World War II and the exclusionary nature of New Deal programs, generated new commitments to fuller visions of democracy. It initiated a new period of starkly defined and opposed racial orders, one seeking transformation toward a more egalitarian politics and society and the other fighting to maintain white supremacy in some form (King and Smith, chapter 4). This struggle played out straightforwardly in the confrontation between members of the mass movement and southern segregationists, but it mapped in more complex ways for organized labor, which symbolically supported civil rights but resisted close examination of racism in its locals and national organizational structure (Gould 1977; Hill 1985; Frymer 2007). In chapter 10, Naomi Murakawa demonstrates that the civil rights era also saw the development of new political alliances that effectively linked conservatism to racial subordination through popular political discourse and ultimately through legislative alliances and pronouncements racializing federal crime policy (see also Lowndes 2008). As Sidney Milkis explains in chapter 11, while Lyndon Johnson endorsed a strong program of building a more egalitarian society and supported the movement structurally and financially, his efforts to cement a core political commitment to a major reallocation of power failed against the shoals of increasingly sophisticated and racialized conservative resistance and the Vietnam War. By the 1968 presidential election, resurgent conservative forces were able to construct a winning coalition that gained strength in the early 1970s by mobilizing around issues like crime, judicial accountability, and busing that invoked race implicitly or explicitly. In chapter 12, Daniel Martinez-HoSang describes this process in relation to state-level political struggles over busing.

The post-civil rights era saw the shaking up of civil rights coalitions around race but race remains a major factor in structuring politics and policies (King and Smith, chapter 4). As Robert C. Lieberman argues in chapter 9, considering this history critically and systematically enables the causal tracing of the long legacy of slavery and other forms of racial subordination to contemporary manifestations of racial inequality across a wide swath of policy areas. State initiative campaigns on racial issues like busing, affirmative action, mandated English language, and immigrants' ability to access state-provided services have proliferated (see, e.g., Martinez-HoSang, chapter 12). And, as Nancy Wadsworth demonstrates in chapter 13, exploring the intersections of race and religion encourages a new analysis of the relationship between cultural and political change as well as highlighting the potentialities for shifting orders and coalitions across multiple axes. Recent developments have generated new questions and cleavages, but these questions and cleavages are configured and play out specifically through their historical, structural, and cultural roots in the struggles over race through time in the United States.

Race and contemporary politics

Historical explorations of racial politics are essential, but not only for history's sake. Analyses of prior political struggles make visible the contingency of what now appear as settled, even natural, social or economic phenomena; be they racially inequitable residential patterns, labor market inequalities, disparate imprisonment rates, the prevalence and severity of certain diseases among populations of color, or starkly different voting behavior. Such patterns and practices are the result of institutional and discursive histories. We cannot hope to gain analytic purchase on deeply entrenched social and political problems without understanding the forces which—intentionally or not—went into their production. This is clearly evident today, when political approaches to racial issues often turn on whether and how history is to be considered.

In an era when "colorblindness" is a widely accepted approach to questions of racial equality in U.S. politics, the past has never been of more importance. Colorblindness is a particularly attractive target for the analysis we advocate, both because of its advocates' prominence in contemporary debates about politics and policy and because of its refusal to engage history. Proponents of colorblind arguments claim that the acknowledgement of race in social policy only serves to reproduce racial hierarchies. This approach is crystallized in the Supreme Court's 2007 landmark ruling striking down school desegregation plans in Louisville and Seattle, which many legal experts see as retreating sharply from the core principle of *Brown v. Board of Education I*. In *Parents Involved in Community Schools*, Chief Justice John Roberts interpreted the Fourteenth Amendment to prohibit policymakers from addressing racial subordination unless a specific, narrow, state-sponsored, and utterly unremediated history of discrimination could be identified, and to permit policymakers to acknowledge racial difference only as an ahistoric and thin conception of diversity.[4] His summary of the Fourteenth Amendment's command to legislators and administrators is telling: "The way to stop discrimination on the basis of race is to stop discriminating on the basis of race." While it is too early to tell how this ruling will shape policies and later controversies, Roberts' ability to muster a majority around the outcome and three justices around this specific principle calls into question the center of the Court's capacity to negotiate more ambivalent rulings like that issued in *Grutter v. Bollinger* upholding affirmative action in 2003.

This assertion actively erases the significance of history, because it claims that past institutional and cultural discrimination must not direct our attempts to remedy their current manifestations. But how are we to determine the "way to stop racial discrimination" without clear, concrete analyses of the institutional arrangements, cultural patterns, and economic dynamics that have produced the racial stratification that demands remedy? Indeed, only historical tools can enable us to make clear sense of the very term "racial discrimination." Roberts' strong focus on individuals as the subjects of law and policy silently endorses a conception of racial discrimination as an individual phenomenon that need only be confined to the private realm to render it constitutionally irrelevant. At the same time, his own (and his concurring justices') narrow understanding of history blinds him to the institutional, cultural, and economic embedding of racial discrimination and its production of intractable patterns of hierarchy, exclusion, and diminished possibilities based on one's racial position in society.

But how exactly are we to make use of the past? From Lyndon Johnson's 1965 Howard University address to the current reparations movement, the argument has been made time and again that past wrongs require attention and redress if we are to ever achieve an egalitarian society (Balfour 2003). However, addressing the relationship between past and present racial hierarchies requires not simply an accounting of past individual and institutional crimes. As Robert Lieberman argues, we must also seek to understand precisely how institutional patterns of racialization have developed over time (chapter 9). Such specificity allows us to better understand and craft law and policy to dismantle racial discrimination today (Katznelson 2005). Analyses of forms of political exclusion built into New Deal legislation and implementation, as well as post-World War II patterns of discrimination produced by the Federal Housing Authority, and the GI Bill among others, gives us better purchase on the dynamics that produced the school segregation with which the Court was grappling. Only through tracing back the interwined institutional and ideological paths that produced the contemporary manifestations of inequality we observe can we effectively formulate policies to address these inequalities—and justify the need to do so.

Race, political science, and interdisciplinarity

Understanding contemporary American politics requires attending to political phenomena like the distribution of power, the organization of participation, the structure of institutions, the shape and scope of the economy, the influence of movements on politics and policy, and the state's interactions with culture and society across time and space. The chapters in this volume demonstrate that the history of the nation as its denizens have dealt with race has critically influenced how all of these phenomena operate today. Since before the founding, the American state's development has been intertwined with the development of race as an ideology and a basis for the allocation of power. The importance of race in development means that studying racialized development provides us with different and richer interpretations of key moments, and can help us to identify crucial moments that otherwise might remain unnoticed. If we believe that the structure of institutions and the organization and distribution of power matter in politics, we should analyze the crucial meaning and influence of race for both. To achieve this, we must use approaches from within and outside of the discipline of political science.

If political scientists want to interrogate and understand the most important issues of our time, then using the analytical tools associated with a racialized political development approach are necessities. Race and concerns about preserving and promoting racial hierarchy and empire were the very raison d'etre for the founding of the discipline of American political science in the late nineteenth century. Early presidents of the American Political Science Association worried publicly about the impact of immigration on emerging Progressive agendas to build good government, and questioned the capacity of new immigrants to engage in mature democratic governance (Fraga et al. 2006: 515). At the same time, such concerns were mirrored in the discipline's approach to the study of non-European nations. In the *Journal of Race Development* (which later became *Foreign Affairs*), political scientists regularly contributed articles on the relative potential that the "darker races" had in becoming civilized and in building modern states. Just as important was the question of what role the United States as an emergent power would play in such development (Vitalis 2003; Blatt 2004). Indeed, as Jessica Blatt has pointed out, these origins make the very notion of development itself problematic (Blatt: 706–7). Yet, as the discipline institutionalized and matured over the twentieth century, for too long, the study of race in American politics was seen as marginal at best to the central questions of the field. Studies of the state and the shift to pluralism in the 1920s cemented political scientists' conceptions of politics around state institutions and those empowered to participate in conventional politics, driving out consideration of the role of identity and the political agency of disempowered groups (Tolleson-Rinehart and Carroll 2006).[5]

One explanation attributes this to the long-term intellectual segregation by race in the discipline. As yet another example of the consequences of racial hierarchies in American society, racialization has often affected what white and non-white scholars "see." Throughout much of the discipline's history, white scholars and scholars of color studied racial politics in significantly different ways: they asked different questions, advanced different theories, and utilized different empirical methods and approaches (Dawson and Wilson 1991; McClain and Garcia 1993).[6] Coming on the heels of the civil rights movement, the 1960s and 1970s portended a dramatic increase in the number of black and Latino scholars into the discipline (Preston and Woodward 1984). Yet at just this moment, disciplinary insurgencies possibly led to greater intellectual segregation by race. The American Political Science Association (APSA) meetings in 1967 were rocked by the political fervor of the times (particularly the civil rights movement and the anti-war movement). But by the 1969 founding of the National Conference of Black Political Scientists, many African-American political scientists had temporarily disengaged from the mainstream discipline they interpreted as inhospitable for studying racial politics.[7] Thus, it is probably no surprise that the prolific body of scholarship produced by black political scientists during the 1970s and 1980s—often employing what we would consider a racialized political development approach—has been and regretfully still is ignored by many scholars of American politics generally, and American political development specifically.[8] To take but one example of the consequences of political science's long marginalization of racial politics, much of the earliest scholarship on race and American political development was advanced by Hanes Walton, Jr.'s body of work on the relationship of black Americans to national political institutions (political parties, bureaucracy, presidency), public policy, political culture, and ideology (Walton 1970, 1972a, 1972b, 1973, 1988).[9]

The nature and location of scholarly output is another dimension of the marginalization of scholarship on racial politics in political science. Consider, for instance, the frequency and nature of articles published on race and politics in the mainstream journals of the discipline. As Dawson and Cohen (2002) point out in their recent overview of the subfield, "research on race enjoys less status in this [political science] field than in any other discipline in the social sciences with the probable exception of economics" (496). A comparative analysis of published articles on race in sociology, history, economics, and political science by Ernest Wilson and Lorrie Frasure (2007) supports their view. From 1970 to 2003, political science ranked third behind history and sociology (but ahead of economics) in the number of articles on race published in the top three journals of the discipline. But not only was scholarship published less frequently and prominently on race and politics, the theoretical nature of such research, when published, differs remarkably as well. In an in-depth analysis of published articles on racial politics in the discipline's major journals over the course of the twentieth century by Walton and his colleagues (1994), the authors found two distinct traditions of scholarship: a "race relations" framework which emphasized "peaceful and consensual relations between the two races, even if the result is the domination of one and subjugation of the other," and an "African American politics" framework which tends to focus on the politics of "parity and empowerment" of marginalized racial groups (Walton et al. 1994: 145–74).

But at this historical juncture in political science, it is not enough to simply make the study of race more central to the discipline, as it was at its founding in pernicious ways with racist consequences. *How* we study the role of race in American politics also matters. Write Dawson and Cohen,

> Part of the reason for our unequal levels of information regarding racial politics in the United States is political science's excessive reliance on the discipline of economics as a source of methodological and theoretical inspiration as well as our constant emphasis on the individual level of analysis. This dependence has led to the emergence of dominant methodological approaches in political science, rooted in the use of economic modeling and the individual as the unit of analysis.

(2002: 488)

The current dominance of behavioral approaches to the study of racial politics has consequences for how we understand and interpret not only racial politics but American politics (King and Smith, chapter 4). Briefly, the study of race and politics in the United States has evolved to encompass four areas of inquiry: political behavior and public opinion; political theory; public/social policy; and race and APD. (A fifth strand of scholarship encompassing comparative studies of racialization is also emerging.) While all four of these areas of scholarship are healthy and thriving, the vast majority of articles on racial politics in the discipline focus on political behavior and racial attitudes. Yet even in the subfield of public opinion and racial attitudes, still lacking are adequate accounts of the historical or institutional sources of the political attitudes of all racial groups (Harris-Lacewell 2007, Reed 1999). At the beginning of the twenty-first century, the study of race and American politics has consolidated firmly around these behavioral approaches. A quick perusal of articles on race and politics in the discipline's flagship journals since 2000—the *American Political Science Review* and the *American Journal of Political Science*—confirm this assessment. This doesn't negate the fact that APD approaches to the study of race might be "segregated" in the subfield's primary organ (*Studies in American Political Development*), although even here, the articles on race in APD have been few and far between (averaging roughly one per year). Further, while some leading figures in APD incorporate racialization as a crucial element of development, others still do not read race centrally into processes of development, the resurgence of conservatism, or the rise of governmental activism in recent American political history (see, e.g., Pierson and Skocpol 2007).

The problem with many contemporary behavioralist and attitudinal approaches—which especially focus on the individual as the unit of their analyses—to racial politics is twofold. First, these approaches leave a range of important political questions unanswered and off the table. The "drunkard's search" for racial politics in easily downloadable survey-based data sets has implications for how we broadly understand the role and place of race in American politics and society (Harris-Lacewell 2007). To take one example addressed further below, analyzing race only in terms of racial attitudes towards inequality or the Bush Administration's failed response to Hurricane Katrina can only explain a limited range of questions related to the disaster. To understand the political origins of a weakened state capacity to act, or to get at the underlying reasons for why Americans were "shocked" at the discovery of racial inequality, a wider cast of analytical approaches are required.[10]

Second, racial attitudes and political preferences are often seen as given and exogenous to the political process and institutions. With a few important exceptions, most notably the work of Michael Dawson, who brings a historical and institutional grounding to black political ideologies and behavior, much work on racial attitudes and political behavior proceeds as if in a historical, contextual and institutional vacuum, devoid of either a causal, constitutive or discursive narrative about racial politics or racialized development. So it should be no surprise that the poverty of theoretical insight into processes or racialization, racial ordering, and racialized political development are also linked to political science's heavy borrowing from and fetishization of individual-based methodological and quantitative approaches. As arguably the most influential political scientist currently working from a behavioral approach, Michael Dawson and his co-author Cathy Cohen argue,

> A close examination of the literature dealing with race and politics, especially that originating from political scientists, however, suggest that far from examining the social processes that racialize, categorize, and constrain the life opportunities of different groupings of people in this country, largely people of color, most of this work has focused on individual manifestations of political differences that correlate with visible and self-identified racial differences. Most of this literature takes racial categories as given as well as the resulting ordering of occupants within these hierarchical categories. Ignored are the historical and social contexts through which the complicated processes of racialization and categorization utilized in this country have developed and evolved.
>
> (Dawson and Cohen 2002: 490)

While behavioral approaches are useful for some questions, we contend that an APD framework is best suited for getting at these larger questions involving the discursive, institutional, and dynamic dimensions of racialized development. For instance, we cannot adequately analyze the racial attitudes of black Americans without an understanding of the processes of "preference formation" (Reed 1999). In the case of black Americans, only through approaches such as historical, institutional, and discursive analyses that uncover the sources of opinion formation in historically segregated African-American communities can one fully understand how and why black public opinion has consistently been radically different from that of mainstream white Americans (Dawson 1994, 2001; Cohen 1999; Savage 1999; Harris-Lacewell 2004, 2007). These modes of analysis could fruitfully be applied to the processes of preference formation for other racial groups as well.

We take seriously Dawson and Cohen's (2002: 493) admonition to "move away from individualist models" that seem to be the raison d'etre of contemporary racial politics and political science scholarship. Presaging King and Smith's argument in their chapter (4) in this volume, they write that "[e]xploring the historical and specific processes of racialization should provide greater insight into such staples of political science inquiry as electoral realignment, public opinion shifts, and interest group proliferation" (Dawson and Cohen 2002: 489). A political developmental approach to studying race and American politics allows us to analyze order and stability on the one hand, and political change on the other. For example, long before King and Smith's (2005) seminal article, both sociologist Loic Wacquant's (2001) and historian Tom Holt's (2000) periodization of distinct racial orders each provided, in their own conceptual and disciplinary language, a political development account of historically specific yet ever-evolving racial orders.[11] Such a conceptual proffering reminds us that processes of racialization are not static; they are instead dynamic and evolve in relation to political institutions, discourses, policies, and their interaction with political actors' strategies and action. What mainstream behavioralist, formal, and quantitative approaches to racial politics do is to freeze historically specific racial orders in place, while also naturalizing racial identities, racial attitudes, and political behavior devoid of context.

Many scholars who study American politics rightfully focus on national political institutions like Congress, the executive branch, and the courts, to understand how struggles over politics work and how policies are made and implemented. Others consider how the public understands and influences this process through studies of political communication, political behavior, political psychology, and social movements. The study of American political development offers critical insights to politics unavailable elsewhere, however, because it is here that we analyze political entities and dynamics as historical constructions and processes. But focusing on development is also distinct either from strictly studying history or using history solely as background to contemporary issues. While many historians are concerned with politics, scholars of political development ask the specific question of how and why the political landscape has changed over time, and what significance these changes have had. These questions necessarily call attention to how regimes, institutions, and discourses have organized and exercised power, and their constitutive or even causal roles in shaping social relations and political phenomena. Where quantitative, behavioral, and rational-choice approaches place individual choices and behaviors at the center, APD expands the scope of analysis to incorporate direct focus on institutions, change, and the political and cultural dynamics that shape them. This focus provides more insight into the structural organization of power as well as its operation in the context of political institutions and identities. Considering power in this disaggregated and specific way in turn enables a deeper understanding of how those acting in the name of the state, within state-based institutions, make, enforce, and interpret policies and practices.

By attending to these questions, the tools of American political development can both gain from and enhance intra- and inter-disciplinary theorizing about race, power, and politics. Within political science, our understanding of racial politics is augmented by a developmental approach, while scholars of American political development stand to gain much by increased attention to race. Racial categorization and hierarchical ranking have been central facets of American history from the colonial era to the present. Racialization has profoundly shaped political dynamics and outcomes where one would expect it, but as Desmond King and Rogers Smith have argued (in their piece reprinted in chapter 4), also in relation to phenomena not ordinarily associated with race. Given the importance of race in every developmental moment that APD scholars have identified as significant, analyses of American political development that do not account for the constitutive role of race should offer reasons for this omission. Put simply, racialized political development *is* American political development, and vice-versa. No analysis of American political development can be comprehensive without situating race centrally.

But the study of racialized development enhances APD research in other fundamental ways as well. Because race is at once a lived experience, a hierarchically ranked social category, and a site of institutional action, the study of how it operates in politics can help us transcend the false divide between culture and identity on the one hand, and institutions and structure on the other. As such, centrally situating race can fruitfully expand our understanding of what in fact we mean by "political development." In contrast to APD approaches that focus on the mechanics, markers, and causal mechanisms of institutional change, the history of racial politics shows that many significant changes wrought on the polity might occur as discursive shifts or in other cultural sites long before they register as what Orren and Skowronek describe as a "durable shift in governing authority" (Orren and Skowronek 2004). Indeed, some significant shifts in racial ordering may never register as a struggle among governmental actors (Wadsworth, chapter 13; Hattam and Lowndes 2007). Further, placing racialized development in the center of the analysis facilitates the study of political dynamics as cultural dynamics and vice versa. Seeing this interplay enables the reading of culture as a phenomenon as complex and ultimately irreducible as institutions themselves. It also produces a richer narrative of how identity interacts with institutions over time to produce and respond to political dynamism. To see the full range of political development, we must expand our visions of politics to incorporate the sociological, cultural, and ideological facets of racial formation. While racialized development registers in the political institutions on which APD research has focused, its incorporation into and reliance upon power relations brings new elements into understandings of the dynamics of development. These elements can be incorporated most effectively by turning to interdisciplinary scholarship on race.

In thinking about how race operates alongside or outside of conventional political spheres, Omi and Winant's appropriation of Gramsci has been critical for understanding how race has shaped hegemonic relations of power. Cultural historians such as Carroll Smith-Rosenberg, Grace Elizabeth Hale, and David Blight have in different ways explored how race is productive of political identity, and have shown how these productions have helped determine how institutional actors interpreted, defended, and practiced white supremacy (Smith-Rosenberg 1992; Hale 1998; Blight 2001).

Work in American Studies, Ethnic Studies and American Literature has likewise opened up avenues for understanding how race shapes politics in culture. Richard Slotkin's groundbreaking work on the uses of frontier myth throughout U.S. history, for instance, has revealed the mechanisms through which the narrative of the striving, self-reliant individual was produced in popular culture and used by political elites to authorize Indian slaughter and capital accumulation; while masking the violent consequences of westward expansion, urban industrialization, and empire-building (Slotkin 1973, 1985, 1992). Toni Morrison's work on the role of race in American literature has shown how American national identity was forged in part out of the narrative placement of people of color in relation to white men, bestowing on the latter a sense of manly independence (Morrison 1992). Philip Deloria's work on white Americans' ambivalent cultural identifications with indigenous peoples further demonstrates just how complex the racial invention of American identity has been (Deloria 1991).

A developmental approach can gain much from how cultural analyses have located racial power in language, symbols, and identity both by demonstrating how political practices are shaped by interpretive frameworks, and how institutions reproduce and alter racialized interests and identities. But given that studies of culture, discourse, and identity only rarely focus on the institutional patterns of racial politics, we think that there is much yet to be done. Considering institutional development and race together raises useful questions about how political institutions participate in constructing race and how their own trajectories are initiated and shaped in relation to the racial politics of the moment. The late Michael Rogin, whose work joined racial demonology to political interests at the center of American political life, helped to bridge the divide between American Studies and Political Science (Rogin 1988). Victoria Hattam's recent work on the interlinked histories of the concepts of 'race' and 'ethnicity' in the twentieth century also traverses the realms of language, identity, and institutional policy (Hattam 2007). The chapters in this volume move this project forward in varied ways, with some complicating narratives of development by incorporating racialization as an intervening process, and others arguing that racialization itself is so firmly interwoven with development as to be indistinguishable from it. Bringing development into these interdisciplinary conversations demonstrates that culture and institutions do not exist as fully distinct phenomena.

Future agendas

The chapters in this volume each make important individual contributions, and collectively shift how we understand the relationship among race, politics, and history in the United States, with significant payoffs for contemporary political science and politics. But we see this volume as the first step in outlining a research as well as practical political agenda for the future. Some questions about race and politics in the U.S. are being addressed by other scholars. Others still await research. And some questions will only arise when the current questions have been explored further. A focus on race and political development opens up an entirely new research agenda within political science and across disciplines. Here we suggest just a few of those directions for future research before we conclude with the ground this volume covers.

In her chapter (13), Nancy Wadsworth presses for an intersectional analysis of race and religious identity in political development. She makes a compelling case for understanding how racial orders and religious orders have intertwined over time, and for why we cannot understand the impact of religion on politics absent race, and vice versa. The same can be said for other aspects of identity. The intersection of race and gender has been significant, to note only a few examples, in shaping how slaves' status was defined and passed on from generation to generation, how the politics of immigration and citizenship in the Progressive Era and afterwards evolved around men's differential capacity to transmit Americanness, how marriage policies encouraged and prohibited relationships based on race, and how the political mobilization of negative racial stereotypes has simultaneously encompassed gender. Likewise, as Paul Frymer's chapter demonstrates, the relationship between class and race in politics is both crucial and complex. We welcome more consideration of questions about the political dynamics that emerged through the Jacksonian-era transformations of racial categories that generated robust conceptions of whiteness across previously more salient class divides. The brief moments of political opportunity presented in racially integrated unions from the late nineteenth century through the 1930s beg further analysis. And research on the racial politics in agrarian and populist movements could enhance both the history of race and development as well as the history of class struggle and land reform. Some other intersections that could contribute valuably to understanding racial politics and development in the United States include race and sexuality, race and citizenship status, and race and disability.

While intersectional research challenges colorblindness directly, colorblindness is but one major ideological trend in how race is situated in American politics and culture. As popular and political endorsements of colorblindness retreat from the category of race, across other dimensions race has re-emerged in its most biological form. From popular discourse to professional medical journals, the assertion of actually existing "races" is becoming commonplace, as are recommendations of policy solutions based on racial categories. Race has been paired with the revolution in genomic research to find solutions for disparities in health and mortality rates in different communities (Stevens 2003; Reed 2004). The fallacy of race has long been agreed on by experts from across the social and hard sciences, so the resurgence of the myth of racial difference requires explanation. The retreat to the concept of race to resolve stubborn social problems has plenty of antecedents in American politics (and political science), from Jeffersonian justifications for slavery to attempts to regulate the behavior of southern and eastern European immigrants at the turn of the twentieth century. Such analyses simultaneously reveal how deeply entrenched racial thinking is in U.S. political culture, how institutional goals get met by racial classification, and finally how definitions of race themselves reflect contemporary imperatives. Thus, the political significance and potential policy outcomes of the re-biologization of race urgently require historical and institutional consideration.

As Robert Lieberman's chapter shows, a more comparative approach to race and political development in the U.S. context is also warranted. While the field of APD has always been implicitly comparative (especially in debates around U.S. exceptionalism), explicitly focusing on political development across national contexts might provide greater analytical leverage on the unique patterns of racialized institutional practices and political discourses in this country. Comparative work on race in the U.S., South Africa, and Brazil has shown how political institutions shape processes of racialization in both different and similar ways, while also providing different political opportunities for racialized groups to mobilize against racial inequality (Greenberg 1980; Fredrickson 1981, 2000; Marx 1998; Nobles 2000). This small foundational "varieties of racialization" literature also points to questions about the inter-relationship of race, political economy, and political institutions.

Raising the comparative political development perspective also directs atten-tion to the role of race, globalization and empire in APD, a topic that Kevin Bruyneel's chapter (5) addresses. The rise of nationalism has been linked with processes of racialization in modernity, and nations' imperial projects have always shaped the internal politics within the home country, sometimes with pernicious and other times with liberating consequences for racially marginal-ized groups (see Bruyneel, chapter 5; Anderson; Plummer 1996; Dudziak 2000; Takaki 2000; Singh 2004). Yet so far, debates about globalization, global inequality and justice, and the continuing relevance of the nation-state have largely proceeded absent either a racial or political development perspective.[12]

Considering race in connection with globalization raises additional questions about the relationship between race and American foreign policy. Too often political scientists hive off the study of domestic from international politics. But as an expansionist nation from the beginning, America's international and domestic politics have always shaped each other. This point is underscored by Richard Young and Jeffrey Meiser's chapter (2) on the antebellum American state, which demonstrates how expansion into "Indian"-held territory secured the stability of the early republic. Likewise, Bruyneel's chapter (5) reveals much about the cultural, economic and political terms under which former Mexican citizens were incorporated into the American nation. Significant research has explored and largely confirmed the Cold War thesis—that people of color tend to see advances in equality during crises when their support is crucial to the war effort and the American creed is used to whip up patriotic support for military action (see, e.g., Klinkner and Smith 1999; Dudziak 2000; Kryder 2000), and that the nature of these advances are themselves circumscribed by wartime political imperatives (Dudziak 2000; Singh 2004). This work raises other questions. How has foreign policy itself configured race and racial difference over time? How has the United States' involvement in international affairs reflected its racial ethos, and how has its racial ethos influenced how, when, where, and why the United States has engaged or disengaged abroad? How have the politics of race contributed to the United States' identity as a warrior state, a nation that has spent far more years involved in some form of military conflict than at peace (Brandon 2005)?

Thinking about geography raises the politics of the border. Immigration has become one of the key issues in contemporary U.S. politics, dividing the electorate and the parties themselves. Race and racialized development have fundamentally shaped questions of immigration from the 1790 Immigration and Naturalization Act through the Chinese Exclusion Act of 1886 until today (Mink 1986; Ngai 2004). Bruyneel uses the U.S. annexation of Mexican territory in the mid-nineteenth century to demonstrate what he calls "internal postcolonialism" and the making of "accidental citizens" out of former Mexican nationals. This political and historical context can help us understand the ambivalent relationship the U.S. has to immigration, celebrating a national ethos of openness toward migrants while reading Latinas and Latinos out of American national identity. The border, racialized since before the foundation of the United States, remains racially politicized today, both through the broad political movement against immigration from Mexico and Central and South America, and through the racial undertones of the "war on terror." We urge deeper understandings of the history of how the border has configured insiders and outsiders, domestic dependent nations or semi-autonomous indigenous states, and the relationship between race and conquest.

Border struggles are intertwined with citizenship. Yet political debates over who is and is not eligible for citizenship, as well as over which elements of citizenship are mandatory and which discretionary for different individuals, have occurred largely along racial lines (Smith 1997). Racial controversies over citizenship were present at the founding, through the latter days of the sectional crisis, in the debates over the Fourteenth Amendment's ratification and early interpretations, at the end of the nineteenth century over Asian immigrants and their children, and into the twentieth century with its restrictive policies seeking assimilation for white immigrants and their children alongside the near total exclusion of immigration by people of color. Recent challenges to the Fourteenth Amendment's guarantee of citizenship for any individual born within the geographic boundaries of the United States have placed these questions back on the agenda. All of these issues, as well as shifts in the gradations and degrees of citizenship offered to people of color, are ripe for further exploration.

Finally, a race and political development approach has much to contribute to long-standing questions in political science about institutional capacity and failure. As the disaster wrought on New Orleans and the Gulf Coast by Hurricane Katrina unfolded in real time during the 2005 meetings of the American Political Science Association, scholars attempted to make sense of the exposed inequality and horrid consequences of the government failure to assist those in most need of help. In the aftermath, scholars have employed a range of analytical tools to understand the failure of the Federal Emergency Management Agency (FEMA) and the Bush Administration to respond adequately to the crisis and separately to consider the continuing racial divisions in public opinion about racial inequality and the role and capacity of government. But a large body of scholarship using a race and political development approach brings together an analysis of race and an analysis of institutions and culture; in fact, it sees these as fundamentally related. Understanding the central role of race in shaping and limiting national political institutions from the founding, through the Civil War and Reconstruction, to post-civil rights racial retrenchment provides a fuller explanation for the failure of local, state, and national political institutional responses to the destruction of the hurricane, and subsequent efforts to reshape New Orleans racially and neoliberally (see, e.g., Frymer et al. 2006).

This list only scratches the surface of a research agenda that is in progress and on the horizon. We hope that this volume will serve as a jumping-off point both for those who wish to explore and contest the empirical stories presented in the individual chapters and for those who want to expand toward different empirical and theoretical questions that lie at the intersections of race, politics, development, and history in the United States. Considering these questions has the potential to advance the study of American politics generally, producing new ways to conceive of political culture and institutions and how they change. At the same time, these questions provoke reflection about where the United States as a nation has been with respect to race, where it is going, and where it might be directed in the future.

The volume

The chapters in this volume offer multiple ways of integrating race into APD. And they do so along a number of different axes, considering the role of elite actors and institutions, social movements, labor politics, cultural politics, ideological development, and the dynamics of structural change. While they by no means exhaust the territory, they do offer quite varied approaches and sites of research. This thematic summary provides a different way of thinking about the volume's agenda than the chronological organization of the book discussed above.

While King and Smith make their case by positing the existence (and centrality?) of racial political orders, examining the role of race in APD can also lead to better understandings of the ways that politics is contingent, ambivalent, and disorderly. Because race has played an important role in party realignments, institutional development, and in the constitution of subjects, the category is a particularly good site to study the links among regimes, institutions, and subjectivity. Such connections can help us understand both political order and political change, both of which are chief research agendas in American political development.

Many of the chapters take up the issue of order and change directly, reconfiguring the relationship between these categories as they are conventionally understood in non-racialized conceptions of periods of American political development. Richard Young and Jeffrey Meiser's chapter (2) on the antebellum "dual state" helps us to understand how the early American Republic could be simultaneously a pluralistic and republican regime on the one hand, and a coercive, white supremacist state on the other. Indeed, they argue that the stability of the new republic required the enforcement of black slavery and "Indian" removal. Pamela Brandwein's chapter (6) engages debates about how to gauge the significance of Reconstruction. Arguing that it was neither completely revolutionary, nor of a piece with the antebellum era, Brandwein outlines the complexities in both Republican views on race and on constitutional change. Most importantly, Brandwein challenges us to get beyond the binary and sequential conceptions of order and change that are all too common in APD. The commonalities between Reconstruction and Jim Crow, along with their differences, point toward a much more complex understanding of institutional change.

Kevin Bruyneel (chapter 5) posits the simultaneous existence of hierarchic and hybrid orders in the mid-to-late nineteenth century, arguing that neither concept fully captures racial ordering in the colonialist assimilation of Mexican territory and citizens acquired through conquest. Kimberly Johnson (chapter 7) complicates the politics of Jim Crow in the New Deal era. Against prevailing accounts that attribute Jim Crow's undoing to grassroots civil rights pressure and federal intervention, she shows that southern moderates, both white and black, played a key role in dismantling it. Nancy Wadsworth (chapter 13) looks at the central role religion has played in racial politics, and shows that any account of race in APD must account for its constitutive character. Failure to do so leaves us unable to understand race, religion, or order and change in American politics. Further, her analysis of the intersection of religion and race demonstrates that considering cultural development as part of institutional development can transform where and when we identify change.

A number of the chapters look to the way that race has mediated specific dynamics between institutions and social movements. Paul Frymer (chapter 7) takes up the complicated relationship of race and class by examining the NAACP's troubled negotiations with organized labor in the mid twentieth century. He shows that labor leaders' belief that racism was the province of a few bigots left them unable to confront its deep roots in labor. Sidney Milkis (chapter 11) considers the complex relationship between social movements and the presidency in his account of the unique—if tortured—relationship between Lyndon Johnson and the Civil Rights movement. Johnson built a relationship with the movement to advance civil rights reform, but ultimately the institutional constraints of the office left him unable to sustain the relationship.

Some chapters attend to conservative efforts to mobilize racial discourse to achieve political and institutional change. Naomi Murakawa (chapter 10) reveals the racialized origins of the carceral state. She demonstrates that uniquely high rates of incarceration in the U.S., as well as the enormous racial disparity in imprisonment rates between whites and blacks, is neither the result of higher crime rates, or even white "backlash" in the 1960s, but rather arises from a longer term strategy by politicians seeking to blunt the progress of civil rights in the U.S. Daniel Martinez-HoSang (chapter 12) considers antibusing efforts in statewide referenda. Historically, the chapter demonstrates the "critical renovations and renewals in political debates over meaning of race and racism during this period." Works like these help us to understand the origins of the contemporary political landscape in post-civil rights era, and so give us purchase on the recent Court decision on school desegregation and other institutional instances of racial retrenchment. Much has been written about racial retrenchment since the 1960s and about colorblind conservatism in the current era, but there are few very good, empirical analyses of how we got from there to here.

Some chapters also show how racialized agendas on the part of political actors strongly influenced or primarily drove institutional change. Desmond King and Rogers Smith (chapter 4) argue that race must always be considered in analyzing the formation, maintenance, and change of political coalitions in the United States. Even in recognizing the foundational presence of race in institutional design, the racial component of these institutional designs has then not always been remembered as the institutions have moved forward in time. Kathleen Sullivan's work (chapter 3) on the antebellum development of police powers shows that strong conceptions of military and regulatory authority on the state level owed much to southern fears of slave revolts. Robert Lieberman (chapter 9) seeks to develop a more general theory about how to locate and understand the concrete legacies of slavery through reconfiguring arguments about causation in contemporary institutional design. And Young and Meiser (chapter 2) attribute major elements of constitutional design, the drive to geographic expansion, and the early development of national institutions to the initial commitment to establish a racialized dual state.

Ultimately, the research questions and agenda raised here and in the volume's chapters are important not for their inherent intellectual interest, nor for their capacity to generate more sophisticated methods and theories to understand the dynamics of change and continuity in American politics. This volume, and the research that follows it, should serve two more fundamental purposes. First, as we noted in opening this chapter, we believe that we must ask and answer questions about history and racialization in the political sphere in order to see the way forward. In an era of debate over whether the state's historic relationship with race should end, it is imperative to foreground how the state was always present and active in the construction, transformation, and preservation of racial hierarchy. Only through exploring the depths and nuance of this political commitment can we see what dismantling it would take, and where the points of resistance might lie.

Recent broad debates among political scientists have generated deep existential anxieties about the discipline as a whole (Monroe 2005; Schram 2006). What are our purposes as a discipline? What political questions, intellectual approaches, and methodologies are appropriate for political scientists to undertake? What knowledge is it our life's work and the work of our profession to contribute, and to whom? If the discipline of political science is to be relevant in helping us interpret and understand the most significant issues of the past, present, and future, combining the centrality of race with a broader analytical perspective of political development must be a pivotal part of the disciplinary equation. We write this volume in the hope that our answer for ourselves and our collaborators can be more than the advancement of narrow forms of knowledge divorced from politics itself. One contribution that this kind of work can make to the discipline as a whole is to reconnect it to politics. Each chapter has implications for normative politics. The take-away messages differ, but overall every author researches politics critically in the hope that these critiques may lead us to see our historical political commitments in a different light and address this history in the public sphere. Only through understanding the political nature of the long intertwined processes of racialization and state-building can we clear the political space to commit concretely to dismantling racialized forms of power in the future.

Notes

1 On Native Americans, see John Marshall's opinion for the Court in *Cherokee Nation v. Georgia*. While Marshall was sympathetic to the Cherokees' claim against Georgia, he did not permit them to articulate it as a sovereign nation. When the Court vindicated the Cherokees in the posture of a suit brought by a white missionary, President Jackson refused to enforce the ruling. In the case of the slave takeover of the ship *Amistad*, the slaves were permitted their freedom only because they had won it in a state of nature, and the judicial avenue of embracing a natural law opposition to slavery narrowed and closed through the imposition of statutory positive law. See Cover 1975.

2 For the seminal race and American political development book on the Civil War, Reconstruction and post-Reconstruction eras, see W.E.B. Du Bois's (1935) *Black Reconstruction*. Arguing against the orthodox historical accounts about the Reconstruction era dominant in the early twentieth century, Du Bois injected black agency into the narrative of the Civil War, while also articulating the long-term implications for American political development of racialization and unequal labor and racial regimes.

3 In the south, constitutionalization took place on two levels: national constitutional interpretation and lawmaking left room for local control and lack of oversight through the adoption of separate but equal as an acceptable constitutional standard, and a wave of southern state constitution-writing sought to legitimate white supremacy as a grounding purpose for state governance. See Novkov 2008.

4 One of the many ironies in Roberts' analysis is his construction of a coherent line of precedent linking racial retrenchment on affirmative action in education in *Grutter* and *Gratz*, voting rights in *Shaw v. Hunt* and *Rice v. Cayetano*, and affirmative action in contracting in *Croson* and *Adarand* back to the NAACP's briefs filed in *Brown I. Parents Involved in Community Schools v. Seattle School District #1*, 551 U.S. __ (2007)

5 Tolleson-Rinehart and Carroll note that, despite the obvious political significance of the campaign for women's suffrage, the *Political Science Quarterly* and the *American Political Science Review* together published only 13 articles on women out of the more than 1,400 pieces they published between 1886 and 1925 (Tolleson-Rinehart and Carroll 2006: 509).

6 Much of the scholarship that examines race and the history of the discipline focus on the binary racial divide between black and white scholars, although more recently Latino, Asian, and Native American scholars and their work have been incorporated into these accounts (see, e.g., Fraga et al. 2006).

7 See, e.g., http://www.ncobps.org/history.htm.

8 See, for instance, the work of Dianne Pinderhughes, Matthew Holden, Lucius and Twiley Barker, Charles Henry, Ralph Bunche, Linda Williams, Adolph Reed, Charles Hamilton, and Hanes Walton, among many others.

9 Arguably, Walton is an early yet ignored pioneer in the field of APD writ large.

10 We would obviously advocate a race and political development approach. For examples of these types of analyses of Hurricane Katrina and its effects, see the spring 2006 issue of *Du Bois Review*.
11 See also political scientist Claire Kim's 2000 book, *Bitter Fruit*, for an account of the dynamic nature of racial orders, or what she calls "racial ordering."
12 Feminist research on globalization is an important exception to our criticism of race's absence. See, e.g., Alexander and Mohanty 1997; Mohanty 2003.

Bibliography

Primary sources

The Amistad Case (United States v. Libellants and Claimants of the Schooner Amistad), 40 U.S. 518 (1841)
Prigg v. Pennsylvania, 41 U.S. 539 (1842)
Cherokee Nation v. Georgia, 30 U.S. 1 (1831)
Dred Scott v. Sandford, 60 U.S. 393 (1857)
Brown v. Board of Education, 347 U.S. 483 (1954)
Richmond v. J. A. Croson Co., 488 U.S. 469 (1989)
Shaw v. Hunt, 517 U. S. 899 (1996)
Rice v. Cayetano, 528 U.S. 495 (2000)
Grutter v. Bollinger, 539 U.S. 306 (2006)
Parents Involved in Community Schools v. Seattle School District #1, 551 U.S. ___ (2007)

References and secondary sources

Alexander, Jacqui and Chandra Mohanty, eds (1997) *Feminist Genealogies, Colonial Legacies, Democratic Futures*, New York: Routledge.
Allen, Theodore (1997) *The Invention of the White Race: The Origin of Racial Oppression in Anglo-America*, London: Verso Press.
Balfour, Lawrie (2003) "Unreconstructed Democracy: W.E.B. Du Bois and the Case for Reparations," *American Political Science Review* 97: 33–44.
Bell, Derrick (1989) *And We Are Not Saved: The Elusive Quest for Racial Justice*, New York: Basic Books.
Blatt, Jessica (2004) "'To Bring Out the Best that is in their Blood': Race, Reform and Civilization in the Journal of Race Development (1910–1919)," *Ethnic and Racial Studies* 25: 691–709.
Blight, David (2001) *Race and Reunion: The Civil War in American Memory*, Cambridge, MA: Harvard University Press.
Brandon, Mark (2005) "War and the American Constitutional Order," in *The Constitution in Wartime: Beyond Alarmism and Complacency*, Mark Tushnet (ed.), 11–39, Durham, NC: Duke University Press.
Brandwein, Pamela (1999) *Reconstructing Reconstruction: The Supreme Court and the Production of Historical Truth*, Durham, NC: Duke University Press.
Brown, Michael K. (1999) *Race, Money, and the American Welfare State*, Ithaca, NY: Cornell University Press.
Bruyneel, Kevin (2007) *The Third Space of Sovereignty: The Postcolonial Politics of U.S.–Indigenous Relations*, Minneapolis: University of Minnesota Press.

Cohen, Cathy J. (1999) *The Boundaries of Blackness: AIDS and the Breakdown of Black Politics*, Chicago: University of Chicago Press.

Cover, Robert (1975) *Justice Accused: Antislavery and the Judicial Process*, New Haven, CT: Yale University Press.

Dawson, Michael C. (1994) *Behind the Mule: Race and Class in African-American Politics*, Princeton, NJ: Princeton University Press.

—— (2001) *Black Visions: The Roots of Contemporary African-American Political Ideologies*, Chicago: University of Chicago Press.

Dawson, Michael C. and Cathy Cohen (2002) "Problems in the Study of the Politics of Race," in *Political Science: The State of the Discipline*, Ira Katznelson and Helen V. Milner (eds), 488–510, New York: W.W. Norton.

Dawson, Michael C. and Ernest J. Wilson (1991) "Paradigms and Paradoxes: Political Science and African American Politics," in *The Theory and Practice of Political Science*, William Crotty (ed.), Evanston, IL: Northwestern University Press.

Deloria, Philip J. (1991) *Playing Indian*, New Haven, CT: Yale University Press.

Du Bois, W.E.B. (1935 [1965]) *Black Reconstruction: An Essay Toward a History of the Past Which Black Folk Played in the Attempt to Reconstruct Democracy in America, 1860–1880*, New York: Meridian Books.

Dudziak, Mary (2000) *Cold War Civil Rights: Race and the Image of American Democracy*, Princeton, NJ: Princeton University Press.

Duster, Troy (2006) "Lessons from History: Why Race and Ethnicity Have Played a Major Role in Biomedical Research," *Journal of Law, Medicine and Ethics* 34: 487–92.

Feldman, Glenn (1999) *Politics, Society, and the Klan in Alabama, 1915–1949*, Tuscaloosa, AL: University of Alabama Press.

Fields, Barbara J. (1982) "Ideology and Race in American History," in *Region, Race, and Reconstruction: Essays in Honor of C. Vann Woodward*, J. Morgan Kousser and James M. McPherson (eds), 143–77, New York: Oxford University Press.

Finkelman, Paul (2001) *Slavery and the Founders: Race and Liberty in the Age of Jefferson*, Armonk, NY, and London: M.E. Sharpe, 2nd edn.

Fraga, Luis R., John A. Garcia, Rodney E. Hero, Michael Jones-Correa, Valerie Martinez-Ebers, and Gary M. Segura (2006) "Su Casa Es Nuestra Casa: Latino Politics Research and the Development of American Political Science," *American Political Science Review* 100: 515–21.

Franke, Katherine (1999) "Becoming a Citizen: Reconstruction Era Regulation of African American Marriages," *Yale Journal of Law and the Humanities* 11: 251–309.

Fredrickson, George M. (1981) *White Supremacy: A Comparative Study in American and South African History*, New York: Oxford University Press.

—— (2000) *The Comparative Imagination: On the History of Racism, Nationalism, and Social Movements*, Berkeley: University of California Press.

Frymer, Paul (2007) *Black and Blue: African Americans, the Labor Movement, and the Decline of the Democratic Party*, Princeton, NJ: Princeton University Press.

Frymer, Paul, Dara Z. Strolovitch, and Dorian T. Warren (2006) "New Orleans Is Not the Exception: Re-politicizing the Study of Racial Inequality," *Du Bois Review* 3: 37–57.

Gould, William B. (1977) *Black Workers in White Unions*, Ithaca, NY: Cornell University Press.

Graber, Mark (2006) *Dred Scott and the Problem of Constitutional Evil*, Cambridge, MA: Cambridge University Press.

Greenberg, Stanley B. (1980) *Race and State in Capitalist Development: Comparative Perspectives*, New Haven, CT: Yale University Press.

Guterl, Matthew Pratt (2001) *The Color of Race in America, 1900–1940*, Cambridge, MA: Harvard University Press.

Hale, Grace Elizabeth (1998) *Making Whiteness: The Culture of Segregation in the South, 1890–1940*, New York: Pantheon Books.

Hamilton, Dona and Charles V. Hamilton (1997) *Dual Agenda: Race and Social Welfare Policies of Civil Rights Organizations*, New York: Columbia University Press.

Harris-Lacewell, Melissa V. (2004) *Barbershops, Bibles, and BET: Everyday Talk and Black Political Thought*, Princeton, NJ: Princeton University Press.

—— (2007) "Political Science and the Study of African American Public Opinion," in *African American Perspectives on Political Science*, Wilbur C. Rich (ed.), 107–129, Philadelphia, PA: Temple University Press.

Hattam, Victoria C. (2007) *In the Shadow of Race: Jews, Latinos, and Immigrant Politics in the United States*, Chicago: University of Chicago Press.

Hattam, Victoria and Joseph Lowndes (2007) "The Ground Beneath Our Feet: Language, Culture, and Political Change," in *Formative Acts: American Politics in the Making*, Stephen Skowronek and Matthew Glassman (eds), 199–222, Philadelphia: University of Pennsylvania Press.

Henry, Charles (1990) *Culture and African American Politics*, Bloomington: Indiana University Press.

Hill, Herbert (1985) *Black Labor and the American Legal System: Race, Work and the Law*, Madison: University of Wisconsin Press.

Holden, Matthew (1973) *The Politics of the Black "Nation,"* New York: Chandler.

Holt, Thomas C. (2000) *The Problem of Race in the 21st Century*, Cambridge, MA: Harvard University Press.

Jacobson, Matthew Frye (1998) *Whiteness of a Different Color: European Immigrants and the Alchemy of Race*, Cambridge, MA: Harvard University Press.

Katznelson, Ira (2005) *When Affirmative Action Was White: An Untold Story of Racial Inequality in Twentieth-Century America*, New York: W.W. Norton.

Kim, Claire (2000) *Bitter Fruit: The Politics of Black–Korean Conflict in New York City*, New Haven: Yale University Press.

Klarman, Michael (2004) *From Jim Crow to Civil Rights: The Supreme Court and the Struggle for Racial Equality*, Oxford: Oxford University Press.

Klinkner, Philip, with Rogers M. Smith (1999) *The Unsteady March: The Rise and Decline of Racial Equality in America*, Chicago: University of Chicago Press.

Kryder, Daniel (2000) *Divided Arsenal: Race and the American State during World War II*, Cambridge: Cambridge University Press.

Lieberman, Robert (1998) *Shifting the Color Line: Race and the American Welfare State*, Cambridge, MA: Harvard University Press.

Lowndes, Joseph (2008) *From the New Deal to the New Right: The Southern Origins of Modern Conservatism, 1945–1976*, New Haven, CT: Yale University Press.

Marx, Anthony W. (1998) *Making Race and Nation: A Comparison of South Africa, the United States, and Brazil*, New York: Cambridge University Press.

McClain, Paula D. and John D. Garcia (1993) "Expanding Disciplinary Boundaries:

Black, Latino, and Racial Minority Groups in Political Science," in *Political Science: State of the Discipline II*, Ada Finifter (ed.), 247–79, Washington, DC: American Political Science Association.

Mink, Gwendolyn (1986) *Old Labor and New Immigrants in American Political Development: Union, Party, and State, 1875–1920*, Ithaca, NY: Cornell University Press.

Mohanty, Chandra Talpade (2003) *Feminism Without Borders: Decolonizing Theory, Practicing Solidarity*, Durham, NC: Duke University Press.

Monroe, Kristen Renwick, ed. (2005) *Perestroika!: The Raucous Rebellion in Political Science*, New Haven, CT: Yale University Press.

Morgan, Edmund S. (1973) *American Slavery, American Freedom: The Ordeal of Colonial Virginia*, New York: Norton.

Morrison, Toni (1991) *Playing in the Dark: Whiteness and the Literary Imagination*, New York: Vintage.

Nash, Gary (2006) *The Forgotten Fifth: African Americans in the Age of Revolution*, Cambridge, MA: Harvard University Press.

National Conference of Black Political Scientists (2007) "History." Online. Available: <http://www.ncobps.org/history.htm>. Accessed October 5, 2007.

Ngai, Mae (2004) *Impossible Subjects: Illegal Aliens and the Making of Modern America, 1924–1965*, Princeton, NJ: Princeton University Press.

Nobles, Melissa (2000) *Shades of Citizenship: Race and the Census in Modern Politics*, Palo Alto, CA: Stanford University Press.

Novkov, Julie (2008) *Racial Union: Law, Intimacy, and the White State in Alabama, 1865–1954.* Ann Arbor: University of Michigan Press.

Olson, Joel (2004) *The Abolition of White Democracy*, Minneapolis: University of Minnesota Press.

Omi, Michael and Howard Winant (1994) *Racial Formation in the United States: From the 1960s to the 1990s*, New York, NY: Routledge, 2nd edn.

Orren, Karen and Stephen Skowronek (2004) *The Search for American Political Development*, New York: Cambridge University Press.

Pascoe, Peggy (1996) "Miscegenation Law, Court Cases, and Ideologies of 'Race' in Twentieth-Century America," *Journal of American History* 83: 44–69.

Pierson, Paul and Theda Skocpol, eds (2007) *The Transformation of American Politics: Activist Government and the Rise of Conservatism*, Princeton, NJ: Princeton University Press.

Plummer, Brenda Gayle (1996) *Rising Wind: Black Americans and U.S. Foreign Affairs, 1935–1960*, Chapel Hill: University of North Carolina Press.

Preston, Michael B. and Maurice Woodward (1984) "The Rise and Decline of Black Political Scientists in the Profession," *PS: Political Science and Politics* 17: 787–92.

Rawick, George (1972) *From Sundown to Sunup: The Making of the Black Community*, Westport, CT: Greenwood Press.

Reed, Adolph, Jr. (1999) *Stirrings in the Jug: Black Politics in the Post-Segregation Era*, Minneapolis: University of Minnesota Press.

—— (2004) "Making Sense of Race," *Journal of Race and Policy* 1: 11–42.

Roediger, David (1991) *The Wages of Whiteness: Race and the Making of the American Working Class*, London: Verso.

Rogin, Michael (1988) *Ronald Reagan The Movie and Other Episodes in Political Demonology*, Berkeley: University of California Press.

Savage, Barbara D. (1999) *Broadcasting Freedom: Radio, War, and the Politics of Race, 1938–1948*, Chapel Hill: University of North Carolina Press.

Schram, Sanford F. and Brian Caterino, eds (2006) *Making Political Science Matter: Debating Knowledge, Research, and Method*, New York: New York University Press.

Singh, Nikhil Pal (2004) *Black Is a Country: Race and the Unfinished Struggle for Democracy*, Cambridge, MA: Harvard University Press.

Skowronek, Stephen (1982) *Building a New American State: The Expansion of National Administrative Capacities, 1877–1920*, Cambridge: Cambridge University Press.

Slotkin, Richard (1973) *Regeneration Through Violence: The Mythology of the American Frontier, 1600–1860*, Middletown, CT: Wesleyan University Press.

—— (1985) *The Fatal Environment: The Myth of the Frontier in the Age of Industrialization, 1800–1890*, Norman: University of Oklahoma Press.

—— (1992) *Gunfighter Nation: The Myth of the Frontier in Twentieth-Century America*, New York: Maxwell McMillan International.

Smith, Rogers (1997) *Civic Ideals: Conflicting Visions of Citizenship in U.S. History*, New Haven, CT: Yale University Press.

Smith-Rosenberg, Carroll (1992) "Dis-covering the Subject of the 'Great Constitutional Discussion,' 1786–1789," *Journal of American History* 79: 841–73.

Stanton, William (1960) *The Leopard's Spots: Scientific Attitudes toward Race in America, 1815–59*, Chicago: University of Chicago Press.

Stevens, Jacqueline (2003) "Racial Meanings and Scientific Methods: Changing Policies for NIH-sponsored Publications Reporting Human Variation," *Journal of Health Policy, Politics, and Law* 28: 1033–98.

Takaki, Ronald (2000) *Double Victory: A Multicultural History of America in World War II*, New York: Little, Brown and Co.

Tolleson-Rinehart, Sue and Susan Carroll (2006) "'Far From Ideal': The Gender Politics of Political Science," *American Political Science Review* 100: 507–13.

Vitalis, Robert (2003) "Birth of a Discipline," in *Imperialism and Internationalism in the Discipline of International Relations*, Brian Schmidt and David Long (eds), Albany: State University of New York Press.

Wacquant, Loic (2001) "Deadly Symbiosis: When Ghetto and Prison Meet and Mesh," *Punishment and Society* 3: 95–133.

Wallenstein, Peter (2002) *Tell the Court I Love My Wife: Race, Marriage, and Law; An American History*, New York: Palgrave.

Walton, Hanes, Jr. (1970) "Black Political Thought: The Problem of Characterization," *Journal of Black Studies* 1: 213–18.

—— (1972) *Black Politics: A Theoretical and Structural Analysis*, Philadelphia, PA: J. B. Lippincott.

—— (1972) *Black Political Parties: An Historical and Political Analysis*, New York: Free Press.

—— (1973) *The Study and Analysis of Black Politics*, Metuchen, NJ: Scarecrow.

—— (1988) *When the Marching Stopped: The Politics of Civil Rights Regulatory Agencies*, Albany: State University of New York Press.

—— (1997) *African American Power and Politics: The Political Context Variable*, New York: Columbia University Press.

Walton, Hanes, Jr., Cheryl Miller, and Joseph McCormick, II (1994) "Race and Political Science: The Dual Traditions of Race Relations Politics and African

American Politics," in *Political Science and its History: Research Programs and Political Traditions*, John Dryzek, James Farr, and Stephen Leonard (eds), 145–74, New York: Cambridge University Press.

Watts, Jerry (2007) "Political Science Confronts Afro-America: A Reconsideration," in *African American Perspectives on Political Science*, Wilbur C. Rich (ed.), 398–433, Philadelphia, PA: Temple University Press.

Williams, Linda Faye (2003) *The Constraint of Race: Legacies of White Skin Privilege in America*, University Park: Pennsylvania State University Press.

Wilson III, Ernest J. and Lorrie A. Frasure (2007) "Still at the Margins: The Persistence of Neglect of African American Issues in Political Science, 1986–2003," in *African American Perspectives on Political Science*, Wilbur C. Rich (ed.), 7–23, Philadelphia, PA: Temple University Press.

Woodward, C. Vann (1974) *The Strange Career of Jim Crow*, New York: Oxford University Press, 3rd edn.

Yamin, Priscilla (2005) "Nuptial Nation: Marriage and the Politics of Civic Membership in the United States," Ph.D. diss., Political Science, New School University, New York.

2 Race and the dual state in the early American republic

Richard Young and Jeffrey Meiser[1]

Ever since the 1960s, American historians have been rewriting American history, demonstrating that since the arrival of Europeans and Africans in the early 1600s, America has been a complex mosaic of different races and cultures. This historical movement has produced an immense literature that not only describes the deep racial and cultural divisions that have existed within American society for centuries, but also explores complex historical patterns of interracial cooperation as well as conflict. However, despite this explosion in American historiography, with only a few exceptions, political scientists continue to discuss and debate the nature of early American political development in Eurocentric terms that would have been familiar to the readers of Charles Beard almost a century ago.

In a sense, this tendency is understandable. White males fully monopolized political and economic power in the United States at least until the Civil War, so it seems appropriate to view American politics from the framing of the Constitution until Lincoln's election as a story of white male institutional creation and evolution and conflicting interests and ideologies. American political scientists have, of course, been aware of slavery and the ethnic cleansing of native peoples, but they have tended to view these historical realities as an ugly, racist sideshow, peripheral to the main events of American political and economic development. We argue the opposite.

Prior to the Civil War, racial exploitation was at the heart of the Anglo-American strategy of political and economic development. Put simply, the Anglo-American state successfully redistributed wealth from Native Americans and African Americans to white males and their families. Native American land was expropriated and sold at low prices or given to Anglo-American settlers fueling the agrarian economies of both the North and South. Chattel slavery deprived African Americans of both the fruits of their labor and their basic human rights. But it also underpinned the rise of cotton production in the South, a major driver of American economic growth in the antebellum period. These developments were not an accidental product of white racism, but the result of a political economy strategy, which created a dual American state: a contract state, premised on the rule of law, that promoted the growth of a prosperous, liberal democratic society of Anglo-Americans, and a predatory state that financed white liberal society through its ruthless exploitation of Indian lands and African American labor.

The hegemony of a white supremacist order in the early American republic

In chapter 4 of this book, Desmond King and Rogers Smith argue that the relationship between race and American political development is best understood in terms of two evolving, competing "racial institutional orders": a "white supremacist" order and an "egalitarian transformative" order. They believe that this conceptual framework is so central to understanding American political development that "no analysis of American politics is likely to be adequate unless the impact of these racial orders is explicitly considered or their disregard explained."

We accept the broad outline of the argument presented by King and Smith, but differ in one key respect: although their analytical framework effectively explains key features of American political development from 1860 to the present, an alternative approach better explains the role of race in the political and economic development of the United States prior to the Civil War. To the extent that an egalitarian transformative order existed during the early decades of the American Republic, it was so marginal to Anglo-American politics as to render King and Smith's racial institutional order framework unhelpful for analyzing the course of American political development during this period. During the American Republic's first half-century, a white racist supremacist order dominated all three regions of the nation—South, West, *and* North— and as a result, the institutionalization of the early Anglo-American state took place almost entirely *within* the context of this single racial institutional order.

In this chapter, we propose an alternative race-centered understanding of American political development from 1787 through the 1830s that conceptualizes early American society as a "plural society" "in which distinct social orders live side by side, but separately, within the same political unit . . . held together by some force exerted from outside" (Furnivall 1944: xv, 405). The "outside force" that maintained the stability of America's plural society was the Anglo-American state.[2] Viewing early America as a plural society captures the social reality of conflictive groups of European Americans, African Americans, and Native Americans, who inhabited the same country, but were socially and culturally divided and only integrated economically and politically through the predatory actions of the Anglo-American state.

The maintenance of America's plural society required an institutional and organizational complexity that descriptions of the early American state often overlook. On the one hand, the state had to sustain its legitimacy through republican accountability to American citizens, i.e., Anglo-American males. On the other hand, state actors had to exercise brutal, coercive control over large groups of non-citizens in order to maintain slavery and promote the geographical expansion necessary for economic growth. Building on Ira Katznelson's (2002) work on the liberal and illiberal aspects of the early American state and Douglass North's (1981) conceptualization of the "predatory state" and "contract state," we believe that the early Anglo-American state can be best described as a dual state: a "predatory state" in its dealings with non-white Americans, but a "contract state" in respect to the internal governance of the dominant group, Anglo-American males. In practice, this duality meant that a prosperous, expanding, liberal democratic, Anglo-American society was made possible by the dispossession of Native Americans from their traditional lands and the enslavement of African Americans.

Both state theory and plural society theory, as described above, tend to reify both states and racial groups as social actors. To escape this problem, and to incorporate both human agency and institutional constraint into our analysis, we treat "political entrepreneurs *and* the preexisting institutional orders in which they operate as the key independent variables in shaping all political change, including racial development" (King and Smith 2005: 76, emphasis in original). The analysis stemming from this eclectic theoretical approach explains *both* the successful institutionalization of the Anglo-American state between 1789 and the late 1830s as well as its inherent instability, which reached crisis proportions in the 1850s. In summary, our chapter advances the following propositions, focusing particularly on the period encompassing the founding era through Jacksonian democratic reform for white men:

1   In order to overcome class and sectional divisions and achieve consensual support from Anglo-American males for the constitutional order devised in 1787, Anglo-American political elites made numerous institutional compromises and pursued a policy of economic growth premised on geographic expansion.

2   This strategy proved to be very successful and led to the institutionalization and growing effectiveness and capacity of *both* the federal and state governments.

3   As the Anglo-American political system democratized during the Jeffersonian and Jacksonian eras, the political pressure for the United States government to acquire ever more western lands increased, as did Southern white demands for the expansion of slavery.

4   During this period, the United States government distributed to its citizenry millions of acres of rich farm land, which had been acquired from American Indians, and took military actions at both the state and federal levels to protect western settlers and enforce slavery. These actions constituted an aggressive intervention by the Anglo-American state in the workings of the national economy.

5   In the Jacksonian era, Anglo-American political entrepreneurs, acting in the context of America's federal institutions, became steadily more partisan, parochial, sectional, and extreme in their political appeals and policy

visions. These developments led to the destabilization of the Anglo-American state despite its success in providing national defense, geographical expansion, liberal democracy, and economic prosperity for its citizenry.

Plural society theory and American social reality

We agree with King and Smith's observation that "American political scientists have historically not been much more successful than America itself in addressing racial issues" (chapter 4). They criticize American political science for its lack of theorizing about race, the focus of the field of American political development on political economy, and the widespread acceptance of Hartz's thesis of a consensual liberal American political culture. We add two additional criticisms: political scientists' implicit assumption of American social and cultural homogeneity arising from a shared intellectual tradition of European social and political thought, and their conceptual exclusion of non-citizens and non-voters from explanatory models of American politics. The intellectual tradition of European social thought, established by liberal contract theorists and extended and criticized by Marx, Bentham, Weber, and Gramsci, assumes social and cultural homogeneity within society and tends to ignore racial divisions (Mills 1997). This tradition has led American scholars—often unwittingly—to base their analyses of American politics upon the assumption that America is a homogeneous society with a single cultural identity. In similar fashion, the old institutionalism, pluralism, public choice theory, and—as King and Smith note—the new historical institutionalism, by focusing on institutional rules and conventional politics, have either ignored racial factors, or relegated them to minor roles, in explaining American political development. Plural society theory corrects this tendency by capturing the reality that since the early 1600s, America has been a complex, multi-racial society, and state theory explains the nature of the relationships that existed between America's racial groups between 1789 and 1861.

Plural society theory was first formulated by J.S. Furnivall (1944), who defined plural societies as societies "in which distinct social orders live side by side, but separately, within the same political unit" (xv). He argued that plural societies arose from the economic considerations that oriented European colonial policy, which led to the immigration and commingling of disparate racial and cultural groups whose only social bond was economic interdependence (405). In conceptualizing the plural society, Furnivall emphasized that, unlike the value consensus and shared sense of national identity that define most European societies, in a plural society, the division of labor tends to be along racial or ethnic lines, and economic inequities tend to coincide with and reinforce social and cultural differences. Without significant value consensus, the constituent groups tend to be conflictive, and the plural society is only "held together by some force exerted from outside" (459, 450; see also van den Berghe 1978). By viewing the United States as a conglomeration of diverse racial groups, plural society theory configures America as a synthetic society created through a process of English colonization and Anglo-American conquest (Ringer 1983). This conceptualization is especially useful in describing and explaining American political developments between 1789 and 1861—the period when the plural society model most accurately fits American social reality.

Early America's plural society and dual state

State theory is central to explaining the dynamics of a plural society because state action determines whether or not a plural society persists, collapses into its constituent social groups, or evolves into a single society. To grasp the nature of the Anglo-American state during its formative years, we focus on two central, but very different, institutional realities and the interactions between them: (1) the internal political dynamics of the dominant racial group (white males), which comprised the Anglo-American "contract state" and (2) the predatory relationship of that state to the two other major racial groups that inhabited the early American republic, Native Americans and African Americans.[3] We believe that this reality of two disparate, but interwoven, sets of state institutions, organizations, public policies, and leadership roles is best captured by the concept of a "dual state."

Ira Katznelson's (2002: 82–110) analysis of the role of the military in early American state-building highlights the paradoxical duality of the early American state in which liberal institutions were entwined with coercive state power. Rejecting characterizations of the Early Republic as a "weak state," Katznelson shows that "[t]he United States may have had a state of limited size and centralization, but this state was flexible, effective and efficient" (86). The Anglo-American military was central to this effectiveness; it was "capable of achieving the greatest task of statebuilders: defining, expanding, and securing boundaries" (91) through its success in displacing and, when necessary, defeating in battle America's indigenous peoples and other challengers to Anglo-American power. In addition, the United States' military enabled the United States to become "the only Western nation to internalize a slave regime" (94). In his conclusion, Katznelson observes that "[i]n addition to the protection of its security and commerce the early American state had two main purposes: the management of a sectionally heterogeneous polity and the extension of its sovereignty and normative reach" (104).

We build on Katznelson's insights by further explaining: (1) the centrality of state action in the economic and political development of the early Anglo-American republic, (2) the role of the Anglo-American state as a predatory instrument of Anglo-American interests in their dealings with other races during this period, and (3) the functional relationship that existed between the liberal and illiberal aspects of Anglo-American politics and public policy. Furthermore, we demonstrate that all these processes happened within a white supremacist institutional order, and that the successful institutionalization of the Anglo-American state strengthened this white supremacist order and gave it monopolistic control over the creation and implementation of American public policy.

Analytically, Douglass North's (1981) distinction between contract and predatory theories of the state best captures the simultaneously liberal and coercive aspects of the Anglo-American state. North asserts two "types of explanation for the state": contract and predatory (21). Contract theories argue that the state "plays the role of wealth maximizer for society . . . [and] because a contract limiting each individual's activity relative to others is essential for there to be economic growth, the contract theory approach offers an explanation for the development of efficient property rights that would promote economic growth" (22). In contrast, predatory theories of the state suggest that the state specifies "a set of property rights that maximize the revenue of the group in power, regardless of its impact on the wealth of the society as a whole. . . . This view considers the state to be the agency of a group or class; its function, to extract income from the rest of the constituents in the interest of that group or class" (22; see also Levi 1988). These two conceptualizations of the state differ in that "contract theory assumes an equal distribution of violence potential amongst the principals. The predatory theory assumes an unequal distribution of power" (North 1981: 22).

North views the contract state and the predatory state as mutually exclusive categories. However, during its formative years, *the United States was both a contract state and a predatory state*, or more precisely, the early Anglo-American state was a predatory state in which the dominant group organized its internal dynamics as a contract state. The framers of the Constitution of 1787 based the national state's authority on the principle of popular sovereignty (Wood 1969: 532–6), and as a system of internal governance for Anglo-American males, the Constitution embodied a Lockean social contract. During the formative years of the new republic, the national government consistently adhered to the constitutional rules of the game in resolving Anglo-American political disputes and implementing public policy. However, as we explain below, the consensual support of Anglo-Americans for this constitutional system depended on constant economic growth, which in an agrarian economy could only be achieved by the creation of an effective predatory state capable of dispossessing the country's Native Americans and enforcing the property rights in humans that African-American slavery required.

The origins of the Anglo-American dual state lay in its colonial and revolutionary past, but the framing, ratification, early amendment, and gradual institutionalization of the Constitution of 1787 created a national state able to govern an "empire of liberty" that rapidly grew to continental proportions. This dynamic process of "state-building" involved shifting coalitions of Anglo-American political elites and their followers, who fashioned a system of evolving political institutions and supportive public policies (Bright 1987). The success of these interconnected institutions and policies required consensual support from the Anglo-American citizenry, which was achieved through a process of public debate, popular election, and frequent—but incremental—policy adjustments, which continued until the Anglo-American state collapsed in 1860.

The framers as accommodating conservatives[4]

The men who wrote the United States Constitution in the summer of 1787 led a unified social elite that dominated Anglo-American society (Hofstadter 1948: 5–17; Wiebe 1984). They believed that a society governed by the wealthy and well-born benefited all its members, and they viewed the Constitution as an institutional device that would preserve the existing social order and their place within it (Riesman 1987). As Douglass North (1981: 190) has observed: "The ideological perspective that [the Constitution] reflected was broader than any particular set of interests but was, within the vision of the framers, generally consistent with their interests." However, while the Framers were protective of their own well-being, they were also ideologically committed to republican principles of governance, and they knew that their constitution's success depended upon public support (Wood 1969; Young 1980). As a result, in writing the Constitution, they curbed their more conservative instincts and attempted to achieve two contradictory goals that had traditionally eluded European statesmen: the protection of the economic interests of the rich and powerful, while anchoring the political system on the consent of "the people."

In the United States of the 1780s, the achievement of these twin goals meant reconciling the interests of the plantation owners of the South and the merchants and lawyers of the Middle States and New England with the concerns of the small, independent farmers, artisans, and laborers, who comprised the bulk of the new nation's citizenry. The Framers resolved these conflicts through a complex, subtle, and evolving strategy that involved: first, a frank recognition of class and regional divisions within Anglo-American society; second, the design of national political institutions that would dilute these divisions; and, finally—after the Constitution was ratified and new patterns of national leadership emerged—a program of geographic and economic expansion that would unite Anglo-Americans in a common enterprise.

When the Framers gathered in Philadelphia in the summer of 1787, they were united in their fear that the state governments had fallen into the hands of radical populists, and "if events in the states ran out of control, redistribution of property would become a reality and social life as gentlemen had known it would disappear" (Riesman 1987: 150). James Madison—the most influential theorist at the Constitutional Convention—argued that the state governments had been captured by majoritarian tyrannies and had passed "unjust laws," which threatened the rights of property owners. Only a strong national government could remedy this situation (Madison cited in Farrand 1937: 135–6).

As David Robertson (2005: 64) notes, "Madison proposed to restructure the national government and to empower national policy makers to pursue the economic interests of the nation as a whole, independent of the interests of the individual states." He wanted the national government to have the power "to monitor and veto state policies at will." But Madison did not achieve these goals. Instead, the convention produced the two-tiered, federal system of government that has structured American political development ever since. It is difficult to imagine the convention doing otherwise. Public support for the new constitution depended upon the preservation of significant state independence, as the ratification debates and the necessity of adding a bill of rights demonstrate (Siemers 2002). A path dependent process, beginning with colonial settlement in the 1600s, had led to the institutionalization of quasi-sovereign states whose autonomy could be restricted, but not eliminated (see Deudney 1995: 210–16, 1996).[5]

The Framers were equally constrained in what they could accomplish in regard to the power of "the people." Despite their serious misgivings regarding democratic governance, the Framers accepted contemporary political realities, and based their new constitution on the principle of popular sovereignty (Wood 1969), while simultaneously erecting a set of procedural obstacles to democratic rule (Young 1980). Madison defended the Framers' handiwork in *The Federalist Papers*, arguing that the "most common and durable source" of conflict among men was the "unequal distribution of property" (Madison 1961: 59). According to Madison, government by the people would inevitably lead to a tyranny of the many over the few *unless* the power of the people was functionally and institutionally diluted (56–65, 347–53). However, contrary to Madison's design, in the decades following the Constitution's ratification, the effectiveness of the institutional barriers to democratic government crumbled as nearly all white males obtained the franchise, and national political parties, which could organize and mobilize the mass electorate, emerged (Hofstadter 1969). Thus, the problem raised by Madison remained: how could the United States government prevent class conflict among its citizens?

Madison himself provided the practical answer to this question in one of his less read essays, *Federalist No. 38*, citing the enormous potential wealth of the western lands:

> It is now no longer a point of speculation and hope that the Western territory is a mine of vast wealth to the United States, and although it is not of such a nature as to extricate them from their present distresses . . . yet must it hereafter be able under proper management both to effect a gradual discharge of the domestic debt and to furnish for a certain period, liberal tributes to the Federal Treasury . . . a rich and fertile country, of an area equal to that inhabited extent of the United States, will soon become a national stock.
>
> (Madison 1961: 248; see also Madison 1977: 98–9)

This "national stock" would be the key to Anglo-American political stability. *In a large and steadily growing republic, the nation's wealth would constantly increase, enabling virtually all of the contestants for political power to experience a steady improvement in their economic and social well-being.* This process of steady economic growth, combined with the fragmentation of political power, would ensure that public policy would engender[6] moderate incremental change, social stability, and widespread public contentment. In a pre-industrial society, this happy state of affairs could only be achieved through the steady expansion of the society's agrarian acreage and the widespread distribution of farm ownership among the citizenry at low cost (McCoy 1980).

These political economy assumptions were as well understood and as widely shared among both the political elite and the general citizenry of the Early Republic as were the philosophical beliefs in popular sovereignty, individual rights, states' rights, separation of powers, and checks and balances (Stourzh 1954; McCoy 1980; Riesman 1983; Bailyn 1986: 60–86). For example, in the colonial era, Benjamin Franklin had argued that the government's provision of land to Anglo-American settlers was the highest form of statesmanship: "the Prince that acquires new Territory, if he finds it vacant, or removes the Natives to give his own People Room . . . may be properly called [a] Father of [his] Nation" (Franklin 1961: 231; emphasis in original). Two years before he chaired the Constitutional Convention, Washington saw the availability of western lands to European settlers as a means of ending all social conflict: "Rather than quarrel about territory, let the poor, the needy, & oppressed of the Earth; and those who want Land, resort to the fertile plains of our Western country, to the second Land of promise, & there dwell in peace" (Washington cited in Rasmussen and Tilton 1999: 100; see also Larson 2001: 4, 11).

The Northwest Ordinances as a foundational public policy paradigm

The nation's founding public policy vision made the Framers' institutional design a successful reality. While the Framers were crafting their constitution in Philadelphia, the nation's Congress, meeting in New York, was finalizing a series of policy decisions that would determine the course of early American economic and political development. Acting under the Articles of Confederation, the original states had voluntarily surrendered their claims to the lands west of the Appalachians, giving Congress the power to administer this immense public domain. Congress responded to this challenge by enacting the Land Ordinance of 1785 and the Northwest Ordinance of 1787, which together founded a comprehensive public policy paradigm for subsequent Anglo-American development (Onuf 1987).[6] The Land Ordinance of 1785 stated the procedures for the measurement and sale of public lands acquired by the national government from Indian tribes; its political counterpart, the Northwest Ordinance of 1787, established the principles of territorial governance and the process by which the territories would become states (Onuf 1987; Rakove 1988; Wright 2003).

The Founders designed this public policy paradigm to govern a large and expanding republic.[7] Their strategy was one of conducting geopolitical and economic expansion in order to protect the sanctity of private property, outlaw primogeniture, guarantee republican governance, promote Anglo-American economic and political cohesion, and support economic growth (McCoy 1980; Onuf 1987; Matson and Onuf 1990; Onuf and Sadosky 2002). Once the Constitution of 1787 was ratified, this vision became an effective national policy. In 1789, the new federal Congress reenacted the Northwest Ordinance ensuring that its provisions were consistent with the new constitution (Onuf 1987: xviii), and in 1790 Congress passed the Southwest Ordinance to govern national expansion south of the Ohio River.

Thomas Jefferson, more than anyone else, was responsible for the initiation of this program. He had written the Land Ordinance of 1784, and his thinking strongly influenced the content of subsequent ordinances (Onuf 1987: 143–5). As an agrarian republican, Jefferson was sympathetic to forging an alliance of Southern planters and Western farmers, and he knew that this coalition would only succeed if enough cheap land was available to allow both large and small farmers to improve their lots (McCoy 1980). As a result, he based his political economy upon small-scale family farming and rapid westward expansion (Oberly 1990: 4; Atack et al. 2000: 285, 288; Sylla 2000: 490, 517). Jefferson saw that the greatest asset of the Anglo-American state was its claim to the immense territories of the West and successfully fought for the principle that the public domain would "pass into secure private ownership and development;" these principles laid "the foundation of future American capitalism— private ownership and control of productive resources" (Hughes 1990: 91). With effective national governance of the West assured, "economic growth would resolve conflicts that grew out of scarcity: all interests would benefit from an expanding pie" (Onuf 1987: 14).

Jefferson and his fellow republicans well understood that in Europe land ownership had been the foundation of the state's power, and they wanted to ensure that no national state, church, or aristocracy would use the public domain as the basis of its power. To achieve this goal, they developed a system by which public land would "be a one-time source of revenue to the national government" and then fall into permanent private ownership (Hughes 1990: 89–91; see also Sylla 2000: 494–5). Through these policies, the national state could abandon its traditional predatory role *within its own ethnic group* and become the provider of land to the Anglo-American citizenry and the protector of their property rights. With immense amounts of land available, speculators could make, or lose, fortunes in the process of privatizing the public domain without pushing land prices beyond the reach of middling farmers (Lebergott 1984: 74–84).

By combining republican values with a commitment to western expansion, the Founders transformed popular sovereignty from a radical proposition threatening to property rights, to a conservative creed that protected property rights, but also celebrated equality of opportunity. Concretely, the chief functions of the new national state would be to gain dominion over hundreds of millions of acres of "wilderness" lands and to distribute these lands at low cost to rich and poor alike. Through its control of the western lands, the federal government could guarantee property rights while still maintaining its republican nature. In a constantly expanding economic universe, class warfare could be averted. Expansion was consistent with the Founders' republican ideology (McCoy 1980), but it also enriched land speculators, northern merchants, and southern planters while promoting a social and political alliance with white family farmers (Matson and Onuf 1990: 149–50). Further support for an expansionist policy came from political leaders whose concerns ranged from simply wanting a steady source of income for the new federal government to preventing threatening European powers from gaining control of the West (Anderson 1987; Lewis 1998; Hietala 2003).

Public land and the contract state

During the half-century following the Constitution's ratification, aggressive government land and labor policies undergirded Anglo-American economic prosperity and the political legitimacy and stability of the Anglo-American state (Feller 1984: xii; Sylla 2000: 483, 489–97). From its colonial beginnings until its antebellum collapse, Anglo-America was largely an agrarian economy and society comprised of individual land owners who grew crops for themselves and the market. As late as 1850, 64 percent of the work force was in agriculture, and half the nation's population lived on farms (Olmstead 2006: 8). On the eve of the Civil War, 55.8 percent of the American labor force was engaged in farm work as opposed to only 13.8 percent who were in manufacturing (Carter 2006: 18). Thus, the federal government's chief contribution to Anglo-American well-being prior to the Civil War was gaining control over the lands that Native Americans had previously occupied for centuries and transferring ownership of that land to millions of Anglo-Americans.

This program of property redistribution was of continental proportions and can be legitimately viewed as one of the most radical and effective entitlement programs in world history (Jensen 2003). The federal government implemented this massive program of land redistribution through a settler-friendly land policy, a program of centralized territorial governance, extensive military intervention against hostile Indian tribes and threatening European nation-states, and support for southern slavery (Atack and Passell 1994; Palmer 1994; Katznelson 2002; Ericson 2005). This system did not produce social equality or the redistribution of wealth among Anglo-Americans (Pessen 1973), but it did allow the United States to develop an expanding economy, which enabled most of its citizens to experience a steady improvement in their economic well-being (Bruchey 1990: 253; Lebergott 1984: 72). In the North, these policies promoted the settlement of lands west of the Appalachians by family farmers and provided a safety valve for the Northeast's rapidly growing population (Lebergott 1984: 88–90). In the South, government policies fostered a similar pattern of white settlement and ensured white social and political solidarity by enabling white planters to rely almost entirely on black slaves for labor. However, maintaining the equilibrium of this system required continuing a state-sponsored program of aggressive geographic expansion.

Between the ratification of the Constitution and the Civil War, the United States government sold (at low prices) or gave individuals more than two hundred million acres of public land (Gates 1964: 28, 1968: 802). The federal government also gave state governments millions of additional acres for the construction of schools, colleges, public buildings, roads, canals, and railroads (Gates 1968: 285–386, 804–6). The public domain provided bounties for military service and pensions for veterans (Gates 1968: 249–84; Oberly 1990; Jensen 2003); it provided security for the national debt and a significant source of national income (Feller 1984); but most importantly, it bought political stability by offering individuals and individual states tangible benefits for remaining loyal to the United States (Lebergott 1985; see also Feller 1984: xii, xiii, 6, 7, 11; Onuf 1987: xix, 2, 5, 31; Atack et al. 2000: 287).

As the Anglo-American political system democratized during the 1820s and 1830s, land policy became highly politicized (Feller 1984), and the Anglo-American contract state became a *patronage state* (Skocpol 1992: 67–101) in which the government dispensed goods and jobs to its political supporters (see Carpenter 2001: 37–63). Because of electoral pressure, as land values increased, the price of public land *decreased*, and land was sold in smaller parcels (Feller 1984; Lebergott 1984: 74–84, 1985; Bruchey 1990: 222–53). In addition, squatters were granted the right of preemption, and veterans were given land warrants (Feller 1984; Oberly 1990; Jensen 2003). However, in forging what was, for them, a benign national state, Anglo-Americans also created an aggressive, racist state, which cruelly exploited other peoples.

The Anglo-American predatory state

Between the American Revolution and the Civil War, the United States government acquired an immense public domain of more than *one billion acres* (Bruchey 1990: 223). Officially, Anglo-Americans gained sovereignty over these lands through war and diplomacy with Great Britain, Jefferson's purchase of Louisiana, diplomacy with Spain, and a war with Mexico (Weeks 1996). In legal theory, the acquisition of this territory rested on the assumption that by right of discovery and conquest, European powers or their post-colonial successors owned North America (Williams 1990; Washburn 1995: 3–74). However, in practice, the successful utilization of these lands meant wrestling them from the native peoples who had occupied them for centuries. It was important to Anglo-Americans that this land be formally purchased or acquired through treaty by the federal government, rather than simply confiscated, in order to establish a firm basis of ownership in Anglo-American law (Banner 2005).

Between the Revolution and the Civil War, Native Americans ceded 772 million acres to the United States (Lebergott 1985: 211–12). In gaining title to these lands, government officials consistently adhered to the legal fiction that they had been purchased through freely negotiated agreements, and by 1868, 374 treaties had been signed (Nabokov 1991: 117–21). However, as Stuart Banner has convincingly documented,

> every land transfer of any form included elements of *law* and elements of *power*. No non-Indian acquiring Indian land thought himself unconstrained by Anglo-American law . . . Law was always present, but so was power. The more powerful whites became relative to Indians, the more they were able to mold the legal system to produce outcomes in their favor.
>
> (4, emphasis in original)

Banner's study shows a clear relationship between the democratization of Anglo-American society and its government's Indian policies. During the colonial era, the government in London felt some concern for the welfare of the American Indians and attempted periodically to maintain good relations with them. For example, in 1763, the British government banned European settlement west of the Appalachian Mountains. However, after Anglo-Americans achieved their independence and created an effective national state, Anglo-American settlers rapidly moved into Indian territory. As the Anglo-American political system became more "democratic," it also became even more racist and sexist as women and free blacks were stripped of rights (Smith 1997: 165–232). The systematic economic exploitation of non-whites was extremely popular among United States citizens, and according to the Jeffersonian theory of legitimacy, the support of the populace would increase as the "people realized that the federal government embodied and served their interests" (Lewis 1998: 20).

Jefferson's program of land distribution pitted the interests of Anglo-Americans directly against those of Native Americans (Wallace 1999). As we have seen, Jefferson and his political allies designed a system in which the national government responded to the pressures of Anglo-American farmers, who constituted the bulk of the electorate, by establishing public control over western land which was subsequently turned over to private owners. This system was self-perpetuating and led to an accelerating demand for land, which, regardless of the intentions or rationales of Anglo-American leaders, produced irresistible political pressure for the redistribution of Indian lands to Anglo-American farmers. By the early 1800s, because of the steady growth in the numbers and power of Anglo-American settlers west of the Appalachians, land sales were, in effect, forced on native peoples (Prucha 1986: 64–77; Cayton 1998; Horsman 1999; Hurt 2002; Banner 2005; L.G. Robertson 2005).

These developments culminated in Andrew Jackson's policy of Indian removal in the 1830s. Jackson, who had gained a national reputation fighting the British and the Indians, was elected president in 1828. Soon after his inauguration, he asked Congress for legislation that would empower the federal government to remove all eastern Indians to a "district West of the Mississippi, and without the limits of any State or Territory, now formed, to be guaranteed to the Indian tribes as long as they shall occupy it" (cited in Wallace 1993: 123). Following Jackson's lead, Congress passed the Indian Removal Act of 1830, which required almost all Indians living in the United States to migrate west of the Mississippi. As a result, the Cherokees—along with the other eastern Indian nations—were forced on a death march to Oklahoma (Wallace 1993).

The Anglo-American state's self-reinforcing structural dynamics facilitated the rapid expansion of the Anglo-American nation during the nineteenth century. In a continental republic, the federal government could purchase land from American Indians, enforce Indian treaties, survey and sell public lands to white settlers, and provide military protection for Anglo-American settlers (Prucha 1969; Millet and Maslowski 1994; Hurt 2002; Katznelson 2002). However, Anglo-Americans could normally rely on state militias and volunteers —recruited from local populations and oriented toward local exigencies—to maintain white hegemony in their areas of settlement (Mahon 1983: 46–96). This division of labor worked extremely well in (1) achieving white control of the "middle ground" between western white settlers and native peoples, and (2) maintaining white hegemony in the South, where every able-bodied white man was expected to serve on slave patrols (Stampp 1956: 214–15; Prucha 1969; Mahon 1983: 46–62; Katznelson 2002, 90–4).

The South's "peculiar institution"

In the North, Indian removal completed the creation of a socially homogeneous region dominated by white family farmers (Hughes 1990: 182). However, in the South, the removal of the indigenous population paved the way for the creation of a plural society of Anglo-Americans and African Americans. The motivation for constructing this biracial society was entirely economic, based significantly upon the rise of cotton as the nation's leading commercial crop.

Paul Finkelman (1987) has convincingly demonstrated that the Framers established a firm institutional basis for the protection and extension of racial slavery. Some of these foundational protections were: the three-fifths clause that allowed slaves to be counted as three-fifths of whites for purposes of computing *white male* representation in Congress (Art. I, Sec. 2); the prohibition for ending the African slave trade before 1808 (Art. I, Sec. 9, Par. 1); and the fugitive slave clause, which prohibited states from emancipating escaped slaves and required that these slaves be returned to their owners (Art. IV, Sec. 2, Par. 3). Finkelman also cites numerous "indirect protections of slavery" in the Constitution of 1787, such as the empowering of Congress to call "forth the Militia" to "Suppress Insurrections" (Art. I, Sec. 8, Par. 15) and the prohibition of taxes on exports (Art I, Sec. 9, Par. 5), which was a direct subsidy to the South's slave economy (191–2; see also Finkelman 1996).

During the colonial era, African-American slaves had labored to produce tobacco, rice, and indigo (Sheridan 1984: 45–55; Engerman 2000: 333, 335). With the invention and development of the cotton gin in the late 1790s and early 1800s, cotton quickly became the nation's dominant commercial crop. During the second and third decades of the nineteenth century, it became the primary basis for the nation's economic development (North 1966). In the seven decades following the ratification of the Constitution, cotton production rose from 3,000 bales in 1790 to 1,348,000 bales in 1840 and 3,841,000 bales in 1860 (Olmstead and Rhode 2006; 110–1). Cotton "was by far the most important single export [and] before the Civil War . . . earned directly more than half the nation's ability to buy needed goods from abroad" (Hughes 1990: 188).

Slavery was integral to United States cotton production, which dominated worldwide production (Engerman 2000: 338). Half of the United States' exports from 1825 to 1850 were from cotton, which supported many other aspects of the American economy (339). Slaves were a good investment right up until the first shot was fired on Fort Sumter, and "southern planters were disproportionately among the wealthiest Americans in 1850 and 1860" (343). "On the eve of the Civil War, the economic value of slaves in the United States was $3 billion in 1860 currency, more than the combined value of all the factories, railroads and banks in the country" (Foner 2000), and comprised 20 percent of the total national wealth (Huston 2003: 27–8) and 44 percent of all wealth in the cotton-growing states of the South (Ransom and Sutch 1988: 138–9).

The centrality of cotton to the South's economy led to an expansionist plural society that displayed the following dynamics:

1   Cotton was labor intensive, and *"the output per slave was markedly higher on the more fertile lands of the West"* (Ransom 1989: 45, emphasis in original). Cotton production was slave based, and the rapid expansion of cotton farming significantly increased the demand for slave labor and made slaves very valuable (46–7). By 1850, more than 90 percent of the South's agricultural wealth was owned by slave-holders, and slaves comprised more than a third of the South's population (Hughes 1990: 190–1).

2   This rapidly growing agrarian economy provided economic opportunities that drove Anglo-Americans westward and led them to disregard Native-American claims to their traditional lands (Wallace 1993).

3   These expansionist dynamics were reinforced by the political necessity to provide Anglo-Americans of all social classes with land opportunities in the West in order to prevent explosive class tensions from developing between the South's white planters and small farmers (Oakes 1982), and to maintain the social solidarity among whites necessary for wresting the western lands from the Indians and controlling the enslaved black population (Fredrickson 1981).

4   All of these factors were mutually reinforcing, and in the first four decades of the nineteenth century, they led to: (a) the institutionalization of slavery

in the South, (b) a national policy of western expansionism that was pursued regardless of its cost to Native Americans (Weeks 1996), (c) the evolution of Anglo-American ethnocentrism into a virulent racist ideology (Fredrickson 1971: 43–70), (d) the steady economic growth and improvement of the average Anglo-Americans' standard of living in both the North and the South (Bruchey 1990: 253; Lebergott 1984: 72), and (e) the institutionalization and legitimation of the American constitutional system.

In securing two of the classic ingredients of a prosperous economy, land and labor, the government insured Anglo-American well-being and the institutionalization of the Anglo-American contract state. But by dispossessing Native Americans and enforcing the enslavement of African Americans, the Anglo-American state was also a predatory state—a *Herrenvolk* democracy that was "democratic for the master race but tyrannical for the subordinate groups" (van den Berghe 1978: 18).

The institutionalization of the Anglo-American dual state

Anglo-American political history from the early 1600s to 1860 can be viewed as a story of institutional continuity. Both the political institutions and the dominant public policy paradigm of the Anglo-American republic resulted from a long developmental process. English common law, well-developed notions of individual rights and property rights, and beliefs in representative and accountable government were brought to America by English colonists and evolved into sophisticated Anglo-American political institutions and ideological beliefs during the colonial and revolutionary periods (Wood 1969; Murrin 1984; Morgan 1988; Bailyn 1992; Hoffer 1998; 131–62). In similar fashion, English agrarian capitalism and slavery were well-established institutions by the seventeenth century, and in North America English colonists were motivated primarily by land hunger (Bailyn 1986; Galenson 1996; Jones 1996; Kulikoff 2000; McDougall 2004, 17–37). The availability of land, if seized from the native peoples, and labor, if provided by slaves, led to a transformation in the relationship between white land owners and laborers from an antagonistic one in England to a cooperative alliance in America (Morgan 1975; Galenson 1996; Jennings 2000).

Thus, prior to the Civil War, Anglo-American political development can be understood as a process of path dependence, positive feedback, and increasing returns (see Pierson 2000, 2004) evolving for more than two centuries through a process of incremental—albeit at times major—institutional change (see Campbell 2004). Even such critical junctures as the American Revolution and the ratification of the Constitution both reinforced and accelerated a path-dependent process, which transformed thirteen English colonies hugging the Atlantic Coast into an agrarian, capitalistic, liberal democratic, racist, Anglo-American republic of continental proportions whose trajectory can be seen in its English and colonial origins.

The Founders' strategy of creating an independent Anglo-American nation governed by a federal state committed to popular sovereignty and economic expansion was enormously successful. During the Anglo-American state's first half-century, it grew steadily in strength and legitimacy. Congress created organizations such as the federal judiciary, Bank of the United States, post office, land office, army, and territorial governments, which displayed high levels of capacity (Skowronek 1982: 19; John 1995, 1997; Kersh 2001; Katznelson 2002). These organizations brought order and coherence to Anglo-American life while providing important services. Investments in internal improvements, whether through direct funding or land grants, also fostered unity and commerce (Larson 2001). Land grants to Anglo-American soldiers and their dependents (Jensen 2003), and, as Katznelson (2002) notes, the army played a major role in fostering national development by promoting "the country's territorial extension, trade, and security" (90).

At an abstract level of analysis, the key factors that drove political development in the Anglo-American state were (1) the principle and institutional realities of popular sovereignty, (2) an expansionist, foundational public policy paradigm, (3) a unifying Anglo-American ideology of white supremacy, and (4) a federal political structure. In existential terms, these institutions, policies, and beliefs were articulated, creatively combined, modified, and communicated to the public by competing Anglo-American political entrepreneurs and their mobilized followers, all acting in the context of an evolving plural society and responding to changing technological, economic, and demographic realities (see Sheingate 2003).

Three key methods—military action, law enforcement, and ideological leadership—enabled Anglo-American political elites, with strong support from their nation's citizenry, to use the Anglo-American state to institutionalize a racially hierarchical social order. In each case, as Katznelson (2002: 86) has demonstrated, the Anglo-American federal state, with its flexibility, effectiveness, and efficiency was well suited for these purposes. And as Katznelson (2002; Katznelson and Lapinski 2006) has also noted, Congress and the military were the most important institutions for making and implementing the predatory policies necessary for the maintenance of an Anglo-American liberal state.

Rogers Smith (1997: 137–242) has shown how Anglo-American political leaders provided intellectual coherence for the dual state's racist policies and military actions by creatively combining republican, liberal, and ascriptive arguments in their defense of Anglo-America's "manifest destiny." At the national level, Anglo-American leaders justified federal Indian policies and created a national consensus in respect to them, while at the same time compromising sectional differences over slavery. Federalism allowed white politicians to make often inconsistent ideological arguments based on ugly racist appeals to their constituents on the western frontier and in the South, while national leaders could invoke—often sincerely—paternalistic language that suggested that the United States' policies toward Native Americans and

African Americans served the best interests of these groups (Fredrickson 1971, 1981; Wallace 1993; Horsman 1999; Hietala 2003; Banner 2005).

Path dependence and positive feedback institutionalized the Anglo-American state, not merely through a process of institutional inertia, but because the state earned white male support and loyalty through its effective governance, which provided both public *and* private goods to the Anglo-American citizenry. In the half-century following the Constitution's ratification, this process steadily reinforced the nation's dominant white supremacist racial institutional order to such an extent that *it was the Anglo-American state*. During the 1840s and 1850s, the Anglo-American republic became more of a market economy, grew more prosperous, offered greater economic opportunities to its citizens, developed a more pluralistic civil society, further democratized its political institutions, and gained greater military strength (Remini 1976; Wiebe 1984; Sellers 1991; Millet and Maslowski 1994; Feller 1995). Given these realities, after reading the scholarly literature on economic and political development (e.g., Lipset and Lakin 2004: 3–238), one would expect the Anglo-American nation to be very stable in respect to its domestic politics and very reluctant to pursue an aggressive foreign policy. However, the Anglo-American state not only increased its exploitation of slaves and Indians, but it invaded a neighboring nation and annexed half its territory, *and ultimately collapsed into disunion and civil war.*

The internal contradictions of the Anglo-American contract state

The Framers of the Constitution dealt successfully with many important problems, but two basic contradictions in the Anglo-American constitutional system remained unresolved: (1) Southern adherence to the Union was purely instrumental, and (2) the North and South's different systems of property rights were incompatible. The federal structure of the Anglo-American state allowed the Founders to avoid confronting these fundamental tensions. Nevertheless, their efforts were eventually undone by their nation's geographical expansion and democratization. This process produced a generation of political entre-preneurs who were far more committed to the interests and ideologies of their constituents than to the preservation of the Anglo-American nation-state.

In his analysis of the Constitutional Convention, David Robertson (2005: xii) argues that the delegates had to "create a government that could produce beneficial policies while at the same time ensuring that its policies would not harm the nation or their own constituents, or interests that they considered vital. They especially wanted a government whose policies would cultivate commerce and protect property." Robertson emphasizes the political rather than the value-dependent nature of the delegates' approach (100). As a result, the Framers crafted "a series of politically expedient compromises aimed at expanding national power while minimizing threats to the delegates' constituencies" (165–6), which created the institutional realities that we today understand as "federalism," "separation of powers," and "checks and balances."

Brilliant as these creative and pragmatic realists were, the Framers' product suffered from two fundamental flaws. First of all, as Finkelman (1987) shows, the white South's attitude toward the Constitution was entirely instrumental: Southern delegates favored states' rights when those principles protected slavery, but voted as nationalists—as they did on the fugitive slave clause—when they did not. The fragility of such conditional loyalty was often forgotten when Southern whites dominated Anglo-American national politics, as they usually did during the seven decades following the Constitution's ratification (Richards 2000; Fehrenbacher 2001), but as the white South's dependence on slavery for its wealth and power steadily increased during the antebellum era, and its dominant role in the federal government came under concerted attack, its loyalty to the Union became increasingly problematic.

But the constitutional system designed to "cultivate commerce and protect property" also contained an inherent structural contradiction (Richards 2000). United as Anglo-Americans might be in their vision of westward expansion, racial superiority, and manifest destiny, they divided fundamentally over whether human beings should be defined as property (Wright 1978, 2006; Huston 2003). James Huston shows that "property rights in Africans" were "the bulwark of all southern white society" and grounded the social pathways of the South (42). As a result, white Southern loyalty to the Union was always contingent upon egoistic calculations over whether the Union would support "the value of property in slaves" (57).

Federalism papered over these sectional divisions, and during its first half-century, Anglo-American political leaders successfully promoted the legitimacy and institutionalization of the Anglo-American state, because the state achieved Anglo-American prosperity through geographic expansionism, while simultaneously protecting the individual and states' rights of its citizens. However, while the Anglo-American state effectively defended America from European intervention and achieved supremacy on the North American continent, it had limited ability to coerce either state governments or the Anglo-American citizenry to support its leadership. As a result, the central paradox of the Anglo-American state was that while it had been remarkably successful in achieving the goals of its creators, its institutional design rendered it totally dependent on skillful, nationally oriented political leadership for its success and even survival. Thus, the Anglo-American state's legitimacy not only depended on its success in pursuing the predatory policies described in this chapter, but it also rested on its leaders' ability to maintain a national consensus by constantly reminding its citizenry, as Jefferson had done, that they were all "brethren of the same principle" united by a shared national vision, purpose, and identity (Smith 1997: 137–242).

Skillful political leadership was needed because the national government could not really force its citizenry to do very much. Strong—and potentially autonomous—state governments held independent and exclusive police powers and could challenge national governmental actions that their publics viewed as tyrannical. Understanding these realities, Washington hungered after consensus, as did Jefferson, and as long as the Founders' generation governed, the Anglo-American nation-state grew steadily in its capacity, legitimacy, and effectiveness. However, as the nation also grew in size, wealth, population, and complexity, and the Founders' generation died off, the Anglo-American political system fell prey to its centrifugal design and devolved from a paternalistic, Eurocentric republic, governed by a unified elite, into a democratic, racist state dominated by political entrepreneurs seeking issues to promote their advancement regardless of the cost to the Union. Ironically, the very success of the Anglo-American predatory state promoted institutional conflict within the federal system. The prosperity and support for the nation's political institutions, which resulted from state actions, led to the institutionalization and the growing effectiveness and capacity of governmental institutions *at both the state and federal level* and strong sectional differences (Novak 1996; Wallis 1999, 2000; Sylla 2000; Wallis and Weingast 2005). The institutional tensions of the two-tiered Anglo-American state—further divided functionally at each level into three separate branches—underlay an inherently unstable political system.

Article IV, Sections 3 and 4, of the Constitution enabled Congress to create new states in the West with republican governments and the same rights and privileges enjoyed by the original eastern states. While these provisions allowed for the development of an "empire of liberty" of continental proportions, they also guaranteed constant political conflict within the Anglo-American political system as the admission of each new state destroyed the existing political equilibrium in Congress and the electoral college, providing political opportunities for a new class of ambitious political entrepreneurs (Meinig 1993: 447–61; Weingast 1998). These western politicians promoted public policies—and espoused innovative ideological justifications for them—that gained strong public support within their own states but often destabilized the Anglo-American nation-state as a whole (Donald 1956; Holt 1978; Gienapp 1996).

During the early years of the Republic, Federalist and Republican divisions were real, and the election of 1800 addressed conflict over fundamental philosophical principles and the essence of the Anglo-American state (Ferling 2004; Weisberger 2000). Nevertheless, despite these ideological rumblings, the new nation was governed by a unified socioeconomic elite, who practiced politics in accordance with republican principles and notions of honor and endorsed a program of national state-building (Hofstadter 1948; Wiebe 1984; Elkins and McKitrick 1993; Sharp 1993). As a result, the period from Jefferson's presidency to the election of Andrew Jackson featured growing national political consensus and unity, spurred by public policy programs that strengthened the national state. However, Jackson's election to the presidency ended this era, as Jackson provided the personal and ideological leadership for a program of radical Anglo-American democratization (Remini, 1976, 1988: 7–44; Feller 1995; Brands 2005: 363–560). The age of Jackson meant the replacement of a national leadership united by Burkean notions of states-manship with a much more divided leadership whose outlook was far more opportunistic, parochial, and partisan.

Jackson was a shrewd political entrepreneur and an effective president, but his impact, and that of his party, on antebellum politics was negative for the national state; his opposition to federal economic institutions and programs of economic development weakened it and promoted sectional conflict. Nevertheless, his program and vision dominated Anglo-American politics until the Civil War. In addition to espousing a radical conceptualization of Anglo-American democracy, Jackson produced a well-integrated program of geographical expansion, Indian removal, the retreat of the national govern-ment from economic activity, and states' rights (Remini 1976; Feller 1995: 160–84). These programs further democratized the Anglo-American contract state, made Anglo-American civil society and political stability even more dependent on predatory state action, and strengthened the white supremacist racial institutional order that governed America (Smith 1997: 197–242).

But these policies also ultimately led to open warfare between northern and southern Anglo-Americans over which section's white supremacist institutional order and policy vision would govern the development of the American West (Fredrickson 1981; Huston 2003). These developments, which culminated in the most destructive war in American history, were not the result of successful uprisings by Native Americans or African Americans or an internal split among Anglo-Americans that led to effective political coalitions with non-whites. Instead, they resulted from internal political conflicts that occurred almost entirely *within* the dominant white supremacist institutional order. Ironically, it was only through a process of civil war between the armies of two sectional, white supremacist institutional orders that African Americans finally became major military and political actors *within the context of the American consti-tutional system*, and American politics became a true struggle between two evolving and competing racial institutional orders.

Notes

1   We would like to thank Adam Sheingate and the editors of this book for their comments on earlier drafts of this chapter.
2   We conceptualize the American state as a set of political institutions and gov-ernmental actors. By "political institutions," we mean the constitutional "rules of the game" that have become so thoroughly institutionalized in the United States that they effectively constrain the choices made by both the general citizenry and governmental actors. Governmental actors are officeholders who comprise the "continuous administrative, legal, bureaucratic, and coercive systems that attempt, not only to structure relationships *between* civil society and public authority in a polity but also to structure many crucial relationships within civil society as well" (Stepan 1978: xii, emphasis in original). Many scholars view the state as either a set of institutions, or a semi-autonomous actor, but in our judgment, it is both (Skocpol 1985, 1992).
3   Because of space limitations, our essay ignores two very important realities of the Anglo-American Republic: the politics of gender, and Native American and African

American agency and the many instances of cooperation that occurred across the racial divide. (For example, see Kerber 1980; Isenberg 1998; Norton 1984; Evans 1989; White 1991; Hurt 2002; Berlin 1998.) Nevertheless, we believe that the fundamental political fault lines in the early American republic were racial, and these realities explain early American political and economic development.

4 We are indebted to Alfred Young (1980, 1993) for our understanding of the politics of the writing and ratification of the Constitution of 1787.

5 The Constitution was also a response to the fear that the United States would devolve into a European-style balance-of-power system. From this perspective, the creation of what Deudney calls the "Philadelphian system" was a conscious choice to establish a new way of organizing the relationships among sovereign states (see Deudney 1995, 1996; Lewis 1998; Hendrickson 2003).

6 Peter Hall defines a public policy paradigm as a "framework of ideas and standards that specifies goals of policy and the kind of instruments that can be used to attain them" (1993: 279).

7 In our usage of the terms, "Framers" and "Founders," the former term applies to the men who wrote the Constitution of 1787, while the latter word describes the national Anglo-American political elite that emerged from the politics of constitutional ratification and amendment and the national elections of 1788 through 1800 (Siemers 2002). Following Jefferson's presidency, the political struggle between Republicans and Federalists slowly evolved into an Anglo-American elite and mass consensus on the broad contours of Anglo-American public policy that was formalized during Monroe's presidency and lasted until Jackson's presidency (Hofstadter 1948; Wiebe 1984).

References and secondary sources

Anderson, T.L. (1987) "The First Privatization Movement," in D.C. Klingaman and R.K. Vedder (eds) *Essays on the Economy of the Old Northwest*, Athens: Ohio University Press.

Atack, J. and Passell, P. (1994) *A New Economic View of American History*, 2nd edn, New York: Norton.

Atack, J., Bateman, F., and Parker, W.N. (2000) "Northern Agriculture and the Westward Movement," in S.L. Engerman and R.E. Gallman (eds) *The Cambridge Economic History of the United States*, vol. II, Cambridge: Cambridge University Press.

Bailyn, B. (1986) *The Peopling of British North America*, New York: Knopf.

—— (1992) *The Ideological Origins of the American Revolution*, enlarged edn, Cambridge, MA: Belknap Press.

Banner, S. (2005) *How the Indians Lost Their Land*, Cambridge, MA: Belknap Press.

Berlin, I. (1998) *Many Thousands Gone: The First Two Centuries of Slavery in North America*, Cambridge, MA: Belknap Press.

Brands, H.W. (2005) *Andrew Jackson: His Life and Times*, New York: Doubleday.

Bright, C.C. (1987) "The State in the United States during the Nineteenth Century," in C. Bright and S. Harding (eds) *Statemaking and Social Movements: Essays in History and Theory*, Ann Arbor: University of Michigan Press.

Bruchey, S. (1990) *Enterprise: The Dynamic Economy of a Free People*, Cambridge, MA: Harvard University Press.

Campbell, J.L. (2004) *Institutional Change and Globalization*, Princeton, NJ: Princeton University Press.

Carpenter, D.P. (2001) *The Forging of Bureaucratic Autonomy*, Princeton, NJ: Princeton University Press.

Carter, S.B. (2006) "Labor Force," in R. Sutch and S.B. Carter (eds) *Historical Statistics of the United States*, vol. II, Cambridge: Cambridge University Press.

Cayton, A.R.L. (1998) "Radicals in the Western World: The Federalist Conquest of Trans-Appalachian North America," in D. Ben-Atar and B.B. Oberg (eds) *Federalists Reconsidered*, Charlottsville: University Press of Virginia.

Deudney, D.H. (1995) "The Philadelphian System: Sovereignty, Arms Control, and Balance of Power in the American States-Union," *International Organization*, 29: 191–228.

—— (1996) "Binding Sovereigns: Authorities, Structures, and Geopolitics in the Philadelphian System," in T.J. Biersteker and C. Weber (eds) *State Sovereignty as a Social Construct*, Cambridge: Cambridge University Press.

Donald, D.H. ([1956] 1993) "An Excess of Democracy," in M. Perman (ed.) *The Coming of the American Civil War*, 3rd edn, Lexington, MA: D.C. Heath.

Elkins, S. and McKitrick, E. (1993) *The Age of Federalism*, New York: Oxford University Press.

Engerman, S. (2000) "Slavery and Its Consequences for the South in the Nineteenth Century," in S.L. Engerman and R.E. Gallman (eds) *The Cambridge Economic History of the United States*, vol. II, Cambridge: Cambridge University Press.

Ericson, D.F. (2005) "The Federal Government and Slavery: Following the Money Trail," *Studies in American Political Development*, 19: 105–16.

Evans, S.M. (1989) *Born for Liberty: A History of Women in America*, New York: Free Press.

Farrand, M. (ed.) (1937) *The Records of the Federal Convention of 1787*, New Haven, CT: Yale University Press.

Fehrenbacher, D.E. (2001) *The Slaveholding Republic*, W.M. McAfee (ed.), New York: Oxford University Press.

Feller, D. (1984) *The Public Lands in Jacksonian Politics*, Madison: University of Wisconsin Press.

—— (1995) *The Jacksonian Promise*, Baltimore, MD: Johns Hopkins University Press.

Ferling, J. (2004) *Adams vs. Jefferson*, New York: Oxford University Press.

Finkelman, P. (1987) "Slavery and the Constitutional Convention: Making a Covenant with Death," in R. Beeman, S. Botein, and E.C. Carter II (eds) *Beyond Confederation: Origins of the Constitution and American National Identity*, Chapel Hill: The University of North Carolina Press.

—— (1996) *Slavery and the Founders*, Armonk, NY: M.E. Sharp.

Foner, E. (2000) "Slavery's Fellow Travelers," *New York Times*, July 13, 2000: 29.

Franklin, B. (1961) *The Papers of Benjamin Franklin*, vol. 4, L.W. Labaree (ed.), New Haven, CT: Yale University Press.

Fredrickson, G.M. (1971) *The Black Image in the White Mind*, New York: Harper & Row.

—— (1981) *White Supremacy: A Comparative Study in American and South African History*, New York: Oxford University Press.

Furnivall, J. S. (1944) *Netherlands India*, New York: Macmillan.

Galenson, D.W. (1996) "The Settlement and Growth of the Colonies," in S.L. Engerman and R.E. Gallman (eds) *The Cambridge Economic History of the United States*, vol. I, Cambridge: Cambridge University Press.

Gates, P.W. (1964) "Charts of Public Land Sales and Entries," *Journal of Economic History*, 24: 22–8.

—— (1968) *History of Public Land Law Development*, Washington, DC: U.S. Government Printing Office.

Gienapp, W.E. (1996) "The Political System and the Coming of the Civil War," in G.S. Boritt (ed.) *Why the Civil War Came*, New York: Oxford University Press.

Greene, J.P. (1994) *Negotiated Authorities: Essays in Colonial Political and Constitutional History*, Charlottesville: University Press of Virginia.

Hall, P.A. (1993) "Policy Paradigms, Social Learning and the State," *Comparative Politics*, 25: 275–96.

Hendrickson, D.C. (2003) *Peace Pact: The Lost World of the American Founding*, Lawrence: University Press of Kansas.

Hietala, T.R. (2003) *Manifest Design*, revised edn, Ithaca: Cornell University Press.

Hoffer, P.C. (1998) *Law and People in Colonial America*, revised edn, Baltimore, MD: Johns Hopkins University Press.

Hofstadter, R. (1948) *The American Political Tradition*, New York: Vintage Books.

—— (1969) *The Idea of a Party System*, Berkeley: University of California Press.

Holt, M.F. (1978) *The Political Crisis of the 1850s*, New York: Norton.

Horsman, R. (1999) "The Indian Policy of an 'Empire for Liberty,'" in F.E. Hoxie, R. Hoffman, and P.J. Albert (eds) *Native Americans and the Early Republic*, Charlottesville: University Press of Virginia.

Hughes, J. (1990) *American Economic History*, 3rd edn, Glenview, IL: Scott, Foresman.

Hurt, R.D. (2002) *The Indian Frontier*, Albuquerque: University of New Mexico Press.

Huston, J.L. (2003) *Calculating the Value of the Union*, Chapel Hill: University of North Carolina Press.

Isenberg, N. (1998) *Sex and Citizenship in Antebellum America*, Chapel Hill: University of North Carolina Press.

Jennings, F. (2000) *The Creation of America*, New York: Cambridge University Press.

Jensen, L. (2003) *Patriots, Settlers, and the Origins of American Social Policy*, Cambridge: Cambridge University Press.

John, R.R. (1995) *Spreading the News: The American Postal System from Franklin to Morse*, Cambridge, MA: Harvard University Press.

—— (1997) "Government Institutions as Agents of Change: Rethinking American Political Development in the Early Republic," *Studies in American Political Development*, 11: 347–80.

Jones, E.L. (1996) "The European Background," in S.L. Engerman and R.E. Gallman (eds) *The Cambridge Economic History of the United States*, vol. I, New York: Cambridge University Press.

Katznelson, I. (2002) "Flexible Capacity: The Military and Early American Statebuilding," in I. Katznelson and M. Shefter (eds) *Shaped by War and Trade: International Influences on American Political Development*, Princeton, NJ: Princeton University Press.

Katznelson, I. and Lapinski, J.S. (2006) "At the Crossroads: Congress and American Political Development," *Perspectives on Politics*, 4: 243–60.

Kerber, L.K. (1980) *Women of the Republic: Intellect and Ideology in Revolutionary America*, Chapel Hill: University of North Carolina Press.

Kersh, R. (2001) *Dreams of a More Perfect Union*, Ithaca, NY: Cornell University Press.

King, D.S. and Smith, R.M. (2005) "Racial Orders in American Political Development," *American Political Science Review*, 99: 75–92.

Kulikoff, A. (2000) *From British Peasants to Colonial American Farmers*, Chapel Hill: University of North Carolina Press.

Larson, J.L. (2001) *Internal Improvement: National Public Works and the Promise of Popular Government in the Early United States*, Chapel Hill: University of North Carolina Press.

Lebergott, S. (1984) *The Americans: An Economic Record*, New York: Norton.

—— (1985) "The Demand for Land: The United States, 1820–1860," *Journal of Economic History*, 45: 181–212.

Levi, M. (1988) *Of Rule and Revenue*, Berkeley: University of California Press.

Lewis, J.E. (1998) *The American Union and the Problem of Neighborhood: The United States and the Collapse of the Spanish Empire, 1783–1829*, Chapel Hill: University of North Carolina Press.

Lipset, S.M. and Lakin, J.M. (2004) *The Democratic Century*, Norman: University of Oklahoma Press.

Madison, J. (1961) *The Federalist*, J.E. Cooke (ed.) Cleveland, OH: Meridian Books.

—— (1977) *The Papers of James Madison*, vol. 10, R.A. Rutland (ed.) Chicago: University of Chicago Press.

Mahon, J.K. (1983) *History of the Militia and the National Guard*, New York: Macmillan.

Matson, C.D. and Onuf, P.S. (1990) *A Union of Interests: Political and Economic Thought in Revolutionary America*, Lawrence: University of Kansas Press.

McCoy, D.R. (1980) *The Elusive Republic: Political Economy in Jeffersonian America*, New York: Norton.

McDougall, W.A. (2004) *Freedom Just Around the Corner: A New American History, 1585–1828*, New York: Harper Collins.

Meinig, D.W. (1993) *Continental America, 1800–1867*, New Haven: Yale University Press.

Millett, A.R. and Maslowski, P. (1994) *For the Common Defense: A Military History of the United States of America*, revised edn, New York: Free Press.

Mills, C.W. (1997) *The Racial Contract*, Ithaca, NY: Cornell University Press.

Morgan, E.S. (1975) *American Slavery, American Freedom: The Ordeal of Colonial Virginia*, New York: Norton.

—— (1988) *Inventing the People*, New York: Norton.

Murrin, J.M. (1984) "Political Development," in J.P. Greene and J.R. Pole (eds) *Colonial British America*, Baltimore, MD: Johns Hopkins University Press.

Nabokov, P. (1991) *Native American Testimony*, New York: Penguin Books.

North, D.C. (1966; 1961) *The Economic Growth of the United States, 1790–1860*, New York: Norton.

—— (1981) *Structure and Change in Economic History*, New York: Norton.

Norton, M.B. (1984) "The Evolution of White Women's Experience in Early America," *American Historical Review*, 89: 593–647.

Novak, W.J. (1996) *The People's Welfare: Law and Regulation in Nineteenth-Century America*, Chapel Hill: University of North Carolina Press.

Oakes, J. (1982) *The Ruling Race: A History of American Slaveholders*, New York: Knopf.

Oberly, J.W. (1990) *Sixty Million Acres: American Veterans and the Public Lands before the Civil War*, Kent, OH: Kent State University Press.

Olmstead, A.L. (2006) "Introduction: Agriculture," in R. Sutch and S.B. Carter (eds) *Historical Statistics of the United States*, vol. IV, Cambridge: Cambridge University Press.

Olmstead, A.L. and Rhode, P.W. (2006) "Crops and Livestock," in R. Sutch and S.B. Carter (eds) *Historical Statistics of the United States*, vol. IV, Cambridge: Cambridge University Press.

Onuf, P.S. (1987) *Statehood and Union*, Bloomington, IN: Indiana University Press.

Onuf, P.S. and Sadosky, L.J. (2002) *Jeffersonian America*, Malden, MA: Blackwell.

Palmer, D.R. (1994) *America, Its Army, and the Birth of a Nation*, Novato, CA: Presidio Press.

Pessen, E. (1973) *Riches, Class, and Power before the Civil War*, Lexington, MA: D.C. Heath.

Pierson, P. (2000) "Increasing Returns, Path Dependence, and the Study of Politics," *American Political Science Review*, 94: 251–67.

—— (2004) *Politics in Time*, Princeton, NJ: Princeton University Press.

Prucha, F.P. (1969) *The Sword of the Republic*, London: Macmillan.

—— (1986) *The Great Father: The United States Government and the American Indians*, abridged edn, Lincoln: University of Nebraska Press.

Rakove, J.N. (1988) "Ambiguous Achievement: The Northwest Ordinance," in F.D. Williams (ed.) *Northwest Ordinance*, East Lansing: Michigan State University Press.

Ransom, R. (1989) *Conflict and Compromise*, New York: Cambridge University Press.

Ransom, R. and Sutch, R. (1988) "Capitalists without Capital: The Burden of Slavery and the Impact of Emancipation," *Agricultural History*, 62: 133–60.

Rasmussen, W.M.S. and Tilton, R.S. (1999) *George Washington: The Man behind the Myths*, Charlottesville: University Press of Virginia.

Remini, R.V. (1976) *The Revolutionary Age of Andrew Jackson*, New York: Harper & Row.

—— (1988) *The Legacy of Andrew Jackson*, Baton Rouge: Louisiana State University Press.

Richards, L.L. (2000) *The Slave Power*, Baton Rouge: Louisiana State University Press.

Riesman, J.A. (1983) "The Origins of American Political Economy, 1690–1781," unpublished thesis, Brown University.

—— (1987) "Money, Credit, and Federalist Political Economy," in R. Beeman, S. Botein, and E.C. Carter II (eds) *Beyond Confederation: Origins of the Constitution and American National Identity*, Chapel Hill: University of North Carolina Press.

Ringer, B.B. (1983) *"We the People" and Others*, New York: Tavistock.

Robertson, D.B. (2005) *The Constitution and America's Destiny*, New York: Cambridge University Press.

Robertson, L.G. (2005) *Conquest by Law*, New York: Oxford University Press.

Sellers, C. (1991) *The Market Revolution*, New York: Oxford University Press.

Sharp, J.R. (1993) *American Politics in the Early Republic*, New Haven, CT: Yale University Press.

Sheingate, A.D. (2003) "Political Entrepreneurship, Institutional Change, and American Political Development," *Studies in American Political Development*, 17: 185–203.

Sheridan, R.B. (1984) "The Domestic Economy," in J.P. Greene and J.R. Pole (eds) *Colonial British America*, Baltimore, MD: Johns Hopkins University Press.

Siemers, D.J. (2002) *Ratifying the Republic*, Stanford, CA: Stanford University Press.

Skocpol, T. (1985) "Bringing the State Back In," in P.B. Evans, D. Rueschemeyer, and T. Skocpol (eds) *Bringing the State Back In*, Cambridge: Cambridge University Press.

—— (1992) *Protecting Soldiers and Mothers: The Political Origins of Social Policy in the United States*, Cambridge, MA: Harvard University Press.

Skowronek, S. (1982) *Building a New American State*, Cambridge: Cambridge University Press.

Smith, R.M. (1997) *Civic Ideals*, New Haven, CT: Yale University Press.

Stampp, K.M. (1956) *The Peculiar Institution*, New York: Vintage Books.

Stepan, A. (1978) *The State and Society*, Princeton, NJ: Princeton University Press.

Stourzh, G. (1954) *Benjamin Franklin and American Foreign Policy*, Chicago: University of Chicago Press.

Sylla, R. (2000) "Experimental Federalism," in S.L. Engerman and R.E. Gallman (eds) *The Cambridge Economic History of the United States*, vol. II, Cambridge: Cambridge University Press.

van den Berghe, P.L. (1978) *Race and Racism*, 2nd edn, New York: Wiley.

Wallace, A.F.C. (1993) *The Long, Bitter Trail*, New York: Hill and Wang.

—— (1999) *Jefferson and the Indians*, Cambridge, MA: Harvard University Press.

Wallis, J.J. (1999) "Early American Federalism and Economic Development, 1790–1840," in A. Panagariya, P.R. Portney, and R.M. Schwab (eds) *Environmental and Public Economics*, Northampton, MA: Edward Elgar.

—— (2000) "American Government Finance in the Long Run: 1790–1990," *Journal of Economic Perspectives*, 14: 61–82.

Wallis, J.J. and Weingast, B.R. (2005) "Equilibrium Impotence: Why the States and Not the American National Government Financed Economic Development in the Antebellum Era," Working Paper 11397, Cambridge, MA: National Bureau of Economic Research.

Washburn, W.E. (1995) *Red Man's Land/White Man's Law: The Past and Present Status of the American Indian*, 2nd edn, Norman: University of Oklahoma Press.

Weeks, W.E. (1996) *Building the Continental Empire*, Chicago: Ivan R. Dee.

Weingast, B.R. (1998) "Political Stability and Civil War: Institutions, Commitment, and American Democracy," in R.H. Bates, A. Greif, M. Levi, J.L. Rosenthal, and B.R. Weingast (eds) *Analytical Narratives*, Princeton, NJ: Princeton University Press.

Weisberger, B.A. (2000) *America Afire*, New York: HarperCollins.

White, R. (1991) *Indians, Empires, and Republics in the Great Lakes Region, 1650–1815*, New York: Cambridge University Press.

Wiebe, R.H. (1984) *The Opening of American Society*, New York: Vintage Books.

Williams, R.A. (1990) *The American Indian in Western Legal Thought: The Discourses of Conquest*, New York: Oxford University Press.

Wood, G.S. (1969) *The Creation of the American Republic, 1776–1787*, Chapel Hill: University of North Carolina Press.

Wright, G. (1978) *The Political Economy of the Cotton South*, New York: Norton.

—— (2003) "The Role of Nationhood in the Economic Development of the U.S.A." in A. Teichova and H. Matis (eds) *Nation, State and the Economy in History*, New York: Cambridge University Press.

—— (2006) *Slavery and American Economic Development*, Baton Rouge: Louisiana State University Press.

Young, A.F. (1980) "Conservatives, the Constitution, and the Spirit of Accommodation," in R.A. Goldwin and W.A. Schambra (eds) *How Democratic Is the Constitution?* Washington, DC: American Enterprise Institute.

—— (1993) "How Radical Was the American Revolution?" in A.F. Young (ed.) *Beyond the American Revolution*, DeKalb: Northern Illinois University Press.

3 Charleston, the Vesey conspiracy, and the development of the police power

Kathleen Sullivan[1]

Whether studying ideas or institutions, American political development has historically equated development with progress. Development has been identified when American laws and policies transitioned from feudal to liberal traditions, or toward greater administrative capacity of the state (Skowronek 1982; Skocpol 1985; Orren 1991). Understood as such, studies of development that address subordinated racial groups would look for a transition from formal attribution of ascriptive status to these groups to constructions of citizenship based on the tenets of liberalism (Smith 1993; Ericson and Bertch Green 1999). The field of American political development is now moving away from Whiggish narratives and identifying more fundamental features of order and change. Racial orders are emerging in studies of citizenship (see chapter 4 of this book). Teleological conceptions of development of institutions are giving way to development understood as a durable shift in governing authority, which results in a "new distribution of authority among persons or organizations within the polity at large or between them and their counterparts outside" (Orren and Skowronek 2004: 123).

Under this modified understanding of development, race can continue to inform studies of citizenship by identifying the state's long entanglement with invidious discrimination. It can likewise inform studies of institutional development, whereby efforts to respond to past invidious discrimination have involved development of the capacities of the administrative state through programs such as the Equal Employment Opportunity Commission. This chapter explores a further opportunity to acknowledge those invidious classifications that have contributed to patterns of governing authority. The American experience with slavery contributed to growth of the early American state (Ericson 2005; Graber 2006). At the same time, it delimited the interpretation of the federal government's constitutional powers, namely its authority under the commerce clause. By tracing race through the capacity to govern, rather than through the rights conferred upon or denied to classes of persons, the role of race in the political order becomes evident in a new guise. In this configuration, race is a resource of routine governmentality rather than some deviation from healthy governance (Foucault 1991). This approach parallels Ruth O'Brien's (2001) consideration of the category of disability which, she argues, has served as a regulatory measure to establish modes of control, normalization, and resistance. As such, state-sponsored recognition of disability in order to aid citizens served as a tool to extend government power into surveillance of citizens. This chapter considers the enlistment of racial categories in the development of police powers by slaveholding states in the period 1820–47. During this period, South Carolina's efforts to strengthen its position in the politics of slavery rested on the development of its historic power to preserve safety, health, and public order. In this history, race was not only an object of state government policy but an instrument of governance itself.

The police power arose from a British, feudal tradition of local regulation. In response to sectional tensions over slavery, it developed as a resource for slaveholding states to protect themselves from federal interference. The Supreme Court acknowledged police powers as powers of states that bounded Congress' power to regulate interstate commerce in *New York v. Miln* in 1837 (36 U.S. 102). Although this case dealt with the question of immigrants arriving in a New York City port, the case was decided against the background conditions of mounting sectional tension over slavery (Wiecek 1977; Finkelman 2003).

The police power emerged from the antebellum period as an implicit and necessary feature of state sovereignty, allowing states to pass legislation for internal regulation free from external interference, whether that regulation focused on sick chickens or racial subordination. The federal power to regulate interstate and foreign commerce became circumscribed by state police powers. Because antebellum doctrinal development strengthened state power without mention of slavery, the structures and operation of police powers were not included in post-Civil War reform. The police power's secure position in federalism remained available for renewed racial categorization in the Jim Crow era (Lofgren 1988).

The influence of the police power went far beyond race, however. Because police powers established the outer limits of congressional power to regulate interstate commerce, their development had consequences for nonracialized federal issues, most notably federal regulation of the economy. Not until the New Deal would the commerce clause be construed on its own, without reference to the extent of power allowed by states. In *U.S. v. Darby* in 1941 (312 U.S. 100), the Court invoked John Marshall's *Gibbons v. Ogden* ((1824) 22 U.S. 1) opinion to declare the power of Congress over interstate commerce to be "complete in itself." This power, furthermore, "can neither be enlarged nor diminished by the exercise or non-exercise of state power" (*U.S. v. Darby* (1941): 114). In *Wickard v. Filburn* in 1942 the Court lamented that "for nearly a century" determination of the commerce clause had begun with the power of the state. "Instead of being what was 'necessary and proper' to the exercise by Congress of its granted power, was often some concept of sovereignty thought to be implicit in the status of statehood" (317 U.S. 111: 121). This renewed commerce clause, unfettered by claims to state sovereignty that had set its limits, would then be put into service to strike at state exercise of the police power that established segregation in the Civil Rights Act of 1964.

While it enjoyed its primary position in the politics of federalism, the police power expanded the power of state governments and restricted the power of the federal government. Had police powers not been enlisted in the sectional politics over slavery, they likely would have been consigned to history as a localized feudal regulatory power. The politics of slavery secured it as a pillar of federalism that long outlasted slavery. As Mark Graber (2006) has pointed out, race can determine structure, while structure can likewise determine the politics of race. The American constitutional order was founded on an implicit agreement to accommodate slavery. Any unresolved tensions over slavery and race were left to be worked out within the structural constraints and opportunities of that constitutional order. Electoral rules and population shifts resulting primarily from the acquisition of territories, influenced the strategies and outcomes of slavery politics. The structure of federalism influenced slavery politics, although the battle lines over federalism were contingent upon historical events. Up until 1820, slave states, certain of representative advantage in Congress, often championed strong federal power and employed nationalist sentiment (Graber 2006: 94). Once the South began to lose its certainty of majority control of Congress, the slaveholders' strategy shifted from emphasizing federal power to state power in struggles over federalism. Structural resources were available in the form of police power, which had long been a part of state and local regulatory power. Slave states drew upon it to regulate internal societies that were based on race, but the police power simultaneously took on an external focus. It was able to absorb attributes of state sovereignty sufficient to resist federal intervention and stalwart enough to limit the extent of federal power to regulate interstate commerce.

The police power

Police powers, the powers to regulate for the health, safety, and welfare of citizens, are one of those feudal traditions rooted in the colonial period that has remained embedded in American law and governance (Orren 1991). The British crown ensured that each colony provided for a well-regulated society, and colonies delegated these powers to counties and municipalities. Regulations covered areas of public safety, construction of a public economy, policing of public space, and restraints on public morals. Specifically, they might include regulations on obstructions on waterways, gambling, selling spirits, nuisances, disorderly houses, slaughterhouses, swimming in waterways, vagrancy, disposal of carcasses, kite flying, burial of the dead, duties of watchmen and police, public lighting, or ferries (Novak 1996: 1). These regulations were pervasive and citizens held few liberties against the government's capacity to regulate. Private property, for example, was easily susceptible to regulation if it posed a fire hazard. A private home could quickly be labeled as a bawdy house if it was considered an affront to good order. Such infringements on liberty rested in the status and regulation of the common law notion of the well-regulated society. This feudal power was not completely out of sync with the notion of American governance when liberty was understood in terms of common-law liberty (Stoner 2003). The purpose of the police power was not to oppress, however. In Christopher Tomlins' (1993) formulation, the police power was initially a republican device for a community to define and pursue the collective good or its vision of happiness. The limitations on freedom exhibit the dynamics of republican governance—a vision of the common good was articulated, citizens gave up rights for that common good, and the government assumed the power to pursue that good.

Localized regulations were administered through the differentiation of citizens and denizens into various statuses that determined their privileges and obligations. Municipalities appropriated the patriarchal rules of household governance under the common law to identify citizens more efficiently in the process of regulation (Dubber 2005). Within the community, citizens were differentiated according to feudal categories of status, drawing on household hierarchies, occupations, and outsider status. Hence the status relations and categories of the common law provided the means to classify citizens and limit their rights in pursuit of the people's general welfare.

The American political development literature has acknowledged feudalism as a historic legacy that gave way to a modern counterpart, at which point scholars identify development. Karen Orren (1991) points to the New Deal as the period when feudal relations between master and servant gave way to liberal employment law. Similarly, after identifying the pervasiveness of the police power in the nineteenth-century United States, William Novak (1996) locates a transition from feudal to administrative regulation in 1877. By the late nineteenth century, governance moved from localized regulation to central administration, the public spirit gave way to the individual as the unit of the society, and common-law rule gave way to constitutional law (238). Novak's periodization supports a notion of development as a progression from state to federal governance and from a feudal to an administrative system. The intro-duction of race, however, complicates the narrative of development. While the employment relation certainly did develop in the New Deal, it maintained the status-like significance of race and sex through the neutral categorization of employment benefits on the basis of employment in a racially and sexually stratified public and private market (Mettler 1998). Likewise, police powers, strengthened by sovereignty arguments by slave states, continued to serve as the source of authority for Jim Crow laws, providing a justification sufficient to thwart federal interference via the Fourteenth Amendment.

Race, then, had an enduring role in the development of federalism, even as shifts occurred in legal and administrative systems. The politics of slavery used the racialization of slavery, which then established the conditions under which a feudal regulatory power modernized. Rather than give way to more modern forms of governance, racialized police powers were inextricably integrated with a strong state power that endured until the twentieth century. The need for such a power is evident in the events that unfolded in Charleston, South Carolina in the 1820s. Race was employed not simply out of racist animus but instead out of a search for authority in the sectional politics of slavery. Race was an available resource to expand state power. The articulation of the police power's suitability for racial regulation and its immunity from federal control took place in a constitutionalism outside the courts. These structural arguments were available for inclusion in judicial doctrine when the Supreme Court endorsed a strong conception of police power in the 1830s and 1840s.

Charleston

The development of the police power was influenced by the distinctive society generated by the urban slaveholding system in Charleston. As a port city, Charleston was a cosmopolitan city, with sailors, traders, and travelers with different ethnicities and languages (Pearson 1999: 41). Charleston enjoyed a postwar boom, with affluence and a high quality of life evident in the city at the turn of the century (40). The number of slaves and free blacks together outnumbered the population of whites (Powers 1994: 10; Pearson 1999: 40).

Slavery in the urban port town of Charleston differed significantly from plantation slavery (Fox-Genovese 1988). Charleston slaves worked in the skilled and unskilled occupations as bricklayers, blacksmiths, carpenters, tailors, bakers, plasterers, coopers, shoemakers, carpenters, maritime occupations, hands and pilots on steamboats and sloops, and in mechanical trades, manufacturing, and mills. These various occupations enabled many slaves to work and live outside of the surveillance of whites. For skilled male artisans, workshops were masculine places for social interchange. Public spaces were available in taverns and grogshops, with opportunities to exchange gossip and hear of news from the outside (Pearson 1999: 53). The streets became sites of alternative public spaces, dominated by slaves, whose work included transporting goods, leveling the streets, removing horse waste, and selling in market stalls (56). Slaves found myriad and regularized opportunities to meet, out of the master's eye, while working on the docks and below the decks of ships (Powers 1994: 14). Church Sunday schools, clandestine schools, and political rallies also enabled slaves and free blacks to get both education and news (15).

While these spaces could be seen as the spaces to which slaves were relegated, they were appropriated to carve out relative freedom. Charleston's slaves were "quick to seize every opportunity to live normal lives and continually acted to enlarge the cracks in the wall of oppression" (Pearson 1999: 9). They occupied a "shadow realm between freedom and bondage" (72) outside the web of social relations of the plantation. Slaves could hire themselves out and earn wages, from which they returned a share to their owners, or the owner received the wage and passed along a share to the slave. With these earnings, slaves could purchase their own freedom.

Charleston's large free black population included slaves in the city and state who had been emancipated. Free blacks, who tended to be of mixed race in the lower South, had been part of the Charleston population since the 1600s. Charleston likewise attracted free blacks and fugitive slaves from rural South Carolina and from other slave states. An increase in manumission between 1790 and 1810 also contributed to growth of the free black community in Charleston (Johnson and Roark 1984: 33). Like other southern cities, Charleston hosted African churches free of white control, as well as schools and benevolent societies (Berlin 1974: 173).

Economic practices influenced social regulations for both slaves and free blacks. Plantation slavery fostered a paternalism that "grew out of the necessity of discipline" (Genovese 1972: 4). Urban centers could not sustain such relations, nor was paternalism necessarily desirable. Some historians of antebellum Charleston have identified a softening of mores concerning race brought about by commerce, with market transactions cutting across patterns of racial subordination (Genovese 1972: 398; Egerton 1999: 67). Ira Berlin (1974) explains that the practice of selective emancipation rested on and encouraged ongoing ties between slaveowners and their freed slaves, with upper-class whites frequenting the shops of free blacks (222). The imperatives of self-interest offer another explanation for the relaxation of regulation. For instance, slaves who went to market were only supposed to buy and sell the commodities of their owners, but white retailers were happy to purchase cheap and accessible slave products (Egerton 1999: 55–6). Likewise, slaves were not supposed to hire themselves out, but the arrangement benefited masters as well as slaves, so masters remained "cheerfully oblivious" (65).

Charleston experienced an increase of legal regulations at the turn of the century. The slave uprising in Saint Dominique was followed by a flood of slaveowning refugees and their slaves in 1793. Reports of insolence among these "French Negroes" spread and whites considered further restrictions and mass expulsion (Berlin 1974: 36). The autonomy of Charleston's free blacks was circumscribed by a system of white supremacy that was continually on the lookout against such insolence. Nevertheless, a prosperous, cultured elite of free, light-skinned blacks developed in Charleston (Powers 1994: 36).

The fostering of this elite social group was made possible by the strategies of free blacks, who had taken pains to distinguish themselves from slaves and to ingratiate themselves with the white community (Berlin 1974: 188; Powers 1994: 57; Egerton 1999: 90). The Brown Fellowship Society maintained social segregation as an exclusive society with membership resting on its initiates' light skin color (Pearson 1999: 52). The routine breaches in the many regulations regarding slaves and free persons of color also helped along relative autonomy. While Charleston technically regulated the lives and work of both slaves and free blacks, these regulations often went unheeded (Genovese 1972: 398; Pearson 1999: 57). Waterfront taverns, frequented by visiting sailors, were sites of fighting and carousing, despite the existence of liquor laws (Pearson 1999: 40). Licenses and badges were required for slaves who hired themselves out, but they were frequently ignored by both slaves and slaveholders (56). Nighttime curfews, if violated, promised imprisonment in the workhouse, but slaves often disregarded them (Powers 1994: 23). Smoking was regulated in open places, and punishments were available for whooping or making a clamorous noise, but residents complained frequently about lack of enforcement. Formal regulations thus did not reflect local practices.

The ordinances became more important for Charleston life as sectional tensions over slavery began to simmer. At the time of the Philadelphia Convention, the North and South were balanced in terms of slavery, and delegates avoided conflict over slavery and race. Territorial acquisition upset that compromise. At the time of the Louisiana Purchase in 1803, North and South each controlled eight states. The Louisiana Purchase was initially not threatening to slaveholding states. By the time the nation considered admitting Missouri as a state in 1819, however, it was clear that the Louisiana Territory would benefit the North. Projections indicated that the North would gain ten free states, and the South three slave states (Freehling 2005: 75–6). Ultimately these projections did not obtain, and slaveholding states still enjoyed ample representation and access to leadership in all branches of government for much of the antebellum period (Finkelman 1994: 250; Graber 2006: 149). Nonetheless, because slaveholding states still had political power at the federal level, the move toward state-level resources can be understood as a response to the disruption in the original constitutional compact over slavery. By 1820, the sectional tension over slavery had begun, and a southern self-consciousness was developing (Wiecek 1977: 125; Powers 1994: 3; Egerton 1999: 209). Constitutional politics over slavery was underway, and slave states felt the imperative to amass appropriate resources.

The states' power to regulate their own internal affairs offered one such resource. In 1820 the South Carolina legislature altered the method of emancipation of slaves, declaring that only the legislature could emancipate slaves as part of an effort to control the size of the free black population (Henry 1914: 177). The police power was an additional source of state power against federal intervention, and readily available as a familiar regulatory power. It was recognized by the Marshall Court in this period as a power "which unquestionably remains, and ought to remain, with the States. . . . The removal or destruction of infectious or unsound articles is, undoubtedly, an exercise of that power, and forms an express exception to the prohibition we are considering. Indeed, the laws of the United States expressly sanction the health laws of a State" (*Brown v. Maryland* (1827) 25 U.S. 419: 443). In *Gibbons v. Ogden* (1824), a case that could be read as establishing strong federal power, Marshall acknowledged the presence and legitimacy of police powers, saying, "They form a portion of that immense mass of legislation, which embraces every thing within the territory of a State, not surrendered to the general government: all which can be most advantageously exercised by the States themselves. Inspection laws, quarantine laws, health laws of every description, as well as laws for regulating the internal commerce of a State, and those which respect turnpike roads, ferries, &c., are component parts of this mass" (22 U.S. 1: 23).

The Supreme Court recognized health regulations, construction of turn-pikes, and inspection laws as legitimate and expected internal regulatory powers. If the constitutional compact had admitted some states as slave states, then regulation responsive to the particular needs of a slaveholding society and economy could likewise be recognized as legitimate. A slave conspiracy constituted an imminent threat that required vigorous exercise of police powers. Slavery required constant maintenance that was particularly vulnerable in the conditions of relative freedom in cities. Hence it was little surprise that Charleston reacted to news of the Vesey conspiracy.

In June 1822, Charleston officials became informed of an attempted plot led by Denmark Vesey, a free black man who had immigrated to Charleston after the Saint Dominique rebellion. Slaves and free blacks had apparently conspired to set fire to the city of Charleston, violently kill all of the whites—men, women, and children—and flee the state by sea. On Friday, June 14, Charleston's intendant, James Hamilton, Jr., mobilized the militia and constabulary in response to informers' testimony. The city council held an emergency meeting, convening a court of freeholders to prosecute captured conspirators. A Committee on Vigilance and Safety was established. On the night of Sunday, June 16, units stood mustered and ready for any disturbance (Pearson 1999: 106–7). There was no uprising that night, which was read as a sign of success of Charleston's vigilance. The "night of terror" was followed by the trials and executions of the alleged conspirators. Charleston's immediate reaction was a combination of arms and a spectacle of power using the visible surveillance of patrols.

Some historians doubt that there was ever any slave conspiracy at all. Michael Johnson has suggested that, however outspoken Denmark Vesey may have been in his opposition to the system of slavery and white supremacy, it is unlikely that he coordinated and armed 9,000 conspirators (2001). In this view, the conspiracy is better understood as a concoction of Charleston officials and the court that tried and executed Vesey and his alleged co-conspirators. Historical accounts of the Vesey conspiracy have reproduced the story of the conspiracy from witnesses' testimony that was, Johnson suggests, coerced from slaves who knew the dynamics of racial hierarchy and delivered the testimony urged by the court for fear of their own safety and lives (Johnson 2001; see also Wade 1964).

The letters of Mary Beach, a Charleston resident, offer further evidence that the insurrection itself was not the danger. After the night of June 16, Charleston was filled with alarming rumors of more insurrections, with responses of the arming of militias and rumors of turning Charleston into a garrison town (Beach July 23, 1822). But overall, Beach did not feel threatened. She reassured her out-of-town sister, "my heart aches my dear sister to read how much you had been exercised from the state of things here this Summer. I am afraid you have suffered more from apprehension than we did here (with the exception of the night of the 16th of June) & I am pretty sure more than there was ground for" (Beach July 5, 1822). Supreme Court Justice William Johnson, a Charleston native, published an anonymous essay in the *Charleston Courier*, "Melancholy Effect of Popular Excitement" (1822), which reminded readers of the overreaction to a conspiracy scare in the previous decade that proved to be an April Fool's joke.

The overreactions to slave conspiracy scares may have been the very point of such scares. Historians have remarked that such fears, both real and fabricated, were most acute in urban areas (Morgan 2002). Cities lacked the system of supervision and close paternalistic control that was available in rural sites of slavery, so that when they felt that their system of slavery and racial hierarchy was vulnerable, they resorted to formal regulation by courts, patrols, and increased surveillance of blacks' social life. The events surrounding the Vesey conspiracy produced a spectacle in the quick mustering of citizen patrols, sending a signal to any conspirators that the white population was vigilant. The trials themselves served as another sort of spectacle. After Justice Johnson's insinuation that the Vesey conspiracy rested on hysteria, the Charleston Court of Magistrates and Freeholders took pains to establish itself as legitimate. To show that it was no kangaroo court, the court produced numerous witnesses testifying to the Vesey conspiracy and convicted dozens of conspirators through the formal operation of the legal system (Johnson 2001: 935–6).

David Brion Davis has suggested that, whatever the reality of the conspiracy, what remained valid is the "traumatic shock, in terms of vulnerability," that the conspiracy raised (2006: 224). Whether there really was a conspiracy is secondary to the response, both socially and legally. With relative ease, South Carolina was able to transform public hysteria and the consequent spectacle of white power into legal regulation. Police powers served as the formal means of codifying this white reaction, rendering the state violence that was so apparent in the summer of 1822 into a set of racially coded regulations. Nevertheless, these regulations appeared to be much more benign than the raw spectacles of power in the gallows and streets, and they obscured the violence of the law (Cover 1986). Such legal regulations served as important resources in the external battles being played out between slaveholding and free states.

After the summer, the South Carolina legislature received a memorial from a group of Charleston citizens, appealing to it to take action. The memorialists referenced a system of slavery and social norms that it had tolerated but now considered too permissive: "Under the influence of mild and generous feelings, the owners of slaves in our state were rearing up a system, which extended many privileges to our negroes; afforded them greater protection; relieved them from numerous restraints; enabled them to assemble without the presence of a white person for the purpose of social intercourse or religious worship; yielding to them the facilities of acquiring most of the comforts and many of the luxuries of improved society" (Citizens of Charleston 1822: 1). Under this system, slaves and free blacks were able to plot an insurrection, requiring a change in rules. The memorialists continued, "although the immediate danger has passed away, yet the causes from which it originated, your memorialists conceive to exist in full vigor and activity, and will, as they conscientiously believe, produce, before many years, a series of the most appalling distresses, unless speedily removed by the most resolute and most determined laws. To the enacting of such laws, the attention of the Legislature is solicited by your memorialists" (2). They appealed for the use of the law for purposes of social control. The response to the threatened conspiracy was not to increase the police force but to strengthen the police power, thereby imposing public order and regulation of persons, their attitudes, and social norms. Their appeal to law was less to call for a response to wrongdoing than to bolster it to assert and display control by the ruling whites through legitimate means.

The state legislature responded in December 1822 with a series of laws that would accord Charleston with the means of social ordering to continue this exhibition of power. South Carolina already had a statute "respecting Free Negroes, Mulattoes, and Mestizoes" (McCord 1836–41: 440). In December 1822, the legislature passed an act "for better regulation of Free Negroes and Persons of Color" (461). An annual tax was instituted on free blacks and persons of color. Free blacks who left the state could not return. One way to preclude any future rebellions was to remove any influential presences who might regale slaves with stories of possibilities of freedom and justice. States could and now did prohibit free blacks from entering the state and talking with slaves. The legislature also passed the Negro Seaman Act, dictating that free negroes or persons of color could not be brought into the state under any circumstances. To accommodate the employment of persons of color on ships that entered Charleston's ports, South Carolina provided that any black crew members would be incarcerated in the local jail for the duration of the ship's stay in port. The captain would retrieve the seamen at his own expense when the ship was ready to leave. In 1823, another statute was passed "more effectively to prohibit Free Negroes and Persons of Color from entering into this state" (McCord 1836–41: 463).

Free blacks in Charleston were required to be assigned a guardian (McCord 1836–41: 461–2). Sumptuary laws were passed as a response to "the expensive dress worn by many of them . . . subversive of that subordination which policy requires to be enforced" (Powers 1994: 22). A city patrol was established, with particular emphasis on Sundays, the day when slaves and free blacks were most likely to travel to visit relatives (Egerton 1999: 212). The state instituted more stringent regulations on liquor licenses, affecting the free black businessowners (215). Racially based laws proliferated across port cities in the Lower South, regulating entry into the state and the lives of free blacks who lived within them.

Modernization of a feudal regulatory regime

While the laws, on their face, appear to rely on race, the Charleston experience demonstrates that the laws constructed racial categories. They erected a black–white distinction upon a social structure of multiple racial categories. The socially recognized categories of free blacks, mulattos, Indians, mestizoes, and other cross-cutting racial categories belied easy distinctions between black and white. The acts of 1822 and those that followed made a binary distinction between black and white. The legislation transformed race and erected a new status of "black" or "negro" that was more rigid than the lived experience of race.

Although police powers were not historically racialized, they did accommodate racial categories quite easily. After all, status went hand-in-hand with the historic exercise of the police power. The common-law categories of head of household, servant, vagrant, etc. were amenable to the addition of race. Howard Gillman (1993) has recovered the importance of the police power in nineteenth-century jurisprudence, but this recovery has not fully contended with the centrality of status. In explaining the economic understandings of *Lochner*-era judges, Gillman recovers police powers' endurance in a Jacksonian ethos of equality. Nineteenth-century courts were on guard, Gillman says, against "class legislation," i.e., legislation that benefited one class or group (7). The Supreme Court emphasized equal rights, understood as the denial of special privileges to any one group. As Thomas Cooley said, the state could have no favorites (56). While police powers advanced principles of fairness, they nevertheless still rested on distinction. Police powers employed a feudal order of categories, in which citizens were identified as husbands or wives, as masters or servants, or apprentices, or guardians or wards. These distinctions remained embedded in law and localized administration into the late nineteenth century (Orren 1991). The status categories upon which police powers rested proved open to a new one—that of race. The use of race as a category is better understood as the modernization of a feudal status regime. Reva Siegel (1994) has identified this phenomenon in movements for egalitarian legal reform that unwittingly serve to preserve and naturalize a system of status. Adding new racial categories to the police power was no reformist movement. Rather, the addition of race preserved the system, expanding the scope of the states' regulatory powers and securing the police power against transition to more modern administrative practices.

Status itself is not necessarily at odds with fairness. A.K. Sandoval-Strausz (2005) recovers the use of status as a form of protection for the vulnerable. Travelers on a journey were vulnerable to physical threats and to being cheated, and so the common law accorded them a distinct legal status (62–3). Fulfilling their obligations under the common law, innkeepers had to take in travelers and provide any available bed and board without overcharging. Public accommodations themselves were not simply private businesses, they were "a public calling subject at all points to regulation by the community" (66). Laura Edwards (2007) has drawn attention to antebellum legal practices in which status enabled slaves to gain access to the legal system in the absence of rights.

Status has played an important role in governing. The status of master and servant rendered employment relations secure while the industrial economy developed (Orren 1991). Gender status served social needs in a liberal order (Ritter 2006). As such, status has already been acknowledged as a means for government to get things accomplished. Charleston's society and economy were based on racial subordination, and it could use its local regulatory power for racial social ordering. Intrusion into individual autonomy was consistent with routine operation of police powers and their reduced expectations of privacy. That said, it remained to be seen just what kind of social ordering the legislation of 1822 and 1823 accomplished.

The racial regulations that followed the Vesey conspiracy scare were primarily aimed at free blacks who were not, in practice, threats to public order. Targeting free blacks, however, was a routine element in the reaction to conspiracy scares. Philip Morgan (2002: 166) points out that slave societies were marked by sporadic moments of white fears reaching "near-hysterical proportions." He notes as well that slave conspiracy scares emerged in cities. Plantations relied on patriarchal culture to control their slave population and white workers (Fox-Genovese 1988). These means of control were weak in urban areas with concentrations of free black residents, particularly in Charleston. When the need for social order arose, municipal regulations, rather than hierarchical personal relations, were readily available. Local regulations governing entry into the state and everyday behavior of free blacks were not responses to wrongdoings by free blacks but, rather, a visible form of discipline by the law and its close regulations. The regulations served to discipline, not punish, free blacks (Foucault 1977).

Nonetheless, as with earlier regulations, free blacks, black slaves, and whites were all happy to ignore or resist regulations (Johnson and Roark 1984: 45). The guardianship acts were not strictly enforced. Initially, Charleston officials did not enforce the Negro Seaman Acts. Perhaps the new regulations would have gone the way of historic regulations by remaining on the books but lightly honored. This pattern was disrupted by the engagement of a white citizens' group—the South Carolina Association—which took on the task of enforcing the law. The South Carolina Association operated as rather an open secret. In 1823, the shipping news in the Charleston newspaper listed incoming ships. Rather ominously, a notice was placed below, calling for a meeting of the Association (*Charleston Mercury*, July 3, 1823: 3; July 16, 1823: 3; July 21, 1823: 3). The Association garnered enough support to actively enforce the law. In the summer of 1823, 154 black sailors from northern states, the West Indies and Great Britain were incarcerated (Bolster 1997: 196).

Constitutional politics inside and outside the courts

With the Negro Seaman Act enforced, British and northern merchants found their black crewmen incarcerated during the duration of their ship's stay in a Charleston port. Their complaints raised the constitutional question of whether South Carolina possessed the power to pass such a law. The first challenge came from Great Britain. In response to the incarceration of British seamen, the British diplomat Stratford Canning appealed to John Quincy Adams, Secretary of State, in February 1823. In June, Adams responded, assuring him the situation would be taken care of, but nothing came of his promise (Ex. Doc. 119 1842). Adams failed to resolve the constitutional question over the Negro Seaman Act at that time. He would go on to engage in the politics over slavery in other roles—as lawyer in *The Amistad* case and as a member of the House of Representatives, when he made this correspondence available to the committee on commerce—but his efforts in 1823 were unsuccessful.

Judicial proceedings over the Negro Seaman Act were not much more helpful. Henry Elkison, a mulatto British seaman, was incarcerated under the Negro Seaman Act and applied for a writ of *habeas corpus*. Justice Johnson, the native Charlestonian presiding over the circuit court decision of *Elkison v. Deliesseline* ((1823) 8 F. Cas. 493), candidly recounted the unconventional politics surrounding this act. He admitted that he found the law to have been written in haste under circumstances of extreme agitation. When British officials and American captains had initially sought relief, Johnson recommended them to file suit in the state judiciary. No formal measures were taken to repeal the act, but local officials did stop enforcing the Act. The Act was enforced again only when, Johnson explained, it was "lately revived by a voluntary Association of gentlemen who have organized themselves into a society to see the laws carried into effect" (Johnson 1823: 4). With a Mr. Holmes, whom Johnson explicitly identified as lawyer for the South Carolina Association, arguing the circuit case instead of the South Carolina Attorney General, Johnson pronounced the execution of the law to be "rather a private than state act" (*Elkison v. Deliesseline* 1823: 494). Additionally, Johnson found the operation of the law to come into conflict with Congress' power to regulate interstate and foreign commerce, as well as treaties between the United States and Great Britain. That said, Johnson pointed out that the writ would have to issue from a state, not a federal, court.

Johnson immediately printed his opinion for public consumption and sought to circulate it, but the local newspaper, the *Charleston Mercury*, refused to print it. In August and September 1823, however, a debate raged in the newspaper between two pseudonymous writers. Caroliniensis published his first essay on August 15, defending the Negro Seaman Act and deriding Johnson for dicta delivered *extra judicially* (*Charleston Mercury*, August 15, 1823: 2). Caroliniensis was disturbed by the candidness of Johnson, who was born and bred in Charleston and knew the conventions of its racial politics. Caroliniensis also took exception to Johnson's presentation of the act as an exhibition of zeal in response to the Vesey conspiracy (*Charleston Mercury*, August 20, 1823: 2). He was particularly troubled by Johnson's outing of the South Carolina Association. Johnson wrote one brief essay under his own name to address his mentioning of Holmes and the South Carolina Association (*Charleston Mercury*, August 21, 1823: 2). The next day, the newspaper reported that 76 new members joined the South Carolina Association at its meeting the previous day. Again, Caroliniensis admonished Johnson for betraying the norms of his hometown, musing that Johnson should have known better. Given the fears raised by the Vesey conspiracy, Johnson should have recognized what had to be done, "namely, the exclusion of these characters, who furnish such an important means of communicating to the domestics of the South, the sentiments and opinions, and horrible schemes of their own colour of the North. The author of this pamphlet was born and has lived amongst us" (*Charleston Mercury*, August 22, 1823: 2). The sense of betrayal by one of their own native sons is evident in these complaints against Justice Johnson.

Soon after, Philonimus—who likely was Johnson himself (Wiecek 1977: 135)—published his first essay. He pointed out that the acts constructed a new category of race, consisting of all persons not white. He noted that the phrase, "persons of color," was not definitively settled, but that it would be interpreted as the converse of white. As such, he identified a new construction of race in police powers that rested on a binary between black and white (*Charleston Mercury*, August 27, 1823: 2). Caroliniensis insisted it applied to blacks—who were understood to be blacks and mulattoes—but not other persons of color, such as Moors, Lascars, Indians, or Mestizoes (*Charleston Mercury*, August 16, 1823: 2). Nevertheless, Johnson, who was indeed familiar with the racial politics of Charleston, highlighted the construction of whiteness at play in the new legislation.

Raising constitutional objections, Philonimus claimed that the Negro Seaman Act interfered with Congress' commerce clause power and commercial treaties (*Charleston Mercury*, August 27, 1823: 2). Caroliniensis responded with reference to the state's own power as paramount to any treaty (*Charleston Mercury* August 28, 1823: 2). The state's police power rested on the doctrine of self-preservation, which is "the first law of nature" (*Charleston Mercury*, September 3, 1823: 2). The right to regulate for public health and safety is so fundamental "that a State never can surrender a right, the exercise of which is indispensable to its safety. It is a right inherent in every sovereign state" (*Charleston Mercury*, September 3, 1823: 2). Racial ordering was particularly required in exercising this power, given that

> free and uninterrupted ingress of a colored population into this State from the North and elsewhere, with their known habits, feelings and principles, animated and emboldened as they are by the philanthropy of the day, and by the events which Europe in its throes and convulsions cast upon mankind, is the most formidable evil which South Carolina has to look upon in these her days of apparent quiet. To permit such persons to have a footing on our soil, is to introduce a moral pestilence which is to destroy the subordination in the slave, and with it the State itself.
>
> (*Charleston Mercury*, September 3: 2).

In identifying free blacks, bringing notions of freedom into the state, as a moral pestilence, Caroliniensis linked racial ordering to traditional police power.

It was just one more kind of quarantine. As such, the regulatory power was already available, rooted in the colonial tradition of regulatory power.

Relying on police power to regulate on the basis of race had not been fully discussed at the national or state constitutional conventions, but Caroliniensis claimed that the lack of discussion conveyed the self-evident nature of the state power. At the time of the constitutional compact, South Carolina was a slave-holding state, and all contracting parties understood that the state itself was the best judge to determine regulation of its colored population (*Charleston Mercury*, September 6, 1823: 2). Additionally, there was no reason to discuss the matter at the convention, since the conventioneers implicitly agreed about the needs of slaveholding states. Times had changed, however: "There were then afloat no doctrines of African emancipation. If they existed at all they existed only in the minds of a few pseudophilanthropists. These doctrines had not stalked abroad, as now, 'shaking from their hair horrid pestilence.' The abolition society of Philadelphia, the *British Association* in London, and the *Amis des noirs* in Paris had not then been formed" (*Charleston Mercury*, September 6, 1823: 2). These ideological movements and projected political change posed the threat to southern control of its population. Arguments like Caroliniensis' indicate the impetus behind the increase of racial regulations as reaction to the Vesey conspiracy. The pressure came not from internal plots or extraordinary threats from free blacks but from external sources—ideological and political changes regarding slavery in the United States. Given changing representative patterns, instability introduced by territories, and emerging ideological theories regarding slavery, slaveholding states increasingly felt the need to control internally, demonstrate power, and be able to defend that power against external influence.

This debate resumed obliquely in *Gibbons v. Ogden* in 1824. This landmark Supreme Court decision, authored by Chief Justice Marshall, affected a broad reading of commerce as navigation and presumed that Congress' power to regulate interstate and foreign commerce was a regulatory power. Should states' exercise of police powers come into conflict with a federal regulation of interstate commerce, the federal law would trump the state law. In his concurring opinion, Justice Johnson interpreted the commerce clause in light of the burgeoning state police powers (Wiecek 1977: 136). Among the areas that Congress' regulatory arm could reach were, notably, "Ship building, the carrying tradition, and propagation of seamen, are such vital agents of commercial prosperity, that the nation which could not legislate over these subjects, would not possess power to regulate commerce" (*Gibbons v. Ogden* (1824) 22 U.S. 1: 230). He then pronounced Congress' power to be exclusive (236). But once again, his strong constitutional argument had little impact on the racialized police powers.

In 1824, Britain resumed its complaint. Another British official wrote to Adams in April, reminding him that the situation with British seamen had not been addressed. The only executive action was an Opinion by Attorney General, William Wirt, who said of the Negro Seaman Act, "Here is a regulation of commerce, of a highly penal character, by a State, superadding new restrictions to those which have been imposed by Congress" (House Report 80 1843). He found the act to be incompatible with the Constitution and, therefore, void. That same year the Governor of South Carolina defended the seamen's act in terms of police powers, citing peace and tranquility of life, infectious disease, and self-preservation (Hamer 1935: 11). With this impasse, the law remained on the books and no federal action was taken.

In 1829, David Walker, who had been a member of a Charleston church that was destroyed in the aftermath of the Vesey conspiracy, published his famous *Appeal*. From his store near the Boston wharves, Walker asked sailors to spread his abolitionist message (Bolster 1997: 197). The perceived threat from the spread of antislavery ideas strengthened recourse to the police power. Southern states responded with stronger seamen's acts as well as laws requiring the death penalty for possession or distribution of Walker's *Appeal* (Crockett 2001). More Southern states restricted the immigration of free blacks (England 1943). President Jackson's Attorney General, John Berrien, determined that the Negro Seaman acts were a necessary measure of internal police.

Nat Turner's 1831 slave insurrection in Southampton County, Virginia, as well as more violent insurrections by British slaves in Barbados, Demerara, and Jamaica, heightened the fears of Southern slaveholders (Davis 2006: 221). Claiming a fear of further insurrection, the Mississippi Constitution of 1832 prohibited the importation of slaves into Mississippi. In Mississippi the population of whites outnumbered blacks by only 4,784 and Mississippi sought to preserve its ratio of whites over blacks. Given the states' historic power to preserve peace and order by prohibiting entry of malefactors, Mississippi could rely on its police powers to limit the interstate slave trade by invoking its powers to maintain order and provide for its self-preservation (*Groves v. Slaughter* (1841) 40 U.S. 449). Free blacks or new slaves with insurrectionary ideas could be reconceptualized as malefactors.

By 1837, Roger Taney sat as chief justice of the Supreme Court. With three southern, Jacksonian, slaveholding justices appointed to the Court, the doctrine of the police powers was poised to serve as a weapon in the arsenal of slaveholding states' constitutional discourse. This phenomenon did not go unnoticed at the time (Peters 1838). The Taney Court would secure the police power as a worthy adversary to congressional power with theories that had already been rehearsed in Charleston in the 1820s.

Justice Barbour soon took advantage in *Mayor of New York v. Miln* ((1837) 36 U.S. 102), in which the police powers doctrine functioned as a buttress against congressional power to regulate interstate commerce. At issue in *Miln* was a New York law that required the master of any ship or vessel arriving in a port of New York City from any foreign country to make a report to the mayor of the names, places of birth, ages, and occupations of the passengers. Furthermore, the master of the vessel was required to issue security for each foreign passenger, in anticipation of those immigrants becoming paupers and burdens upon the city.

The measure clearly raised questions of conflict with Congress' power to regulate foreign commerce, and yet the New York law reflected long-standing practices of the police power. States and localities were responsible for poor relief under the police powers doctrine. Because they administered to residents with settlement in the municipality, local governments had the incentive to race to the bottom, foist the settlement of the poor onto other towns, and disclaim responsibility for indigents. Requiring a ship captain to post security was not much different from one town claiming that another town was the legal settlement of a pauper. New York's regulation of the entry of poor immigrants raised a constitutional question of whether its traditional powers of regulating the entry of paupers, whom the state would have to support, conflicted with federal control of immigration in international ports. Had the Court framed the issue as a matter of commerce, then any federal regulation would trump state regulation, offering a precedent for the regulation of interstate and foreign commerce to trump the Negro Seaman Act and other measures to restrict the entry of free blacks and abolitionist literature.

The 1842 decision of *Prigg v. Pennsylvania* (41 U.S. 539) demonstrated how the politics of federalism could be reversed when police powers were employed on behalf of abolitionist interests. In response to the regular escape of fugitive slaves from nearby Maryland, followed by slavecatchers hired to capture them, Pennsylvania passed a personal liberty law. This exercise of the police power made it a felony to capture blacks or mulattos for the purpose of selling or disposing of them into slavery. In this case, the constitutional question was raised not by the commerce clause but by the Fugitive Slave Clause. Justice Story, faced with upholding the state police powers and an anti-slavery outcome, or issuing a nationalist opinion, chose the latter. His opinion held the Pennsylvania law to be unconstitutional by constructing a historical argument that placed the fugitive slave clause as a *sine qua non* at the constitutional convention (Plaag 2004). This history was inaccurate, but it did capture the tension of his time. Preferring the nationalist commitment of his Federalist partisanship rather than his personal commitment to antislavery, Story made the decision that he calculated would preserve national stability in his own day (Finkelman 1994: 264).

The Court's nationalist decision in *Prigg* did not transfer to other police powers cases. Police powers continued to be recognized as a strong state powers doctrine that could thwart federal interference when the conflict was between the commerce clause and police power. The extent of the police power was confirmed in the *License Cases* in 1847. In a case involving the sale of liquor bought in Boston and sold in New Hampshire without a license, the Court determined that New Hampshire could issue licenses on spirits because it possessed police powers. "But what are the police powers of a State?" the Court asked. "They are nothing more or less than the powers of government inherent in every sovereignty to the extent of its dominions" (*Pierce v. New Hampshire* (1847) 46 U.S. 504: 583). By 1847, police powers were acknowledged as a matter of sovereignty and it would be difficult for Congress to legitimize its breach when exercising its regulation of interstate commerce.

The formal police power doctrine produced a rather innocuous space for states to regulate for the health, safety, and welfare of their communities as they saw fit. Only two of the cases dealt with slavery, and none of them with race. The doctrine, therefore, appeared to support a power that was quite independent of the system of slavery. The exclusion of explicit references to race and slavery in burgeoning police powers doctrine and courts' and legislatures' reliance on racially neutral grounds such as state sovereignty failed to convey the increased social control wrought by the newly racialized police powers. The violence upon bodies, the construction of new racial categories, and enforced compliance with those categories and regulations went unacknowledged in formal doctrine. Hence, the legacy of slavery and its racial social ordering remained embedded deep in American constitutional structure.

Considering the racialization of police powers likewise exposes features of governance itself. While police powers were appropriated to sustain a system of white supremacy, the tools for racial regulation were already available in the traditional police powers. The power to infringe upon citizens' bodies and freedom, the ability to muster a vision of a good society, and the reliance on status were all part of local regulation. The recovery of these features indicates that the study of race in American political development informs not only the American experience with race but the resources of authority embedded in governing institutions.

Note

1　Thanks to the Institute for Constitutional Studies, Paul Finkelman, Linda Tvrdy, the South Carolina Historical Society, and to the editors of this volume.

Bibliography

Primary sources

Beach, M. (1822) *Letters to Elizabeth Gilchrist, Germantown, Pennsylvania. Beach, Mary Lamboll Thomas, 1770–1851*, Mary Lamboll Thomas Beach papers, 1822–90 (43/225): South Carolina Historical Society.
Citizens of Charleston (1822) *Memorial of the Citizens of Charleston to the Senate and House of Representatives of the State of South-Carolina*, Charleston: Duke & Browne.

Government documents

Ex. Doc. 119. (1842) 27th Congress, 2nd sess.
House Report 80 (1843) 27th Congress, 2nd sess.

Cases cited

Brown v. Maryland (1827) 25 U.S. 419
Elkison v. Deliesseline (1823) 8 F. Cas. 493
Gibbons v. Ogden (1824) 22 U.S. 1
Groves v. Slaughter (1841) 40 U.S. 449
Mayor of New York v. Miln (1837) 36 U.S. 102
Pierce v. New Hampshire (1847) 46 U.S. 504
Prigg v. Pennsylvania (1842) 41 U.S. 539
United States v. Darby (1941) 312 U.S. 100
Wickard v. Filburn (1942) 317 U.S. 111

References and secondary sources

Berlin, I. (1974) *Slaves without Masters: The Free Negro in the Antebellum South*, New York: Pantheon Books.

Bolster, W.J. (1997) *Black Jacks: African American Seamen in the Age of Sail*, Cambridge: Harvard University Press.

Cover, R. (1986) "Violence and the Word," *Yale Law Journal*, 95: 1601–29.

Crockett, H. (2001) "The Incendiary Pamphlet: David Walker's *Appeal* in Georgia," *Journal of Negro History*, 86: 305–18.

Davis, D.B. (2006) *Inhuman Bondage: The Rise and Fall of Slavery in the New World*, New York: Oxford University Press.

Dubber, M. (2005) *The Police Power: Patriarchy and the Foundations of American Government*, New York: Columbia University Press.

Edwards, L. (2007) "Status without Rights: African Americans and the Tangled History of Law and Governance in Nineteenth-Century U.S. South," *American Historical Review*, 112: 365–93.

Egerton, D. (1999) *He Shall Go Out Free: The Lives of Denmark Vesey*, Madison: Madison House.

England, J.M. (1943) "The Free Negro in Ante-Bellum Tennessee," *Journal of Southern History*, 9: 37–58.

Ericson, D. (2005) "The Federal Government and Slavery: Following the Money Trail," *Studies in American Political Development*, 19: 105–16.

—— and Green, L.B. (ed.) (1999) *The Liberal Tradition in American Politics: Assessing the Legacy of American Liberalism*, New York: Routledge.

Finkelman, P. (1994) "Story Telling on the Supreme Court: *Prigg v. Pennsylvania* and Justice Joseph Story's Judicial Nationalism," *Supreme Court Review*, 1994: 247–94.

—— (2003) "Civil Rights: Looking Back—Looking Forward: The Root of the Problem: How the Proslavery Constitution Shaped American Race Relations," *Barry Law Review*, 4: 1–19.

Foucault, M. (1977) *Discipline and Publish: The Birth of the Prison*, New York: Random House.

—— (1991) "Governmentality," trans. R. Braidotti and revised by C. Gordon, in G. Burchell, C. Gordon, and P. Miller (eds) *The Foucault Effect: Studies in Governmentality*, Chicago: University of Chicago Press, 87–104.

Fox-Genovese, E. (1988) *Within the Plantation Household: Black and White Women of the Old South*, Chapel Hill: University of North Carolina Press.

Freehling, W. (2005) "The Louisiana Purchase and the Coming of the Civil War," in S. Levinson and B. Sparrow (eds) *The Louisiana Purchase and American Expansion, 1803–1898*, Lanham: Rowman & Littlefield.

Genovese, E. (1972) *Roll, Jordan, Roll: The World the Slaves Made*, New York: Vintage Books.

Gillman, H. (1993) *The Constitution Besieged: The Rise and Demise of Lochner Era Police Powers Jurisprudence*, Durham, NC: Duke University Press.

Graber, M. (2006) *Dred Scott and the Problem of Constitutional Evil*, New York: Cambridge University Press.

Hamer, P. (1935) "Great Britain, the United States, and the Negro Seamen's Acts, 1822–1848," *Journal of Southern History*, 1: 3–28.

Henry, H.M. ([1914] 1968) *The Police Control of the Slave in South Carolina*, reprint New York: Negro Universities Press.

Johnson, M.P. (2001) "Denmark Vesey and His Co-Conspirators," *William and Mary Quarterly*, 58: 915–76.

—— and Roark, J. (1984) *Black Masters: A Free Family of Color in the Old South*, New York: W.W. Norton & Co.

Johnson, W. (1822) "Melancholy Effect of Popular Excitement," *Charleston Courier. Louisville Public Advertiser*, July 31, 1822: Column A.

—— (1823) "The Opinion of the Hon. William Johnson, delivered on the 7th of August, 1823," Charleston: C.C. Sebring.

Lofgren, C. (1988) *The Plessy Case: A Legal-Historical Interpretation*, New York: Oxford University Press.

McCord, D. (ed.) (1836–41) *The Statutes at Large of South Carolina*, Columbia: A.S. Johnston.

Mettler, S. (1998) *Divided Citizens: Gender and Federalism in New Deal Public Policy*, Ithaca, NY: Cornell University Press.

Morgan, P. (2002) "Conspiracy Scares," *William and Mary Quarterly*, 59: 159–66.

Novak, W. (1996) *The People's Welfare: Law and Regulation in Nineteenth-Century America*, Chapel Hill: University of North Carolina Press.

O'Brien, R. (2001) *Crippled Justice: The History of Modern Disability Policy in the Workplace*, Chicago: University of Chicago Press.

—— (2005) *Bodies in Revolt: Gender, Disability, and a Workplace Ethic of Care*, New York: Routledge.

Orren, K. (1991) *Belated Feudalism: Labor, the Law and Political Development in the United States*, New York: Cambridge University Press.

—— and Skowronek, S. (2004) *The Search for American Political Development*, New York: Cambridge University Press.

Pearson, E. (1999) *"Designs against Charleston" The Trial Record of the Denmark Vesey Slave Conspiracy of 1822*, Chapel Hill: University of North Carolina Press.

Peters, R. (1838) "Reports of Cases Argued and Adjudged in the Supreme Court of the United States," *North American Review*, 46: 126–55.

Plaag, E. (2004) "'Let the Constitution Perish:' *Prigg v. Pennsylvania*, Joseph Story, and the Flawed Doctrine of Historical Necessity," *Slavery and Abolition*, 25: 76–101.

Powers, B. (1994) *Black Charlestonians: A Social History, 1822–1885*, Fayetteville: University of Arkansas Press.

Ritter, G. (2006) *The Constitution as Social Design: Gender and Civic Membership in the American Constitutional Order*, Stanford, CA: Stanford University Press.

Sandoval-Strausz, A.K. (2005) "Travelers, Strangers, and Jim Crow: Law, Public Accommodation, and Civil Rights in America," *Law and History Review*, 23: 53–94.

Siegel, R. (1994) "The Modernization of Marital Status Law: Adjudicating Wives' Rights to Earnings," *Georgetown Law Journal*, 82: 2127–225.

Skocpol, T. (1985) "Bringing the State Back In: Strategies of Analysis in Current Research," P. Evans, D. Rueschmeyer, and T. Skocpol (eds) *Bringing the State Back In*, New York: Cambridge University Press.

Skowronek, S. (1982) *Building a New American State: The Expansion of National Administrative Capacities 1877–1920*, Cambridge: Cambridge University Press.

Smith, R. (1993) "Beyond Tocqueville, Myrdal, and Hartz: The Multiple Traditions in America," *American Political Science Review*, 87: 549–66.

—— (1997) *Civic Ideals: Conflicting Visions of Citizenship in U.S. History*, New Haven, CT: Yale University Press.

Stoner, J. (2003) *Common Law Liberty: Rethinking American Constitutionalism*, Lawrence: University of Kansas Press.

Tomlins, C. (1993) *Law, Labor, and Ideology in the Early American Republic*, New York: Cambridge University Press.

Wade, R.C. (1964) "The Vesey Plot: A Reconsideration," *Journal of Southern History*, 30: 143–61.

Walker, D. ([1830] 1968) *David Walker's Appeal to the Coloured Citizens of the World*, P. Hinks (ed.) University Park: Pennsylvania State University Press.

Wiecek, W. (1977) *The Sources of Antislavery Constitutionalism in America: 1760–1848*, New York: Cornell University Press.

4 · Racial orders in American political development[1]

Desmond S. King and Rogers M. Smith

Whether race is *the* "American Dilemma," racial inequities have been and remain confounding features of U.S. experience. Has racial injustice been a great aberration within a fundamentally democratic, rights-respecting regime? Has the United States instead been an intrinsically racist society? Has racial discrimination been the spawn of psychological or cultural pathologies, or a tool of class exploitation, or a political "card" to be played in power games, or something else?

One might expect political science in the United States to be the center of debates, if not answers, on such questions. But American political scientists have historically not been much more successful than America itself in addressing racial issues. We seek to do so by connecting theoretical frameworks emerging in the subfield of American political development, including King (1995), Lieberman (2002), Orren and Skowronek (1994, 1996, 1999, 2002), and Smith (1993, 1997), with insights from scholars of race in other areas of political science and other disciplines (e.g., Omi and Winant 1994; Dawson and Cohen 2002; Wacquant 2002). We argue that American politics has historically been constituted, in part, by two evolving but linked "racial institutional orders:" a set of "white supremacist" orders and a competing set of "transformative egalitarian" orders. Each of these orders has had distinct phases, and someday the United States may transcend them entirely— though that prospect is not in sight.

This "racial orders" thesis rejects claims that racial injustices are aberrations in America, for it elaborates how the nation has been pervasively constituted by systems of racial hierarchy since its inception. Yet more than many approaches, it also captures how those injustices have been contested by those they have injured and by other political institutions and actors. It does not deny that the nation's "white supremacist" racial orders have often served vicious economic exploitation or that their persistence reveals psychological and cultural pathologies. Instead it provides a framework to organize empirical evidence of the extent and manner in which structures of racial inequalities have been interwoven with economic as well as gender and religious hierarchies and social institutions.

But more than many scholars, our approach analyzes the "political economy" of American racial systems by stressing the "political," not the "economy." We see all political institutional orders as *coalitions of state institutions and other political actors and organizations that seek to secure and exercise governing power in demographically, economically, and ideologically structured contexts that define the range of opportunities open to political actors.* "Institutional orders" are thus more diversely constituted and loosely bound than state agencies; but they are also more institutionalized, authoritatively empowered, and enduring than many political movements. *Racial* institutional orders are ones in which political actors have adopted (and often adapted) racial concepts, commitments, and aims in order to help bind together their coalitions and structure governing institutions that express and serve the interests of their architects. As in any coalition, the members of a racial order support it out of varied motives. Economic aims are central for many, but others seek political power for its own sake, or to quiet social anxieties, or to further ideological goals. Leaders hold them together by gaining broad agreement on the desirability of certain publicly authorized arrangements that predictably distribute power, status, and resources along what are seen as racial lines. Hence these alliances necessarily combine what scholars have often treated as distinct "ideational" and "institutional" orders (cf., e.g., Smith 1997; Lieberman 2002; Orren and Skowronek 2004). And though the racial institutions they create at least seem to serve many members' economic interests, their coalitional nature means that their unifying aim must be power for many purposes, not just profits (cf. Goldfield 1997: 30–1, 91).

By presenting racial orders as political coalitions, we build on Omi and Winant's (1994: 53–76) depiction of "racial formation" as a product of many elite led "racial projects." But in their account, political actors or "intellectuals" attacking or defending the dominant racial ideology drive racial transformations (86). Like many other scholars of American political development, we treat political entrepreneurs *and* the preexisting institutional orders in which they operate as the key independent variables shaping all political change, including racial development. We also disagree that, despite some forces working at cross purposes, the American state has preserved "an overall unity" as a "racial state," granting "no political legitimacy" to "oppositional racial ideologies" or "competing racially defined political projects" (80, 84). Instead, we see the American state as comprised of multiple institutional orders, including competing racial orders with conflicting ideologies. Though the rival orders have always had unequal power, to understand change we must recognize both that competing racial orders have long existed and that all have included some governing institutions. No American racial "project" has gone far without aid from some such institutions, and no racial conflict can be grasped without seeing how these institutions have shaped the sincere aims of the actors involved and their strategic calculations. Rather than seeing racial change as many sociologists do, as "the product of the interaction of racially based social movements and the state" (Omi and Winant 1994: 88; Wacquant 2002: 52), we see it as the product of the interaction of opposing racial orders, as well as other political orders, all of which include some state institutions and some nonstate political actors and organizations.

The balance of power in those interactions has shifted over time in part because, like most politically constructed coalitions, America's racial orders have been complex and breakable. Most political actors possess partly conflicting identities and interests, and there are always many goals they might like to pursue. But because preexisting contexts define the problems and options actors face, politics usually involves choosing sides among two or three major approaches to what are widely seen as the dominant issues of the day, even if the prevailing approaches and issues do not express one's concerns fully. To accomplish much at all, American political actors have generally felt compelled to join either their current form of white supremacist order or its more egalitarian opponent. This means, however, that the competing racial orders have always included some members whose alignment was tentative and alterable, while others in each era have at least sought to remain unaligned or to forge a third direction. Because of the limits of politics, the latter choices have usually meant effectively aiding one order more than the other, or becoming politically unimportant, until exceptional circumstances have opened up new coalitional options and policy directions.

In the antebellum era, for example, many supported institutions of white supremacy as buttresses to African-American chattel slavery and the acquisition of Native American lands. Others simply wanted institutional protections against aggrieved nonwhites, or a socially recognized superior status, while some displayed psychological aversions, even genocidal impulses, toward people "of color." Though most of these white supremacists sided with slavery when it was the issue of the day, some did so reluctantly, and others opposed it, temporarily allying with advocates of an egalitarianism they did not share. Given these internal tensions and changing demographic contexts, in order to sustain a coalition powerful enough to control key governing institutions, antebellum white supremacists sometimes had to modify prevailing legal definitions of "whiteness," "blackness," and other racial categories. They slowly concluded that they had to label all with any African ancestry "black" and accept the Irish and many other immigrants as "white" (Jacobson 1998; Williamson 1984: 17–21). Yet they remained largely unified around the goal of maintaining the U.S. as a "white man's nation."

The internal tensions among those championing egalitarian changes over the content of egalitarian goals and the means for pursuing them have been greater still. American discourses and institutions promising equal rights burgeoned in opposition to British aristocracy. Initially few British colonists thought them inconsistent with African slavery. But from the start, many black and some white Americans did; and some who opposed slavery favored full racial equality. Yet they worked in alliance with many more who were antislavery advocates of less extreme forms of white supremacy, such as "tutelary" status or colonization for nonwhites. And throughout history, many who have rejected all versions of white supremacy still have differed on whether priority should be given to seeking economic equity, equal political status, or cultural recognition. Hence even when they were allied on issues such as ending slavery or segregation, advocates of racial change have disagreed over whether their ultimate goal should be full integration or some form of more egalitarian racial pluralism. Over time there have been major shifts in the degree and kinds of egalitarianism that have predominated among reformist institutions and actors, defining the phases of the nation's transformative egalitarian racial orders.

Changes have occurred in part because individuals positioned on the margins of racial orders, in relation either to the aims or to the power structures of those orders, have sometimes switched their dominant allegiances at critical junctures. Such was true of Andrew Johnson, who was ardently antislavery but otherwise did not favor altering systems of white supremacy; and Harry Truman, who had never been a strong racial egalitarian but who concluded for domestic, international, and personal reasons that it was wiser to ally with antisegregationist northern Democrats than white supremacist southerners (Klinkner with Smith 1999: 77–9, 206–24).

Despite these complexities, in particular settings it is not hard to discern what were commonly seen as the main proposals on the nation's agenda that promised to increase or decrease racial equality of conditions in the near term. Scholars can recognize that issues such as slavery, Jim Crow segregation, and racially targeted aid programs have at different times been the central disputes around which political battle lines have formed. Hence in each era scholars can identify empirically the main institutions and actors allied to sustain the then-dominant forms of white supremacy, thereby comprising that period's "white supremacist" order, and the leading institutions and actors working for more egalitarian racial conditions, its "transformative egalitarian" order. The existence and analytical utility of these racial orders are not discredited by the presence of internal tensions in the orders, including marginal and "dual" members who may change sides, by some who seek to stay unaligned, or by the fact that the orders modify their goals and members over time. Rather, these features add to their explanatory force. The processes of change wrought by the problems leaders face in sustaining these orders amidst internal tensions, by the conflicts of the orders with each other, by the defection of actors and institutions from one order to its rival, and by their interactions with other actors and institutions comprising American life, all have been engines of significant political development.

The "racial orders" approach is a theoretical framework that can enable empirical studies of racial systems to falsify hypotheses. If a racial order works against the economic interests of many participants, as antebellum laws banning free blacks in Old Northwest states arguably did for many employers and even white workers, as Jim Crow laws clearly did for transportation companies, and as race-based immigration restrictions probably did for many wealthy supporters, it is hard to claim their economic aims drove that order. And if the systems of economic and political inequality sanctioned by a racial order come to be greatly modified, as in the shattering of the interweaving of white supremacy and slavery before the rise of de jure segregation systems, it is implausible to deny that the order has undergone true development. Thus this approach can also help scholars map the stages and extent of the nation's real but incomplete progress toward racial equity and the political contests through which progress has come. And insofar as our framework can unify and strengthen empirical findings on racial developments, it can also vindicate the claim that these contests have been fundamentally political.

Useful as this framework is for making sense of racial development, our main claim here is that a "racial institutional orders" approach helps explain many features of American politics that may appear *unrelated* to race, such as congressional organization and bureaucratic autonomy. We conclude that the internal developments, clashes, and broader impacts of American racial orders have been and remain so central that all scholars of American politics ought always to consider how far "racial order" variables affect the phenomena they examine. Analysts should inquire whether the activities of institutions and actors chiefly concerned either to protect or to erode white supremacist arrangements help to account for the behavior and changes in the nation's political institutions, coalitions, and contests they study. Any choice not to consider racial dimensions requires explicit justification.

This is so precisely because racial orders have been constitutively interwoven with many other highly significant institutional orders, including gender and class hierarchies. Still, we recognize that African Americans, Asian Americans, Latinos, and Native Americans, like all others, have had political concerns that are best captured by stressing their membership in other such orders, not their racial positioning (Reed 2003). We hope that the framework we advance here will aid the study of all these political orders, providing us with ways to identify and measure their profound intersections with racial institutions and conflicts. We suspect that these intersections will show how the unusual prominence of racial orders in America's development has also given distinctive shape to its gender and class systems.

Placing race in American political development

Work on race has exploded in political science in recent decades. Yet leading scholars still see a "need for a firm theoretical foundation on which to conduct empirical research" into American racial politics (Dawson and Cohen 2002: 488–9). We reach the key concept of our theoretical framework, "racial institutional orders," by combining arguments for the prominence of America's racial traditions in the nation's "multiple traditions" (e.g., King 1995; Goldfield 1997; Smith 1997) with the "multiple institutional orders" approach to political development advanced by Karen Orren and Stephen Skowronek and also explored by historical institutionalist scholars (e.g., Lieberman 2002; Pierson and Skocpol 2002). To clarify this framework, we begin with "institutions," then "institutional orders," and then "racial" institutional orders.

We follow Orren and Skowronek (2004: 82–5) in defining "institutions" as organizations that (1) have broad but discernible purposes, (2) establish norms and rules, 3) assign roles to participants, and (4) have boundaries marking those inside and outside the institutions. We extend Orren and Skowronek's framework by defining an "institutional order" as a coalition of governing state institutions, nonstate political institutions, and political actors that is bound together by broadly similar senses of the goals, rules, roles, and boundaries that members of each order wish to see shaping political life in certain areas. Such orders contain constitutional provisions, statutes, and administratively made or judge-made rules that formally establish and govern those areas; legislative bodies, executive agencies, and/or courts involved in implementing those legal doctrines; and all political parties and civil groups that make their positions on how the areas should be managed central to their activities. Such groups are usually drawn from the economic and social actors and organizations regulated and partly constituted by an order's rules.

"Racial" institutional orders seek and exercise governing power in ways that predictably shape people's statuses, resources, and opportunities by their placement in "racial" categories. The orders rarely originate such categories. But their proponents often modify inherited racial conceptions to attract new supporters while retaining old ones and stigmatizing opponents. At times, "white" has meant most northern Europeans, all Europeans, most Middle Easterners, and those with one-eighth African or one-fourth Native American ancestry (Kennedy 1959: 48; Jacobson 1998). The shifting ways in which actors in racial orders institutionalize these categories partly constitute persons' senses of racial identity.

In this approach, meaningful "development" occurs when one predominant order gives way to another, or when the prevailing order's leading concepts of racial goals, rules, roles, and boundaries are substantially revised, as when most white supremacists felt compelled to abandon slavery or when most racial egalitarians came to insist on equal voting rights, not just civil rights. Such development can arise from struggles among partly dissonant groups within an institutional order, from the interactions of racial orders with other orders, such as labor and party systems, and from broad social, economic, and inter-national changes, all of which may strengthen some participants in an order and weaken others, or add new players and policy challenges for the order to confront (Orren and Skowronek 2002: 747–54; Pierson and Skocpol 2002: 698–704). The "racial orders" framework does not postulate priority for any of these factors, though if scholars regularly take the institutions and actors comprising racial alliances into account, we may eventually be able to judge which causes have mattered most.

While the concept of an "institutional order" builds on work in the American political development subfield, our focus on racial orders is novel. The subfield grew out of the efforts of pioneering scholars including Bensel (1984), Skocpol (1979), and Skowronek (1982) to "bring the state back in," a quest that led to the "claim that institutions have an independent and formative influence on politics" (Orren and Skowronek 1986: vii). But little of that work addressed race, because for many, the impetus to grasp the roles of "states" and "institutions" came from dissatisfaction with analyzing politics in Marxist "class" or liberal "group" terms. Those approaches seemed unable to explain why America had weaker redistributive and regulatory programs than much of Europe. This new historical institutionalist literature thus had an economy centered sense of "political economy." Most writers also viewed American politics as shaped by a common though internally conflicted "liberal" political culture (e.g., Greenstone 1986: 1–49).

There remains a strong tendency in the American political development literature, tracing to Louis Hartz (1955), to theorize racial issues as ultimately products of the antebellum "master/slave" order (e.g. Greenstone 1993: 95–117; Ericson 1999, 2000; Orren and Skowronek 2004). This tendency endures in the "liberal culture" premise of much early American political development work, and for some major topics it is appropriate. The slave system was deeply interwoven with American racial patterns, and clashes over the extension of slavery formed the chief cause of the Civil War. Yet to grasp the politics of *race* in the antebellum era; to explain Reconstruction; to analyze later racial developments; and to see the impact of racial contests on American development generally, "multiple orders" analyses must encompass not only this "master/slave" order, but, especially, America's racial orders.

Both evidence and parsimony lead us to posit two potent, evolving racial systems at work: first, the set of "white supremacist orders" created to defend slavery and also the displacement of the tribes. Even the Declaration of Independence sought to justify tribal subjugation (by denouncing "merciless Indian Savages") and to avoid criticism of chattel slavery (by excising Jefferson's language attacking the slave trade) (Ellis 2000: 81–119). From then on, fueled by the spread of slavery, by desires to justify westward expansion into tribal and Mexican lands as racial "manifest destiny," and, at times, by anxieties about immigrants, political leaders extended the nation's white supremacist order into spheres that eventually went well beyond master/slave relationships (Horsman 1981).

Along with the state and national laws that upheld the master/slave order, this white supremacist system was comprised by statutes at the national as well as the state level, in the north and south, that accorded even free black citizens restricted political, economic, and mobility rights (Berwanger 1967: 42–9, 140; Fuchs 1990: 91–3; Litwack 1961: 31, 70–93, 113–15). We stress that while most of the actors and institutions in the antebellum white supremacist order supported slavery, some did not, because the latter played pivotal political roles. In an 1857 Oregon constitutional referendum, 74 percent of Oregon voters rejected permitting slavery in their state, but 89 percent favored excluding all blacks (Berwanger 1967: 93). Analysts have struggled to explain such positions as somehow due to white workers' economic interests, while terming those views a misguided, racist "blind spot" (Goldfield 1997: 79–80, 92, 108–11). Though worker fears of cheap competitors surely played a part, so great an antiblack vote in a state seeking immigrant labor indicates that many saw all nonwhites as undesirable (Hutchinson 1981: 24, 35–9; Fuchs 1990: 24). A racial orders approach suggests they did so not only from misconceived economic motives but also out of beliefs in black inferiority, fear of racial strife, and desires to reserve power for those with whom they identified racially. On many racial measures these Oregonians could side with slaveholders, unless and until the issue became slavery and blacks in their own backyard.

The core of the antebellum white supremacist order included much of the Senate and most presidents, products of electoral systems that overrepresented the slave states; most of the state officials in those states; and all proslavery Whigs and Jeffersonian, then Jacksonian, Democrats. The more tenuous members were white supremacist but antislavery Whigs and Free Soil Democrats. The order also included politically active church and scholarly leaders who justified slavery and white rule (Takaki 1993: 173–6; Bay 2000). This institutional order had a broadly shared goal, extending white domination. It had rules and norms, including racialized slavery laws and other denials of equal rights that assigned different political, economic, and social roles to whites and various nonwhites. And it had boundaries, for there were always rival institutions and actors.

This white supremacist order made explicitly racial identities seem natural and vital to millions. It habituated many it privileged as "white" to think of their racial status as a primary feature of their lives (Du Bois [1935] 1992: 700–1). Its imposed inequalities gave many white farmers and workers as well as slaveholders a sense of economic dependency on the maintenance of racial restrictions that seemed to make their lands, jobs, and wages more secure. It also generated in many a sense of racial entitlement, which most defended in religious and biological terms. It did all these things by creating politically powerful institutions in which all whites could officially share, along with public policies that advantaged whites in relation to blacks, even if some whites benefited far more than others. All of this made most whom governing institutions deemed "white" resistant to radical transformations in the white supremacist order, even those who wished to see slavery and blacks expunged from America.

Yet U.S. history displays a rival, expanding "transformative egalitarian racial order" that built on doctrines and institutions of equal rights also present from the nation's inception. The American revolutionaries rejected monarchy and aristocracy for democratic republics, and systems of primogeniture and entail for greater individual powers over property. Then they created many new political, economic, and cultural institutions to pursue the broad goals of "equal rights" and "equality before the law," and that provided greater equality to European-descended men than ever before. Its rules and roles called for courts that upheld equal justice, a comparatively broad suffrage, market systems promising equal rights to all participants, equal opportunities for worship, and general adherence to the natural rights doctrines used to support these claims (Kesler 1998: 13–23). The fuel to ignite those doctrines and institutions into conflict with white supremacist ones came largely from "free labor" economic and political interests, but also from the moral indignation that slavery fostered in virtually all blacks and some whites. Of the two great antebellum slavery issues, the most decisive conflict, opposition to the expansion of slavery, was predominantly driven by "free labor" commitments; but outrage against southern efforts to recapture fugitive slaves came chiefly from allied racially egalitarian reformers (Wiecek 1977: 153–62, 216–48; Foner 1988: 75–87, 124–6, 543– 7; Takaki 1993: 129–30).

Through this alliance, specifically racial egalitarian principles won limited institutionalizations in the antebellum years, and then growing numbers of activists invoked them to champion black rights. These institutions included, first, the Revolutionary-era laws ending slavery in the north and promoting manumission in the south, and the congressional ban on slavery in the Northwest Territory; then, beginning with the 1820 Missouri controversy, congressional advocacy and some judicial rulings claiming Article IV "privileges and immunities" of citizenship for free blacks; then the statutory and procedural obstacles to the return of fugitive slaves erected by some northern legislatures and courts, prodded by more egalitarian white and black churches and antislavery organizations (Goldfield 1997: 93–104; Morris 1974: 94–120, 219–22; Zilversmit 1967: 135–42). Even if white abolitionists like William Lloyd Garrison had trouble accepting blacks like Frederick Douglass as equals, together their efforts were enough to spark repressive responses. The northwest states banned entry of free blacks, and all states denied them full civic equality. Still, in most northeastern states blacks kept their political, educational, and economic statutory rights and used them to work for more (Litwack 1961: 70–5, 84–104, 153–70; Berlin 1974: 225–9, 316–33, 360–4; McFeely 1991: 175–7).

When southern demands forced antislavery white supremacists to decide whether to side with more racially egalitarian actors and institutions to stop slavery's spread, many did so. Exemplary here is Pennsylvania Democrat David Wilmot, author of the proviso that sought to ban slavery in the western territories. Wilmot feared slave competition with "free white labor," thought blacks inferior, and hated the notion of sharing power with them. But faced by slavery's expansion, he became a Republican and, while urging peace with the South, supported President Lincoln as a wartime Senator before withdrawing to a judgeship.

Lincoln's Republicans, the center of the late antebellum transformative alliance, came to power championing only an end to slavery in the territories and the equal claim of all races to the limited rights of the Declaration of Independence, but those views were enough to spur southern secession. Lincoln preferred war to slavery's expansion (Greenstone 1993: 245–85). The war's polarizations and the key military contributions of blacks then pushed Lincoln and many others farther. Believing that, "as He died to make men holy," they were called to make men free, Republicans passed statutes and constitutional amendments at the state and national levels that banned slavery and elaborated a far more extensive and egalitarian racial order. After white southerners showed at the war's end that they still sought to oppress the ex-slaves via new Black Codes, many angry northerners even supported black voting rights. Though few whites saw much economic benefit in paying to aid the freedmen, by the late 1860s the electoral needs of many white Republicans, the interests of their black partisans, and the moral goals of the now-prestigious reform groups all pushed hard for political equality (Kousser 1974: 27–9, 241–2; Valelly 1995). After the Fifteenth Amendment in 1870, the expanded egalitarian order centered on new constitutional guarantees of formal racial equality in political as well as economic and civil rights. Its proponents included many congressional Republicans, new Reconstruction agencies like the Freedmen's Bureau and the Freedmen's Saving Bank, many Republican state officials including black officeholders, religious reform groups, and the numer-ous new black schools and civil groups they helped create (Du Bois [1935] 1992: 220–32, 599–600; Goldfield 1997: 115–23; Nelson 1988: 123–47).

Those developments are made more comprehensible by adding a "racial orders" stress on power and ideological goals to the more traditional emphasis on economic interests embodied in the effort of Orren and Skowronek (2004: 133–43) to explain the politics of this period in terms of allies of former masters contesting with allies of former slaves. That approach has difficulty making sense of the pivotal actors who were antislavery but also white supremacist, like the great foe of Reconstruction, President Andrew Johnson, and others in the new coalition he sought to form. It is hard to use Johnson's economic interests to explain why he sided with his old opponents, the former masters, against the slaves he had once supported. But when seen as an effort to build a new, nonslavery white supremacist order, his conduct was not foolish. Slavery was no longer on the agenda. Preserving white supremacy against egalitarian reformers was. Most white southerners, most Democrats, and even many Republicans welcomed a chance to stop the equal rights crusaders' assaults on white privilege. Johnson simply moved too crudely and abruptly to succeed (Foner 1988: 216–27, 247–51). Nonetheless, from 1867 on, many voters showed renewed willingness to support white supremacist Democrats. Even after defeating Johnson and enfranchising blacks, many Republicans decided by the early 1870s that they could advance their power and economic interests by largely relinquishing support for African Americans, beyond maintaining black voting rights. Yet in so doing, they permitted hostile white supremacist forces to strengthen; and they were also on the unpopular side of the leading nonracial issue of the day, whether money policies would favor credit seeking farmers and workers, or creditors. Amidst declining electoral fortunes, and after a last gasp effort to protect black voters, the Federal Elections Bill of 1890 only helped the Democrats win in 1892; most Republicans defected entirely to the resurgent white supremacist order. Many joined the Democrats in repealing Reconstruction-era election laws in 1894, and Republican justices upheld de jure segregation in *Plessy v. Ferguson* (1896) 163 U.S. 537 (Logan [1954] 1965: 43–75, 140– 1; Gillette 1979: 18–49; Foner 1988: 488–511).

The modified white supremacist order they constructed included not only antiblack Jim Crow measures but also similar laws and practices aimed at Mexicans in the Southwest, Asians in California, and Native Americans in many western states, as well as, first, Chinese exclusion, then racially justified imperial conquest and governance of Filipinos, Puerto Ricans, and various Pacific Islanders, and eventually race-based immigration quotas (Fuchs 1990: 80–6, 110–22; Ngai 1999). These other forms of domination and exclusion differed in some ways from the Jim Crow system and could reasonably be viewed as relatively autonomous racial orders. But they were created via alliances of western whites and northern imperialists and immigration restrictionists with the southern architects of black segregation, and much of their ideological content defined how far those they subordinated should be treated like blacks (Williams 1980; Takaki 1993: 148–9, 209–13; Jacobson 1998: 203–45).

Equivocally before, but overwhelmingly after 1892 up to the 1930s, this "second-phase" white supremacist order encompassed majorities in all three branches of the federal government, virtually all southern and many western officeholders, and many other local officials and police forces. It centered on some national and many state and local statutes, executive policies, and judicial doctrines that enacted explicit forms of racial apartheid, race-based immigration and naturalization restrictions, and exclusionary housing, educational, and employment practices, along with titularly race-neutral vagrancy laws, tenant farming rules, criminal statutes, and voter registration and jury selection systems administered to maintain white supremacy (and used also to disempower poor whites where they failed to cooperate). The order was supported by new intellectual justifications for the "tutelary" subordination of less "civilized" and "evolved" nonwhites (Fuchs 1990: 96–8; Almaguer 1994; Oshinsky 1996: 40–1). That content, and the formally neutral measures, show how the American systems of white supremacy had to be restructured because of the successes of the transformative egalitarian order in institutionalizing enduring bans on overt racial subordination. But restructured as it was, this system of segregation, disfranchisement, and immigrant exclusion remained a white supremacist order that made largely formal, limited concessions to the more egalitarian institutions and actors that opposed it.

Yet just as the Civil War egalitarians did not succeed in removing all institutional bases for the resurgence of the white supremacists, so their new system did not eradicate the postwar egalitarian racial order. The constitutional provisions and some national and state statutes remained available for judges willing to apply them. Often dissenters and sometimes even majorities did so, as when the Supreme Court upheld birthright citizenship for Chinese Americans and struck down laws that overtly banned blacks from juries and prevented whites from selling housing to blacks (*U.S. v. Wong Kim Ark* (1898) 169 U.S. 649; *Rogers v. Alabama* (1904) 192 U.S. 226; *Buchanan v. Warley* (1917) 245 U.S. 60). Both the Declaration and the Reconstruction amendments and statutes also were central to the rhetoric and the tactics of black protest organizations such as Ida Wells-Barnett's Negro Fellowship League, William

Monroe Trotter's New England Suffrage League, and the NAACP, founded in 1909 and soon focused on winning court decisions and legislation that could realize the egalitarian principles therein proclaimed. They had white allies among journalists like Oswald Garrison Villard, urban social workers like Jane Addams, some church and labor leaders, socialists, and some Republican legislators like Congressman Leonidas Dyer, who pushed for antilynching legislation (Nieman 1991: 122–30). But white supremacists dominated Congress, the executive branch, and most courts, so transformative egalitarians won little more than sporadic judicial victories in these years.

In the early 1920s hundreds of thousands of alienated African Americans supported Marcus Garvey's separatist Universal Negro Improvement Association, which rejected white supremacy, yet at times made common cause with segregationists (Cronon [1955] 1969: 189–95). If, in creating a network of black vocational schools, Garvey's hero Booker T. Washington tried to operate in both racial orders at once, Garvey strove instead to create a third, black institutional order. Both men inspired millions of African Americans. Still, their public acceptance of racial separatism helped legitimate the Jim Crow system, leading W. E. B. Du Bois to charge that they were on balance aiding white supremacy (Franklin and Moss 1988: 244–50; Balfour 2003). On a racial orders analysis, it is hard to disagree.

But World War I and industrialization created new demands for black labor. The ensuing migration of blacks to northern industrial cities made them a potentially important voting bloc and generated new activist African American organizations, including the National Negro Congress, Philip Randolph's Brotherhood of Sleeping Car Porters, and some interracial CIO unions. The Depression then brought many northern liberals into national offices, and the Communist Party launched efforts to win rights for black Americans such as the famous "Scottsboro Cases." All these developments strengthened transformative egalitarian forces (Meier and Rudwick 1976: 314–32; Franklin and Moss 1988: 339–48). Many New Dealers in Congress, the new executive agencies, on courts, and in northern state and local governments wished to include black Americans in the economic restructuring they were pursuing.

But aided by the seniority system, white supremacist representatives of the one-party Democratic south held many key congressional posts and were strongly represented in FDR's executive branch and the courts. They also dominated many of the state and local governments that implemented most New Deal programs. Hence proponents of Jim Crow were able to gain exclusionary concessions from Roosevelt and racially liberal New Deal policymakers in the design or administration of programs like old age insurance, unemployment compensation, housing aid, the Civilian Conservation Corps, and new labor laws. The concessions meant that these new institutions largely maintained the white supremacist order, embittering activists like Randolph, who concluded that whites should never provide movement leadership (Bates 2001). African Americans did benefit from many New Deal programs over time, and through some of his appointments to administrative agencies and, particularly, to the judiciary, FDR made the nation's conflicting racial orders less unequal in power. But he shaped political development most with regard to the nation's economic and federalist structures, not its racial ones (Katznelson et al. 1993; Quadagno 1994; Lieberman 1998; McMahon 2003).

Change came in the post-World War II years through further migration of blacks to the north; a convergence of litigative, lobbying, and militant protest actions by leading black groups including the NAACP, the Urban League, the Southern Christian Leadership Council, and others; and Cold War pressures to make the nation less vulnerable to Communist criticism. In this context many northern Democrats in Congress, and first Harry Truman and later Presidents Kennedy and Johnson, along with the Warren Court, decided that both national and partisan interests could best be served by repudiating racial segregation and disfranchisement and white supremacist ideologies and reviving the Reconstruction amendments and statutes (Dudziak 2000). The manner in which, in response to domestic and international pressures, key actors and institutions joined the transformative egalitarian order seems even more central to explaining change than the heightened "resource mobilization" or the adoption of new concepts of "black identity" by "minority movements" rightly stressed by scholars using "social movements and the state" frameworks (e.g., McAdam 1984; Omi and Winant 1994: 98–9).

White supremacists in Congress, and in many state and local offices, and some judges resisted ferociously, but these altered political contexts left them more isolated and less powerful. The resulting civil rights congressional and state laws, the executive endorsements they received, the expansion of civil rights enforcement and administrative capacities they authorized, and the supportive judicial rulings of the era all constituted genuine development in Orren and Skowronek's terms. They brought the nation's transformative egalitarian racial order to predominance, for it now encompassed the national legislative, executive, and judicial branches and included many new officials and institutions, including the Equal Employment Opportunity Commission, the HEW Office for Civil Rights, and the Department of Labor's Office of Contract Compliance. And though the struggle had centered on the rights of blacks, egalitarian institutions and actors soon expanded their aims to include women, Latinos, Native Americans, Asian Americans, and the disabled (Skrentny 2002: 8–20).

Yet though overtly white supremacist policies were discredited and egalitarian principles widely proclaimed, many whites north and south remained protective of arrangements that the Jim Crow system had generated, especially de facto residential and school racial segregation, various legal limits on national powers to interfere with state and local practices, and the overrepresentation of whites at the top of most American political and economic institutions. In addition, many white and some black supporters of egalitarian change were troubled by the disruptions and resistance those changes engendered. Once again, some white reformers felt anxious that they might lose control of the extent and pace of social transformations. Many others felt daunted or exhausted by the costs of continuing the changes the civil rights era had begun, much less by the greater ones posed by expansions of those efforts to more and more groups. In ascendancy, the modern transformative egalitarian alliance soon became more uncertain of its agenda than its predecessors had ever been. The chief beneficiary of these discontents was the Republican Party. The GOP added to its traditional base the support of prosegregationist George Wallace Democrats as well as formerly Democratic "neo-cons" who felt the Sixties had gone too far. Conservatives created a coalition that, aided by Ronald Reagan's charisma, eventually came to power in all three federal branches, led by southern and western Republicans such as Newt Gingrich, Trent Lott, William Rehnquist, and both the elder and the younger George Bush (O'Reilly 1995; Carter 1996).

One can easily find in modern conservative ranks many actors and institutions who once opposed desegregation and modern civil rights laws, as Bush and Rehnquist did, and who still oppose policies promising near-term decreases in material racial inequalities. Still, it is not correct to portray this coalition as merely a continuation of the old white supremacist orders. The transformative egalitarian order, once nearly invisible, then constitutionally enshrined but politically dominated, is now authoritative in American law and many governing agencies. As a result, the terrain of the clashes between America's rival racial institutional orders has shifted. Most institutional occupants of what we see as the current descendant of "white supremacist" racial orders steadfastly and sincerely reject that label—so it is appropriate to describe their contemporary variant as an "antitransformative" racial order. As Swain (2002) documents, there remain overtly white supremacist forces in American life, but though they provide some support to the modern antitransformative order, they do not define it.

Nonetheless, one major contribution of the "racial orders" framework is to compel recognition of a disturbing reality. The contemporary "antitransformative" alliance does have a widely recognized racial agenda, though a negative one. Its actors and institutions oppose measures explicitly aimed at reducing racial inequalities. Because many of the institutionalized inequities in schooling, jobs, education, and political offices created by the Jim Crow order still endure, this opposition helps maintain many superior white statuses and privileges for the near term, however much some who espouse "colorblind" policies hope for greater equality in the long run. It is also likely that others are attracted to such policies precisely because they may slow alterations in segregated, unequal arrangements.

Because racial egalitarians cannot accept that negative racial agenda, the context between today's orders has come to center largely on clashes between transformative egalitarian actors and institutions who support many kinds of direct action to reduce material racial inequalities in the near term—including most Democrats, many administrative agencies, some federal and state judges, many educational institutions, some corporations, and many liberal and minority reform groups—and an antitransformative order united by rejection of such actions, including most Republican national and state elected officials and partisans, many federal and state judges, and conservative religious, ethnic, corporate, and activist groups. In that contest, each of today's racial orders has strengths and weaknesses. The widespread resistance to racial change means that American political actors can still make appeals to white interests when discussing policies like affirmative action, racial profiling, housing and school desegregation, and economic aid to minority communities. But with egalitarian precepts more deeply institutionalized, they now must generally do so indirectly or covertly (Kinder and Sanders 1996; Gilens 1999; Mendelberg 2001). Rhetorical allegiance to egalitarian ideals has become de rigueur—even though that often means reinterpreting civil rights slogans such as "color-blindness" and "equality of opportunity" to justify resistance to changes in unequal racial statuses. Many Americans who honestly reject white supremacy are receptive to those reinterpretations, feeling that principles of equal justice and practical realities limit the ways in which governments can legitimately and effectively pursue a more racially egalitarian society (Sniderman and Piazza 1993). Many still wish to see entrenched racial disadvantages reduced; but this rejection of direct efforts leaves few options for doing so. The main recent policy response has been unprecedented levels of mass incarceration, overwhelmingly of nonwhites (Wacquant 2002). That has not prevented significant reversals in racial arenas such as school desegregation, with a smaller percentage of blacks now attending majority white schools than at any time since 1968, with white students the most segregated of all groups, and with the Supreme Court voiding most forms of affirmative action (Frankenberg et al. (2003): 4, 6; *Gratz v. Bollinger* (2003) 439 U.S. 249). Though these are victories for antitransformative forces, they do not generate faith that racial problems are fading.

Those victories do show that while many of the newer egalitarian institutions and policies of the 1960s and early 1970s continue to work for greater racial equality, the problems facing modern transformative egalitarian forces are great. They have struggled in the last quarter century to find a unifying agenda. Today's African American activists pursue many different "black visions" of civic equality and community flourishing (Dawson 1994, 2001). For some like Louis Farrakhan, the transformative order of the civil rights era has failed, so other, more separatist or Black Nationalist routes to greater prosperity must be sought. Though the Nation of Islam's control of governing institutions is too limited to form a rival racial order, its leaders often opt out of working with the modern racially egalitarian coalition. Critics call those choices misguided, self-marginalizing acquiescence to antitransformative forces and urge a traditional civil rights agenda. But with much of that agenda formally accomplished, black leaders face heightened, often conflicting demands to focus more on suppressed concerns of class, gender, and sexual orientation, rather than race alone (Cohen 1999; Reed 1999, 2003).

The new immigrant groups from Asia and Latin America, moreover, confront modern versions of old pressures to situate themselves in relation to today's transformative egalitarian and antitransformative racial orders. If they seem to embrace the latter, by seeking to be seen as "model minorities" within what they affirm to be a just system of equal opportunities, they face condemnation from many civil rights organizations and their allies. If they seem to choose the former, by joining in calls for reparations, group rights, and multiculturalism, they risk getting locked out of avenues to social mobility that, for many, were what coming to America was all about (Smelser et al. 2001; Waters 2001). If they, too, seek somehow to opt out of American racial politics or to build orders of their own, again those choices may end up helping existing systems of racial inequality to remain largely unchanged.

We hope it is clear at this point that, just as a racial orders framework helps explain much about America's past, many key features of what analysts have deemed today's "postsegregation era" (Reed 1999) or period of "advanced marginalization" of African Americans (Cohen 1999) can be illuminated by viewing them as clashes between the modern, internally conflicted "transformative egalitarian" racial order and the resurgent "antitransformative" racial order. But valuable as those contributions are, they may be the lesser part of the intellectual gains that can come from a racial orders approach. From the nation's inception to the present, the impacts of these orders have not been confined to each other. The white supremacist and egalitarian transformative orders have also interacted with most of the nation's other "multiple orders," with far-ranging consequences for many aspects of American life that may seem distant from race. The frequent failure to grasp these connections may well represent the greatest weakness of political science in grasping the place of race in American politics.

The unseen impacts of racial orders

Many features of the U.S. political system, from national powers over commerce and other economic concerns, to states' rights and voting rights, to structures of congressional representation, to immigration and naturalization, the scope of free expression, criminal justice procedures, and much more, have never developed apart from pressures to alter or to maintain the nation's racial ordering. The pattern continues today. The operations of the federal civil service; the organization of Congress; the content of major pieces of social policy during the New Deal and the War on Poverty; the opposition to "big government," "tax and spend programs," and "welfare" from the Reagan administration on; and the activism of modern courts, among other matters, have all been driven in major ways by battles over how far racial hierarchies would be kept or changed. When political scientists ignore these impacts, or analyze them without a suitable theoretical framework, they often neglect or misunderstand the conduct of actors who are responding to the tensions and opportunities generated by America's racial orders. As a result, not only are these writings inadequate in their discussions of race, but they fall short in their accounts of the apparently nonracial topics they address.

Because it is the literature on which we build, we illustrate these shortcomings with some otherwise outstanding recent contributions to the American political development field. Though these works afford a wealth of valuable insights, many nonetheless exhibit several deficiencies.

First, they do not employ theoretical frameworks that ask whether the governing institutions and political behavior they examine have been involved in explicitly racial conflicts. Second, partly as a result, their historical narratives often omit glaring ways in which racial orderings have shaped the institutional goals, structures, procedures, and political actions they examine, as well as the ways in which those institutional features and actions have worked to perpetuate or reconfigure American racial patterns. Third, many scholars neglect, in particular, both the internal and the external politics of political communities defined and subordinated through racial categories. Because African Americans, Latinos, Native Americans, Asian Americans, and others have been disempowered historically, scholars tend to ignore them as politically irrelevant, either acquiescent or ineffectual. But precisely because racial orders have been so important in the United States, the politics within such communities, and their often masked resistance to the larger orders in American life, have always mattered greatly (Kelley 1994: 35–53; Yu 2001).

Bureaucracy

From the post-Reconstruction years on, federal departments such as Agriculture, Interior, Treasury, State and the Post Office bestowed upon African Americans two sorts of experiences. First, they discriminated against blacks in hiring practices, routinely segregated them, and confined them to low-level positions. Discrimination came via measures such as the 'rule of three,' whereby for every opening, the U.S. Civil Service Commission provided a list of three eligible applicants to the hiring department, which then picked one. In this way an African American candidate could be on the list three times without being selected. From 1914, the same Commission attached a photograph to each name included in the list of three eligible, with predictable effect. No African Americans rose to senior office.

Second, federal departments helped to devise, implement, and monitor the segregationist order legally in place between 1896 and 1954. Before the 1950s, federal officials, especially middle rank bureaucrats, assiduously upheld "separate but equal" arrangements or introduced them where they had not existed. The Federal Bureau of Prisons, for example, repeatedly sought from the 1920s to the 1950s to ensure that penitentiaries guaranteed segregated accommodations, eating, and working arrangements (King 1995). The War Department was also a notorious enforcer of segregation during World War II (Kryder 2000). We believe, then, that federal bureaucracies were profoundly shaped by and active in constituting America's post-Reconstruction racial structure, in ways that a racial orders analysis can bring out.

Contrast in this regard Daniel Carpenter's *The Forging of Bureaucratic Autonomy* (2001), a sterling example of American political development themes and methods. Carpenter deploys quantitative analyses as components in three comparative historical narratives that provide powerful support for his central claim. He argues that executive agency bureaucrats achieved policy-making autonomy from "politicians and organized interests" earlier and more extensively than many scholars have seen (2).

Yet Carpenter largely omits from his analysis the politics that led to the overwhelming confinement of African Americans to lower level positions in the postal service; the failure of the Agriculture Department to confront, and its frequent complicity in, the exploitation of black tenant farmers; and the Interior Department's toleration of practices that limited African Americans' access to public lands while it also transferred Indian lands to public and private white hands.[2] Such patterns strongly suggest that these bureaucrats either were not autonomous from the white supremacist order and its efforts to resist racial transformations, or they were choosing to assist it. Either way, the case for bureaucratic autonomy and its significance cannot be made fully unless those issues are addressed. This point applies to the whole literature "bringing the state back in." Scholars have failed to reflect on how far the internal structures and goals of "autonomous" agencies have been constituted by racial orders.

When considering the efforts of Woodrow Wilson's Postmaster General Albert Burleson to squash union organization amongst postal workers (Carpenter 2001, 170–1), for example, it would be illuminating to explore the degree of autonomy we should attribute to Burleson's role in entrenching segregation among postal employees. Was it a "divide and conquer" tactic? Was it done at Burleson's discretion, or in response to powerful white supremacist congressional committee members, or the ardently segregationist President, or other political actors? It would also be valuable to consider to what extent the employees thus organized on race lines helped to secure the "white suprema-cist" order. The roles of Burleson and his agency appear not inconsiderable in these regards. The Postmaster General advocated increased segregation to President Wilson's Cabinet in April 1913, complaining on behalf of white mail clerks: "it is very unpleasant for them to work in a car with negroes where it is almost impossible to have different drinking vessels and different towels, or places to wash." Burleson then promoted measures "to segregate white and negro employees in all Departments of Government" (cited in Cronon [1955] 1963: 32). This policy was adopted throughout the federal government (NAACP 1913; Weiss 1969: 64–5).

If the Postmaster General had autonomy in this sphere, then his use of it contributed substantially to patterns of segregation throughout the federal government, in ways that helped define racial practices throughout American society. That is a feature of bureaucratic autonomy that seems worth noting. And if these bureaucrats were not autonomous in these regards, if they were complying with powerful southern congressmen, the President, or other officials, then Carpenter's argument is seriously undercut.

The same questions about the character of government complicity in white supremacist arrangements can also be asked of the Department of Agriculture, for like the Post Office it was at the time of segregation's spread an old department that had long been engaged with African Americans. We might also ask whether segregation in labor unions, specifically, should be seen more as a cause of discriminatory governmental employment practices, more as a result, or as equally shaped by a broader white supremacist order. Conversely, we might ask whether the persistence of patronage appointments instead of civil service positions in public employment worked to strengthen the white supremacist order. But no such questions surface in Carpenter's work, because the relationship of bureaucratic autonomy to racial hierarchies is not raised. Mostly race does not make it into the index, let alone the text. Hence his case for bureaucratic autonomy and its significance is less compelling than it otherwise might be.

Congress

The political importance of Congress to the United States' racial orders hardly needs elaboration, so its interactions with those orders might seem an inescapable theme of most congressional studies. Yet Eric Schickler's *Disjointed Pluralism* (2001) is a historically sweeping and methodologically sophisticated account of institutional change within Congress that gives little attention to this dimension of congressional politics. Schickler makes a strong case for understanding institutional change in Congress as "disjointed pluralism." He argues that a variety of actors, interests, and conditions, rather than any single engine of change, have long shaped congressional institutional innovations. His analysis finds enduring tensions in conflicting efforts to centralize power in the parties and institutional leadership, among strong committees and their chairs, and in decentralizing initiatives from new members of the House or Senate wishing to use their chamber for policy or personal entrepreneurship (5–18). There is no single direction in which those tensions have been resolved and no single winner in the processes of change.

However, it is striking how Schickler's approach leads him to underplay the powerful racial dynamics structuring many of the changes he discusses, as well as the consequences for America's racial ordering that each involves. All of his four periods (1890–1910, 1919–32, 1937–52, and 1970–89) coincide with racial conflicts that were brought directly into congressional politics and national policy-making. They were never peripheral and often central to the changes in congressional behavior Schickler documents, in terms of both causes and effects.

Schickler's theoretical framework has room for race chiefly as a "policy interest," which may be "ideologically" as well as sectionally based, though racial considerations also play into individual member "electoral interests" and "party interests" (11–12). Though otherwise reasonable, this approach has the undesirable effect of fragmenting the "white supremacist" order and rendering it invisible. It fails to grasp theoretically the reality that individual and party ideologies, sectional, and electoral interests were significantly *constituted* in these periods by where individuals, parties, and the dominant forces in various regions stood on the great questions of whether and how America's racial hierarchies were to be preserved or dismantled. Hence it makes interests and actors appear more "disjointed" than they often were. In Schickler's first period (1890–1910), patterns of speakership and committee powers shifted several times in important ways. In discussing these developments, Schickler does note that Republican Party interests led many to support a bill to protect African American voting rights in 1890, but that they were sharply divided, and that this was the one element of their legislative package they failed to enact. Nonetheless, the Democrats denounced this "force bill," among other centralizing measures, at the next election and won the majority (34–5, 42–3). We would explain those events as products of the internal conflicts and electoral decline of the postwar transformative egalitarian order. Schickler leaves them unexplained, and does not note their consequence: the Democrats went on to repeal the last vestiges of Reconstruction voting rights protections for blacks and the Republicans largely abandoned the cause of black voting rights (Kousser 1974: 27–9, 49, 241, 363; Valelly 1995). The GOP soon regained power but strictly as a party of economic interests, not civil rights. Its members then cooperated to promote congressional efficiency on a fairly bipartisan basis—the same basis on which the nation moved to rebuild the white supremacist order in the form of segregation and race based imperialism. With the not-so-coincidental sanction of the Court in *Plessy v. Ferguson,* segregation laws spread, the number of lynchings increased steeply, and annexations of Puerto Rico and the Philippines extended the American white supremacist order to new realms while helping to legitimate it at home. In sum, Republican efforts in 1890 to restructure Congress on behalf of its partisan interests, then aligned with the transformative egalitarian order, collided with the nation's white supremacist order in ways that contributed greatly to the shifts in congressional structure Schickler examines. Those shifts contributed in turn to a repositioning of the Republican Party in the nation's racial ordering, and the expansion of the white supremacist order, in ways Schickler does not examine.

The realities of this acquiescence by both parties in the Jim Crow system meant that during Schickler's second period, 1919–32, a key effort of resistance by transformative egalitarian forces, the vigorous NAACP-led campaign to enact antilynching legislation, found only a few official champions and no success (Zangrando 1980). Instead, bipartisan organizational reforms resulted in fewer but stronger committees, making seniority in terms of committee service, as well as chamber membership, a source of great power (Schickler 2001: 95–8). Though Republicans introduced these changes, much support came from white supremacist southern Democrats, who virtually always won reelection. The increased importance of seniority then embedded Congress even more firmly in the white supremacist order, so that legislative efforts to transform that order went for naught. In this period the rules of cloture and filibustering in the Senate were also cast. Both became bulwarks of white supremacy, used to dilute the 1957 civil rights bill and to pose the major hurdle to the 1964 Civil Rights Act.

Schickler notes that in his third period, 1937–52, the Rules Committee became "the principal institutional power base in the House" for a "cross-party conservative coalition" consisting of "Dixiecrats" and conservative Republicans and that it enabled "southerners to block legislation that just might have driven them from the party" (163–6). He also notes that a 1949 liberal rebellion against the Rules Committee only ended up strengthening the power of committee chairs, where southern seniority conferred similar advantages (178). Yet he does not observe that it was consistently legislation threatening the white supremacist order, such as antilynching laws, voting bills and other civil rights proposals, and economic and welfare legislation that might benefit black farm and domestic workers that Dixiecrats opposed. Republican conservatives won their support through allying with them in support of white supremacy. Or to put it more strongly, because race was its linchpin, Schickler's "conservative coalition" should be seen as an institutional component of the white supremacist order.

Schickler instead follows Bensel (1984) in presenting southern interests simply as collective "sectional interests." If we believe that southern and conservative interests stem from attachments to a racial order that cannot be analyzed as simply a class system or a sectional system, then more than Schickler acknowledges, his history provides evidence not just for "disjointed pluralism," but for the special role of conflicting racial orders in shaping congressional structures during much of the twentieth century. A portrait of "racist-constrained pluralism" conveys a very different sense of congressional organization than his more open-ended "disjointed" pluralism. In sum, in theory Schickler employs an approach that fragments what are arguably manifestations of an interlocked white supremacist order into a variety of apparently separate interests, and in his historical studies he gives only slight attention to the interactions of congressional structuring with the nation's clashing racial structures. The result may be to portray the congressional forest without recognizing the common seeds of many of its trees.

Conclusion

Today, racially inflected contests in courts, legislatures, electoral campaigns, and popular discussions over affirmative action; school and residential segregation; felon disfranchisement; majority-minority districts; racial profiling; the disparate racial impact of incarcerations and the death penalty; hate crimes; reparations for slavery; Native American rights; immigration policies; bilingualism; multiculturalism; "model minority" stereotyping; and racial discrimination in housing, auto, and credit markets, and in hiring and promotions, all still roil American political waters. Many putatively nonracial issues, such as restraints on free speech, vouchers for private schools, the revival of federalism, and disputes over public health, environmental, and social assistance policies, all continue to be shaped by race-related struggles. Few of these issues, or the wider developments with which they are linked, can be understood without exploring the enduring tensions between and within the nation's racial orders.

Our argument has not been that race explains everything in American politics, or even that race is always important for every dimension of American political development. Many of the apparently nonracial issues just listed, and many more, are indeed heavily shaped by other concerns. But we maintain that the internal dynamics of American racial orders, and their interactions with each other and with other aspects of American political life, have so often been so important that the question of what role race may be playing should always be part of political science inquiries. The failure of political scientists to deal adequately with race in their scholarship has been all too much a part of the failure of Americans to deal adequately with race in their common lives. That is why this failure is one that our discipline has a special need, and a special duty, to rectify.

Notes

1   King, Desmond S. and Smith, Rogers M. "Racial Orders in American Political Development." *American Political Science Review*, Vol. 99, No. 01 (February 2005), pp. 75–92. Copyright © 2005 by the American Political Science Association. Reprinted with the permission of Cambridge University Press.

2   Carpenter makes one brief reference to discrimination against blacks in the postal service (2001: 74). For more on the racial patterns of farm and land policies, see Hoxie (1984: 44–72); Foner (1988: 542, 592–8); and Fuchs (1990: 92–8).

Bibliography

Primary sources

Court cases

Buchanan v. Warley (1919) 245 U.S. 60
Gratz v. Bollinger (2003) 439 U.S. 249
Plessy v. Ferguson (1896) 163 U.S. 537
Rogers v. Alabama (1904) 192 U.S. 226
U.S. v. Wong Kim Ark (1898) 169 U.S. 649

Study

NAACP (1913) "Segregation in the Government Departments in Washington," Washington DC: NAACP.

References and secondary sources

Almaguer, T. (1994) *Racial Fault Lines: The Historical Origins of White Supremacy in California*, Berkeley: University of California Press.

Balfour, L. (2003) "Unreconstructed Democracy: W.E.B. Du Bois and the Case for Reparations," *American Political Science Review*, 97: 33–44.

Bates, B.T. (2001) *Pullman Porters and the Rise of Protest Politics in Black America 1925–1945*, Chapel Hill: University of North Carolina Press.

Bay, M. (2000) *The White Image in the Black Mind*, New York: Oxford University Press.

Bensel, R.F. (1984) *Sectionalism and American Political Development, 1880–1980*, Madison: University of Wisconsin Press.

Berlin, I. (1974) *Slaves Without Masters: The Free Negro in the Antebellum South*, New York: Pantheon.

Berwanger, E.H. (1967) *The Frontier against Slavery: Western Anti-Negro Prejudice and the Slavery Extension Controversy*, Urbana: University of Illinois Press.

Carpenter, D.P. (2001) *The Forging of Bureaucratic Autonomy: Reputations, Networks and Policy Innovation in Executive Agencies 1862–1928*, Princeton, NJ: Princeton University Press.

Carter, D.T. (1996) *From George Wallace to Newt Gingrich: Race in the Conservative Counterrevolution, 1963–1994*, Baton Rouge: Louisiana State University Press.

Cohen, C.J. (1999) *The Boundaries of Blackness: AIDS and the Breakdown of Black Politics*, Chicago: University of Chicago Press.

Cronon, E.D. (ed.) (1963) *The Cabinet Diaries of Josephus Daniels 1913–1921*, Lincoln: University of Nebraska Press.

—— ([1955] 1969) *Black Moses: The Story of Marcus Garvey and the Universal Negro Improvement Association*, Madison: University of Wisconsin Press.

Dawson, M.C. (1994) *Behind the Mule*, Princeton, NJ: Princeton, University Press.

—— (2001) *Black Visions: The Roots of Contemporary African American Political Ideologies*, Chicago: University of Chicago Press.

Dawson, M.C. and Cohen, C. (2002) "Problems in the Study of the Politics of Race," in I. Katznelson and H.V. Milner (eds) *Political Science: The State of the Discipline*, New York: W.W. Norton: 488–510.

Du Bois, W.E.B. ([1935] 1992) *Black Reconstruction in America*, New York: Atheneum.

Dudziak, M.L. (2000) *Cold War Civil Rights: Race and the Image of American Democracy*, Princeton, NJ: Princeton University Press.

Ellis, J.J. (2000) *Founding Brothers*, New York: Alfred Knopf.

Ericson, D.F. (1999) "Dew, Fitzhugh, and Proslavery Liberalism," in D. F. Ericson and L. B. Green (eds) *The Liberal Tradition in American Politics: Reassessing the Legacy of American Liberalism*, New York: Routledge.

—— (2000) *The Debate over Slavery: Antislavery and Proslavery Liberalism in Antebellum America*, New York: New York University Press.

Foner, E. (1988) *Reconstruction: America's Unfinished Revolution, 1863–1877*, New York: Harper and Row.

Frankenberg, E., Lee, C., and Orfield, G. (2003) "A Multiracial Society with Segregated Schools: Are We Losing the Dream?" The Civil Rights Project, Harvard University. Online. Available: <http://www.civilrightsproject.harvard.edu/research/reseg03/AreWeLosingtheDream.pdf.> (accessed April 18, 2004).

Franklin, J.H. and Moss Jr., A.A. (1988) *From Slavery to Freedom: A History of Negro Americans*, 6th edn, New York: Alfred A. Knopf.

Fuchs, L.H. (1990) *The American Kaleidoscope: Race, Ethnicity, and the Civic Culture*, Hanover, NH: University Press of New England.

Gilens, M. (1999) *Why Americans Hate Welfare*, Chicago: University of Chicago Press.

Gillette, W. (1979) *Retreat From Reconstruction 1869–1879*, Baton Rouge: Louisiana State University Press.

Goldfield, M. (1997) *The Color of Politics: Race and the Mainsprings of American Politics*, New York: New Press.

Greenstone, J.D. (1986) "Political Culture and American Political Development: Liberty, Union, and the Liberal Bipolarity," *Studies in American Political Development*, 1: 1–49.

—— (1993) *The Lincoln Persuasion: Remaking American Liberalism*, Princeton, NJ: Princeton University Press.

Hartz, L. (1955) *The Liberal Tradition in America: An Interpretation of American Political Thought Since the Revolution*, New York: Harcourt, Brace.

Horsman, R. (1981) *Race and Manifest Destiny*, Cambridge, MA: Harvard University Press.

Hoxie, F.E. (1984) *A Final Promise: The Campaign to Assimilate the Indians, 1880–1920*, Lincoln: University of Nebraska Press.

Hutchinson, E.P. (1981) *Legislative History of American Immigration Policy, 1798–1965*, Philadelphia: University of Pennsylvania Press.

Jacobson, M.F. (1998) *Whiteness of a Different Color: European Immigrants and the Alchemy of Race*, Cambridge, MA: Harvard University Press.

Katznelson, I., Geiger, K., and Kryder D. (1993) "Limiting Liberalism: The Southern Veto in Congress 1933–1950," *Political Science Quarterly*, 108: 283–306.

Kelley, R.R.D. (1994) *Race Rebels*, New York: Free Press.

Kennedy, S. (1959) *Jim Crow Guide: The Way It Was*, Boca Raton: Florida Atlantic University Press.

Kesler, C.R. (1998) "The Promise of American Citizenship," in N. Pickus (ed.) *Immigration and Citizenship in the Twenty-First Century*, Boston: Rowman and Littlefield.

Kinder, D.R. and Sanders, L. (1996) *Divided by Color*, Chicago: University of Chicago Press.

King, D. (1995) *Separate and Unequal: Black Americans and the U.S. Federal Government*, Oxford: Oxford University Press.

Klinkner, P.A. with Smith, R.M. (1999) *The Unsteady March: The Rise and Decline of Racial Equality in America*, Chicago: University of Chicago Press.

Kousser, J.M. (1974) *The Shaping of Southern Politics: Suffrage Restriction and the Establishment of the One-Party South, 1880–1910*, New Haven, CT: Yale University Press.

Kryder, D. (2000) *Divided Arsenal*, New York: Cambridge University Press.

Lieberman, R. (1998) *Shifting the Color Line*, Cambridge, MA: Harvard University Press.

—— (2002) "Ideas, Institutions, and Political Order: Explaining Political Change," *American Political Science Review*, 96: 697–712.

Litwack, L.F. (1961) *North of Slavery: The Negro in the Free States, 1790–1860*, Chicago: University of Chicago Press.

Logan, R.W. ([1954] 1965) *The Betrayal of the Negro from Rutherford B. Hayes to Woodrow Wilson*, New York: Collier Books.

McAdam, D. (1984) *Political Process and the Development of Black Insurgency*, Chicago: University of Chicago Press.

McFeely, W.S. (1991) *Frederick Douglass*, New York: W.W. Norton.

McMahon, K.J. (2003) *Reconsidering Roosevelt on Race: How the Presidency Paved the Road to Brown*, Chicago: University of Chicago Press.

Meier, A. and Rudwick, E. (1976) "The Origins of Nonviolent Direct Action in Afro-American Protest: A Note on Historical Discontinuities," in A. Meier and E. Rudwick (eds) *Along the Color Line: Exploring the Black Experience*, Urbana: University of Illinois Press: 314–32.

Mendelberg, T. (2001) *The Race Card: Campaign Strategy, Implicit Messages, and the Norm of Equality*, Princeton, NJ: Princeton University Press.

Morris, T.D. (1974) *Free Men All: The Personal Liberty Laws of the North*, Baltimore, MD: Johns Hopkins University Press.

Nelson, W.E. (1988) *The Fourteenth Amendment: From Political Principle to Judicial Doctrine*, Cambridge, MA: Harvard University Press.

Ngai, M.M. (1999) "The Architecture of American Immigration Law: A Reexamination of the Immigration Act of 1924," *Journal of American History* 86: 67–92.

Nieman, D.G. (1991) *Promises to Keep: African Americans and the Constitutional Order, 1776 to the Present*, New York: Oxford University Press.

Omi, M. and Winant, H. (1994) *Racial Formation in the United States: From the 1960s to the 1990s*, 2nd edn, New York: Routledge.

O'Reilly, K. (1995) *Nixon's Piano: Presidents and Racial Politics from Washington to Clinton*, New York: Free Press.

Orren, K. and Skowronek, S. (1986) "Editor's preface," *Studies in American Political Development*, 1: vii–viii.

—— (1994) "Beyond the Iconography of Order: Notes for a 'New Institutionalism,'" in L.C. Dodd and C. Jillson (eds) *The Dynamics of American Politics: Approaches and Interpretations*, Boulder, CO: Westview Press, 311–30.

—— (1996) "Institutions and Intercurrence: Theory Building in the Fullness of Time," in I. Shapiro and R. Hardin (eds) *Nomos XXXVIII: Political Order*, New York: New York University Press: 111–46.

—— (1999) "In Search of Political Development," in D.F. Ericson and L.E. Bertch Green. (eds) *The Liberal Tradition in American Politics: Reassessing the Legacy of American Liberalism*, New York: Routledge: 29–41.

—— (2002) "The Study of American Political Development," in I. Katznelson and H. V. Milner (eds) *Political Science: The State of the Discipline*, New York: W.W. Norton: 722–54.

—— (2004) *The Search for American Political Development*, Cambridge: Cambridge University Press.

Oshinsky, D.M. (1996) *Worse Than Slavery: Parchman Farm and the Ordeal of Jim Crow Justice*, New York: Free Press.

Pierson, P. and Skocpol, T. (2002) "Historical Institutionalism in Contemporary Political Science," in I. Katznelson and H. V. Milner (eds) *Political Science: The State of the Discipline*, New York: W.W. Norton: 693–721.

Quadagno, J. (1994) *The Color of Welfare: How Racism Undermined the War on Poverty*, New York: Oxford University Press.

Reed, A. (1999) *Stirrings in the Jug: Black Politics in the Post-Segregation Era*, Minneapolis: University of Minnesota Press.

—— (2003) "The Study of Black Politics and the Practice of Black Politics: Their Historical Relation and Evolution," paper presented at the Yale Conference on Problems and Methods in the Study of Politics, December 2003. Online. Available: <http://www.yale.edu/probmeth/main> (accessed September 21, 2007).

Schickler, E. (2001) *Disjointed Pluralism: Institutional Innovation and the Development of the U.S. Congress*, Princeton, NJ: Princeton University Press.

Skocpol, T. (1979) *States and Social Revolutions*, New York: Cambridge University Press.

Skowronek, S. (1982) *Building a New American State*, Cambridge: Cambridge University Press.

Skrentny, J.D. (2002) *The Minority Rights Revolution*, Cambridge, MA: Belknap Press.

Smelser, N.J., Wilson, W.J., and Mitchell, F. (eds) (2001) *America Becoming*, Washington, DC: National Academy of Sciences.

Smith, R.M. (1993) "Beyond Tocqueville, Myrdal and Hartz: The Multiple Traditions in America," *American Political Science Review*, 87: 549–66.

—— (1997)) *Civic Ideals: Conflicting Visions of Citizenship in U.S. History*, New Haven, CT: Yale University Press.

Sniderman, P.M. and Piazza, T. (1993) *The Scar of Race*, Cambridge, MA: Harvard University Press.

Swain, C.M. (2002) *The New White Nationalism in America: Its Challenge to Integration*, New York: Cambridge University Press.

Takaki, R. (1993) *A Different Mirror: A History of Multicultural America*, Boston: Little, Brown.

Valelly, R.M. (1995) "National Parties and Racial Disfranchisement," in P. E. Peterson (ed.) *Classifying by Race*, Princeton, NJ: Princeton University Press.

Wacquant, L. (2002) "From Slavery to Mass Incarceration: Rethinking the 'Race Question' in the U.S," *New Left Review*, 13: 41–60.

Waters, M. (2001) *Black Identities: West Indian Immigrant Dreams and American Realities*, Cambridge, MA: Harvard University Press.

Weiss, N.J. (1969) "The Negro and the New Freedom: Fighting Wilsonian Segregation" *Political Science Quarterly*, 84: 61–79.

Wiecek, W.M. (1977) *The Sources of Antislavery Constitutionalism in America, 1760–1860*, Ithaca, NY: Cornell University Press.

Williams, W.L. (1980) "United States Indian Policy and the Debate over Philippine Annexation: Implications for the Origins of American Imperialism," *Journal of American History*, 66: 810–31.

Williamson, J. (1984) *New People: Miscegenation and Mulattoes in the United States*, New York: Free Press.

Yu, H. (2001) *Thinking Orientals: Migration, Contact and Exoticism in Modern America*, New York: Oxford University Press.

Zangrando, R.L. (1980) *The NAACP Crusade Against Lynching 1909–1950*, Philadelphia, PA: Temple University Press.

Zilversmit, A. (1967) *The First Emancipation* Chicago: University of Chicago Press.

5 Hierarchy and hybridity: the internal postcolonialism of mid-nineteenth-century American expansionism

Kevin Bruyneel

Introduction

One does not need to look far and wide in contemporary U.S. politics to locate anti-immigrant discourse directed at, especially, Mexican immigrants and by correlation Mexican Americans. In particular, Congressman Tom Tancredo (R-CO) and Cable News Network anchor Lou Dobbs have led the way in articulating an anti-immigrant political discourse that envisions Mexicans, in particular, as a force that threatens American nation-space by transgressing U.S. borders and laws, challenging American national identity by waving Mexican flags at rallies, and, in some cases seeking to "re-conquer" American territory. In all, a consistent demand of these anti-immigrant voices is for Mexicans in the United States to "go back to where they came from."[1] Along with being racist and nationalist, this political discourse is generally ahistorical, masking the complicated relationship between state, space, and identity that has constituted the Mexican and Mexican-American relationship to U.S. politics and American nationhood. This chapter does not refer to the contemporary situation directly, but, rather, seeks to shed light on the colonialist relationship between race and U.S. political development as it concerns Mexicans and Mexican Americans. Shedding light is the appropriate term here, as the approach I employ in this chapter offers a way to make visible the colonialist practices woven into American nation- and state-building over time. Specifically, I read the story of mid-nineteenth century American expansionism as one of neither simple exploitation nor inclusion, but rather as a reflection of what I call the internal postcolonial dynamics of U.S. nation-building, where racial hierarchies are persistent but not static, subject to hybridic developments in racial identity and relations over time.

From 1845 to 1854, the United States expanded its territory by 1,228,743 square miles, adding the states of Texas and California as well as the land that would eventually become the states of Nevada, Arizona, Utah, Oregon, Washington, and sizable portions of present-day New Mexico, Colorado, Kansas, and Wyoming, enlarging U.S. territory to a little over 3 million square miles. All but the Oregon and Washington territory was acquired, by force and ostensible negotiation, from Mexico, accounting for 945,304 square miles. The

Mexico-related expansion occurred in three parts: via the incorporation of Texas as a state in 1845 nine years after Texas had won its independence from Mexico; through land settlements agreed to in the Treaty of Guadalupe Hidalgo that brought an end to the U.S.-Mexican War (1846–8); and through the 1853–4 Gadsden Treaty/Purchase with Mexico. In nine years, the U.S. boundary moved rapidly westward from about the line of the Rocky Mountains all the way to the Pacific Coast, and significantly southward to and in places beyond the Rio Grande and Gila Rivers. Altogether, these territorial acquisitions comprised 31 percent of U.S. territory by 1854 and concomitantly reduced Mexican territory by over 50 percent. Overall, then, the 1845–54 period stands as the high tide of the American expansionary doctrine of *manifest destiny*—the notion first articulated in 1845 in defense of the annexation of Texas as another step in "the fulfillment of our manifest destiny to overspread the continent allotted by Providence for the free development of our yearly multiplying millions" (Sullivan 1845: 5).[2] In so doing, the U.S. federal government not only engaged in a project of national territorial expansion that exceeded that of the Louisiana Purchase, it also significantly added to the demographic diversity of the U.S. population.

While manifest destiny specifically referred to and foresaw the "multiplying millions" of primarily European immigrants and American settlers moving west as part of the "providential" expansion of the white American nation, this ambition could only be achieved through the imperial practice of conquering and absorbing the lands, subjects, and residents of foreign nations. Specifically, mid-nineteenth-century American acquisition of over half of Mexico added to the resident U.S. population 120,000 Mexican citizens who lived and owned property in this vast former Mexican territory (Ruiz Cameron 2000: 10). Furthermore, these newly expanded U.S. boundaries now contained within them a multitude of indigenous tribes and nations, such as the Apache and Navajo that had previously existed outside the American domestic realm. A number of indigenous communities even found their traditional lands cleaved in two by American expansion, to devastating effect. Notably, in this regard, "the Gadsden Purchase included approximately half of the Tohono O'odham traditional homelands" that had been under Mexican state purview prior to 1853, and as a result "contacts between families were severed and the political history and government structure diverged sharply" (Luna-Firebaugh 2002: 166). To this day, the O'odham continue to struggle with American border impositions across their land; impositions that are a living legacy of American actions a century and half earlier.[3]

The fact that American expansionism led to the incorporation of non-white peoples in this way also raises questions about what sort of nation was being produced, or reproduced, especially in light of the fact that the preservation and strengthening of the white nation was a defining, if certainly contested, objective that shaped American policymaking, institutions, and political culture.[4] Did the imperial ambitions for nation-building defined and driven by political leaders like President James Polk contradict the maintenance of racial hierarchies that had so shaped the nation? Does the study of race in American political development disclose a tension between the contested and complicated racial and imperial aims of the nation's citizens and leaders? There are no easy answers to these questions, but in this chapter I argue that in some of the key documents, policies, and governing practices of mid-nineteenth-century American expansionism we can see the compatible workings of *hierarchy* and *hybridity* in the relationship between race and nation in U.S. politics and history. Hierarchy and hybridity are the twinned components that I introduce to better account for the complexity of the interplay between racial inequality and American nation-building.

To develop this argument, I begin by explaining what I mean by hierarchy and hybridity, how I put them together, and in what way they can offer a precise analysis of the colonialist dynamics shaping persistent group inequality in a liberal democratic setting such as the United States. For the purposes of this chapter, the main focus of my analysis will be the Treaty of Guadalupe Hidalgo and its consequences.[5] With this focus in mind, I see in a few of the Treaty's key clauses, as well as in subsequent legislation such as the California Land Act of 1851, the internal postcolonial process by which Mexican citizens were drawn into the American polity on hierarchical and hybridic terms, requiring both their subjugation in the politics, culture, and economy of the United States, and the creation of a new ethnic identity for them that would assume a liminal place within the nation's racial order.

Hierarchy and hybridity

Pairing hierarchy and hybridity in this account reveals how group-based inequities endure and evolve through a mutually constitutive relationship to national and sub-national identities over time. In short, hierarchies endure but not in the same form, and in fact they endure because they can change form, via hybridic developments in group and national identities. The hybridic element generates dynamism in American racial hierarchies, allowing for the adaptation and implication of these hierarchies in political developments such as that of American expansionism. While hybridity can be invoked as a recombinant force that fosters the pursuit of racial equality and liberation it can and often does serve to forestall this very same pursuit, the latter being the main direction of internal postcolonialism in American political development.[6]

The *internal* of internal postcolonialism denotes a focus on the creation and maintenance of relations of inequality within U.S. boundaries, including those created in the production, through expansion in this case, of those boundaries. At the same time, the term *postcolonial* signals attentiveness to the idea that colonialist practices persist in cultural, institutional, and political forms within contexts that are not classically colonial or that may see themselves as having moved beyond colonialism. In this regard, the postcolonial perspective refuses the linear narrative of colonialist history—a before, during, and after colonialism—and does so in a way that allows for analysis of how colonialist tropes and practices are often premised upon the perpetuation of temporal and spatial disjunctures between dominant and non-dominant groups, marking ways subaltern groups are left behind.[7] In this sense, postcoloniality, as Gayatri Spivak (1995: 178) sums it up, derives from and references the "failure of decolonization," and implores us to seek out and expose colonial institutions and practices embedded in and woven into contemporary contexts, often co-existent with liberal-democratic principles and practices. More pointedly, Homi Bhabha (1994: 251) argues along postcolonial lines that the "nation must be reconceived liminally as the *dynastic-in-the-democratic*" (emphasis added). The "dynastic-in-the-democratic" elegantly captures the interplay of hierarchy and hybridity in the political history of race and American political development, as the "dynastic" stands for persistent hierarchies that benefit from and forestall the nation's liminal "democratic" possibilities. To situate my approach in the academic discourse, I suggest that an internal postcolonial emphasis on hybridity generates a more fluid, dynamic reading of the role of racial hierarchies in American political development than that offered by the most notable academic and political critique of colonial practices in the U.S. setting, that being internal colonialism.

The internal colonial model reached its peak of influence during the post-World War II era at the height of anti-colonial revolutionary action around the globe, when it turned the attention of, especially, American activists and academics to the structural sources and consequences of group inequality in the United States, seeing colonial rule at work here. Internal colonialism thus focused on the utilization of colonial practices and processes in a dominant nation's domestic setting, which contrasts with the classical form by which nations, predominantly European nations, subjugated foreign populations and territories for the sake of garnering influence and resources from beyond the colonizing nation's domestic boundaries. Drawing from the classical paradigm, scholars of internal colonialism such as Jennifer Hurstfield (1975: 138) have devised five processes that generally comprise colonial rule in an internal setting; they are: (1) coerced social and political location and status; (2) persistent structural economic inequality; (3) racially alien administrative rule; (4) cultural domination; and (5) the production and imposition of racial ideology and practices. The crux of the matter for those working from the internal colonial thesis is that inequality involves the creation of a perpetual dependent class, and this is the consequence of the structural impositions generated by the dominant group. Sociologist Robert Blauner is likely the most notable scholar to examine the U.S. context through the internal colonialism perspective. In his 1972 work, *Racial Oppression in America*, Blauner argued that racial and ethnic group relations are fundamentally and rigidly hierarchical. For Blauner, the racial dynamic that most clearly exemplified American internal colonialism was that concerning black–white relations. He pointed to a number of concrete features of the history and the contemporary condition of black–white relations in the United States that justify this internal colonial argument, including the construction of the ghetto as a colonized spatial realm (1969: 404, 407). To Blauner, internal colonialism captures the fundamental features of an American racial order in which race is central to the nation's political life, where "racism is institutionalized," rather than being an agentic matter of individual prejudices or a factor that becomes diluted through assimilation into the dominant national identity (1972: 9).[8] In all, then, proponents of the internal colonialism approach saw the existence of rigid racial and ethnic hierarchies, with clearly defined spatial, socio-economic, and political demarcations between groups that allow for little fluidity or change without deep structural transformations, along the lines of an anti-colonialist revolution.

While internal colonialism's emphasis on persistent racial hierarchies in political societies such as the United States stands as a worthwhile insight, the most glaring failing in this approach is an inability to either conceptualize the complexity of group interaction, movement, and identity formation in settler societies and/or connect these to political developments over time. The internal colonialism approach focuses on enduring features of racial inequality without being able to account for that which is changing (for better or worse), and because of that failing it does not adequately capture the complexity of those endurances. What is lacking, then, is a sense of the intricate, constitutive relationship between group identity (be it race, ethnicity, gender, class), nation, and state in American political development. In this regard, Michael Omi and Howard Winant (1994: 46) seem to have it right when arguing that the internal colonial approach neglects "extensive interpenetration in the U.S. of minority and majority societies" and "the broader cultural dynamic." What is missing here in the effort to understand and critique hierarchy, then, is the role of hybridity as a force of dynamism in race relations in liberal democratic settler societies such as the United States, which is what I seek to bring to the analysis. It is with this aim in mind that I turn now to analyze the internal postcolonial dynamics of mid-nineteenth-century American expansionism, beginning with the Treaty of Guadalupe Hidalgo.

The Treaty Of Guadalupe Hidalgo

When Article V of the Treaty of Guadalupe Hidalgo ("the Treaty") began by setting out that "the boundary line between the two Republics shall commence in the Gulf of Mexico, three leagues from land, opposite the mouth of the Rio Grande" the immediate effect of these words, as noted earlier, would be to significantly expand U.S. territory through the historic extension of American boundaries. But the Treaty and such clauses did more than expand American space. This action by the American state remade space by remaking the U.S.-Mexico boundary, and in so doing provoked the remaking of sub-national and national identities of that space. These developments necessarily called for the continued role of the state to determine who is a citizen and who has a legitimate claim to property within the new U.S. boundaries. It is too simple to say that state remakes boundary and space, which then remake nation and identity, which then remake state, but in terms of mid-nineteenth-century American expansionism, this description provides at least some purchase in seeing the dynamics of race and U.S. political development. We can see this relation between space-making and identity-making in Article VIII.

Taken as a whole, the Treaty enacts a political and economic relationship between the United States and Mexicans that is clearly hierarchical but necessarily hybridic as well, because it either explicitly asserts or implicitly requires the reconstruction of sub-national and national identities in the American political context. Given that the United States suddenly gained sovereignty over territory that from the time of Mexican independence in 1821 had been under Mexican sovereignty, the hierarchical consequences for the day-to-day standing of Mexicans were rather clear. Around 120,000 Mexican citizens were now living in a foreign country where the predominant language was English, the dominant majority was white, and the political institutions and culture were explicitly and increasingly white supremacist. As it concerns the American racial order of this time, Mexican identity was constructed less as its own distinct racial identity than as one generally deemed in political, legal, and cultural realms to be *non-white*, or in the very least lacking the qualities required to attain the full racial privileges of unadulterated whiteness.[9] The production of Mexican identity (as well the encompassing, subsequent identities of Latino, Hispanic, and Chicano)—sometimes as race, sometimes as ethnicity, sometimes as both—developed over time and continues to do so, often with varying constructs emerging depending upon in which institutional, cultural, and/or regional setting the issue is being fought.[10] But for all these cases the historical and political origin of these fights and struggles in the United States is the conquest consolidated by the Treaty of Guadalupe Hidalgo.[11] With this in mind, it is interesting to see that as it concerned their immediate legal and political status, Article VIII of the Treaty set out the following options, promises, and stipulations to "Mexicans now established in territories previously belonging to Mexico:"

[They] shall be free to continue where they now reside, or to remove at any time to the Mexican Republic, retaining the property which they possess in the said territories. . . .

Those who shall prefer to remain in the said territories may either retain the title and rights of Mexican citizens, or acquire those of citizens of the United States. But they shall be under the obligation to make their election within one year from the date of the exchange of ratifications of this treaty; *and those who shall remain in the said territories after the expiration of that year, without having declared their intention to retain the character of Mexicans, shall be considered to have elected to become citizens of the United States.*

In the said territories, property of every kind, now belonging to Mexicans not established there, shall be inviolably respected.

(emphasis added)

Article IX goes on to support Article VIII by assuring that those who "shall not preserve the character of the citizens of the Mexican Republic . . . [shall enjoy] the rights of citizens of the United States . . . maintained and protected in the free enjoyment of their liberty and property." Given that these Article provisions are part of a document that codifies U.S. gains from its expansionist effort against Mexico, they seem on the surface to be strikingly egalitarian, even anti-imperialist, in their openness to non-white foreign citizens becoming U.S. citizens and property-owners and even to these non-white foreigners owning property within the American nation-space. On closer look, however, what may seem to be egalitarian gestures are, I suggest, hybridic, a distinction with a difference.

Article VIII reflects two key concerns, *citizenship* and *property*, and for each one can easily get the idea that agency and fluidity shape the relationship between state, space, and identity. If one is to take these provisions at their word, a person could live within the boundaries of the United States as an American or a Mexican citizen, and/or one could own property in American nation-space whether she or he was an American citizen of Mexican origins, a Mexican citizen residing in the United States, or a Mexican citizen living in Mexico. By this quick reading, then, national boundaries do not determine identity and ownership, the concepts 'domestic' and 'foreign' are flexible descriptors subject to the individual choices of residents, and identity has little constitutive relationship to space. However, in considering citizenship, to start, we find the creation of a hybridic identity in which boundaries, space, and state played a clear role in the construction and positioning of a 'new group' in the American racial hierarchy.

Regarding the constitutive relationship between the Treaty, space, and identity, writer Lalo López's (2007) assessment is apt:

> The treaty didn't just create the American Southwest; it also created Chicanos. By definition, Chicanos, or Mexican Americans, are U.S.-born or -raised Mexicans. With one stroke of the pen, the treaty assigned a new national status to the Mexican residents of the former northern Mexico.

While it is technically not correct to say that a *Mexican-American* identity was created at the "stroke of a pen," it is not that far off the mark. Before the ink had time to dry, Mexicans were faced with a choice to declare within a year "their intention to retain the character of Mexicans"—that is, retain Mexican citizenship—or by their inaction "be considered to have elected to become citizens of the United States." Even a rough determination of the number of people who decided to leave for post-1848 Mexican territory and/or elected to maintain Mexican citizenship is difficult,[12] in no small part because a hybrid sub-national identity, unknown and thus uncounted, was constructed by means of and as a consequence of the Treaty. While the Treaty poses a seeming 'choice' for Mexican residents, like many other conquered peoples in history and around the globe they were not the actual agents involved in the formation of the Treaty. As Katherine Franke (2000: 1685) points out, they were "the objects of treaties entered into by other contracting parties on their behalf . . . [which] created or transformed their political identity by virtue of positive law." This issue of agency—or lack of same—is pertinent for elaborating the hybrid elements of Mexican American identity, and connecting them to the place of Mexican Americans in the racial hierarchy over time and the role of colonial practices in this process.

The Treaty, and Article VIII in particular, engage in a process of hybrid identity construction by means of the creation of a hybrid political agency for Mexicans in the newly American territory. They were offered a citizenship choice in response to a rapidly and radically altered political, cultural, and racial context over which they had no choice. In fact, Article VIII allowed Mexican citizens residing within the newly expanded boundaries of the United States to become U.S. citizens without making an affirmative, explicit choice on the matter. One became a U.S. citizen just by remaining for a year in the vast territory conquered by the United States. As such, the agency at work here is hybrid, a decision neither simply voluntary nor involuntary. One cannot view Mexicans who became U.S. citizens in this way as voluntary immigrants who moved to a new country, nor can one deem them to be entirely involuntary conquered subjects forced into the American nation, because they had the option to maintain Mexican citizenship. Instead, I suggest that those who became Mexican Americans at this time, and possibly their descendents, might be more accurately classified as "accidental citizens," a term I adapt from the work of Peter Nyers (2006). This notion provides a way to connect hybridity to hierarchy in the context of the colonial practices of the American nation-space, because as it concerns the status of those who became citizens in this way "the opposition becomes not one of citizen vs. non-citizen, but between those citizens who are deemed essential and necessary and those who are dismissed as accidental and dispensable" (Nyers: 24).[13] In turning to connect the issue of citizenship to that of property rights and claims, we begin to see the codification of the "dispensability" of the hybrid, accidental Mexican American citizen in the American nation-space. In this colonialist process, the hybridity of identity and agency helps to constitute the liminal positioning of Mexican Americans in the American racial hierarchy.

As noted above, Article VIII promised that in the new American territory Mexicans were free to retain the "property which they possess" and those residing in Mexico were assured that their American property holdings would "be inviolably respected." This promise appeared to be further secured by Article X, the first sentence of which stated:

> All grants of land made by the Mexican government or by the competent authorities, in territories previously appertaining to Mexico, and remaining of the future within the limits of the United States, shall be respected as valid, to the same extent that the same grants would be valid, if said territories had remained within the limits of Mexico.

The Article also provided the "grantees of land in Texas" a period of time to ratify their grants according to Mexican law to compensate for the difficulties in doing so due to the "troubles between Texas and the Mexican government." The provisions of this article were put in at the request of the Mexican government, and by their presence would compel the U.S. federal government to accept the validity of any property claim deemed legitimate by the Mexican government—or farther back to the Spanish sovereign—prior to the war, and to allow Mexicans in Texas time to get their papers in order. The article thus presumed equivalence between Mexican-based property claims and U.S.-based property claims, leaving the United States little room to deny land grants that had the Mexican state imprimatur. In this sense, according to one legal scholar, "Article X was fully consistent with the existing practice under international law to recognize the preexisting legal status of property rights in lands colonized by acts of war" (Tsosie 2000: 1626). Despite, or maybe because of, extant legal practice, Article X never made it to the final version of the document, as the Polk administration excised it from the Treaty before sending it to the Senate for ratification. In response to the Mexican government's concern with this deletion, the two governments agreed to the "Protocol of Querétero," in which the U.S. promised that "legitimate titles to every description of property personal and real, existing in the ceded territories, are those which were legitimate titles under the Mexican law in California and New Mexico up to May 13, 1846, and in Texas up to March 2, 1836." However, the Polk administration did not deem the U.S. to be legally bound by the protocol, a view clearly demonstrated by the fact that Polk did not include it as part of the Treaty documents submitted to the Senate, and the very existence of the protocol was kept secret for six months.

My concern here is less with the precise motivations and machinations of the Polk administration and federal government in the Treaty's formulation than with the consequences for Mexicans of the document that was ratified by the Senate. Without Article X, the property claims of Mexicans in New Mexico, California, and Texas could only be secured through Articles VIII and IX, neither of which mentions Mexican (or Spanish) state standards or actions; this absence shifted the relationship between state, space, and identity from that imagined in the original Treaty. With the Mexican state basically removed from the formal treaty document, the property rights of Mexicans now existed entirely under U.S. sovereignty and jurisdiction, subject to the authority which U.S. courts, in particular, were willing to give the Treaty.

Henceforth, the authority of Mexican and Spanish state documents, norms, and practices that may have certified the land grants of Mexican claimants was uncertain, subject to the awareness, whims and/or interests of judges, legislators, and commissioners. Uncertainty is the apt description here, as it is the hybridity of the embryonic Mexican-American identity in relationship to U.S. state authority and national space that helped undermine the development of a consistent process of adjudicating these claims, allowing for the refusal of some claims and not others. In her study of Chicano/Chicana land tenure cases stemming from this period, Guadalupe Luna (1998: 47–8) captures this relationship between hierarchy and hybridity:

> By subjecting them to shifting legal norms, American courts subordinated Mexican grantees and their heirs as outsiders to the American legal system, thereby diminishing their status as citizens, sacrificing basic principles of law, and ultimately privileging the dominant population.

Note here the distinction Luna makes and how it recalls the notion of the accidental citizen. The status of Mexican grantees as U.S. citizens is subordinated not because they are deemed non-citizens in the legal sense, but, rather, because they are treated as dispensable or non-essential citizens in the racial and colonialist sense of "privileging the dominant population." The hybridity of identity here allowed for the positioning of Mexican Americans as domestically located aliens in the American racial hierarchy; domestic by accident and alien by intent. We can see this colonialist process at work in the U.S. effort to address the conflicts over land claims in California in the years immediately following the ratification of the Treaty.

The California Land Act of 1851

The California gold rush of 1848–9 increased the region's population from about 15,000 to between 150,000 and 200,000, and the Compromise of 1850 brought California into the Union as a state. Combined, these developments placed immense pressure on land claims in the nation's newest state, as "against a backdrop of confusion and uncertainty many American settlers dismissed the validity of Mexican titles and squatted on the land on the assumption that the United States government would eventually decide in their favor" (Hombeck 1979: 438). In response to these escalating conflicts and to resolve the "confusion," the Congress passed the California Land Act in March of 1851. Among other things, the Act established a Board of Land Commission to "decide upon the validity" of the claims based upon "any right or title derived from the Spanish or Mexican government." The Board's decisions were to be "governed by the treaty of Guadalupe Hidalgo . . . [and] the laws, usages, and customs of the government from which the claim is derived, the principles of equity, and the decisions of the Supreme Court of the United States, so far as they are applicable" (California Land Act 1851: Ch. 41, 9. Stat. 632, 633). Individuals had two years to present their claims with supporting documents and testimony, and could appeal commission decisions to the district court and the Supreme Court (Ruiz Cameron 2000: 7). The Act also provided for the presence of a secretary, and if the President so desired, an agent, fluent in Spanish and English for the sake of interpreting documents and testimony. The process created by the Act, from the Land Commission hearings to the judicial appeals process, eventually led to the patenting of almost nine million acres of land to individuals in California. The overall picture of the Act's effect on the status and property rights of Mexicans is a complicated one—not a one-dimensional story of either simple inclusion or outright exploitation—as Mexican claims were both recognized and forestalled, and Mexicans were included and disempowered, with institutional, political, and cultural dynamics all at work here. The long-term results of the California Land Act were the patenting of numerous Mexican land grants, but not right away—in fact not for decades—which thereby allowed time for Anglo claimants to have the first crack at the best property, and for the development of the racialized relationship among state, space, and identity in California. In this regard, the California Land Act is an expression and institutionalization of internal postcolonialism— a process of nation-building perpetuated upon securing the 'dynastic-in-the-democratic'—because it allowed for the entry and recognition of Mexicans as hybrid citizens of the American nation-space while fostering both the delay in the certification of actual Mexicans claims and the submergence of Mexican American identity into the American racial hierarchy.

Examination of a few well researched studies of the consequences of the California Land Act exposes a complicated picture of an internal postcolonial institution, one which requires us to look at what happened prior to and during the Commission hearings and then what occurred in the wake of them over the course of many decades. The immediate determinations following from the Act give the image of an inclusive, hybrid approach to Mexican land claims. Geographer David Hornbeck (1979: 439) finds that the Land Commission weighed "each claim on the basis of the spirit of the law and what was morally correct. More emphasis was placed on custom than law . . . In effect, the Commission sided with the Mexican claimants, while the government through its representative supported the American settlers' position." By 1856, the Commission had heard 794 claims, and it confirmed 514 and rejected 280. However, while the Act clearly sought to adjudicate claims premised upon grants from the Mexican or Spanish government, by the time the Commission started hearing cases, a good portion of the claims were not being made by Mexicans, but were instead made by white Americans, be they settlers or squatters. To be precise, historian Paul Gates (1971: 410) discovered that 346 of the 794 claims, or 43.5 percent, "were presented by non-Mexicans, [i.e. white Americans]. In addition, a considerable number of claims had either passed to non-Mexicans by 1851 or by the time they were patented, but the litigation was carried in the name of the original grantees." The fact that so many of the claims were taken over by Anglos prior to the start of the Commission hearing lends validity to the argument of Christopher David Ruiz Cameron (2000: 8) that in "post-conquest California" Mexicans "become invisible . . . conspicuous by their absence among not only the landholding class but also the land claimant class."

Combined, the Treaty and the Land Act acknowledge the legitimate place of Mexican titles and Mexican claimants in the process of securing status and rights in the American nation-space, and this is a hybridic vision. But the development of this hybrid vision can only be fully understood in relationship to the emerging hierarchical relationship between Anglo-Americans and Mexicans/Mexican Americans, where the former used the hybridic standing of the latter—neither fully inside nor outside American political culture and institutions—as the means by which to absorb and secure land claims in California. Specifically, at the Land Commission white Americans presented claims based upon Mexican titles (titles conferred in some way by the Mexican or Spanish states) in a process in which "custom"—that being Mexican custom —took some precedence over the strictures of U.S. law. In the end, these claims, along with those made by Mexicans themselves (still almost 57 percent of the total claims made), were by a significant majority waived through and approved by the Commission. This picture of the shifting locus of property holdings from Mexicans to whites prior to and during the Commission hearings is only further sharpened when we look at what Mexican claimants had to deal with afterward, and the benefits which accrued to white Americans as a consequence.

In the end, the decisions by the California Land Commission served as the final word on the matter for only 3 of those 794 claims, leaving almost all claimants to deal with the implicit and explicit challenges of the post-Commission appellate process (figures compiled from Hornbeck (1979: 439–40) and Clay (1999: 134)). This process took the claimants to the U.S. district court and/or to the U.S. Supreme Court. In turning now to look at the post-Commission appeals process and history, what we find is the working of internal postcolonialism in the inter-relationship among state, space, and identity in constructing the location of Mexican Americans in the American racial hierarchy.

To Ruiz Cameron, the California Land Act's "true evil:"

> lay in its formality, which ensured delay, which in turn ensured costly litigation. To negotiate the three levels of adjudicatory apparatus (board, district court, and Supreme Court,) a claimant could ill afford to proceed without counsel, who often took the mortgage in the disputed title as part of the fee (6).

Ruiz Cameron highlights the more implicit hierarchical and colonialist processes at work in the claims process. These processes become evident when one examines the longer-term institutional, cultural, and spatial dynamics of the Land Act. Step by step, from the Commission process through to the pursuit of an appeal, a claimant could expect to have to spend $500–$1,500 to bring a claim to the land commission, $100–$500 to appeal to the district court, and $600–$1,000 to take the appeal all the way to the Supreme Court, or part of the payment could well be title to part of the land under claim. And even if claimants had the resources to cover the process, they had to be patient, as it took on average 17 years from the time one presented an initial claim to when one finally received a confirmed, legal land patent (Clay 1999: 134). For Mexican claimants, however, the situation was even worse, as the 17-year average refers to all claimants—Anglos and Mexicans—but the historical evidence clearly shows that Anglo Americans moved through the process at a much more rapid pace.

Hornbeck's study of the Land Act finds that while they were formally included in the land claims process by treaty and law, "Mexican claimants were confused and lost in the maze of hearings, appeals, and trials" (1979: 440). In this way, the Land Act forestalled Mexican landholders from "developing their land under American rule" because they had to work through and certify their claims in a language, institutions, and a culture foreign to them, and for this reason "they struggled in an alien legal system to obtain undisputed title to their land" (446). Here we see 'accidental citizens' who are in certain formal ways (by means of the Treaty and the Land Act for example) recognized in their hybrid identity as comprising the American domestic space as citizens—or potential citizens—while functionally standing as aliens to the legal and political system that is supposed to serve to secure their rights of citizenship. On the other hand, as Mexican claimants struggled to figure out how to work through the political institutions and culture of the conquering American nation: "In the early stages of patenting, [white] American settlers were success-ful because they were familiar with the dominant legal and land-tenure systems and had the financial resources to survive the bureaucratic entanglements of the California Land Act" (442).

As a consequence, through the advantages of colonial rule, Anglo-American settlers, sitting at the top of the racial hierarchy, were able to "clear title to their claims early to escape protracted legal disputes, and to bring the land into productive use more quickly than were Mexican claimants. The large number of American claimants reflected the government's inability to protect the original grantees from the increasing demand for land" (443–4). Furthermore, in having the racial, cultural, and political status to get out ahead in the land claims process, white Americans were able to claim the most valuable, arable land of northern California. The temporal and spatial implications of the process set out by the internal postcolonial institution of the California Land Act are rather easy to see: "Claims patented by the persons with Anglo names were more numerous in northern California, especially before 1870. In contrast, Mexican claimants received the majority of land patents in the south after 1870" (445). Here, then, we get a spatially specific rendering of American internal postcolonialism articulated through the relationship between hierarchy and hybridity. Over many decades, Mexicans who remained residents in the post-1848 expanded territory of the United States became U.S. citizens, incorporated into the American nation via the production of a hybrid identity, as Mexican Americans liminally positioned in the American racial order. Over time, Mexican Americans also attained patents to some of the land originally granted to them by Mexican or Spanish title, but the quantity was much less overall than they had held at the time of the Treaty, and the majority of their landholdings were located in southern California, closer to the Mexican border.

The predominance of Mexican-American holdings in the south and Anglo-Americans in the north represents and enacts the racial hierarchy within which Mexican Americans henceforth, from the 1850s on, have had to exist, struggle, and adapt. This analysis of the internal postcolonial dynamics at work in the relationship between race and American political development reveals how the dynastic-in-the-democratic persists as a key feature of American nation-building. Specifically, the relationship between state, space, and identity was a mutually constitutive product of the laws and institutions that brought Mexicans into the American nation-space and political community, as accidental citizens rather than intentional ones through the construction of hybrid identity that helped make Mexican status and title dispensable, institutionally and culturally ceding way to the urgent and loud desire of Anglo-American settlers for land.

Conclusion

To close, I consider two contrasting scholarly assessments of the California Land Act, and briefly note why these views show the need for an approach that appreciates the complex role of colonial practices in the relationship between race and American political development. Ruiz Cameron (2000: 4, 8) offers a stark picture when looking at the long term consequences of the Treaty of Guadalupe Hidalgo and the Land Act: "between 1854 and 1930, Mexican litigants or their heirs prevailed in just one-quarter of all cases presenting land title claims decided by the Court during the period," and this "all but wiped out [Mexicans] as a landholding class in the Southwestern United States. Their transformation from masters to servants had been completed, and set the stage for a new chapter in U.S.-Mexico relations: the exploitation of low-wage, migratory Mexican and Mexican labor." By contrast, Karen Clay (1999: 140) praises the U.S. Congress, for in devising a means to deal with the land conflicts of that time and place: "the institution it chose balanced the interests of the government, American owners of land grants, and American squatters and settlers . . . the institution established by the California Land Grant was the most successful institution to date."

For Ruiz Cameron, the end results of the Treaty and Land Act are clear; they generated a subaltern population that meets the criteria of colonized subjects noted earlier: coerced location and status, structural economic inequality, racially alien administrative rule, cultural domination, and the imposition of a racial ideology and practices. But while all of this is hard to dispute, especially when it is this same subaltern group that has become the object of persistent racial and nationalist invective by the likes of Tom Tancredo and Lou Dobbs, Clay's praise for the Land Act may shed even more light on the persistence of colonialist institutions and practices in American political development. In a way that Ruiz Cameron would undoubtedly appreciate by way of critique, to Clay, Mexicans are invisible in the California Land Act's formulation, institutionalization, and practices. This invisibility is a product of either not seeing

Mexican interests as relevant to the Congress, which could well be the case although Clay never makes mention of this in her study (or of Mexicans at all), and/or not distinguishing Mexican interests from that which she generally refers to as that of "American owners," and thus not accounting for their concerns in her assessment of the Act, which is just as likely the case. Either way, and let us assume it is a bit of both, what Clay's assessment implicitly reveals is the success of the Treaty of Guadalupe Hidalgo and California Land Act in fostering colonial practices within a liberal democratic settler polity; in other words, as expressions of internal postcolonialism.

The Treaty and Land Act are state expressions of internal postcolonialism because they fostered the expansion of American nation-space and the endurance of American racial hierarchies through, in part, the creation and absorption of a hybrid identity, that of Mexican American. In terms of our understanding of the role of race in American political development, it is important to see the functioning of the relationship between state, space, and identity at work here. The colonialist practices articulated and institutional-ized in these mid-nineteenth-century U.S. policies are too often made invisible in analyses that read this moment to be fundamentally about state and space, without due consideration to the national and sub-national identity issues that are also constitutive of this political moment and its consequences. This is not to say that this period should be read as solely a story of American colo-nization of Mexican people and the production and liminal positioning of Mexican-American identity in the American racial hierarchy. It is about that, but that is not the whole story. If one were to read this moment entirely through, say, the internal colonialist model, one would sacrifice an under-standing of the dynamism and complexity of the construction and location of Mexican-American identity in the U.S. political, socio-economic, and cultural landscape, and thereby be at a loss to explain the more nuanced functioning of the liberal democratic polity as it concerns matters such as race and ethnic relations. At the same time, any reading of the long-term effect of mid-nineteenth-century U.S. expansionist policies that does not account for the colonialist sources, traces, and practices woven into and constitutive of the liberal democratic political culture and institutions we live with to this day cannot explain fully the persistence and mutability of racial hierarchies over time.

The political story I have traced and analyzed in this chapter cannot be framed as a matter of simple exclusion or inclusion, outright domination or liberation. Instead, it is a story of colonialism in a liberal democratic setting, and both elements need to be recognized with concern for their compatibilities as well as their tensions. It is, to be sure, the colonialist element of this relation-ship which is too easily rendered invisible, read as irrelevant, ancient, and/or inapplicable in the study of U.S. politics and history. In the political science subfield of American political development, in particular, there is a notable absence of studies that take seriously the role of colonialist traces and practices in U.S. political culture and institutions, in terms of their production, iterations, and long-term political impact. My effort to define and expose the practices of American internal postcolonialism seeks to offer a way for APD scholars, among others, to get an analytical grip on the role of colonialist practices in U.S. politics without falling into the trap of reproducing the limited and rigid internal colonial model. Thus, as we seek to discern the colonialist dynamics embedded in the relationship between race and American political development —as I argue we need to—we should not see the views of scholars such as Ruiz Cameron and Clay as representing distinct, disconnected perspectives. To the contrary, an approach that draws out the functioning of American internal postcolonialism locates the mutually constitutive connection between viewpoints such as the former's expressly colonialist diagnosis and the latter's more ideologically liberal praise of U.S. policies and institutions. These two scholars are viewing the same developments through their own lenses, but what is necessary to analyze the functioning of colonialist practices in liberal democracies is to widen this vision, to make these and other parties understand that they are seeing parts of a more complicated whole. I hope this chapter has at least begun to stake out a way to do this by exposing the interplay between the transformation and persistence of hierarchy and the construction and deployment of hybridity in the development of American nation-space, state institutions, and identity over time.

Notes

1 For a summary, critique and contextualization of contemporary anti-immigrant views, see Fraga and Segura (2006).
2 These are the words of journalist John L. Sullivan (a pro-Democratic Party journalist) in his essay entitled "Annexation." Along with the passage cited in the text, he goes on to articulate a vision in which over the next century these millions will 'multiply' into a population of "*two hundred and fifty million* (if not more), is too evident to leave us in doubt of the manifest design of Providence in regard to the occupation of the continent" (O'Sullivan 1845: 7, emphasis in original).
3 For an example of contemporary border issues confronting the Tohono O'odham, see Archibold (2006).
4 Not that this claim is really up for much debate—for example Smith (1997) entitles his chapter on this period in U.S. political history, "High Noon of the White Republic." Also, for example, the *Statistical View of the United States*, published by the federal government in 1854, contains a section on the "White Population of the United States," including tables entitled "Relative Rank of the States and Territories according to their White Population" and "Progress of Population— Increase of the White Population of the United States under each Census from 1790–1850" (47).
5 While this document specifically, and this time period generally, very much involves the concerns and status of indigenous people and African Americans in the racial politics of American expansionism, for this chapter I will focus on the case of Mexicans, but with the understanding that the insights articulated here must be brought into conversation and context with those of the other two notable subaltern racial groups to get a full picture of the situation.
6 For another critical view of the notion of hybridity in the functioning of identity in politics, see Beltran (2004). It is important to make clear that while Beltran offers

a critique of hybridity in this article, her specific focus and the direction of the argument is quite different from my own. Specifically, her focus is on the hybridity of *mestizaje* identity as a "central trope in Chicano and Latino thought" such as that of Gloria Anzaldúa, which "celebrates multiplicity and fluidity over stability and singularity" (596). Beltran's critique is that there is a deeper, constraining essentialism at work in the employment of hybridity in this literature. My approach to hybridity, by contrast, focuses not on *mestizaje* but rather on Mexican-American identity and its construction and deployment within U.S. political discourse, institutions, and policies. In contrast to Beltran, I do define hybridity as representing fluidity and multiplicity, but see it utilized from the top down in order to secure and perpetuate the American racial hierarchy. Finally, Beltran's reference to hierarchies is, again, very different, as she is referencing the hierarchy *of* hybridity, where the liberatory construction of *mestizaje* in Chicano and Latino thought ranks the Indian part of this identity above the Spanish part because "indigenous ancestry is the site of group unity and collective resistance" (599). By contrast, my argument about hierarchy *and* hybridity focuses on the discursive and institutional construction of American racial hierarchies that perpetuate a white supremacist racial order.

7   On this point, consider that in the introduction to the edited collection entitled *After Colonialism* (1995), a book with essays by postcolonial writers including Edward Said and Homi Bhabha, editor Gayan Prakash states that the essays in this collection seek to challenge the way in which Western history "sequestered colonialism tightly in the airless container of History, and casts postcoloniality as a new beginning, one in which certain modes of domination may persist and acquire new forms of sustenance but one that marks the end of an era. To pry open the reading of colonialism from this prison-house of historicism requires more than the concept of neocolonialism. For at stake is not simply the issue as to whether or not former colonies have become free from domination, but also the question as to how the history of colonialism and colonialism's disciplining of history can be shaken loose from the domination of categories and ideas it produced" (5).

8   Other important work from the internal colonial perspective worthy of note, include the following: Curtin (1974); Moore (1976); Anders (1979); Maldonado (1979); Ritter (1979); and Hechter (1999).

9   Given that citizens and descendents of Mexico can trace and construct their identities as of primarily or solely Spanish origin, or of indigenous origin, or most commonly that of mestizo as a mixture of Spanish and indigenous, pinning down a Mexican racial identity relative to whiteness was and remains a complicated matter. As mentioned, what is important for the case presented in this chapter is that from a U.S. perspective, the most politically pertinent mid-nineteenth century construct of Mexican racial identity was as non-white. We can see this, for example, in how governmental and party officials, in particular members of the Whig Party, opposed the U.S.–Mexican War partially on the basis that Mexicans, as a "mongrel race," should not have the right nor were they prepared to engage in American republican governance (cited in Morrison (1992: 39). For more on white perceptions of Mexican Americans in the mid-nineteenth-century, see Greenfield and Kates (1975: 694–710). In this section, they cite explicit racial othering views that emanated from the U.S. Senate, the press, and the Southwest region in the decades following the U.S.–Mexican War.

10   For a recent, excellent study of the complicated racial and ethnic construction of, among others, Latino identity in U.S. politics, see Hattam (2007).

11   From the Treaty on through the twentieth century and to our time, the complicated construction of the Mexican (and/or Hispanic, Latino, Chicano) racial identity, specifically in relation to whiteness, also reflects the dynamics of hierarchy and hybridity, whereby Mexicans are drawn into and out of being read as

white—variously deemed "another white race" or "white by law" to quote two scholars cited below—for the purpose of both securing and re-arranging the American racial order. For a sampling of historical and legal analyses of these developments in U.S. racial politics, please see: Menchaca (1993); López (1997); Gómez (2000); and Sheridan (2003). Also, for the role of indigenous identity in "coloring" Mexican racial identity, and the complicated matter and status of the potentially "white Mexican," see Saldaña-Portilla (2004).

12 The 1850 and 1860 U.S. censuses offer no clear numbers on these questions.

13 The original source for the notion of the "accidental citizen" comes from the work of Paul Virilio—whom Nyers credits—but it is in Nyers' rendering of the concept to race and ethnic relations in the U.S. context that I draw the most value.

References and secondary sources

Anders, G. (1979) "The Internal Colonization of Cherokee Native Americans," *Development and Change*, 10: 41–55.

Archibold, R.C. (2006) "Border Fence Must Skirt Objections from Arizona Tribe," *New York Times*, September 20: 24.

Beltran, C. (2004) "Patrolling Borders: Hybrids, Hierarchies, and the Challenge of the Mestizaje," *Political Research Quarterly*, 57: 595–607.

Bhabha, H. (1994) *The Location of Culture*, New York: Routledge.

Blauner, R. (1969) "Internal Colonialism and Ghetto Revolt," *Social Problems*, 16: 393–408.

—— (1972) *Racial Oppression in America*, Berkeley, CA: University of Berkeley.

Clay, K.B. (1999) "Property Rights and Institutions: Congress and the California Land Act of 1851," *Journal of Economic History*, 59: 122–42.

Curtin, P.D. (1974) "The Black Experience of Colonialism and Imperialism," *Daedalus: Proceedings of the American Academy of Arts and Sciences*, 103: 17–29.

Fraga, L.F. and Segura, G.M. (2006) "Culture Clash? Contesting Notions of American Identity and the Effects of Latin American Immigration," *Perspectives on Politics*, 4: 279–87.

Franke, K.M. (2000) "The Uses of History in Struggles for Racial Justice: Colonizing the Past and Managing Memory," *UCLA Law Review*, 47: 1673–88.

Gates, P. (1971) "The California Land Act of 1851," *California Historical Quarterly*, 50: 395–430.

Gómez, L.E. (2000) "Race, Colonialism, and Criminal Law: Mexicans and the American Criminal Justice System in Territorial New Mexico," *Law and Society Review*, 34: 1129–202.

Greenfield, G. and Kates Jr., D.B. (1975) "Mexican Americans, Racial Discrimination, and the Civil Rights Act of 1866," *California Law Review*, 63: 694–710.

Hattam, V. (2007) *In the Shadow of Race: Jews, Latinos, and Immigrant Politics in the United States*, Chicago: University of Chicago Press.

Hechter, M. (1999) *Internal Colonialism: The Celtic Fringe in British National Development*, New Brunswick and London: Transaction Publishers.

Hornbeck, D. (1979) "The Patenting of California's Private Land Claims, 1851–1885," *Geographical Review*, 69: 434–48.

Hurstfield, J. (1975) "The Educational Experiences of Mexican Americans: 'Cultural Pluralism' or 'Internal Colonialism'?" *Oxford Review of Education*, 1: 137–49.

López, I.H. (1997) *White By Law: The Legal Construction of Race*, New York: New York University Press.

López, L. (2007) "Legacy of a Land Grab," *Hispanic Online—Hispanic Heritage Plaza 2002*. Online. Available: http://www.hispaniconline.com/hh02/history_ legacy_guadalupe_hidalgo.html (accessed September 21, 2007).

Luna, G.T. (1998) "Chicana/Chicano Land Tenure in the Agrarian Domain: On the Edge of a 'Naked Knife,'" *Michigan Journal of Race & Law*, 4: 39–144.

Luna-Firebaugh, E.M. (2002) "The Border Crossed Us: Border Crossing Issues of the Indigenous Peoples of the Americas," *Wicazo Sa Review: A Journal of Native American Studies*, Special Issue on Sovereignty and Governance, 17: 159–81.

Maldonado, L.A. (1979) "Internal Colonialism and Triangulation: A Research Example," *Social Service Review*, 53: 464–73.

Menchaca, M. (1993) "Chicano Indianism: A Historical Account of Racial Repression in the United States," *American Ethnologist*, 20: 583–603.

Moore, J.W. (1976). "American Minorities and 'New Nation' Perspectives," *Pacific Sociological Review*, 19: 447–68.

Morrison, M.A. (1992) "'New Territory versus No Territory': The Whig Party and the Politics of Western Expansionism, 1846–1848," *Western Historical Quarterly*, 23: 25–51.

Nyers, P. (2006) "The Accidental Citizen: Acts of Sovereignty and (Un)making Citizenship," *Economy and Society*, 35: 22–41.

Omi, M. and Winant, H. (1994) *Racial Formation in the United States: From the 1960s to the 1990s*, 2nd edn, New York and London: Routledge.

O'Sullivan, J.L. (1845) "Annexation," *United States Magazine and Democratic Review*, 17: 5–10.

Prakash, G. (ed.) (1995) *After Colonialism: Imperial Histories and Postcolonial Displacements*, Princeton, NJ: University of Princeton Press.

Ritter, K. (1979) "Internal Colonialism and Industrial Development in Alaska," *Ethnic and Racial Studies*, 2: 319–40.

Ruiz Cameron, C.D. (2000) "One Hundred Fifty Years of Solitude: Reflections on the End of the History Academy's Dominance of Scholarship on the Treaty of Guadalupe Hidalgo," *Bilingual Review*, 25: 1–22.

Saldaña-Portilla, M.J. (2004) "'Wavering on the Horizon of Social Being:' The Treaty of Guadalupe Hidalgo and the Legacy of its Racial Character in Américo Paredes's *George Washington Gómez*," *Radical History Review*, 89: 135–64.

Sheridan, C. (2003) "'Another White Race': Mexican Americans and the Paradox of Whiteness in Jury Selection," *Law and History Review*, 21: 109–44.

Smith, R. (1997) *Civic Ideals*, New Haven, CT: Yale University Press.

Spivak, G. (1995) "Teaching for the Times," in J.N. Pieterse and B. Parekh (eds) *The Decolonization of the Imagination*, London and New Jersey: Zed Books Ltd.

Tsosie, R. (2000) "'Sacred Obligations' Intercultural Justice and the Discourse of Treaty Rights," *UCLA Law Review*, 47: 1615–72.

United States Census Office (1854) *Statistical View of the United States: Being a Compendium of the Seventh Census*, J.D.B. DeBow, Superintendent of the United States Census, Washington: Beverly Tucker, Senate Printer.

6 Reconstruction, race, and revolution

Pamela Brandwein[1]

It is common today to regard the period of Reconstruction as a revolution, albeit an unfinished one.[2] In the crucible of the 1860s, a war was fought, slavery was forbidden, birthright citizenship was established, and the principle of equality under law was enshrined in the Fourteenth Amendment. In 1870, the freedmen became members of the American political community, marking another momentous step in this critical era.[3] If the architects of Reconstruction described themselves as "in the midst of a revolution,"[4] this hardly seems surprising.

But not all scholars accept the characterization of this turbulent era as revolutionary. An earlier body of historical work (Kelly 1966; Meier 1967; Benedict 1974; Paludan 1975; Litwack 1979) stresses the themes of racism, conservatism, and continuity with the antebellum order. Pointing to a persistent belief in white supremacy and emphasizing the limited commitment of Republicans to the freedmen, C.V. Woodward argues that Reconstruction was "essentially non-revolutionary and conservative" (Woodward 1979: 26). For Herman Belz, the Reconstruction Amendments were a "nonrevolutionary extension to black persons of guarantees of liberty and equality contained in the original Constitution" (Belz 1998: 13).

My purpose here is not to referee this dispute. Rather, my goal is to begin thinking about the concept of revolution scholars use to debate the character of Reconstruction.[5] These scholars, it turns out, work with a concept of revolution that lacks precision and rigor. To put the matter more bluntly, Reconstruction scholars are using the term *revolution* in a fairly sloppy way. Their thinly elaborated notion of revolution leaves undefined the criteria for distinguishing between revolution and reform. Unspecified, too, are the criteria or thresholds that mark the success of revolutionary efforts. This underspecification, in fact, permits the debate.[6] Without criteria for distinguishing between revolution and reform and without clear thresholds for marking the success of efforts by the freedmen and on behalf of them, a thin concept of revolution permits opposite conclusions about whether Reconstruction witnessed a revolution.

What happens to our understanding of Reconstruction if a more rigorous concept of revolution is introduced? What new view of Reconstruction emerges? And why does it matter? What is at stake in reconsidering the revolutionary character of Reconstruction with a more elaborate conception of revolution in place? In this chapter, I begin to address these questions, especially as they bear on the political transition from Reconstruction to Jim Crow.

For a tighter conception of revolution, I turn to the political theorist Hannah Arendt (1963). Arendt is by no means the last word on revolution, but certain features of her concept offer a more precise way of thinking about Reconstruction. Detailed in *On Revolution*, these features include an understanding of revolution as political, a republican understanding of freedom where "subjects become the rulers themselves" (1963: 34), and a need for institutional consolidation. Arendt's concept of political revolution is different from Marxist notions of social revolution, which focus on class structure, and it offers a distinctive entry into thinking about race and reform in the crucial post–Civil War period.

But there is a secondary reason, too, for turning to Arendt. Ackerman explicitly appeals to Arendt to formulate the idea of a revolutionary constitutional moment (1991: 204–12). Because one of my goals is to show that an Arendtian concept of revolution actually injures Ackerman's Reconstruction narrative, it is necessary to present her concept in more complete form.

Here is Arendt's summary definition, which provides an initial glimpse of her notion of revolution:

> Only where change occurs in the sense of a new beginning, where violence is used to constitute an altogether different form of government, to bring about the formation of a new body politic, where the liberation from oppression aims at least at the constitution of freedom can we speak of revolution.
>
> (1963: 28)

All of the main features of Arendt's concept of revolution are present: the idea of an "entirely new story," a distinction between "freedom" and "liberation," and the need for institutional consolidation.[7] An Arendtian concept of politics is implicit here, as well.[8]

The turn to Arendt yields a new understanding of Reconstruction as a failed revolution. A revolution arguably started with black soldiering during the Civil War, Major General William T. Sherman's order for land redistribution,[9] and the formation of the Sea Islands communities. The formation of a Southern biracial political coalition in 1867–8 can also be seen as an early stage of a revolutionary effort. But revolutionary action failed at key institutional thresholds and the attempt to secure black political participation collapsed after temporary victories and a period of unevenness and decline. A new political regime and black political freedom were never institutionalized.

The conventional view today, as already noted, is that a revolution succeeded before it failed. The historian James McPherson is an exemplar of this common view. Reconstruction "was a revolution," states McPherson (1988: 76) "though the success of the southern counterrevolution made it an unfinished one." The view that follows from Arendt is that a revolution never succeeded in the first place. It passed through early stages but was never set or consolidated in lasting institutions.

Recent scholarship in political science supports this understanding of Reconstruction as a failed revolution. Richard Valelly, for example, identifies the political participation of blacks as potentially the most radical aspect of Reconstruction. The Reconstruction Act of 1867 (which extended the vote to black men in the South) and the Fifteenth Amendment held "revolutionary potential" (Valelly 2004: 138) but a revolution did not happen. Change fell short of specific developmental thresholds and the biracial political coalition of 1867–8 was "incompletely institutionalized" (Valelly 2004: 47–71). Valelly, notably, declines to choose between the two sides in the revolution debate, offering instead the understanding of Reconstruction as a "quasi-revolutionary era" (2004: ix).

Why does it matter if Reconstruction is understood as a revolution or a failed revolution? Historical stakes, of course, attach to the question of whether a revolution "happened." But there are stakes here, too, for political scientists and law professors, as understandings of Reconstruction bear on understandings of political and constitutional development in the United States. There are contemporary constitutional stakes, as well. Assertions and denials of the revolutionary character of Reconstruction are linked to heated disputes about federalism and the power of the national government to protect rights. All of these stakes can be briefly laid out.

First, understandings of Reconstruction bear on understandings of American political development, especially the complex path from the antebellum slavery system to the Reconstruction-era racial order to Jim Crow institutions. The revolution thesis is associated with the premise that the antebellum state's relationship to race can be—and was—completely changed. Here, I underscore the difficulty of this, pointing to the ways antebellum institutions and ways of thinking bounded post-war political agency. Reinforcing this point on a general level, the historical-comparative literature on institutional change has repeatedly pointed to what Weir (1992) calls "bounded innovation" (see also Skocpol 1979 and Thelen 2003).[10]

Even the weak version of the revolution thesis—captured in Foner's expression "unfinished revolution"—breaks down in the face of Arendt: the expression becomes visible as aspirational rather than analytical. As an aspirational phrase, this locution has its eyes set on the Second Reconstruction (the civil rights era of the 1950s and 1960s). The turn to Arendt not only helps to clarify the relationship between the First and Second Reconstructions, i.e., why the Second was necessary (this is the question of American political development taken up by Valelly 2004). The Second Reconstruction has become the prism for seeing the First, and it is important to disentangle the aspirational content in Reconstruction histories from the historical and analytic content.

An understanding of Reconstruction thus provides a building block for stories about American political development. But in addition to this, understandings of Reconstruction matter for stories about constitutional development. Arendt's concept of revolution, as I suggested earlier, does great damage to Ackerman's strong version of the revolution narrative. Ackerman, a law professor, advances a model of constitutional development in which the "the People" play a central, creative, and revolutionary role in legitimizing irregular (i.e., non-Article V) constitutional change. It is well known that Republicans used irregular procedures to gain passage of the Fourteenth Amendment, as ex-Confederate states were excluded from the Congress that passed the Amendment (see Nelson 1988: 93–6). For Ackerman, the People's revolution, expressed in both the passage of the Amendment and the elections of 1866 and 1868, supplies legitimacy for these unconventional procedures. Ackerman's project, then, makes him highly dependent on asserting the success of the revolution, since a constitutional moment only exists if the People's engagement produces and legitimizes a genuine revolution. The turn to Arendt injures Ackerman because Arendt's emphasis on institutional consolidation (i.e., the establishment of a new body politic that enacts the revolutionary vision) is a threshold Ackerman cannot meet. The turn to Arendt also injures Foner, but not nearly as much. This is because Foner's goal is to provide a comprehensive synthesis of revisionist[11] and post-revisionist[12] scholarship on Reconstruction; many of the conservative and continuous elements of Reconstruction are already built into his account.

Contemporary constitutional stakes, finally, attach to assertions and denials of the revolutionary character of Reconstruction. Constitutional scholars wedded to originalism and critical of the Warren Court, such as Raoul Berger (1977), have seized upon post-revisionist understandings of Reconstruction to justify a state-centered federalism. Arguing that the Fourteenth Amendment did not originally apply the Bill of Rights to the states, Berger claims that "the key to an understanding of the Fourteenth Amendment is that the North was shot through with Negrophobia" (1977: 10). Lashing back at Berger, constitutional scholars (Curtis 1986; Kaczorowski 1986) who support strong national authority to protect rights turn to the revisionist scholarship of Foner and his predecessors.

What happens in constitutional law if Reconstruction is understood as a failed revolution? Originalists like Berger will find little comfort in the answer, since the "failed" part of the "failed revolution" pertains primarily to the absence of predictable enforcement of Reconstruction legislation like the Civil Rights Act of 1866[13] and the Ku Klux Klan Act of 1871.[14] While space prevents me from addressing this matter, the understanding of Reconstruction as a failed revolution does not rob the Reconstruction Amendments of legal force. In saying this, however, I am not endorsing the "revolutionary constitutionalism" thesis formulated by Kaczorowski (1986). Of all the contributors to the revolution debate, Kaczorowski draws the brightest line between antebellum constitutionalism and Republican constitutionalism. While I do not deliver here on my suggestion that he has a flawed understanding of Republican constitutionalism,[15] his picture of Republican constitutionalism presupposes the idea that the state's relationship to race and the organizing federal principles that govern race relations can be readily and completely converted. If we should beware this presupposition (and we should), it remains to understand the ways in which institutions mattered in constraining post–Civil War transformations in the racial and political order.

This chapter, then, puts into a place a clear and rigorous concept of revolution, generating a new understanding of Reconstruction as a failed revolution. But there is a second result, as well.

Arendt's vision of republicanism and her prioritization of "the political" can be used to clarify the stakes that attached to the conventional division or "hierarchy" of rights that characterized the Reconstruction era. Central in this respect is the Moderate, or centrist, Republican stance on black rights: support for "civil rights" (e.g., property, contract and physical security rights) and "political rights" (e.g., voting and holding office) but a rejection of "social rights" (e.g., equal access to public accommodations and integrated schools). What is at stake in this rejection of social rights? Clearly, it was a loss for the freedmen and it marked the limits of the centrist Republican understanding of "equality under law." But even deeper stakes can be identified using Arendt's infamous essay, "Reflections on Little Rock" (1959), in which she claimed legitimacy for the social custom of segregation.

Key here is the centrist Republican assumption that civil and political equality were possible when social rights were denied. I use Arendt's essay to challenge this assumption and to suggest they may have held an impossible vision. Whether they did or not depended on how they viewed the relationship among the civil, political, and social realms. If centrists thought that once blacks "proved themselves" in the civil and political realms, they would advance irresistibly toward social equality, then their vision can be saved. But as I explain, the documentary evidence is unclear on this matter. Centrist Republicans never clearly articulated a view—any view—of the relationship among these realms. A clear view of this relationship emerged only later in the 1890s as the Jim Crow regime solidified. The majority in *Plessy v. Ferguson* (1896), for example, viewed the boundary between the civil/political realm and the social realm as natural and permanent. And with such a view, the possibility of securing civil and political equality in the absence of social rights evaporated.

The final section of this chapter turns to "Reflections" to think about whether civil and political equality were possible without social equality. What role, moreover, did the centrist Republican rejection of social rights play in the political transition to Jim Crow? In framing these questions, my broader goal is to use shifting understandings of the tripartite division of rights as a window on how the nation moved from the uncertain threshold of revolution to Jim Crow at century's end.

Rogers Smith's (1993) multiple-traditions thesis[16] applies to this final piece of the chapter, as the combination of republican and "ascriptive inegalitarian" traditions that characterized the centrist Republican stance on black rights is associated with particular tensions and inconsistencies. In other words, the centrists' support for civil and political rights coupled with a rejection of social rights brought specific contradictions. This is because social recognition was in fact necessary for freedom. These tensions got worse as Jim Crow institutions and social exclusion were established in more rigid fashion. When "the political" is privileged over the social (as in Arendt's "Reflections"), these tensions and contradictions are obscured, indeed, denied. Arendt's privileging of the political thus leaves us unable to perceive and trace the tensions and contradictions that characterized the transition from Reconstruction to Jim Crow.

To sum things up, the main part of this chapter treats Arendt's notion of political revolution as unproblematic for the purpose of criticizing the conventional Reconstruction-as-revolution narrative. The last section problematizes her privileging of the political in order to consider the stakes that attach to the centrist Republican rejection of social rights. It is important to acknowledge, finally, that a deeper engagement with Arendt is necessary in order to fully support the rethinkings proposed here.[17] Necessary, as well, is greater engagement with the comparative social science literature on revolution, which takes up questions about the causes, processes, and outcomes of revolution.[18]

The rest of this chapter is organized in the following way. First, a more detailed presentation of Arendt's concept of revolution and its institutional character is offered. The section that follows shows how this concept allows us to rethink the question of whether a revolution happened or succeeded. Finally, Arendt's Little Rock essay is used to examine the stakes that attach to the centrist Republican view of the post-Civil War "hierarchy of rights."

Arendt's concept of revolution

Arendt's concept of revolution can be found in her case study, *On Revolution*, which compared the basic experiences of the French and the Americans before, during, and after their Revolutions. Arendt had a very positive view of the American experience. Finding that a "taste for public liberty" was crucial to the American Revolution, Arendt offers what her biographer Elisabeth Young-Bruehl (2006: 128) calls a "song of praise to all the state and federal institutions —all the world-building—of the founding fathers." But Arendt also cautions against judging the failure of the French Revolution against the success of the American Revolution. Her reasons for this caution are relevant to our understanding of Reconstruction.

In France, revolutionaries were confronted by massive abject poverty and "the social question." The social question referred to the predicament of mass poverty: the desperately poor formed the majority of the population but did not belong to "the people." The conditions of America's revolutionary success, Arendt emphasizes, included not just an absence of massive abject poverty, but also the presence of a slave system, which enabled white America's relative freedom from acute poverty. In the United States then, unlike France, the social question was absent. Slavery was not perceived as presenting "the social question" (more on this shortly). This changed only during the Civil War and Reconstruction, when large numbers of political actors came to regard slavery as presenting the social question, or some version of it. Doubt about the inevitability of acute misery (slavery) among the degraded (blacks)—a population excluded from "the people"—now generated widespread claims to birthright equality and national belonging. If we take a cue from Arendt's cautions about judging French failure against American success, we ought to be careful, too, in judging the failure of Reconstruction-era revolutionaries against the success of their colonial antecedents.

I now sketch the three relevant features of Arendt's concept of revolution in more detail: the idea of an "entirely new story," a distinction between freedom and liberation, and the need for institutional consolidation.

For Arendt, revolution is bound up with the idea that "the course of history suddenly begins anew" (1963: 21). There is an "entirely new story" (30). Contrasting an "altogether different form of government" with "mere changes" (13), Arendt explains that revolutions "are the only political events which confront us directly and inevitably with the problem of beginning" (13).[19] What kind of "entirely new story" does Arendt have in mind? The answer: "A change so radical that "subjects become the rulers themselves" (34). In revolution, an entirely new beginning and the goal of freedom coincide (22).

Her notion of freedom is central. Arendt subscribes to a form of republicanism, which can be discerned in her distinction between liberation and freedom. She defines liberation as the absence of government restraint (140–41) and the "power of locomotion." She defines freedom as political freedom, and claims that political freedom "generally speaking means the right to be a participator in government" (1963: 221). Freedom means "participation in public affairs, or admission to the public realm" (25). Or in another repeated phrase, "subjects become the rulers themselves" (1963: 69).[20] Remarking on Arendt's republicanism, Michelman (1996: 205) observes, "The fundamental Arendtian right is the right of political inclusion."

Arendt's view of agency is related here. Indeed, what Michelman takes to be special in Arendt's view of rights is her "distinctive grasp of the relationship between agency and rights" (1996: 204). Michelman offers his own rendering of this relationship: "It's a condition of my having a right that I have, myself, contributed to the production of it, and that I cannot do this on my own, can't do it without membership, can't do it except as a correspondent and co-producer with others in a social group in which I have membership standing" (205). People come to have rights, then, only through their agency, which depends on membership in the social group and social recognition.

The lack of social recognition defines the boundaries of the social question. As previously noted, the social question refers primarily to the predicament of mass poverty and it plays a key role in revolutions. The poverty-stricken multitudes formed the majority of the population in France without ever belonging to the people. Doubt that their misery was inevitable or inherent in the human condition—and was instead the product of human-made institutions—germinated the modern notion of equality, i.e., the idea that every person is born or created equal, and that this is a birthright. This doubt was the match, according to Arendt, that lit the flame of revolution, whose goal was freedom for the poverty-stricken. Talking, persuading, deciding, and acting with others as equals in the public realm, i.e. (republican) freedom—was for the desperately poor as well as the rich.

When social recognition is based on racial status, the boundaries of the social question are drawn differently. For blacks in the United States, of course, gaining even the most basic form of social recognition (self-ownership) was an ordeal. The fact that it was an ordeal relates to a point Arendt emphasizes, namely, that both Americans and Europeans were blind to slavery as presenting the social question (1963: 66). The American colonial experience could generate doubt about the inevitability of abject misery among France's multitudes only because the social question was perceived to be absent in America. As William Penn put it, the United States was "a good poor man's country" (1963: 65) due to the absence of European-style poverty. But the United States was a good poor *white* man's country. As Arendt carefully notes, the absence of the social question from America's landscape was "quite deceptive and that abject, degrading misery was present everywhere in the form of slavery and Negro labor" (1963: 65). The goodness of the poor white man's country thus depended heavily on black labor and black misery (1963: 66).[21] Slavery, she states, was "the one great crime in America's history" (Arendt 1959: 46).

Arendt's acknowledgment of slavery extends (at least in name) the social question to race in black and white terms. Arendt did not, however, discuss the Civil War or Reconstruction, when a significant number of political actors finally perceived in slavery the presence of the social question.[22]

With the social question therefore at the center of revolutionary efforts, the task of foundation is the last among several stages of revolution.[23] This culminating task consists of "devising and imposing upon men a new authority" (31). Power, then, must not only be "won," it must be "duly constituted" (87), and this job includes both lawmaking and the predictable enforcement of new laws. Revolutionaries must build "stable and durable institutions" (225), i.e., an "entirely new power center" (152) that is "lasting" (81). This is the task of institutional "consolidation" (152); these durable institutions set the new beginning.

Consolidation, then, concerns the developmental boundaries of revolution. Arendt refers to the success of the American Revolution, which lasted "13 years" (68–9) and so we can conclude that the addition of the Bill of Rights in 1789 marked the consolidation and success of the American Revolution. It is important to keep in mind, again, that abject poverty was absent among whites and that racial slavery was not perceived as presenting the social question. The addition of the Bill of Rights to the Constitution, therefore, indicates little about the markers of a successful revolution where the social question is present. Because the social question was at the center of Reconstruction, it is folly to treat the passage of new laws and amendments as marking the success of revolutionary efforts without attending to the enforcement of those laws, i.e., the "imposing upon men" of the revolutionary vision.

Here, then, is Arendt's more fully defined concept of revolution. In the next section, I return to Foner and Ackerman and present their revolution theses in more detail. While some elements of Arendt's conception of revolution, e.g., an entirely new beginning, justify the conclusion that a revolution was attempted during Reconstruction, most of the criteria and thresholds just canvassed cannot be met. Only partial civil and political freedom were gained, and even these partial gains were temporary. Moreover, "the social question" was never fully confronted, as the group of centrist Republicans who held the balance of power denied social rights to blacks. Reconstruction undeniably witnessed profoundly important changes and many forms of discontinuity, as well as a new vision of national belonging. But with a more specified concept of revolution in place, this is not enough to warrant the revolution thesis, even the "unfinished revolution" thesis of Eric Foner.

Reconstruction as a failed revolution

The Reconstruction-as-revolution thesis comes in several forms. Bruce Ackerman expresses the strong version of this thesis while Foner's account is much more nuanced. Foner, for example, emphasizes the dual (conserving and transformative) elements of Republican legislation while the conserving elements drop out in Ackerman. There are, however, a host of commonalities. This is not surprising, as Foner's account is standard not just in history departments but also in law schools. It is worth noting, as well, that neither writer treats land redistribution as a requirement of revolution. (Cf. Du Bois 1935; Trelease 1971).[24]

I now highlight the key features of Foner's and Ackerman's narratives, beginning with the commonalities. For both, the new legal status of the freedmen (as holders of equal civil and political rights) was a revolutionary achievement. Just a decade earlier, of course, blacks had been regarded as "so far inferior, that they had no rights which the white man was bound to respect."[25] The Republican vision of a robust national citizenship is also a revolutionary change,[26] as are changes in federalism. Republicans, as both scholars explain, provided new federal power to protect rights when states denied these rights. Federal intervention, however, was conditioned or predicated on state denial of rights, i.e. state action.[27] Even though original control over rights remained with the states (a characteristic of antebellum federalism), Foner and Ackerman both define the provision of federal oversight as revolutionary.[28]

Foner, indeed, reflects on the shortcomings of the post-revisionist narrative. The view of Reconstruction as conservative and continuous, he states, does not seem fully persuasive when one considers that "it took the nation fully a century to implement its most basic demands, while others are yet to be fulfilled" (Foner 1988: xxiii). The post-revisionist view, he emphasizes, misses the new beginning that Reconstruction launched. "Prodded by the demands of four million men and women just emerging from slavery, Americans made their first attempt to live up to the noble professions of their political creed—something few societies have ever done" (xxvii). Drawing an explicit parallel with the American Revolution, Foner explains that Reconstruction, too, "was an era when the foundations of public life were thrown open for discussion" (1988: 278).[29]

Changes in law mark the success of this new beginning, according to Foner. Reconstruction generated "enduring changes in the laws and Constitution that fundamentally altered federal–state relations and redefined the meaning of American citizenship" (1988: xxvi).[30] What emerged was a "national state possessing vastly expanded authority and a new set of purposes, including an unprecedented commitment to the ideal of a national citizenship whose equal rights belonged to all Americans regardless of race" (1988: xxvi). With this "radical departure" codified in law (1988: 278), the nation thus began its first experiment of interracial democracy. Foner's focus, then, is on the passage of new Amendments and laws, not their implementation.

For Ackerman, too, Reconstruction was a transformative and revolutionary moment in constitutional history (1998: 164, 207, 385, 393). Ackerman defines a revolution as "a successful effort to transform the governing principles and practices of a basic aspect of life through an act of collective and self-conscious mobilization" (Ackerman 1992: 5–6). Building a model of constitutional development in which "the People" accomplish dramatic, non-Article V upheavals, Ackerman presents Reconstruction as a period that witnessed a "revolutionary redefinition of nationhood" (1998: 238). The Republicans were the party of "revolutionary nationalism" (238), and the Thirteenth and Fourteenth Amendments were "both revolutionary reforms, committing the national government to intervene when the states trampled upon newly defined rights that adhered to Americans as Americans" (121). Laws on-the-books are thus central for Ackerman, as well.

Note Ackerman's view that both principles and practices transform in revolutions. As Ackerman states (1991: 207), revolutions are marked by "the triumphant construction of a political order by the revolutionary generation." The creation of "a new world of political meaning" (207) thus means "the construction of a novo ordo seclorum" (205).[31]

The transcendence of racism, by Republicans and "the People," is a critical part of Ackerman's narrative. Focusing on the "revolutionary commitment" of the Republicans "to equal freedom for all," Ackerman declares that Republicans "transcended" their racism (1998: 164).[32]

An overwhelming majority of white Americans—North as well as South—were racists. When Northerners emancipated slaves before the Civil War, it was on legal terms that emphasized their continuing inferiority; indeed, some Western states prohibited 'free' blacks from entering their borders. Only in the Northeast could black men vote. And yet Republicans were proposing to defy this pervasive prejudice. Not only did their Fourteenth Amendment guarantee all blacks the privileges and immunities of citizens of the United States; it gave them the right to break down borders by claiming citizenship in any state they wished. Not only did it require all states to provide equal protection of the laws; it reduced the Congressional representation of states that denied blacks the vote. To vindicate such revolutionary reforms, Republicans would have to persuade their fellow countrymen to transcend their racist impulses. The real surprise is not that they encountered resistance, but that they managed to win sustained popular support for such a radical challenge to entrenched political, legal, and social practices.

(1998: 164)

The popular transcendence of racism is central for Ackerman. Indeed, he hammers down the point: "This is the fundamental weakness in interpretations of the amendment that emphasize the pervasive racism of the time. The amendment stands as proof of the possibility that Americans can transcend their racist instincts in response to the ideal of equal citizenship" (1998: 164). The elections of 1866 and 1868, which returned strong wins for Republicans, are also evidence of this transcendence (1998:164). As key indicators of revolutionary success, these elections legitimate the Fourteenth Amendment (which, remember, was passed using irregular procedures). Ackerman thus posits a revolutionary Fourteenth Amendment that is legitimated by "the People" in an act of transcendence.

It is with this formulation—a revolutionary Fourteenth Amendment legitimated by the popular transcendence of racism—that I begin my analysis. An analytic difficulty lurks here. Ackerman needs popular transcendence to legitimate the revolution, just as he needs "the People." His assertion about transcendence, however, is self-validating. Here is what I mean: because he posits a revolutionary amendment, popular support for it must necessarily be transcendent.

There are two ways of exposing the analytical problem here. The first way is to show that there were conservative elements to the Fourteenth Amendment, e.g., the absence of protection for "social rights" and "social equality". If the Amendment contained conservative elements, (and it did), then evidence for a "transcendence of racism" gets muddy (more on this shortly).

The second way to expose the analytic problem is to show that the elections of 1866 and 1868 could mean a variety of things. Popular support for the

Fourteenth Amendment could have merely reflected the view that the Black Codes of 1865–6 were invalid and that formally equal laws were required. However, formal equality hardly qualifies as revolutionary change without the administration and enforcement of equal laws. Ackerman provides no evidence that the population was attentive to issues of administration and enforcement. Support for the Amendment could also be interpreted as a rebuke to President Andrew Johnson, who was perceived to be giving away the fruits of the war when he vetoed the Civil Rights bill of 1866. Finally, the meaning of "civil equality" evolved over the course of Reconstruction. Not until 1870–1, when Republicans began to address the problem of unpunished Klan violence, did they begin to articulate the view that civil equality required not just equal laws but the equal enforcement of laws (Zuckert 1986). How could the revolution have succeeded by 1868 if this meaning of civil equality was not yet generated, much less endorsed by the population?

All of this is to say that Ackerman paints with too broad a brush in claiming Republican and popular transcendence of racism. But let me take, in turn, the elements of Arendt's concept of revolution. This permits a systematic assessment of the revolution thesis, including Ackerman's formulation above.

We can begin by asking whether Reconstruction was an "entirely new story." Pertinent here is the recognition by both Foner and Ackerman that Reconstruction was not a total break. Indeed both writers take the position that a partial break might still constitute a revolution. Ackerman's narrative, for example, contains a mysterious distinction between total revolution and revolution. Stating that Reconstruction was not a "total revolution," which he defines as a root-and-branch repudiation that destroys the entire matrix of preexisting institutions (1998: 12), Ackerman distinguishes between total revolution and "revolutionary reform" (1991: 211). He does not explain, however, how much of the old matrix must be destroyed in order for a "moment" to count as revolutionary reform. The implicit distinction—between revolutionary reform and non-revolutionary reform—is nowhere defined.

Foner, too, notes that Reconstruction was not a complete break with principles of federalism. While Republicans aimed to provide national protection of basic rights, he notes that "[f]ew Republicans wished to break completely with principles of federalism. Only if state governments failed to protect citizens rights would federal action become necessary" (1988: 259). In light of comments like this, the absence of criteria to distinguish between revision and revolution is all the more noticeable.

So was Reconstruction a "new beginning"? The answer is surely yes when it comes to the status of blacks and the attempt to define a robust national citizenship. The provision of new federal oversight permits both answers (yes and no), as federal oversight was conditioned on state denial of rights; states retained original (but no longer exclusive) jurisdiction.

We can move on to a critical, two-part question: (1) Did the goal of freedom, as Arendt defines it, characterize the Civil Rights Act of 1866 and the Fourteenth Amendment, which both Foner and Ackerman define as revolutionary? (2) If the goal of freedom was later incorporated into Republican legislation, did Republicans establish stable and durable institutions? Recall that for Arendt, the institutional "consolidation" (152) of freedom is a requirement of revolution.

With regard to the first question, the goal of freedom was certainly held by black soldiers, black settlers in the Sea Islands, and black members of the biracial political coalition of 1867–8. The answer is more complex if one considers white Republicans, who acted on behalf of the freedmen and whose action was necessary for the passage of Reconstruction legislation. Central here is the post-Civil War concept of a hierarchy-of-rights, which distinguished among "civil rights," "political rights," and "social rights." To lay out these rights distinctions, it is useful to think in terms of realms of equality.[33]

During the post-war period, political and legal actors conceived of three realms of equality. These realms were organized hierarchically and each was associated with a type of rights (the hierarchy-of-rights). The realm of civil equality related to labor and economic life. This was the most basic realm and a core group of "civil rights" was considered fundamental to economic opportunity: property, contract, suing, testifying in court, and physical security. This small package of rights separated "free labor" from slave labor, and from the earliest days of Reconstruction centrist Republicans identified these rights as belonging to blacks on an equal basis (Hyman & Wiecek 1982). The nation's first civil rights law, the Civil Rights Act of 1866, protected black civil equality. After President Andrew Johnson vetoed the bill, outraged Republicans promptly and easily overrode the veto. The Moderate, or centrist, Republicans, it should be noted, held the balance of power in the Reconstruction Congresses. While the more radical Republicans were the visionaries in the party and consistently ahead of their centrist colleagues in supporting emancipation and black suffrage, the radicals were never able to secure consensus on their broader definition of "civil rights," which included access to public accommodations and integrated schools. Centrists had a more narrow definition of civil freedom, and it was limited to the rights protected in the Civil Rights Act of 1866.

If freedom consists mainly in the right to vote and equal political participation, as Arendt suggests, then the initial goals of the centrist Republicans, expressed in the Civil Rights Act of 1866 and the Fourteenth Amendment, cannot be described as revolutionary. Centrists did support extending to blacks the rights of free speech and free association/assembly, writing this guarantee into the Civil Rights Act of 1866 and the Fourteenth Amendment.[34] Because Arendt refers to these rights as part of political freedom, she perhaps would identify the centrists' initial goals as containing a revolutionary element. But for her, the continued denial of suffrage would loom large.

The promise of political freedom came with the Reconstruction Act of 1867, the Fifteenth Amendment, and powerful voting rights enforcement legislation such as the Ku Klux Klan Act of 1871. Republicans conceived of this lawmaking as protecting "political rights,"[35] and it resulted from a fusion of principle and pragmatism (Foner 1988; Wang 1997; Valelly 2004). Some immediate changes followed the passage of this legislation. In 1870, Hiram Revels of Mississippi became the first black man elected to the U.S. Senate—indeed, Democratic protests to his seating and Republican defenses of it offer a window on contemporary conceptions of race and political belonging (Primus 2006). In 1870, too, Joseph Hayne Rainey became the first black member of the House of Representatives. In 1871, the forty-second Congress included five black members in the House of Representatives.

The years 1871 to 1873 were the high-water mark for enforcement of the Klan Act (see Wang 1997: 300), but this enforcement was never consistent or predictable. The Klan trials of South Carolina in 1871 (Williams 1996) testified to the effectiveness of hard-fisted enforcement, but an economic panic occurred in 1873 and a depression set in for the rest of the decade. After this, more changes occurred as Democrats won big in the 1874 election and took control of the House of Representatives by a wide margin. This takeover had significant effects on Republican policy and criminal prosecutions under the Enforcement Acts. The 1874 election, indeed, marks the beginning of a two-decade stretch when national elections were decided by razor-thin margins (Silbey 1991) and when Republican use of sectionalism and black rights to build Southern Republicanism took on a pattern of vacillation. As Republicans tried multiple strategies for building the Southern wing of the party, only to be thwarted by Democratic fraud and violence, they kept returning (with some successes) to black rights (Hirshson 1962). Enforcement therefore was sporadic and uneven through the 1880s and spiked for one final time during the Republican administration of Benjamin Harrison (1888–92), when Republicans secured both the Congress and the Presidency for the first time since Reconstruction (see Valelly 2007 on this "policy window"). Enforcement stopped completely in the early 1890s after the failure of the Lodge Elections bill in 1892, the Republican party's political abandonment of blacks in the wake of this defeat, and the Democratic repeal of most voting rights laws in 1894 (Wang 1997; Valelly 2004; Calhoun 2005).

If the consistent and predictable enforcement of Reconstruction laws is defined as necessary for revolution, then a revolution did not happen during Reconstruction. Black subjects never "became the rulers themselves" at the national level. At the state level, political participation was highly uneven. Did blacks, then, achieve freedom in an Arendtian sense? No. Their efforts, and efforts on their behalf, failed.

It should be noted, at this point, that Ackerman does not adhere to his own definition of revolution, which requires the "construction of a novo ordo seclorum," i.e., a new political order (1991: 205). By any definition of political order (see, e.g., Shapiro & Hardin 1993), laws on-the-books are only one piece of a political order. So forget Arendt on the need for institutional consolidation. Ackerman cannot meet his own definition of revolution, which requires the successful transformation of principles *and practices.*

To return, finally, to Ackerman's claim that Republicans transcended racism, we can say that this is partly right but also partly wrong. Ackerman's broad-brushed assertions about the transcendence of racism obscures the complex character of centrist Republican racial beliefs, which were radical, conservative, and ambivalent all at once.[36] The transformation they were attempting was only a partial one, and the ideal of equal citizenship must be understood with reference to the tripartite rights hierarchy that was dominant at the time (i.e., not with reference to our own categories; indeed, Republican legislation looks like a full or complete transformation only when our own, broader notion of civil rights is taken for granted).

It was in the third realm of equality, the so-called "social" realm, where centrist Republicans (and black agency) reached their limits. This realm related to social life. While centrists were genuinely committed to securing blacks' equal rights to property, contract, and physical security, these Republicans also accepted the antebellum view that blacks were unfit for social interaction and social assimilation with whites. As noted earlier, they supported anti-miscegenation laws (Novkov 2006) and segregation in public schools.[37] They also rejected black claims to public accommodation rights.[38] Congress indeed passed a public accommodation statute in 1875 guaranteeing blacks "full and equal" enjoyment of inns, public theatres and the like, but these provisions have long been misinterpreted as a sign that centrists were committed to public accommodation rights. A lame duck Congress passed them after the devastating election of 1874 (which returned the House to Democratic control) and many Republicans perceived these provisions as a tribute to the radical abolitionist Charles Sumner, who had just died (Lofgren 1987). While the bill contained provisions protecting jury service rights that were later upheld by the Supreme Court, the public accommodation provisions were regarded as dead on arrival. The Moderate, or centrist, Republican racial outlook, in short, fit comfortably into neither the "transcendent" nor "racist" categories, qualifying more as a transitional or intermediate positioning (Brandwein 2007). In the minds of these white Republicans, then, the black image generated ambivalence.

The centrists' rejection of social rights, finally, marked the limits of black agency (black agency is at the center of Foner's narrative). Recall Michelman's rendering of the relationship between rights and agency in Arendt: "It's a condition of my having a right that I have, myself, contributed to the pro-duction of it, and that I cannot do this on my own, can't do it without membership, can't do it except as a correspondent and co-producer with others in a social group in which I have membership standing" (Michelman 1996: 205). While blacks gained partial recognition as "co-producers" through their soldiering and activism and thus gained civil and political rights, they could not overcome centrist Republican beliefs about black unfitness for social assimilation with whites, which carried over from the antebellum period. Black agency was thus partial; it could not overcome social exclusion. This denial of social equality, indeed, held important implications, which I examine in the next section.

To sum up so far, the tripartite division of rights during Reconstruction bears directly on assertions about the revolutionary character of the Civil Rights Act of 1866 and the Fourteenth Amendment, as well as assertions about Republican transcendence of white supremacist beliefs. The failure to consistently and predictably enforce Reconstruction era laws, however, is especially devastating to the revolution thesis. The Republican failure to consolidate their vision of equal civil and political rights institutionally forces the view of Reconstruction as a failed revolution. Republicans devised a new system of government, but they were unable to "impose upon men" this new plan.

"The social question" and desegregation

In 1957, a national drama unfolded in Little Rock, Arkansas. A federal court ordered the admission of nine black students to Central High School in Little Rock, prompting Arkansas Governor Orval E. Faubus to order the National Guard to bar their entrance. With this move, Faubus courted a showdown with President Dwight D. Eisenhower, who responded by federalizing the guardsmen. On September 4, the nine students entered Central High School under the protection of federal troops. An iconic photograph of Elizabeth Eckford, one of the nine, captured a white woman surrounded by a white mob hurling invectives at a steely Eckford.

This episode was the basis for a controversial essay by Arendt (1959), which earned her the condemnation of liberals.[39] In "Reflections on Little Rock," Arendt criticized the NAACP and the federal government for their efforts on behalf of school desegregation. The focus on desegregation was misplaced, according to Arendt, and at the heart of her criticism lay her conceptualization of three realms: the political, the social, and the private.[40]

This section identifies the stakes that attach to the post-Civil War hierarchy-of-rights concept, and more particularly, the centrist Republican rejection of social rights. A defining feature of "Reflections" is Arendt's belief that civil and political equality can co-exist with social discrimination. Centrist Republicans believed the same thing. By pointing to the criticism directed at "Reflections," my purpose is not to sign on to this criticism (though I do) but to consider whether the centrists' rejection of social rights jeopardized their project of advancing civil and political equality. Their project was threatened, and was indeed defeated, by more immediate things, that is, Democratic violence and fraud. But the viability of the centrist vision is nevertheless an important subject. If the centrists' rejection of social rights would have doomed their project for civil and political equality, then this is a much deeper reason for conceiving of Reconstruction as a failed revolution.

Let me first summarize Arendt's reasons for criticizing federally mandated desegregation. The place to start is her prioritization of the political realm, and this should come as no surprise at this point. Equality, she emphasized, was the principle of the body politic. "Only there are we all equals. Under modern conditions, this equality has its most important embodiment in the right to vote, according to which the judgment and opinion of the most exalted citizen are on a par with the judgment and opinion of the hardly literate" (1959: 50). The right to hold office was also an "inalienable right of every citizen" (50).

The private realm was located on the opposite side of Arendt's tripartite framework. "Here," she explained, "we choose those with whom we wish to spend our lives, personal friends and those we love" (52). These choices aim "inexplicably and unerringly, at one person in his uniqueness" (53). Government, in her view, must not only safeguard equality in the political realm. It must also "safeguard the rights of every person to do as he pleases within the four walls of his own home" (53). Arendt called these "rights of privacy" (55).[41]

In the middle was the social realm. Here, in her view discrimination—by custom, not by law—was permissible. "[E]ach time we leave the protective four walls of our private homes and cross over the threshold into the public world," stated Arendt, "we enter first, not the political realm of equality, but the social sphere. We are driven into this sphere by the need to earn a living . . . Once we have entered it, we become subject to the old adage of 'like attracts like' which controls the whole realm of society in the innumerable variety of its groups and associations" (51). While equality is the principle of the political realm, discrimination is the principle of the social realm.

Arendt argued that customary segregation in public schools was acceptable. The legal requirement of segregation, however, was not. According to Arendt, government must not legalize discrimination in the social sphere. "The moment social discrimination is legally enforced, it becomes persecution . . . It is not the social custom of segregation that is unconstitutional, but its legal enforcement" (53). Government, then, must neither legalize nor bar segregation in public schools. It must leave the matter to social custom and private choice.

Arendt also thought customary exclusions in vacation resorts and places of public amusement were perfectly acceptable:

> If as a Jew I wish to spend my vacations only in the company of Jews, I cannot see how anyone can reasonably prevent my doing so; just as I see no reason why other resorts should not cater to a clientele that wishes not to see Jews while on a holiday. There cannot be a "right to go into any hotel or recreation area or place of amusement," because many of these are in the realm of the purely social where the right to free association, and therefore to discrimination, has greater validity than the principle of equality.
>
> (52)

An immediate qualification, however, followed: "This does not apply to theaters and museums, where people obviously do not congregate for the purpose of associating with each other" (52). Another important qualification appeared later, when she stated that the principle of equality governed public transportation, and hotels and restaurants in business districts. Arendt explained, "we are dealing with services which, whether privately or publicly owned, are in fact public services that everyone needs in order to pursue his business and lead his life. Though not strictly in the political realm, such services are clearly in the public domain where all men are equal" (52).

Here, Arendt blurred the distinction between the political and the social. Regarding public schools (where one can imagine a similar blurring), Arendt acknowledged a political dimension. This political dimension, however, justified only compulsory education. Public schools, as she saw it, were located at the intersection of the private, social, and political realms. Parents had the right to educate their children as they wished, subject only to the requirement of compulsory education. Parents thus had association rights.[42] There were political considerations, i.e., government's concern to prepare children for citizenship,[43] but these could go no further than legitimizing the enactment of compulsory education laws.

For Arendt, then, the effort to integrate public schools forcibly was a mistake. Efforts in the political realm took priority. Though she supported a just, integrated society, the color question was "soluble only within the political . . . framework of the Republic" (46). Arendt thus opposed the prioritization of desegregation in public schools and predicted it would fail. As she saw it, after the Supreme Court issued *Brown v. Board of Education* (1954), "the general situation in the South has deteriorated" (48).

It would have been better, she implied, to challenge segregation in hotels and restaurants in business districts, which were part of the public domain and which were governed by the principle of equality.[44] "The most startling part of the whole business was the Federal decision to start integration in, of all places, the public schools" (50). Not only were schools at the juncture of the private, social, and political, the schools campaign burdened children.[45]

While much can be said (and has been said) about "Reflections," I want to use her essay for a particular purpose: to think about the viability of the centrist Republican vision of the polity, a vision that combined civil and political equality with a rejection of social equality. What did the centrists' investment in black social exclusion mean for their vision of civil and political freedom? This discussion opens a window on the transition from Reconstruction to Jim Crow.

The place to start is Arendt's view of the boundary between the political realm and the social realm. For her, these realms can be separated (though recall her qualifications on segregation in theaters, museums, and public accommodations in business districts).[46] Now, if these realms can be separated, and indeed if the political realm is privileged, what we can say about the centrist Republican vision of the polity? We can conclude that the centrists can achieve civil and political freedom for blacks while at the same time supporting the social custom of segregation and social exclusion. In other words, their vision of civil and political equality is viable, even if social rights are denied. However, if we question the separability of these realms as well as the privileging of the political, the centrist Republican vision of civil and political freedom for blacks under conditions of social exclusion becomes impossible. In other words, it can be argued that without social inclusion, the vision of civil and political freedom will fail. Centrist Republicans assumed they could achieve civil and political equality while denying social equality, but what if they were wrong? The work of legal scholar Charles Black suggests that they were indeed wrong.

For Black and many others, segregation embodied the intimate connection of the political and the social. For Black, segregation in public schools was part of a system that denied equal citizenship. "[I]f a whole race of people finds itself confined within a system which is set up and continued for the very purpose of keeping it in an inferior station, and if the question is then solemnly propounded whether such a race is being treated 'equally,' I think we ought to exercise one of the sovereign prerogatives of philosophers—that of laughter" (Black 1960: 424). In making the point that it was impossible to separate the social and political realms, Black pointed to the history and purpose of segregation: "Segregation in the South comes down in apostolic succession from slavery and the *Dred Scott* case. The South fought to keep slavery, and lost. Then it tried the Black Codes, and lost. Then it looked around for something else and found segregation. The movement for segregation was an integral part of the movement to maintain and further white supremacy" (1960: 424–5). The picture, Black emphasized, "is not of mutual separation . . . but of one in-group enjoying full normal communal life and one out-group that is barred from this life and forced into an interior life of its own" (425).

Charles Black pointed as well to extralegal patterns of discrimination where blacks were subject to "unwritten law" pertaining to "job opportunities, social intercourse, patterns of housing, going to the back door, being called by the first name, saying 'Sir,' and the rest of the whole sorry business" (1960: 425). Southern society "extralegally imposes on [blacks] every humiliating mark of low caste that until yesterday kept him in line by lynching" (426). Segregation, then, was a system, a complex of practices that comprise "a whole regional culture" (426). The prospect of political equality under these conditions is thus fanciful, as the out-group is also "barred from the common political life of the community" (425).

To be sure, Black was discussing segregation imposed by law.[47] He was also discussing the system of segregation that grew up in the 1890s and the first decade of the twentieth century. During Reconstruction, segregation replaced exclusion (Rabinowitz 2002). The Jim Crow regime came later (Van Woodward 1955). Nevertheless, the in-group, out-group dynamic identified by Black pertained during Reconstruction.

If Black is correct that the political and social realms cannot be separated in a segregation culture (and if Arendt errs in separating the two), is there any way to preserve the viability of the centrist Republican vision of the polity, despite their rejection of social rights? The key issue here is their view of the relationship among the economic, political, and social realms. What was the centrists' view of this relationship? Did they think that once blacks succeeded in the civil and political realms and gained recognition as "co-producers," they would advance irresistibly and inexorably up the ladder toward social rights and social equality? Or did centrists view these realms as permanently separate, with no necessary connection, so that social rights would be permanently withheld?

If centrist Republicans imagined no necessary connection between civil/ political rights and social rights, they imagined a polity where social caste (customary segregation in public transportation, public accommodations and public schools) could exist alongside political equality.[48] This returns us to the arguably impossible nature of their vision of the polity. But did they actually think this way? On this critical matter, the answer is unknown. The documentary record is simply unclear on their view of the relationship between civil and social rights. If centrists indeed imagined an inexorable and inevitable climb up the ladder, then movement toward social equality could save the possibility of achieving civil and political equality, i.e., save their vision.

Republican clarity on the relationship among these spheres of life emerges only later. The emergence of clarity, indeed, is an important feature of the political transition from Reconstruction to Jim Crow. In *Plessy v. Ferguson* (1896), Justice Henry Billings Brown gives a clear view of the relationship between civil and political rights on the one hand and social rights on the other. Grounding this distinction in "nature," Brown asserts that the civil and political realms are permanently separate from the social realm.

> The object of the amendment was undoubtedly to enforce the absolute equality of the two races before the law, but in the nature of things it could not have been intended to abolish distinctions based upon color, or to enforce social, as distinguished from political equality, or a commingling of the two races.[49]

> If the civil and political rights of both races be equal one cannot be inferior to the other civilly or politically. If one race be inferior to the other socially, the Constitution of the United States cannot put them upon the same plane.[50]

Justice Brown thus invoked hierarchy of rights categories, which remained part of the discourse, in order to assert the permanence of these distinctions and to justify Jim Crow segregation. But the meaning of these categories had changed: assertions of a permanent boundary were now present. This clear answer to the question about the relationship between the civil/political realm and the social realm replaced the uncertainty and ambiguity of earlier decades. Indeed, the fact that centrist Republicans during the Reconstruction era never clarified their view of the relationship between these realms is significant: this ambiguity bespeaks the transitional character of Reconstruction. Clarity emerged only during the 1890s, as the Jim Crow regime solidified. Justice

Brown, we must remember, was not a Reconstruction-era Republican. And as a general matter, the Waite Court (1874–1888) and the Fuller Court (1888–1910) took sharply different approaches on matters of civil rights (Benedict 1974). *Plessy*, in short, is representative of a new era.

Conclusion

Institutional change has been a subject that has vexed social scientists. As noted by Kathleen Thelen (2003: 208), "Despite the importance assigned by many scholars to the role of institutions in structuring political life, the issue of how these institutions are themselves shaped and reconfigured over time has not received the attention it is due." Institutional changes during Reconstruction have not generally vexed social scientists, but this is not because these changes are easily explained. It is because one of two views of Reconstruction has been too readily adopted: either the war permitted a revolution, which was followed naturally by counter-revolution (hence the easy revolution–counterrevolution narrative) or continuity reigned (hence the lack of change in the first place).

Arendt's concept of revolution disrupts both of these views and offers new ways of puzzling over institutional change—both political and racial—during the Reconstruction era. Reconstruction, I have suggested here, is best conceptualized as a failed revolution. When the matter turned from devising a new system of government to imposing it, there was failure: inadequate enforcement of Reconstruction legislation was followed by vacillation, decline, and finally in the 1890s, the political and judicial abandonment of blacks. I have also suggested that the centrist Republican vision of the polity was viable only insofar as the boundary between the civil/political realm and the social realm was conceived as permeable. The ambiguity of centrist Republicans on this matter is instructive and suggests not just uncertainty but genuine and substantial flux. After all, at the height of Reconstruction between 1866 and 1871, the centrist vision of civil and political equality looked possible. Indeed, it looked like a revolution in the making.

Notes

1 I would like to extend my deepest thanks to Julie Novkov for her steady encouragement and criticism. Writing under difficult conditions and experiencing both false starts and blind alleys, I was never quite sure a coherent piece would emerge. That a chapter is here is due to her midwifing. She is, of course, not responsible for any problems that remain, but I owe her a debt of gratitude for anything the chapter might get right. Thanks go, as well, to Douglas Dow, whose helpful comments and remarks improved the quality of the chapter.
2 See, e.g., Foner 1988, Ackerman 1998, Wills 1992, McPherson 1991, Kaczorowski 1986. Progressive era scholarship on Reconstruction also regards it as a radical period, but for different reasons. Viewing Reconstruction through an economic lens and the late nineteenth-century rise of Northern industrialists, Charles and Mary Beard (1939) coined the term "Second American Revolution" to describe a transfer in power from the South's planting aristocracy to Northern capitalists. The

Beards had little to say about emancipation and the transformed status of the freedmen, events that are central in the revolution narrative of today.

3 With the passage of the Fifteenth Amendment, which barred states from denying the right to vote on the basis of race, this biracial polity now included blacks as well as whites. The large number of Chinese immigrants on the west coast remained excluded from membership. While Congress included "aliens" in the 1874 revision of Reconstruction-era civil rights laws, the Naturalization Act of 1792 limited naturalized citizenship to "free white persons," which was interpreted to bar naturalization of the Chinese and other "yellow" races (Lopez 1996). Native Americans, too, were generally excluded from citizenship and voting. In 1884, the Supreme Court ruled in *Elk v. Wilkins* that Native Americans "were not a part of the people of the United States." While Congress could make citizens out of Native Americans and Native American tribes, it had not so acted with respect to Elk's tribe, and so Elk was not a citizen, even after the passage of the Fourteenth Amendment, and so Elk could not vote (112 U.S. 94). Mexicans living in California, Arizona, Texas, and New Mexico were given U.S. citizenship by the 1848 Treaty of Guadalupe-Hidalgo, which ended the Mexican-American war, but their voting was thwarted by English-literacy and property qualifications for voting, as well as violence and fraud.

4 See, e.g., Sen. Lot M. Morrill (Maine), 39th Cong., 1st sess., 570 (Feb. 1, 1866). For James A. Garfield, the country experienced a "gigantic revolution . . . a revolution of even wider scope than the Revolution of 1776." Quoted in Wang, 1997:140. The *Nation* called Reconstruction a "revolutionary period" (*Nation*, April 19, 1877, 230–1); The New York *Herald* referred to "the fiery ordeal of a mighty revolution," quoted in Foner 1988: 271.

5 Many of these scholars are law professors and legal historians, which should not be surprising as "[m]uch of the history of Reconstruction has been constitutional history" (Benedict 1999: 2019).

6 As I discuss below, Ackerman (1991, 1998) uses law-on-the-books plus the elections of 1866 and 1868 to assert that a transformation "happened." But it is also possible to use law-in-action and the elections of 1874 and 1876 to argue that little change occurred and that a revolution in black rights would have to await the Second Reconstruction. Constitutionalism does not map onto differences in how change is measured. For example, scholars on both sides of the revolution debate claim that law-on-the-books vindicates their view. On one side, see Ackerman (1991) and Curtis (1986). On the other side, see Fairman (1949) and Belz (1998).

7 These elements do not exhaust Arendt's concept of revolution, which also includes the idea of historical necessity, the role of compassion and solidarity, and secularization. I do not discuss these elements. I also do not discuss the element of violence. Arendt (1970) has written famously about the relationship among violence, power, and authority, arguing that violence must be distinguished from other forms of domination. As a result of the complexity that inheres in her concept of violence, a consideration of how it helps in recasting thinking about Reconstruction and revolution is beyond the scope of this chapter.

8 For Arendt, politics refers "to human beings acting—discoursing, persuading, deciding on specific deeds, doing them—in the public realm" (Young-Bruehl 2006: 83). This way of thinking about politics is "crucial to her effort to understand how human freedom is experienced and can be preserved" (Young-Bruehl 2006: 84). Yet another Arendtian concept, power, is present as well, as Arendt's way of thinking about politics emphasizes the power that people have when they come together as talking, promising, and acting beings. "Binding and promising, combining and covenanting are the means by which power [of the people] is kept in existence" (Arendt 1963: 174). On Arendt's concept of power, see Young-Bruehl 2006: 90–2.

9 Sherman issued Field Order No. 15 (January 16, 1865) in part at the urging of 20 black leaders (mostly ministers) of the Savannah, Georgia community. The Field Order, approved by Lincoln for a variety of reasons, redistributed roughly 400,000 acres of land in coastal South Carolina and Georgia to the freedmen. The order stated: "The islands from Charleston, [South Carolina], the abandoned rice fields along the rivers for thirty miles back from the sea, and the country bordering the St. Johns river, are reserved and set apart for the settlement of the Negroes now made free by the acts of war and the proclamation of the President of the United States." Sherman ordered Brig. Gen. Rufus Saxton to distribute to the head of each black family "not more than forty acres of tillable land," to police the land, and to ensure legal title of the land for the black settlers. In the fall of 1865, President Andrew Johnson ordered the land restored to the planters who originally owned it, over the objections of General Oliver O. Howard, head of the Bureau of Refugees, Freedmen, and Abandoned Land (the Freedmen's Bureau).

10 See, e.g., Skocpol (1979:171): "Revolutionary crises are not total breakdowns in history that suddenly make anything at all possible if only it is envisaged by willful revolutionaries! . . . For one thing, revolutionary crises have particular forms, and create specific concatenations of possibilities and impossibilities, according to how these crises are originally generated in given old regimes under given circumstances. Furthermore, although a revolutionary crisis does entail institutional breakdowns and class conflicts that quickly change the parameters of what is possible in the given society, many conditions—especially socioeconomic conditions— always 'carry over' from the old regime. These, too, create specific possibilities and impossibilities within which revolutionaries must operate. . . . And so do the given world historical and international contexts within which the entire revolutionary transformation occurs." This understanding is easily adaptable to include racial conflict and racial conditions.

11 In the historical literature, the scholars who assert the revolutionary character of Reconstruction are called revisionists, for they overthrew then-standard Dunning School interpretations of Reconstruction. While Dunning School interpretations condemned Reconstruction as a mistake, labeled blacks as unfit for freedom, and celebrated the Klan, revisionist historians celebrated Reconstruction, resuscitated the reputation of Radical Republicans, and hailed their equal rights program. See Du Bois (1935: 726) for an early critique of Dunning School history. "One fact and one alone," Du Bois stated, "explains the attitude of most recent writers toward Reconstruction; they cannot conceive of Negroes as men."

12 In the historical literature on Reconstruction, the historians who deny the revolutionary character of Reconstruction are called post-revisionists.

13 14 Stat. 27.

14 17 Stat. 13.

15 See Brandwein, *The Supreme Court, "State Action," and Civil Rights: Rethinking the Judicial Settlement of Reconstruction* (Cambridge University Press, forthcoming).

16 "At its heart, the multiple-traditions thesis holds that the definitive feature of American political culture is not its liberal, republican or "ascriptive Americanist" elements but, rather, [a] more complex pattern of apparently inconsistent combinations of the traditions, accompanied by recurring conflicts. Because standard accounts [of the American political tradition] neglect this pattern, they do not explore how and why Americans have tried to uphold aspects of all three of these heterogeneous traditions in combinations that are longer on political and psychological appeal than on intellectual coherency" (Smith 1993: 558).

17 *On Revolution* is a case study that accompanies *The Human Condition* (1958), where Arendt lays out a new and challenging theoretical lexicon, including the distinctions (among the political, social, and private) she invokes in her essay on

Little Rock. The books are guided, as Young-Bruehl (2006: 80) explains, by the same vision. It would be necessary to engage the earlier work to fully elaborate my claim about the distinctive entrance Arendt provides for thinking about Reconstruction and race.

18 Goldstone (2001) divides this literature into four generations, tracking the evolving definitions and theories of revolution. As Goldstone explains in his brief summary (2001: 140–2), the first two generations offered only "simple descriptive generalizations" and "analyses that rested on broad single factors such as 'modernization' or 'relative deprivation.' A flowering occurred in the third generation, which focused on the "great revolutions" of France (1789), Russia (1917) and China (1949) and which offered a structural, class-based understanding of revolutions. In her classic analysis, which capped this third generation, Skocpol defined revolutions as "rapid, basic transformations of a society's state and class structures . . . accompanied and in part carried through by class-based revolts from below" (Skocpol 1979: 4). Events of the 1970s through the 1990s spurred a fourth generation, which (1) applied the structural theory of revolution to many cases beyond the "great" social revolutions (2) extended analytic attention to the roles of agency, ideology and culture, and to contingency in the course and outcome of revolutions, and (3) combined insights from the literature on social movements and revolutions, as many features of revolution such as mass mobilization, ideological conflicts, and confrontation with authorities had been extensively studied in the social movements literature. Offering a contemporary definition that encompasses all generations, Goldstone (2001: 142) defines revolution as "an effort to transform the political institutions and the justifications for political authority in a society, accompanied by formal or informal mass mobilization and noninstitutionalized actions [such as mass demonstrations, protests, strikes, or violence] that undermine existing authorities."

19 Arendt uses a variety of expressions to denote this new beginning, such as the "absolutely new" (1963: 29), a "new form of government" (1963: 17), a "story never known or told before" (1963: 21), and an "entirely new era" (1963: 21).

20 As liberation is a condition of republican freedom, it is "frequently very difficult" to say where liberation ends and freedom begins. But the distinction holds according to Arendt because liberation could take place under a monarchy, though not a tyrannical one. Freedom, she explains, demands the constitution of a republic (25).

21 The United States, it should also be noted, had land. The Western frontier, despite the presence of Native Americans, was treated as an available supply of land. Regarded as America's safety valve, the western frontier was the source of America's confidence that it could escape European-style poverty and class stratification (Foner 1980).

22 Arendt wrote without referencing DuBois (1935), whose Reconstruction narrative began with this original crime and included the role of black labor in attempting to reconstruct the basis of democracy. DuBois also told of a "counter-revolution of property" (1935: 580–636) that defeated the attempt to build "a real democracy of industry for the masses of men" (580).

23 Revolutions run "a course" (Arendt 1963: 21, 30).

24 See, e.g., Cruden (1969: 161): "If freedom were to be meaningful and equality assured, then the federal government must assume physical protection of the black man, promote his welfare, and underwrite his independence by land distribution." See also Trelease 1971: 24, 27.

25 *Dred Scott v. Sandford*, 60 U.S. 393, 407 (1857).

26 In the secondary literature, see Benedict (1992: 789) ("the rhetoric of the debates suggested a vague but general belief that all Americans, white and black, had certain fundamental rights that had been violated in the interest of slavery and that should henceforth be secured against infringement"). See also Eric Foner (1988: 258)

("In establishing the primacy of a national citizenship whose common rights the states could not abridge, Republicans carried forward the state-building process born of the Civil War"). In the primary literature, see, e.g., *Congressional Globe*, 39th Cong. 1st Sess., p. 2542 ("There was a want hitherto, and there remains a want now, in the Constitution of our country, which the proposed [fourteenth] amendment will supply. What is that? It is the power . . . to protect by national law the privileges and immunities of all the citizens of the Republic and the inborn rights of every person within its jurisdiction" [Bingham]). See also the primary sources gathered by Foner 1988: 228–80.

27 See Zuckert (1986) for evidence that Republican Congressmen understood state action to include state failure to equally enforce the law. The question of federal enforcement of the Thirteenth Amendment is complex. The Thirteenth Amendment contained no state action limitation. However, the Civil Rights Act of 1866, passed to enforce the Thirteenth Amendment, contained the requirement that individual interference in black civil rights have "the color of law . . . or custom" before the federal government could intervene. The Act of 1866, in other words, contained a state action limitation on federal intervention. In the *Civil Rights Cases* (1883), the Supreme Court upheld the Act of 1866 as valid enforcement legislation under the Fourteenth Amendment.

28 Opponents of the revolution thesis (e.g., Benedict 1974) suggest that only original federal power over rights, i.e., federal power to protect rights regardless of state behavior/action, counts as a revolutionary change in federalism.

29 In discussing the Fifteenth Amendment, Foner also identifies stages of Reconstruction (1988: 277). McPherson's concept of revolution contains the notion of stages, as well. "By 1863 the Civil War had become a revolution of freedom for 4 million slaves. The antislavery crusade however had envisaged not just a negative freedom—the absence of chattelism—but a positive guarantee of equal protection of the laws to all men. Once freedom was won, most abolitionists were ready to proceed with the next step in the revolution—equality" (quoted in H.B.R. (1967: 106)).

30 Foner (1988: 244) identifies the Civil Rights Act of 1866 a "profound change in federal-state relations."

31 The phrase "Novus Ordo Seculorum" appears on the back of the U.S. dollar bill. According to a website maintained by the United States Bureau of Engraving and Printing, it means "a new order of the ages," standing for the new American era, beginning in 1776. http://www.moneyfactory.com/document.cfm/18/2041.

32 Robert Kaczorowksi, another proponent of the revolution thesis, agrees, stating "Congressional Republicans put aside racial prejudice" (1987: 52).

33 Tushnet (1987) identifies three realms of equality. On the tripartite typology as it relates to Supreme Court jurisprudence during the 1870s and 1880s, see Brandwein (2007).

34 See, generally Curtis 1986 and Amar 1998, who argue that the Fourteenth Amendment "incorporated" the Bill of Rights, i.e., applied the Bill of Rights to the states.

35 Recall that the realm of political equality related to political life, and political rights included voting, office holding, and sometimes jury service (though jury service was more frequently conceived as a "civil" right; jury service was unstable and slippery in the rights hierarchy). Political rights were seen as a privilege, granted (or not) by already existing members of the political community. After black suffrage was secured, voting moved (in uneven fashion) into the "civil rights" category.

36 A brief comment here is also in order regarding post-revisionist assertions about the non-revolutionary character of Reconstruction. In this literature, Republicans are presented as supporters of white supremacy with only weak commitments to the freedmen. But if this is true, the violent resistance of the Klan makes no sense. Why

would the Klan unleash such violence and terror if there was no threat from the Republicans? The threat to the white order was real, even if it was limited to the "civil" and "political" realms, and the Klan knew it. The "no revolution" thesis thus wipes out certain dimensions of Republican racial thought as well, but from the other direction.

37 Alexander Bickel (1955) famously explored the history of the Fourteenth Amendment as it pertained to racial segregation in public schools, concluding that segregation was perceived as legitimate (Cf. McConnell 1995).

38 See Hyman and Wiecek (1982: 395–6) and Tushnet (1987: 884–90). Though the Supreme Court decision, the *Civil Rights Cases* (1883) falls in the post-Reconstruction period, the refusal to identify public accommodation rights as part of the essence of "freedom" is unmistakable. "Congress did not assume under the authority given by the Thirteenth Amendment," stated Justice Joseph P. Bradley, "to adjust what may be called the social rights of men and races in the community; but only to declare and vindicate those fundamental rights which appertain to the essence of citizenship." According to Bradley, the Thirteenth Amendment, which barred slavery and involuntary servitude, permitted the exclusion of blacks from public accommodations. "It would be running the slavery argument into the ground to make it apply to every act of discrimination which a person may see fit to make as to the guests he will entertain, or as to the people he will take into his coach or cab or car, or admit to his concert or theatre, or deal with in other matters of intercourse or business" (109 U.S. at 24–5).

39 Appearing in the journal *Dissent* in 1959, the piece was originally written for *Commentary*, a then-liberal magazine. The essay provoked so much hostility among the editors that Arendt withdrew it. When her essay appeared in *Dissent*, it was followed by two comments. See Spitz (1959) and Tumin (1959).

40 She fully articulates these distinctions in *The Human Condition* (1958).

41 Anti-miscegenation laws violated the right of privacy. Stated Arendt, "The Civil Rights bill did not go far enough, for it left untouched the most outrageous law of Southern states," she wrote, "the law which makes mixed marriage a criminal offense" (1959: 49).

42 The same year "Reflections" appeared, Herbert Wechsler (1959) argued famously that segregation in public schools could be defended on the basis of freedom of association. "[W]here the state must practically choose between denying the association to those individuals who wish it or imposing it on those who would avoid it, is there a basis in neutral principles for holding that the Constitution demands that the claims for association should prevail? I should like to think there is, but I confess that I have not yet written the opinion."

43 The Supreme Court, of course, used this citizenship argument in *Brown v. Board of Education* (1954) to help justify the invalidation of legal segregation in public schools.

44 An equality-based justification for Title II of the Civil Rights Act of 1964 (which desegregated public accommodation) was blocked by the *Civil Rights Cases* (1883) and state action doctrine, or so proponents of this landmark legislation believed (Cortner 2001: 25). For practical reasons, then, proponents turned to the commerce clause to authorize this legislation.

45 "It certainly did not require too much imagination to see that this was to burden children, black and white, with the working out of a problem which adults for generations have confessed themselves unable to solve . . . Have we now come to the point where it is the children who are being asked to change or improve the world? And do we intend to have our political battles fought out in the school yards?" (1959: 50)

46 It is difficult to see where this qualification might end today, for what doesn't count as a business district these days?

47 "Our question is whether discrimination inheres in that segregation which is imposed by law in the twentieth century in certain specific states in the American Union" (1960: 427). He is not addressing what he calls the metaphysics of sociology (1960: 427): "Must Segregation Amount to Discrimination?"
48 An important difference between Arendt and the Moderate Republicans should be noted. Arendt puts labor/employment into the social realm. For Arendt, then, work is governed by the principle of discrimination. For Republicans, work is not in the social realm; it is in the "civil" realm. Civil rights, which are conceived as protecting "free labor," are fundamental for Republicans, and labor is governed by the principle of equality.
49 163 U.S. 537, 544.
50 163 U.S. 537, 551–2.

Bibliography

Primary sources

Cases cited

Brown v. Board of Education (1954) 347 U.S. 483.
Civil Rights Cases (1883) 109 U.S. 3.
Dred Scott v. Sandford (1857) 60 U.S. 393.
Elk v. Wilkins (1884) 112 U.S. 94.
Plessy v. Ferguson (1896) 163 U.S. 537.

Statutes cited

Civil Rights Act of 1866, 14 Stat. 27.
Ku Klux Klan Act of 1871, 17 Stat. 13.

References and secondary sources

Ackerman, B. (1991) *We the People: Foundations*, Cambridge, MA: Harvard University Press.
—— (1992) *The Future of Liberal Revolution*, New Haven, CT: Yale University Press.
—— (1998) *We the People: Transformations*, Cambridge, MA: Harvard University Press.
Amar, A.R. (1998) *The Bill of Rights: Creation and Reconstruction*, New Haven, CT: Yale University Press.
Arendt, H. (1958) *The Human Condition*, Chicago: University of Chicago Press.
—— (1959) "Reflections on Little Rock," *Dissent*, 6: 45–56.
—— (1963) *On Revolution*, New York: Viking Press.
—— (1970) *On Violence*, New York: Harcourt, Brace & World.
Beard, C. and Beard, M. (1939) *The Making of Civilization*, New York: Macmillan.
Belz, H. (1988) "Abraham Lincoln and American Constitutionalism," *Review of Politics*, 50: 169–97.
—— (1998) *Abraham Lincoln, Constitutionalism, and Equal Rights in the Civil War Era*, New York: Fordham University Press.

Benedict, M.L. (1974) "Preserving the Constitution: The Conservative Basis of Radical Reconstruction," *Journal of American History*, 61: 65–90.

—— (1992) "The Slaughterhouse Cases," in K.L. Hall (ed.) *The Oxford Companion to the Supreme Court*, New York: Oxford University Press.

—— (1999) "Constitutional History and Constitutional Theory: Reflections on Ackerman, Reconstruction, and the Transformation of the American Constitution," *Yale Law Journal*, 108: 2011–38.

Berger, R. (1977) *Government By Judiciary: The Transformation of the Fourteenth Amendment*, Cambridge, MA: Harvard University Press.

Bickel, A. (1955) "The Original Understanding and the Segregation Decision," *Harvard Law Review*, 69: 1–65.

Black, C.L. Jr. (1960) "The Lawfulness of the Segregation Decisions," *Yale Law Journal*, 69: 421–30.

Brandwein, P. (2007) "A Judicial Abandonment of Blacks? Rethinking the "State Action" Cases of the Waite Court," *Law & Society Review*, 41: 343–86.

—— (forthcoming) *The Supreme Court, State Action and Civil Rights: Rethinking the Supreme Court's Settlement of Reconstruction*, New York: Cambridge University Press.

Calhoun, C. (2005) *Benjamin Harrison*, New York: Henry Holt.

Cortner, R.C. (2001) *Civil Rights and Public Accommodations: The Heart of Atlanta and McClung Cases*, Lawrence: University Press of Kansas.

Cruden, R. (1969) *The Negro in Reconstruction*, Englewood Cliffs, NJ: Prentice-Hall.

Curtis, M.K. (1986) *No State Shall Abridge: The Fourteenth Amendment and the Bill of Rights*, Durham, NC: Duke University Press.

Du Bois, W.E.B. (1935) *Black Reconstruction in America, 1860–1880*, New York: Free Press.

Fairman, C. (1949) "Does the Fourteenth Amendment Incorporate the Bill of Rights?" *Stanford Law Review*, 2: 5–139.

Foner, E. (1988) *Reconstruction: America's Unfinished Revolution, 1863–1877*, New York: Free Press.

Goldstone, J.A. (2001) "Towards a Fourth Generation of Revolutionary Theory," *Annual Review of Political Science*, 4: 139–87.

H.B.R. (1967) "New Evidence on Issues of the Civil War and Reconstruction" review of Charles Crowe, (ed.), *The Age of Civil War and Reconstruction, 1830–1900: A Book of Interpretive Essays) Phylon*, 28: 102–8.

Hirshson, S. P. (1962) *Farewell to the Bloody Shirt: Northern Republicans and the Southern Negro, 1877–1963*, Chicago: Quadrangle Books.

Hyman, H.M. and Wiecek, W.M. (1982) *Equal Justice Under Law: Constitutional Development 1835–1875*, New York: Harper & Row.

Kaczorowski, R.J. (1986) "Revolutionary Constitutionalism in the Era of the Civil War and Reconstruction," *New York University Law Review*, 61: 863–941.

—— (1987) "To Begin the Nation Anew: Congress, Citizenship, and Civil Rights after the Civil War," *American Historical Review*, 92: 45–68.

Kelly, A.H. (1966) "Comment on Harold M. Hyman's Paper," in H.M. Hyman (ed.), *New Frontiers of the American Reconstruction*, Urbana: University of Illinois Press.

Litwack, L.F. (1979) *Been in the Storm So Long: The Aftermath of Slavery*, New York: Knopf.

Lofgren, C.A. (1987) *The Plessy Case: A Legal-historical Interpretation*, New York: Oxford University Press.

Lopez, I.H. (1996) *White by Law: The Legal Construction of Race*, New York: New York University Press.

McConnell, M. (1995) "Originalism and the Desegregation Decisions," *Virginia Law Review*, 81: 947–1140.

McPherson, J. (1988) "Reconstruction Reconsidered" (book review) *The Atlantic*, 261: 75–7.

—— (1991) *Abraham Lincoln and the Second American Revolution*, New York: Oxford University Press.

Meier, A. (1967) "Negroes in the First and Second Reconstructions of the South," *Civil War History*, 13: 114–30.

Michelman, F. (1996) "Parsing 'A Right to Have Rights,'" *Constellations*, 3: 200–8.

Nelson, W.E. (1988) *The Fourteenth Amendment: From Political Principle to Judicial Doctrine*, Cambridge, MA: Harvard University Press.

Novkov, J. (2006) "*Pace v. Alabama*: Interracial Love, the Marriage Contract, and the Postbellum Foundations of the Family," in R. Kahn and K. Kersch (eds) *The Supreme Court & American Political Development*, Lawrence: University Press of Kansas.

Paludan, P. (1975) *A Covenant With Death: The Constitution, Law, and Equality in the Civil War Era*, Urbana: University of Illinois Press.

Primus, R. (2006) "The Riddle of Hiram Revels," *Harvard Law Review*, 119: 1680–1734.

Rabinowitz, H.N. (2002) "From Exclusion to Segregation: Southern Race Relations, 1865–1890," in J.D. Smith (ed.) *When Did Southern Segregation Begin?* Boston, MA: Bedford Books.

Shapiro, I. and Hardin, R. (1993) *Political Order: Nomos XXXVIII*, New York: New York University Press.

Silbey, J.H. (1991) *The American Political Nation, 1838–1893*, Stanford, CA: Stanford University Press.

Skocpol, T. (1979) *States and Social Revolutions: A Comparative Analysis of France, Russia, and China*, New York: Cambridge University Press.

Smith, R.M. (1993) "Beyond Tocqueville, Myrdal and Hartz: The Multiple Traditions in America," *American Political Science Review*, 87: 549–666.

Spitz, D. (1959) "Politics and the Realms of Being," *Dissent*, 6: 56–65.

Thelen, K. (2003) "How Institutions Evolve: Insights from Comparative Historical Analysis," in J. Mahoney and D. Rueschemeyer (eds) *Comparative Historical Analysis in the Social Sciences*, New York: Cambridge University Press.

Trelease, A.W. (1971) *Reconstruction: The Great Experiment*, New York: Harper & Row.

Tumin, M. (1959) "Pie in the Sky," *Dissent*, 6: 65–71.

Tushnet, M. (1987) "The Politics of Equality in Constitutional Law: The Equal Protection Clause, Dr. Du Bois, and Charles Hamilton Houston," *Journal of American History*, 74: 884–903.

Valelly, R.M. (2004) *The Two Reconstructions: The Struggle for Black Enfranchisement*, Chicago: University of Chicago Press.

—— (2007) "Partisan Entrepreneurship and Policy Windows: George Frisbie Hoar and the 1890 Federal Elections Bill," in S. Skowronek and M. Glassman (eds) *Formative Acts: American Politics in the Making*, Philadelphia: University of Pennsylvania Press.

Wang, X. (1997) *The Trial of Democracy: Black Suffrage and Northern Republicans, 1860–1910*, Athens: University of Georgia Press.

Wechsler, H. (1959) "Toward Neutral Principles of Constitutional Law," *Harvard Law Review*, 73: 1–35.

Weir, M. (1992) "Ideas and the Politics of Bounded Innovation," in S. Steinmo, K. Thelen, and F. Longstreth (eds) *Structuring Politics: Historical Institutionalism in Comparative Analysis*, New York: Cambridge University Press.

Williams, L.F. (1996) *The Great South Carolina Ku Klux Klan Trials, 1871–1872*, Athens: University of Georgia Press.

Wills, G. (1992) *Lincoln at Gettysburg: The Words that Remade America*, New York: Simon & Schuster.

Woodward, C.V. (1955) *The Strange Career of Jim Crow*, New York: Oxford University Press.

—— (1979) "Review of *The Confederate Nation*," *New Republic*, March 17, 26.

Young-Bruehl, E. (2006) *Why Arendt Matters*, New Haven, CT: Yale University Press.

Zuckert, M.P. (1986) "Congressional Power Under the Fourteenth Amendment: The Original Understanding," *Constitutional Commentary* 3: 123–56.

7   Jim Crow reform and the democratization of the south

Kimberley S. Johnson

Introduction

In the decade or so before the *Brown v. Board of Education* (1954) decision, the South as well as the United States experienced broad social, economic, and political changes. By 1945, the American creed was in the ascendancy as exemplified by Gunnar Myrdal's best-selling *An American Dilemma* (1944). The democratic rhetoric of World War II sparked the beginning of a growing aversion to the South's crude racialism (Myrdal 1944) as part of the U.S.'s "democratic revival" (Sosna 2003). During the war, African Americans were buoyed by the "Double-V" campaign for democracy abroad and at home.[1] After the war, changing political configurations and America's growing engagement in the Cold War restructured and reordered the political objectives on the part of national Democratic leaders, and favored greater national involvement in civil rights issues.[2]

The South, as a result of New Deal policy and war production, benefited from a massive inflow of not only funds, but also of new people and new ideas. The economic stimulus of war jobs, as well as the continued mechanization of farming, hastened the shift of white and black southerners from farm to city, and from the South to points north and west. After the war, returning veterans (black and white) began to link their fight for democracy abroad to the limitations of southern government at home.[3] As a result of these broad macro-socio-economic processes, tentative national government action, and increasing African American mobilization, the modern civil rights movement emerged. Squeezed from forces outside of it, from above and below, the southern order collapsed and with it southern exceptionalism. The U.S.'s claim to be a modern liberal democracy was finally fulfilled.

This image of the white South undermined by broad macro-social processes and then overthrown by forces from above and below, or subject to the shifting fortunes of different racial orders, however, too quickly dismisses the role that the South itself played in shaping not only its responses, but also in forging its own path. Southerners, both white and black, did not simply wait for change to come to them, nor were they passive or minor actors within a larger cycle of change. The story of the struggle over the transformation of the South has largely been portrayed in cinematic terms, with forces of good arrayed against the forces of evil. Yet most struggles have elements of ambiguity, of compromise, and of uncertainty.

This chapter explores the role of southern reformers in the democratization of the South by looking at the anti-poll tax movement of the 1930s and 1940s. By returning to this largely forgotten moment in southern politics, we can trace how ideas such as "democracy" and "citizenship," which were important to the New Deal but central to the wartime rhetoric of World War II and the Cold War, were given new meaning and interpretations by southerners. These meanings were shaped in part by the commitments and aims of what I call the Jim Crow order, but also by southern reformers' new understandings of these ideas.

Most accounts of this campaign have focused on the unsuccessful national efforts to enact federal law. This focus on the national campaign ignores the success of poll tax reform in the southern states during this same period. The ability of state-level reform to succeed where national-level action failed shows how the South attempted to reconcile demands for greater democracy against a defense of white supremacy. Poll tax reform demonstrated the potential power and limitations of those trying to reform the southern order.

At the national level, the campaign for anti-poll tax legislation that began in 1938 constituted the first discussion of America's democratic commitments since the end of Reconstruction. Debates over the poll tax bill were the first congressional debates over elections in the South since the defeat of the Lodge Force bill in 1891. In the South, at the state level, poll tax repeal or reform was the site for the first relatively widespread discussion of democracy since the ascendancy of the Jim Crow order. The anti-poll tax campaign also built the first broad-based (though not mass) civil rights coalition in the post-Reconstruction era. Unlike efforts to enact a federal anti-lynching bill, the debate over the poll tax touched on some of the core questions that concern all orders: Who comprised the members of this order? Who had the power to decide what interests and voices were heard? Southern reformers played an important role in this process of shaping and defining the Jim Crow order through a campaign to democratize the South, albeit for whites only. The consequence of this whites-only democratization has implications for linking southern politics and the civil rights movement to broader theories of American political development.

The Jim Crow order

Racial illiberalism, or white supremacy, has been influential, though in varying intensities, across much of the history of the U.S (Smith 1993; chapter 4 of this volume). Supremacy was, however, most thoroughly institutionalized in the South, first through slavery and then in the post-Reconstruction settlement. Differences between the South and everywhere else were not simply a matter of degree; in many respects the form of supremacy itself fundamentally differed. While outside of the South white supremacy had social as well as some legal bases, in the South white supremacy was a particular legal-socioeconomic-political-historical-cultural-ideological manifestation that did not exist anywhere else.

From 1877 to 1964, federalism and national party politics allowed the South to create a political order comprised of a "constellation of rules, institutions, practices, and ideas that [hung] together over time, a bundle of patterns . . . exhibiting coherence and predictability while other things change[d] around them" (Orren and Skowronek 2004: 14–15). The South's post-Civil War political order was a racial institutional order based upon a "complex system of myths, authority, law, statecraft, prejudice, domination, and psychopathology" that arose out of a particular set of political, economic, and social circumstances (Shabazz 2004: 10).[4] While white southerners may or may not have embraced ascriptive inequality or white supremacy any more or less than other white Americans, the differences in southern politics wrought by the American federal system gave the white supremacist order located there an enduring (with the exception of the ten-year Reconstruction interregnum) political and institutional base from which to affect national politics.[5] Calling the white supremacist order of the South that existed from 1877 to 1964 a Jim Crow order locates this particular racial order both in time and in space.

Under the southern Jim Crow order, by 1910 the political exclusion and economic subordination of African Americans was near total. By sharp and significant contrast, the North (as well as many other parts of the United States) still practiced a key tenet of what Rogers Smith has called the "transformative egalitarian order." This order established by Civil War amendments, created near equal political inclusion via universal suffrage for male citizens, whether white or African American. By 1920, with the ratification of the Nineteenth Amendment, this inclusion would extend to all female citizens as well. Through migration elsewhere, but especially to the North, African Americans gained access to this politically inclusive order.

By the New Deal, the growing political inclusion of African Americans in the urban North enabled them in part to change the political configurations of national politics and especially of the Democratic Party. Regionalism (and federalism) grounded changes in political and institutional configurations (Moon 1948; Frymer 1999; McMahon 2004; Valelly 2004). This new configuration is striking and meaningful because it developed alongside of, and in growing conflict with, the opposing Jim Crow order, which was itself engaged in the process of order maintenance.

Claiming that regional difference must be recognized does not necessarily incorporate claims of southern universalism or uniformity. As both C. Vann Woodward and V.O. Key forcefully noted, there were multiple accommodations to the Jim Crow order and multiple "Souths" (Woodward 1974; Key 1984 [1949]). This chapter explores precisely these differences within the South and within the Jim Crow order. The Jim Crow order, like other regimes or orders, constantly had to refine, rearticulate, and adapt the (racial) concepts, commitments, and aims it had adopted in order to sustain itself. To maintain this order and bind together the coalition that sustained it, old commitments would have to be solidified while new arrangements developed to draw in new members to the coalition, or at least quell challenges to the order.

The consolidation of the Jim Crow order in 1910 only began a process of engaging the South in regime maintenance. By the 1930s and 1940s the problem of regime maintenance became more transparent as the Jim Crow order was increasingly subjected not only to external challenges, but also to internal ones caused by the different layers of discordant and sometimes conflicting commitments, aims, and understandings that underlay the main-tenance of the order's legitimacy and power. "Jim Crow reform" was one result of this process of regime maintenance.

Jim Crow reform was a multi-faceted attempt to reshape and reform the Jim Crow order from within. Although a number of reforms were proposed during this period, three were inextricably linked together: political enfran-chisement, economic opportunity and growth, and government reform and modernization. In a break with earlier southern Progressive Era reformers, these reforms were increasingly seen and defined as complementary (Tindall 1963; Hackney 1969; Link 1992). Yet these reformers were by definition not revolutionaries. They accepted, for a variety of reasons, the boundaries of the Jim Crow order. They did not seek to eliminate the order; they simply wanted to perfect it.

For some Jim Crow reformers, expanding the white (and in a limited way the black) southern electorate would loosen the hold of southern elites and empower what V.O. Key called the South's "have-nots." Increasing economic opportunity for all, but especially for southern whites, would blunt the economic competition and anxiety that elites had stoked between whites and blacks in order to maintain their hold on power. Southern white reformers hoped that by offering limited political inclusion and greater economic opportunity to blacks, they could head off what they perceived as a growing assertiveness among southern blacks. They perceived this assertiveness as aggravating the anger and discontent of lower-class whites, whom these largely elite reformers both feared and disdained. Southern blacks would also benefit somewhat from these reforms. For southern black reformers, increased access to formal political inclusion and greater economic opportunity could allow them to wrest more resources and opportunities for individuals and institu-tions within the African American community. Finally, reforming government would decrease the informal power of elites, while establishing and enhancing the institutional power of the states, and not so coincidentally, the power of the reformers who pushed for these changes. Governing would be based on rules and regulations, not on personal ties and "courthouse gangs." In short, the South could only leave the shackles of the past by embracing both democratization and modernization (González and King 2004: 193–210). Southern reformers were prepared to lead the way.

Jim Crow reformers

Jim Crow reform emerged from a variety of institutional sources: interracial organizations, southern universities, religious organizations, women's groups, and civic groups. Participants in these groups ranged over the professions. Many of the most prominent were journalists, others were academics or lawyers; some were members of the clergy, while a few were civic-minded businessmen. Although southern reformers crossed professions and were both white and black, they comprised a small, educated elite. They embraced the strong belief in the South that managed race relations were best left to the "better classes" of both races (Smith 2002). Although individuals often advanced a reform agenda through their own positions, the institutional sources of southern reform were heavily reliant on aid from non-southern foundations, or from state support (in the case of southern state universities).

Although these individuals and groups have been typically categorized as "southern liberals," a better way to categorize them is under the rubric of southern liberal reform. First, southern liberalism has typically been identified with a small sub-set of whites, and has tended to ignore southern blacks who also played an important role during this period. Second, the label of "liberalism" in the context of the Jim Crow order obscures more than it explains. "Liberal" does not capture one of the essential qualities of this period, which is that reformers, for a variety of reasons, accepted the boundaries of the Jim Crow order and worked for change within this order.

The consolidation of the Jim Crow order by the early twentieth century had created two separate racial worlds. Those who openly questioned this order had been excised from white southern society: some critics left the South, while others simply went silent.[6] In the new Jim Crow order, whites and blacks operated on a set of mutually understood norms, violations of which were quickly and sometimes savagely policed. Yet not all southerners (black and white) were content with these closed worlds. By the 1920s, with the Jim Crow order secure and indeed seeming to be an immutable fact of life, young southerners began to cautiously question the tenets of this order.

Reformers pushed for "sane and sensible" solutions to the shortcomings of the Jim Crow order. Not all of this support for reform was grounded in a sense of morality or paternalism. Pragmatism drove much of it. Reducing the frictions Jim Crow caused was essential for keeping social peace and encouraging economic development. Reformers relied on what they called "interracialism:" cooperation and communication between the races through education, through appeals to religious sentiment, and by the leadership of the better classes of both groups. While the violence of the post-Word War I period influenced both white and black reformers, white reformers in particular were shaped by the dominant, conservative, Dunning School historical interpretation of the Reconstruction Era. These memories produced a group focused on averting what they saw as an ever-present threat of violence and instability.

Despite this emphasis on order and stability, southern liberal reform lent "encouragement to the timid" and "unshackle[d] the large number of potential liberals who could not face the prospect of isolation and martyrdom in the community for holding more progressive ideas" (Bunche 1973: 39). In addition to creating a small window for individuals who dared to dissent from parts of the Jim Crow order, the rise of organizations gave reformers a "sense of solidarity and contact with each other" (42; see also Myrdal 1944: 466–74, 842–50). Thus, even though these reformers were bounded by the limits of the Jim Crow order, their valuable efforts opened up the South's ideological and discursive space.

Journalists and the papers they edited or owned played an important role in opening up this space. During this period, they offered an alternative, less reactionary view of southern life and fostered a dialogue (however indirect) between the white and black worlds. Although many scholars have considered white journalists such as Virginius Dabney of the Richmond *Times-Dispatch*, John Temple Graves of the Birmingham *Age-Herald*, and Ralph McDaniel of the *Atlanta Constitution*, few have attended to the role played by African American journalists in shaping southern reform, such as P.B. Young, editor and publisher of the *Journal and Guide* (Norfolk, VA) and Carter Wesley, editor and publisher of the *Houston Informer, Dallas Express*, and the *New Orleans Sentinel* (Suggs 1988; see also Shabazz 2004).

Organized Jim Crow reform had its roots in the World War I outbreak of violence against African Americans. The Committee on Interracial Cooperation (CIC) was founded in 1919 to bring together these separate worlds and through a process of elite leadership, education, and persuasion ease the "maladjustments" between the white and black worlds (Ellis 1976; Sosna 1977; Pilkington 1985; McDonough 1993). By the late 1920s, the CIC had engaged in the broad campaign against lynching. The anti-lynching campaign reflected the conflicted and at times reactive nature of southern reform. Pressure at the national level in terms of anti-lynching bills and the efforts of African American activists such as Ida Wells-Barnett put pressure on a South eager to portray itself as a peaceful region open for investment. The means by which southern reformers pressed the South to address the lynching issue reflected the limits of the period and of Jim Crow reform.

The campaign against lynching rested partly on paternalism towards blacks and an appeal to southern "chivalry" by southern white women. Lynching not only betrayed the caretaker role that whites held over blacks, the act was also a misplaced display of protection toward southern women. Thus while pressure from above may have influenced (mostly elite) white southerners' attitudes towards lynching, more influential were southern reformers whose framing of the issue allowed these elites to develop their own justifications for opposing lynching. At the same time this approach was followed, reformers also developed a new approach based in their Progressive faith in science and expertise. They believed that a sober, objective, fact-based analysis of lynching would be more effective in changing white southern attitudes than appeals to sentiment.

The result of this approach was a landmark study of lynching that the CIC sponsored, *The Tragedy of Lynching*, written by Arthur Raper.[7]

The role of southern women in the southern anti-lynching campaign highlights the active role that women's groups played in shaping southern reform. An important regional women's group was the CIC adjunct, the Association of Southern Women for the Prevention of Lynching. Other groups included state and local chapters of national organizations such as the League of Women Voters, the Business and Professional Women's Clubs, and the Association of American University Women. Within each state, a host of both white and black local women's organizations pushed for a wide variety of reform issues (Gordon 1991; Frederickson 1993).

Southern universities were an important home, as well as source, of southern reform. Most notable of these university sites was the University of North Carolina home of Howard Odum, one of the South's leading social scientists. North Carolina would also serve as the platform for its president Frank Porter Graham. Graham, who would become the state's U.S. Senator and one of the last of the South's New Deal liberals, would be defeated in the wave of reaction that began to sweep the South in 1950. Although the University of North Carolina would play a preeminent role in this movement, the overall upgrading of southern universities and colleges that had occurred during the 1920s had produced a pool of individuals by the 1930s and 1940s who sympathized with the aims of southern reform (Dennis 2001).

For southern black universities and colleges, the picture was less bright. Most African American institutions remained absolutely unequal to white ones.[8] Despite this inequality, like their white counterparts these institutions hosted a number of southern reformers such as Benjamin Mays, president of Morehouse College; Horace Mann Bond, president of Fort Valley State College; Gordon Hancock, President of Virginia Union College; and academics such as Luther Porter Jackson of Virginia College for Negroes. With northern foundation money, from 1931 to 1938 Hancock created and ran the Torrance School of Race Relations, the first of its kind (Gavins 1974: 216). In particular, Fisk University played an important organizational role in southern reform though the leadership of its president, Charles Johnson.[9]

Like their white counterparts, these black academicians were neo-Progressives as they believed that the race problem could be "scientifically analyzed" as a "social problem, that as such, [was] not essentially different form any other social problem . . . and by reason of this fact . . . respond[ed] to the same processes of adjustment or maladjustment" (Gavins 1974: 217–8). Yet what distinguished Johnson and other African Americans like him from their predecessors is that they viewed the Jim Crow order through a pragmatic rather than fully accommodationist lens. As pragmatic accommodationists, they saw their actions as a "middle ground" between the "old politics [of Washington] and the new, between the timid politics of indirection and the undisguised use and organization [of African-American political resources]" (Weare 1973: 212–13). Thus, if separate and equal was the law of the land, then they argued the South must live up to its obligations to generate equality. Not only was this important for moral reasons, but also for practical social and economic ones as well. Employing the planning rhetoric of the New Deal, these black reformers argued that the South could not advance if a significant portion of its "human resources" (i.e., African Americans) remained underdeveloped, and they noted the potential for social instability as a result of this under-development.

By the late New Deal, while Jim Crow reform looked remarkably different in terms of individual participation and organizational form from the 1920s, it did not stray far from its essential limitation. It remained bounded reform, aiming to reconcile and smooth over the stresses and strains within the disparate elements of the Jim Crow order and between the Jim Crow order and other existing orders within the American state. It did not directly challenge that order, although individual members of the reform movement may have wished to do so. The campaign for southern democracy reflected both the strengths as well as the fundamental weaknesses of Jim Crow reform.

The New Deal and Jim Crow reform

The New Deal expanded the horizons of individual southerners and stimulated the formation of new groups who worked with established southern reform groups. A number of southern reformers such as Will Alexander and Jonathan Daniels would become members of the Roosevelt administration (Dykman and Stokely 1962; Eagles 1982). By 1938, with the publication of the National Resource Council's *Report on Economic Conditions in the South*, the southern New Dealers had a template for action. The Southern Policy Committee was set up in Washington DC to focus more attention on the South. The group included southerners such as Clifford Durr and Brooks Hays.[10] This group spawned a number of others at the state level in Arkansas, Alabama, Georgia, and Virginia. The reports issued by these groups on issues such as voting and administrative or economic reform were important in opening up the policy discourse in these states. More concretely, as a result of New Deal policies, southern reformers could develop more permanent bases within state government.

While Jim Crow reform during the New Deal was, as before, still shaped by the desire to avoid issues of race and to avert what they foresaw as an ever-present threat of racial violence, economic liberalism now drove it powerfully. Southern New Dealers perceived the South's problems as fundamentally economic in nature. Once these problems were solved, so too would be other problems (e.g., the race problem).[11] According to Supreme Court Justice Hugo Black, one of the most visible of these southern reformers, "the core of the problem is economic," solve those problems and the "race problem will work itself out" (Bunche 1973: 386). Yet Black's economic liberalism was still tinged by the reformers' overall elitism; they believed that neither blacks nor average whites were ready to "vote intelligently," making them "ready game for corrupt and demagogic politicians." Southern elites, including reformers, still feared undiluted democracy.

By the end of the New Deal, Jim Crow reformers uneasily straddled the increasing divisions between traditional southern Democrats and the national Democratic Party organization. The first clear strain occurred in 1936 when the party at its National Convention voted to abolish the two-thirds rule for nominating candidates in favor of a simple majority vote. The two-thirds rule had been used by the South to ensure that Democratic candidates would be beholden to southern interests. Coupled with this rule change, were the growing criticisms from liberal Democrats that the South's "rotten districts" exercised disproportionate power over national policymaking (Rowan 1940). Some activists suggested threatening the South with actually enforcing the punitive provisions of the Fourteenth Amendment, which in its text reduced a state's representation by the proportion of citizens over 21 that were denied the right to vote in federal elections. Enforcement would take the South's representation in the House from 69 to 9 members (National Committee to Abolish the Poll Tax 1943).

These kinds of threats offered southern reformers a two-pronged opportunity. First, southern reformers would argue that southern leadership had to expand the southern (white) electorate in order for southern Democrats to continue to influence the Democratic Party. Second, by expanding the electorate to the South's (white) "have-nots," southern reformers hoped to create an important new source of support for southern politicians loyal to the New Deal. Protecting the New Deal meant the protection of the economic liberalism that would modernize the South. By the late 1930s, southern reformers realized that a small dose of democratization was needed now, rather than later, in order to achieve this goal.[12]

Poll taxes and Southern politics

In the post-Reconstruction era, the poll tax emerged in the South as one of the elements used by whites to secure the Jim Crow order (Ogden 1958; Lewinson 1963 [1932]; Kousser 1974; Woodward 1974; Lawson 1976; Key 1984: 578–618). Along with other disenfranchising techniques such as literacy tests and understanding clauses, the poll tax was designed to evade the reach of the Fifteenth Amendment and any other federal intervention. In the aftermath of the political upheaval of Populism in the late 1890s, the poll tax also became one of the key instruments that southern political elites used to decrease if not entirely negate the influence of lower-class whites on southern politics. For southern political elites, support for the poll tax was first and foremost an important rhetorical device used to uphold white supremacy by creating solidarity across (white) class lines. Despite this solidarity with lower class whites, the poll tax was also seen by elites as a way to purify southern politics of the influences of these lower classes of people, and to ensure only the participation of the "better elements."

By 1908, all of the southern states had enacted a poll tax (see table 7.1). Poll taxes, along with the white primary, were crucial for securing and maintaining political power for the southern political and business elite. For poor whites, the poll tax symbolized their privileged white standing (Feldman 2004). These privileges notwithstanding, by the 1930s, as a result of the poll tax, scholars estimate that white electoral participation had dropped to less than a third of the total white voting age population.

The effect of this diminished electorate was the creation of a small political and economic elite that perpetuated its power at both the national and state levels to protect the political and economic interests of the Jim Crow order. By the middle of the 1930s, southern members of Congress who had initially welcomed the material benefits of the New Deal became increasingly alarmed at the economic and social upheavals these benefits posed to the Jim Crow order. Increasingly they turned against Roosevelt and the New Deal, blocking the enactment of important legislation (Katznelson et al. 1993; Brinkley 1995).

In 1938, Roosevelt dramatically signaled his frustration with the South with his open support of attempts to unseat incumbent southern Democrats, and his support for abolishing the poll tax. This new, and as it turned out temporary, national stance against the South encouraged the formation of a new group, the Southern Conference on Human Welfare (SCHW). The SCHW for the first time brought together groups who had rarely found common ground with each other, from traditional southern reformers to groups such as the CIO. Unlike the CIC, the SCHW was willing to publicly challenge the Jim Crow social order, most famously by ignoring segregation ordinances in its meeting. Aided by its link to FDR via the participation of Eleanor Roosevelt, the SCHW became one of the first southern groups to press openly for

Table 7.1 Poll tax in the South

State	Poll tax enacted	Rate	Cumulative	Poll tax Reform/Abolish
Alabama	1901	$1.50	To $36.00	1944 (R); 1953 (R)
Arkansas	1893	$1		1938(A)*; 1941 (R); 1949 (R); 1956 (A)*
Florida	1889	$1	To $2	1937 (A)
Georgia	1908		To $47	1945 (A)
Louisiana	1898	$1	To $2	1934 (A)
Mississippi	1890	$2	To $4	
North Carolina	1900	$1.43		1920 (A)
South Carolina	1895	$1		1951 (A)
Tennessee	1890	$1		1943 (A)*; 1949 (R); 1951 (A)
Texas	1902	$1.50		1949 (A)*
Virginia	1902	$1.50	To $4.50	1949 (A)*

Notes: $1(1940) = $14.49 (2006). A= Abolish; R=Reform; * = Failed to Pass

poll tax reform. Despite being more democratic and inclusive, the SCHW's argument for poll tax reform still rested on the basis of economic liberalism (Krueger 1967; Klibaner 1989; Reed 1991).

White (both southern and northern) supporters would make and emphasize the following non-racial arguments about the need for poll tax reform. First, far from purifying southern politics from corruption, the poll tax largely contributed to growing corruption. Critics cited repeated instances of the buying and manipulation of votes through the payment of poll taxes (e.g. Dabney 1939; Stoney 1940). The second argument that reformers offered against the poll tax was its anti-democratic tendencies. The abolition of the poll tax would upend the notion that southern government belonged to the "better classes of people," and out of the hands of "corrupt, the illiterate, the ignorant, the disinterested, and the trifling" (Strong 1944: 697–8).[13] Democracy should be for the masses (of whites), not a small and corrupt elite.

Although African Americans did not approach poll tax reform with the same ardor as white reformers, poll tax reform was not unimportant to them. Poll tax reform mattered to African Americans on several levels. For example, as the Chicago Defender argued, poll tax reform would "hasten the advent of certain white progressives to power . . . [who would] implement state laws as to usher in a new era of justice and quality to a mass of inarticulate whites and Negroes" (Lawson 1976: 55). Poll tax reform was unlikely to happen through congressional legislation or judicial decision; nevertheless, a victory in one of these arenas would provide a valuable tool in the overall fight for African American political rights by establishing a precedent, for the first time since Reconstruction, for federal intervention into southern political institutions.

Of all the aspects of the Jim Crow order, in retrospect it is not surprising that the poll tax emerged as the key organizing issue around which southern white reformers coalesced, and which southern black reformers would support in a limited way. As white supporters of poll tax reform would repeatedly argue, the poll tax affected more whites than blacks. Thus, although some blacks would benefit from the abolition or liberalization of the poll tax, southern white reformers repeatedly emphasized that all whites, in an absolute sense, would benefit from ending the poll tax. For black reformers, given the boundaries of the Jim Crow order, poll tax reform "as such represents progress" (Brewer 1944: 299). For Jim Crow reformers, given their boundaries, the poll tax issue was the "ideal meeting point" for reconciling Jim Crow with the rest of the United States (Bunche 1973: 210).

In 1939, Rep. Lee Geyer (D-CA) introduced a poll tax reform bill (H.R. 7534) in the House. Although the bill went nowhere, it spurred further national level organizing around the issue. In 1941, Sen. Claude Pepper of Florida, one of the last staunch southern New Dealers, introduced another poll tax bill, the Geyer-Pepper bill (S. 1280). This attempt to enact poll tax reform in Congress was successful in the House, passing on a 254 to 84 vote. The bill, however, was filibustered by southern senators. Although Roosevelt had raised the issue of poll tax reform in his brief attack against southern Democrats,

Roosevelt declined to expend any more political capital on the issue. Now mustering limited presidential support, poll tax reform was also thwarted by the perception that it was not only an intra-party dispute, but also fundamentally only a southern issue.

Although poll tax reform ran into the implacable opposition of southern members of Congress, state-level campaigns for abolishing or reforming the poll tax were initiated or reenergized. The most visible of this New Deal-inspired reform was in Florida where Sen. Claude Pepper led efforts to repeal the state's tax in 1937. In Arkansas, a coalition of forces managed to get a referendum on the ballot in 1938 to abolish the poll tax. Roosevelt's open support for poll tax reform, however, was cited as one of the reasons that the referendum failed. Although Louisiana's repeal of the poll tax occurred under different political conditions, southern reformers gave qualified approval to the reform as it demonstrated how New Deal economic liberalism could be supported. By 1940, four of the eleven southern states had abolished the poll tax, enacted limited reform, or held a state constitutional referendum on the tax (see table 7.1).

Nonetheless, despite these state reforms, the poll tax issue seemed to be headed in the same direction as efforts to pass a federal anti-lynching law: a regional and racial issue had merited sympathetic hearing, but not any significant political support, from other political actors (Rable 1985: 201–20). Indeed a brief and not very in-depth overview of poll tax legislation at the national level reveals a familiar pattern to American reformers: an attentive House passes legislation over a period of years, largely for symbolic reasons but then the Senate, usually at the behest of a small group of opponents, continually stymies this legislation until the issue loses its potency and energy and supporters passed to another new issue. In all five poll tax bills that the House passed, southern representatives were remarkably united: in no instance did fewer than 70 percent of southerners vote against any particular bill (Ogden 1958: 241–80).

The South and America's war for democracy

The beginnings of World War II transformed this internal and regional issue into a national one, and shook up a stalled legislative dynamic. World War II provoked a remarkable "democratic revival" (Sosna 2003). As the war in Europe expanded and democratic countries fell to Nazism and fascism, a growing consensus emerged that these countries (with the exception of Britain) were defeated because of the weakness of their democratic spirit and institutions. The U.S. could withstand this threat and save the world only if its own democratic house was in order. The U.S. could not fight for democracy if it did not confidently believe that the American creed was matched in its execution.

As a result, the emphasis of Jim Crow reformers on economic liberalism and democratic gradualism during the New Deal was challenged and then pushed aside. The turn toward war effectively ended the New Deal and sent many of the white southerners who had been working in Washington back to the South. These return migrants would form part of the state-based reform movements that operated during the 1940s. More importantly, as a result of the war, the democratic rhetoric of World War II pressed Jim Crow reformers to address the South's "democratic deficit" directly. Unlike the aftermath of World War I, World War II was preceded by nearly two decades of organizational activity and institution building, which provided a means of translating the rhetoric, limited reforms, and slim political openings created by the war for democracy into action.

A war-driven emphasis on asserting that the American creed was strong and unsullied turned the spotlight onto some, though not all, of America's undemocratic practices.[14] The South by virtue of its own assertion of separateness again came under scrutiny. Whereas during the New Deal, observers focused on the South's economic impoverishment and underdevelopment, this new scrutiny focused on the region's democratic deficit. Critics looked at the South as the U.S.'s weak link. How could the American creed be used as a part of war effort, if it suffered from a fundamental internal weakness? The South's defenders sought to come up with answers to questions like these from critics (e.g. Maverick 1940; Daniels 1941; Hughes 1943; Wright 1945; Odum 1997 [1943]: 14–7).

The South, and by extension, many white southern reformers, was in an ideological and political quandary. Both fearing and lacking the capacity to imagine a fundamental transformation of the Jim Crow order, reformers attempted to square the American creed with what Howard Odum (1997 [1943]: 17–21), a leading southern sociologist, regionalist, and white southern liberal reformer, called the "southern credo:" a political, institutional and cultural commitment to white supremacy (see also Cash 1991 [1941]). In order to align these belief systems, southern white reformers would have to reinvent and reshape the meaning of democracy into an idea that could easily fit into their capacity for creating change, but also accommodate the essentially anti-democratic nature of southern political institutions. This complex restructuring entailed redefining the poll tax issue as an issue of *white* democracy. By writing out or eliminating race from the issue, reformers could square the American democratic revival with the Jim Crow order. Abolishing the poll tax became a way of reasserting the South's adherence to democratic norms (albeit for whites only).

Although the discussion has focused on the reframing of poll tax reform as an issue of white democracy and on the role of white reformers, African Americans, particularly southern ones, were part of the story. For African Americans, despite the way that the poll tax issue had been framed, the existence of a device that locked out not only millions of blacks but also millions of whites from American democracy supported African Americans' contentions that America had failed to live up to its democratic premises. Second, the fight for poll tax reform was also another means for African-American civic groups to extend the process of citizenship training that had begun during World War II. The struggle helped southern African-American leaders focus on a device that could bring tangible results. While the poll tax could be shown to be anti-democratic, efforts to mobilize protest against it could be used to develop and exploit a limited range of political influence. Alongside campaigns to support the elimination of the poll tax were campaigns to encourage the paying of poll taxes. In states like Virginia and Arkansas where other barriers to participation such as literacy and understanding clauses were absent, encouraging the payment of poll taxes developed new African American voters (Cothran and Phillips 1957; Kirk 2002; Dennis 2004).

Fighting and voting for democracy

The South's opposition to federal action on the poll tax was breached by the effective coupling of the rhetoric of democracy with that of military duty and sacrifice. America could not deny the right to vote to millions of military personnel who were fighting to protect American democracy. This coupling led to the enactment of the Soldier's Vote Act of 1942 (PL 712), and the first clear linkage between the war's democratic revival and the poll tax. The law provided an absentee "war-ballot" for military personnel so that they could vote for candidates for federal office (president, vice-president, U.S. Senate and House of Representatives), provided that these individuals satisfied the registration and suffrage requirements of their state of residence.[15] What worried southerners, however, were proposed amendments to the legislation that would have exempted military personnel from paying a poll tax in order to vote for state offices. Even though two poll tax states, Mississippi and South Carolina, exempted active service members from the poll tax, representatives from these states as well as other southern states saw this law as yet another assault on the South. Although southerners were able to amend the legislation so that states controlled the distribution of ballots, the first legislative linkage between the war for democracy abroad and the war for democracy at home had been created. As a result of the timing of the legislation, the actual turnout of military voters was small, less than 2 percent of the estimated 5.5 million active-duty military personnel.

In 1943, the Green–Lucas bill (S. 1285) was introduced to amend and strengthen the Soldier's Vote Act by creating a bi-partisan War Ballot Commission. Among other features of the bill, the Commission would replace the largely ineffectual system of state-supplied ballots that southerners inserted into the original legislation. In addition, the bill would have set aside all state poll tax requirements. Roosevelt announced his support for this bill in 1944. This attempt to amend the legislation created even more southern congressional anger. For example, Senator James Eastland of Mississippi direly predicted that the bill would "send carpetbaggers into the South to control elections." Again showing their unity and the growing cooperation with Republicans, southerners were able to block the Green–Lucas bill and other proposals, substituting instead an act that essentially protected the status quo established by the 1942 Act. Although a War Ballot Commission was created, states still retained the right to control who had access to the "war-ballot."

Given their reluctant acquiescence to the Soldier's Vote Act, southerners were in no mood to compromise on the poll tax bills introduced afterward. Southerners repeatedly and openly declared that national anti-poll tax bills were part of a plot to "enfranchise the Negro in the South" (Lawson 1976: 67). To ward off the possibility of so-called federal interference into southern affairs, southerners sought a "southern solution to its problems." Poll tax reform at the state level would resolve the impasse created by changing national political configurations as well as changing ideas about the meaning of democracy. By championing state-level poll tax reform, southerners could define and control the tenor of democratization in the South, lessening pressure from above in the form of national legislation, and minimizing the increased dissonance between America's competing racial orders.

Democracy for the white South

By framing poll tax reform as an issue of redeeming white democracy, southern reformers accomplished several things. First, they reframed the issue from a regional issue led by national actors and interests to a national issue that had to be led by regional actors and interests. Thus, pressure at the national level could be recalibrated to address the shifting needs of the various actors, interests, and institutions that comprised the Jim Crow order. Southern members of Congress could delay poll tax reform legislation at the national level by claiming that the South was making a credible internal effort to address the issue. Reformers at the state level could use ongoing national attention to the South's democratic deficit to put poll tax reform on the southern public and legislative agenda.

The campaign to redeem white democracy had the added benefit of eroding the political and social power of southern political elites. In the wake of Jim Crow's establishment with the mass disenfranchisement of African Americans and de-incorporation of lower class whites, a restrictive definition of southern democracy was put forth. This version framed democracy as an issue of individual moral fitness. The ability to pay a poll tax certainly drew a line between those worthy to engage in politics and in short be citizens, and those who were unworthy. Since the ability to pay was seen as a choice of whether or not one wanted to pay (i.e., if one was willing to sacrifice a dollar for democracy), then non-payment suggested that one was unworthy for citizenship, and was certainly not ready to participate in politics. To maintain the Jim Crow order, however, southern democracy had to be redefined. A democracy for all (whites) could not be based on economic distinctions. Political engagement was the right and the privilege of all (white) Americans, not simply the "better class."

The expansion of poll tax reform as an issue of white democracy caught the eyes of southern politicians at the state level. The South's one-party system with its varied levels of factionalism had led to a perennial condition of political "ins" and "outs" (Key 1984: 15–18). Manipulation of electoral rules was one of the favorite instruments used to gain power. If restricting the white franchise had worked to benefit one group, why couldn't extending the white franchise be used to benefit another group? If poll tax reform was simply an issue of white democracy and not, as its supporters claimed, a threat to white supremacy, who could credibly argue against the expansion of the electorate? And what politician could resist the possibility of creating a new and more potent electoral coalition from these new votes? Eugene Talmadge—Georgia's governor and a quintessential Jim Crow politician—was quoted by one southern journalist as saying, "When you control the machine you want as few voters as possible so that the machine's proportion will be as big as possible. But when somebody else's machine controls, you need some new voters . . . to swamp it" (Ogden 1958: 157, quoting John Temple Graves). The "inexorable law of American politics," Ralph Bunche observed, "is to get the vote, and once vote hungry candidates taste a helpful vote . . . it is relished" (Bunche 1973: 75–6).

Other practical considerations—such as the rising cost of corruption—also came into play. For example, poll tax reform garnered labor support not only because it was consistent with democratic practice and values, but also because it would facilitate voting for white, and in some cases black, union members. The accepted practice of paying the poll tax bills of political supporters (i.e. voters) was simply too high a cost for most unions, given the uncertain outcomes of elections. Even state politicians realized that winning elections meant facing the ever-higher costs inherent in poll tax receipt buying.

Thus by reframing poll tax reform as an issue of democracy, southern reformers could build a much broader coalition at both the national and the state levels. The national coalition generated the coalition of groups that would later support the modern civil rights movement. While each state had a different configuration of groups pressing for poll tax reform, what is remarkable about each coalition is that they featured groups that would become the elements of the "new" New South: business moderates, suburban voters, and urban "good government" advocates. By 1948, these coalitions had picked up an important new source of support: returning World War II veterans who realized that their fight for democracy was now a domestic one. These veterans' groups played important roles in leading the fight for state-level reform in Arkansas, Georgia, and Tennessee (Lester 1976; Key 1984: 201–4; Spinney 1995; Brooks 2004). In poll tax reform campaign, many of these groups saw a way to clean up the South's image and divert southern government onto a more responsive, orderly, and businesslike path.

Of the eight remaining states that still had poll tax laws, two states, Georgia and Tennessee (albeit temporarily), abolished them during the 1940s (see table 7.1). Georgia, under the leadership of pro-New Deal Governor Ellis Arnall, abolished its poll tax in 1945. Tennessee's legislature, under pressure from a variety of reform groups, also abolished the poll tax in 1943. The state's Supreme Court, whose justices were beholden to the Crump machine which relied on poll tax fraud, overturned this action. Nonetheless, reformers were able to get significant changes in the tax enacted in 1949, leading to the effective abolishment of the tax in 1951.

In the remaining states, poll tax reform came in much more limited steps. In Arkansas, despite the defeat of the referendum in 1938, significant reforms were enacted in 1941 and 1949. In 1956, supporters got a referendum on abolishing the tax on the ballot; however, it failed. In Texas and Virginia, poll tax referenda were on the ballot in 1949. In Texas, the campaign for poll tax reform was led not only by traditional southern reform groups and leading liberal figures like Maury Maverick, but also by state legislators who represented heavily Mexican American districts that were mobilized by returning Mexican-American World War II veterans (Ogden 1958: 216–24). In Virginia, a long campaign by reformers taking place in both the judicial and legislative arenas culminated in the Byrd machine's craftily putting up a poll tax reform measure that would have substituted the tax with even more restrictive suffrage restrictions. Instead of mobilizing voters to vote for the measure, reformers found themselves mobilizing voters against the machine's version of reform (Dennis 2004). South Carolina, after exhausting its appeals against the *Smith v. Allwright* decision, abolished its poll tax in 1951.[16] By 1953, Alabama became the last southern state to address the poll tax issue. Although outright repeal failed, the tax was significantly altered to allow for many new Alabamians to participate in the political system. The last holdout was Mississippi. Although several governors had supported some type of reform, and the state's most liberal governor, James Folsom, had pressed for outright abolition, Mississippi's black-belt dominated legislature refused to allow any consideration of the issue to make it onto the legislative agenda. Mississippi remained the only state where poll tax reform failed to have a significant public or legislative debate.

Although their actual success in reforming or abolishing the poll tax in the South was mixed, southern reformers were remarkably successful in changing the South's level of support for the tax. In 1941, only 43 percent of southerners were in favor of abolishing the poll tax, compared to 63 percent outside of the South.

By 1953, opinion on the issue had moved (see figure 7.1). First, the number of southerners in favor of abolishing the poll tax increased to 59 percent of those surveyed. Second, the gap between the South and the nation on this issue narrowed. Whereas in 1943 there was a 20-percentage point gap, by 1953 this gap narrowed to a smaller 12-percentage point gap ("Gallop and Fortune Poll" 1941; "Public Opinion Polls" 1943; "The Quarter's Polls" 1948, 1949; Ogden 1958: 252).

The democratization of the white South, with the exception of Mississippi, Texas, and Virginia, had begun. Although contemporary analysts of the poll tax like V.O. Key and his student Frederic Ogden were correct in asserting that the repeal of poll taxes would not bring in the tens of millions of voters that

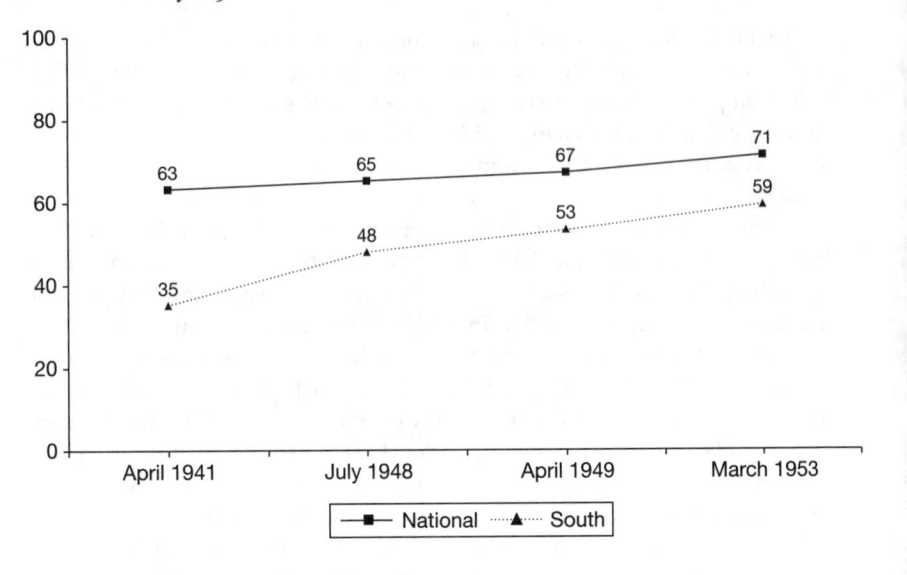

Figure 7.1 Public support for poll tax reform

Source: "Gallup and Fortune Poll" (1941: 470); "The Quarter's Polls" (1948: 567); "The Quarter's Polls" (1949: 557); Ogden (1958: 252)

supporters of reform claimed, they were wrong in their understanding of how these millions of new voters would be incorporated into the political system. Most of the supporters (as well as the critics) of poll tax reform had worked from a New Dealish assumption that the South would experience a liberal democratic revival through inclusion of the white have-nots.

By framing poll tax reform as an issue of reconstitution or reinvigoration of *white* democracy, the extension of political and economic rights and benefits to blacks became even more problematic. How could white southern politicians promise newly incorporated white voters that the foundation of the new white democracy was safe in the face of rising African American political mobilization and increasing national attention to civil rights issues? By the early 1950s, before the *Brown* decision, on the heels of increasing white democratization came attempts to limit the spread of this democratization to blacks. Thus Alabama enacted its infamous (and later overturned) Boswell Amendment in 1946, which strengthened the discretionary and arbitrary powers of local voter registrars. Georgia, with the Talmadge forces back in charge, changed its voting laws in the late 1940s to allow the massive purging of newly registered African American voters (see Bernd and Holland 1959; Lawson 1976; Bernd 1982). Poll tax reform had allowed the South to begin to rejoin the United States. However, like their forebears of the late nineteenth and early twentieth centuries, many white southerners still defined democracy as a privilege restricted to and enjoyed only by whites.

The poll tax issue faded quickly. Although state-level poll tax reform had started off as a movement "with the endorsement of the best leadership and thought of the South" and as the "most forward political step there since the Civil War," by the 1950s its time had come and gone (Brewer 1944: 299). In light of the deeper bitter struggle for civil rights that followed, the poll tax seemed to be a narrow technical issue like lynching that had been largely bypassed by history. Yet it left a significant impact on southern and national politics.

For the masses of southern whites, widespread democratization was a resounding success. A long-standing elite notion of a democracy restricted to the better class of whites was resoundingly and publicly discredited. As a result, millions of whites (re-) gained the franchise. Indeed this forgotten revolution created a new white electorate that responded to the broader pressures from below and above in ways not anticipated, or desired, by southern liberals. The democratization efforts of the Jim Crow reformers brought in millions of newly enfranchised white voters and opened up the political terrain in many states to new voices and new opportunities for political entrepreneurs. Higher levels of education and income coupled with greater urbanization, and new patterns of suburbanization meant that these new voters lay outside of the control of traditional white elites (see Thornton 2002). These new white voters, who held no automatic allegiance to traditional political elites, proved open to the appeals of southern politicians who themselves were not members of the traditional political elite, and were in many ways creatures of a "new" New South. These new politicians would help to pave the way for the eventual entry of these voters into the Republican Party. They used the possibilities opened up by Jim Crow reform, and later the Civil Rights movement, as means to incorporate new white voters.[17] Thus, although most analyses point to race, and in particular the Democrats' support of civil rights as driving working-class whites out of the party and into the welcoming arms of the Republican party, the path to this destination was not as clear cut or straightforward as the conventional narrative has it.

The story of the 1940s campaign for poll tax reform and democratization of the South challenges much conventional wisdom about the South and about the shaping of modern American politics. In understanding how the democratization of the U.S. has unfolded, poll tax reform points out not only the significance of region, but also of ideas. Democratization is not only the achievement of new mechanisms of political inclusion but also the development of new ideas that undergird and justify these democratic extensions. The democratization of the white South showed that by 1954 the solid South was not quite so solid. For a political order that was seemingly resistant to electoral pressure, and was by the 1940s only beginning to face significant judicial assaults, it is surprising that these political reforms occurred. These reforms' success contradicts common assumptions about the impregnability of the Jim Crow order in the pre-*Brown* era. The varieties of "Souths" and their diverse paths towards democratization created a multiplicity of openings for the civil rights activists who would displace southern reformers in shaping and ultimately ending the Jim Crow order.

Notes

1 For discussion of African American politics during the 1940s, see Dalfiume (1968); McCoy and Ruetten (1969); Egerton (1994); Kellogg (1979); and Kryder (2000). See also Sitkoff (1978).

2 On national politics, the crisis of New Deal liberalism, and civil rights, see Berman (1970); Plotke (1996). On the Cold War's impact on race relations see McAuliffe (1978); Dudziak (1988, 2000).

3 On the history of South and the impact of World War II, see Bartley (1995) as well as Sosna (1987); McMillen (1997); and Tyler (2002). For discussion of the economic changes in the South see Schulman (1991) and Cobb (1993).

4 See also Cash (1991 [1941]: viii) who argued that while the South "not quite a nation within a nation [it was] the next thing to it."

5 Indeed as Nicholas Lemann (2006) has argued, the political and cultural power of the Southern order was such that while it may have lost the battles of the Civil War, it had won the war over how the Civil War would be interpreted.

6 For overview of southern liberalism, see Sosna (1977); Kneebone (1985); and Southern (1976); in addition see Sullivan (1996). For a contemporary expression of this see Dabney (1932).

7 On lynching see, Hall (1993). Although lynchings did not completely disappear as a result of this movement, there was a significant drop in the number of lynchings from 1920 onward. See Tolnay and Beck (1995).

8 With the *Gaines v. Canada* (1938) decision, this situation began to change, with some states very slowly increasing funding to black institutions.

9 Johnson, a sociologist trained by University of Chicago's Robert Park, co-authored one of the CIC's most important reports, *The Collapse of Cotton Tenancy*, which resulted in the enactment of the Bankhead-Jones Tenant Farm Act (1937). See Gilpin and Gasman (2003) and Dunne (1998).

10 Durr was a lawyer for the Reconstruction Finance Corporation. His wife, Virginia Durr, also a prominent activist, was Supreme Court Justice Hugo Black's sister-in-law. See Durr (1985).

11 Bunche (1973: 39) called this economic liberalism a "kind of infantile economic determinism."

12 Sarah Wilkerson-Freeman (2002: 333–74) argues that renewed attention by liberal Democrats in the 1930s to the poll tax issue was the result of post–suffrage era southern feminists who continued to secure the political realization of the Nineteenth Amendment. They worked at the state level, through the national Democratic Party Woman's committee, and their personal contact with Eleanor Roosevelt. These women kept poll tax reform alive and with the Great Depression focused attention on the disproportionate effect it had on (white) women.

13 This anti-democratic view is reported in a number of sources including Woodward (1974) and Kousser (1974).

14 For example, in Senate hearings in 1943, the United Christian Council for Democracy argued that "We shall be in a much stronger moral position to be the champions of freedom and democracy among the nations if this injustice in our own country is corrected at once" (Senate hearings on S. 1280, part I, p. 330, March 14, 1942).

15 In fact, the legislation was perhaps more symbolic than practical. The logistics of distributing ballots to millions of service members located all over the world and covered under hundreds of different electoral jurisdictions were daunting. See Martin (1945) and Lawson (1976: 66–85).

16 The *Smith v. Allwright*, 321 U.S. 649 (1944) decision overturned the white primary. For an overview of the case see Zelden (2004).

17 Massive white resistance was not however mobilized by a unified southern elite.

While some elites strategically used racial antagonism as an electoral resource, other elites saw massive resistance as potentially undermining the political and economic gains that were beginning to accrue from the South's repositioning as part of the sunbelt. See for example, Black and Black (2005).

Bibliography

Primary sources

Cases cited

Brown v. Board of Education (1954) 347 U.S. 483
Gaines v. Canada (1938) 305 U.S. 337
Smith v. Allwright (1944) 321 U.S. 649

Other primary sources

National Committee to Abolish the Poll Tax, *Fact Sheet*, April 1943.
Senate hearings on S. 1280 (1942) part I, March 14: 330.

References and secondary sources

Bartley, N.V. (1995) *The New South, 1945–1980*, Baton Rouge: Louisiana State University Press.
Berman, W.C. (1970) *The Politics of Civil Rights in the Truman Administration*, Columbus: Ohio University Press.
Bernd, J.L. (1982) "White Supremacy and the Disenfranchisement of Blacks in Georgia, 1946," *The Georgia Historical Quarterly*, 64: 492–513.
Bernd, J.L. and Holland, L.M. (1959) "Recent Restrictions upon Negro Suffrage: The Case of Georgia," *Journal of Politics*, 21: 487–513.
Black, E. and Black, M. (2005) *Politics and Society in the South*, Cambridge, MA: Harvard University Press.
Borstelmann, T. (2003) *The Cold War and the Color Line: American Race Relations in the Global Arena*, Cambridge, MA: Harvard University Press.
Brewer, W.M. (1944) "The Poll Tax and Poll Taxers," *Journal of Negro History*, 29: 260–99.
Brinkley, A. (1995) *The End of Reform: the New Deal in Recession and War*, New York: Knopf.
Brooks, J. (2004) *Defining the Peace: World War II Veterans, Race and the Remaking of Southern Political Tradition*, Chapel Hill: University of North Carolina Press.
Bunche, R. (1973) *The Political Status of the Negro in the Age of FDR*, Chicago: University of Chicago Press.
Cash, W.J. (1991 [1941]) *The Mind of the South*, New York: Random House, Inc.
Cobb, J.C. (1993) *The Selling of the South: The Southern Crusade for Industrial Development 1936–1990*, Urbana: University of Illinois Press.
Cothran, T.C. and Phillips, W.M. (1957) "Expansion of Negro Suffrage in Arkansas," *Journal of Negro Education*, 26: 287–96.

Dabney, V. (1932) *Liberalism in the South*, Chapel Hill: University of North Carolina Press.

—— (1939) "Shall the South's Poll Tax Go?" *New York Times Magazine*, February 12: 9.

Dalfiume, R.M. (1968) "The 'Forgotten Years' of the Negro Revolution," *Journal of American History*, 55: 90–106.

Daniels, J. (1941) "Dictators and Poll Taxes," *Nation*, February 22: 213.

Dennis, M. (2001) *Lessons in Progress: State Universities and Progressivism in the New South, 1880–1920*, Urbana: University of Illinois Press.

—— (2004) *Luther P. Jackson and a Life for Civil Rights*, Gainesville: University of Florida Press.

Dudziak, M.L. (1988) "Desegregation as a Cold War Imperative," *Stanford Law Review*, 41: 61–120.

—— (2000) *Cold War Civil Rights: Race and the Image of American Democracy*, Princeton, NJ: Princeton University Press.

Dunne, M.W. (1998) "Next Steps: Charles S. Johnson and Southern Liberalism," *Journal of Negro History*, 83: 1–34.

Durr, V. (1985) *Outside the Magic Circle: The Autobiography of Virginia Foster Durr*, H.F. Barnard (ed.), Tuscaloosa: University of Alabama Press.

Dykman, W. and Stokely, J. (1962) *Seeds of Southern Change: The Life of Will Alexander*, Chicago: University of Chicago Press.

Eagles, C.W. (1982) *Jonathan Daniels and Race Relations: The Evolution of a Southern Liberal*, Knoxville: University of Tennessee Press.

Egerton, J. (1994) *Speak Now against the Day: The Generation before the Civil Rights Movement in the South*, New York: Knopf.

Ellis, A.W. (1976) "The Commission on Interracial Cooperation, 1919–1944: Its Activities and Results," unpublished thesis, Georgia State University.

Feldman, G. (2004) *The Disenfranchisement Myth: Poor Whites and Suffrage Restriction in Alabama*, Athens: University of Georgia Press.

Frederickson, M.E. (1993) "'Each One is Dependent on the Other': Southern Churchwomen, Racial Reform, and the Process of Transformation, 1880–1940," in N.A. Hewitt and S. Lebsock (eds) *Visible Women*, Urbana: University of Illinois Press.

Frymer, P. (1999) *Uneasy Alliances: Race and Party in America*, Princeton, NJ: Princeton University Press.

"Gallup and Fortune Poll" (1941) *Public Opinion Quarterly*, 5: 470–97.

Gavins, R. (1974) "Gordon Blaine Hancock: A Black Profile from the New South," *Journal of Negro History*, 59: 207–27.

Gilpin, P.J. and Gasman, M. (2003) *Charles S. Johnson: Leadership beyond the Veil in the Age of Jim Crow*, Albany: State University of New York Press.

González, F.E. and King, D. (2004) "The State and Democratization: The United States in Comparative Perspective," *British Journal of Political Science*, 34: 193–210.

Gordon, L. (1991) "Black and White Visions of Welfare: Women's Welfare Activism: 1890–1945," *Journal of American History*, 78: 559–90.

Hackney, S. (1969) *Populism to Progressivism in Alabama*, Princeton, NJ: Princeton University Press.

Hall, J.D. (1993) *Revolt against Chivalry: Jessie Daniel Ames and the Women's Campaign against Lynching*, revised edn, New York: Columbia University Press.

Hughes, L. (1943) "Democracy Begins at Home: What Shall We Do About the South?" *Common Ground*, winter: 3–6.

Katznelson, I., Geiger, K. and Kryder, D. (1993) "Limiting Liberalism: The Southern Veto in Congress, 1933–1950," *Political Science Quarterly*, 108: 283–306.

Kellogg, P.J. (1979) "Civil Rights Consciousness in the 1940s," *Historian*, 42: 18–41.

Key, V.O. (1984 [1949]) *Southern Politics in State and Nation*, Knoxville: University of Tennessee.

Kirk, J.A. (2002) *Redefining the Color Line: Black Activism in Little Rock, Arkansas, 1940–1970*, Gainesville: University of Florida Press.

Klibaner, I. (1989) *Conscience of a Troubled South: The Southern Conference Education Fund, 1946–1966*, Brooklyn, NY: Carlson Publishing, Inc.

Kneebone, J.T. (1985) *Southern Liberal Journalists and the Issue of Race, 1920–1944*, Chapel Hill: University of North Carolina Press.

Kousser, J.M. (1974) *The Shaping of Southern Politics: Suffrage Restriction and the Establishment of the One-Party South, 1880–1910*, New Haven, CT: Yale University Press.

Krueger, T.A. (1967) *And Promises to Keep: The Southern Conference for Human Welfare, 1938–1948*, Nashville, TN: Vanderbilt University Press.

Kryder, D. (2000) *Divided Arsenal: Race and the American State During World War II*, New York: Cambridge University Press.

Lawson, S.A. (1976) *Black Ballots: Voting Rights in the South*, New York: Columbia University Press.

Lemann, N. (2006) *Redemption: The Last Battle of the Civil War*, New York: Farrar, Straus and Giroux.

Lester, J. (1976) *A Man for Arkansas: Sid McMath and the Southern Reform Tradition*, Little Rock, AR: Rose Publishing Co.

Lewinson, P. (1963 [1932]) *Race, Class, and Party: A History of Negro Suffrage and White Politics in the South*, New York: Russell & Russell.

Link, W.A. (1992) *The Paradox of Southern Progressivism, 1880–1930*, Chapel Hill: University of North Carolina Press.

McAuliffe, M.S. (1978) *Crisis on the Left: Cold War Politics and American Liberals, 1947–1954*, Amherst: University of Massachusetts Press.

McCoy, D.R. and Ruetten, R.T. (1969) "The Civil Rights Movement: 1940–1954," *Midwest Quarterly*, 11: 11–34.

McDonough, J.A. (1993) "Men and Women of Good Will: A History of the Commission on Interracial Cooperation and the Southern Regional Council, 1919–1954," unpublished thesis, University of Virginia.

McMahon, K.J. (2004) *Reconsidering Roosevelt on Race*, Chicago: University of Chicago Press.

McMillen, N.R. (ed.) (1997) *Remaking Dixie: The Impact of World War II on the American South*, Jackson: University Press of Mississippi.

Martin, B.C. (1945) "The Service Vote in the Elections of 1944," *American Political Science Review*, 39: 720–32.

Maverick, M. (1940) "Let's Join the United States," *Nation*, May 11: 592–4.

Moon, H.L. (1948) *Balance of Power: The Negro Vote*, New York: Doubleday.

Myrdal, Gunnar K. (1944) *An American Dilemma: The Negro Problem and Modern Democracy*, New York: Harper & Brothers.

Odum, H. (1997) [1943] *Race and Rumors of Race: The American South in the Early Forties*, Baltimore, MD: Johns Hopkins University Press.

Ogden, F. (1958) *The Poll Tax in the South*, University: University of Alabama Press.

Orren, K. and Skowronek, S. (2004) *The Search for American Political Development*, New York: Cambridge University Press.

Pilkington, C.K. (1985) "The Trials of Brotherhood: The Founding of the Commission on Interracial Cooperation," *Georgia Historical Quarterly*, 69: 55–80.

Plotke, D. (1996) *Building a Democratic Political Order: Reshaping American Liberalism in the 1930s and 1940s*, New York: Cambridge University Press.

"Public Opinion Polls" (1943) *Public Opinion Quarterly*, 7: 478–505.

"The Quarter's Polls" (1948) *Public Opinion Quarterly*, 12: 530–77.

—— (1949) *Public Opinion Quarterly*, 13: 537–61.

Rable, G.C. (1985) "The South and the Politics of Anti-lynching Legislation, 1920–1940," *Journal of Southern History*, 51: 201–20.

Reed, L. (1991) *Simple Decency and Common Sense: The Southern Conference Movement, 1938–1963*, Bloomington: Indiana University Press.

Rowan, S. (1940) "American Rotten Districts," *Common Sense*, October: 8.

Schulman, B.J. (1991) *From Cotton Belt to Sun Belt: Federal Policy, Economic Development, and the Transformation of the South, 1938–1980*, New York: Oxford University Press.

Shabazz, A. (2004) *Advancing Democracy: and the Struggle for Access and Equity in Higher Education in Texas*, Chapel Hill: University of North Carolina Press.

Sitkoff, H. (1978) *A New Deal for Blacks: The Emergence of Civil Rights as a National Issue: The Depression Decade*, New York: Oxford University Press.

Smith, J.D. (2002) *Managing White Supremacy*, Chapel Hill: University of North Carolina Press.

Smith, R.M. (1993) "Beyond Tocqueville, Myrdal and Hartz: The Multiple Traditions in America," *American Political Science Review*, 87: 549–66.

Sosna, M. (1977) *In Search of the Silent South*, New York: Columbia University Press.

—— (1987) "More Important Than the Civil War? The Impact of World War II on the South," in J.C. Cobb and C.R. Wilson (eds) *Perspectives on the American South: An Annual Review of Society, Politics and Culture*, New York: Gordon and Breach Publishers.

—— (2003) "World War II, Democracy and the South: The Birth of the Southern Regional Council," unpublished paper, Conference on the Southern Regional Council and the Civil Rights Movement, University of Florida, October 23–6.

Southern, D.W. (1976) "An *American Dilemma* Revisited: Myrdalism and White Southern Liberals," *South Atlantic Quarterly*, 71: 189–92.

Spinney, R.G. (1995) "Municipal Government in Nashville, Tennessee, 1938–1951: World War II and the Growth of the Public Sector," *Journal of Southern History*, 61: 77–112.

Stoney, G.C. (1940) "Suffrage in the South: Part I," *Survey Graphic*, 29(1): 5–9, 41–3.

Strong, D. (1944) "The Poll Tax: The Case of Texas," *American Political Science Review*, 38(4): 693–709.

Suggs, H.L. (1988) *P.B. Young, Newspaperman: Race, Politics, and Journalism in the New South, 1910–1962*, Charlottesville: University Press of Virginia.

Sullivan, P. (1996) *Days of Hope: Race and Democracy in the New Deal Era*, Chapel Hill: University of North Carolina Press.

Thornton, J.M. III (2002) *Dividing Lines: Municipal Politics and the Struggle for Civil*

Rights in Montgomery, Birmingham and Selma, Tuscaloosa: University of Alabama Press.

Tindall, G.B. (1963) "Business Progressivism: Southern Politics in the Twenties," *South Atlantic Quarterly*, 62: 92–106.

Tolnay, S.E. and Beck, E.M. (1995) *A Festival of Violence: An Analysis of Southern Lynchings, 1882–1930*, Chicago: University of Illinois Press.

Tyler, P. (2002) "The Impact of the New Deal and World War II on the South," in J.B. Boles (ed.) *A Companion to the American South*, Malden: Blackwell.

Valelly, R.M. (2004) *The Two Reconstructions*, Chicago: University of Chicago Press.

Weare, W.B. (1973) *Black Business in the New South*, Chicago: University of Illinois Press.

Wilkerson-Freeman, S. (2002) "The Second Battle for Woman Suffrage: Alabama White Women, the Poll Tax, and V.O. Key's Master Narrative of Southern Politics," *Journal of Southern History*, 68: 333–74.

Woodward, C.V. (1974) *The Strange Career of Jim Crow*, 3rd revised edn, New York: Oxford University Press.

Wright, L.B. (1945) "Myth Makers and the South's Dilemma," *Sewanee Review*, 53: 544–58.

Zelden, C.L. (2004) *The Battle for the Black Ballot: Smith v. Allwright and the Defeat of the Texas White Primary*, Lawrence: University of Kansas Press.

8   Race's reality: the NAACP confronts racism and inequality in the labor movement, 1940–65

Paul Frymer

The prescience of W.E.B. Du Bois's declaring the problem of the twentieth century to be that of the "color-line" overshadows the fact that the century should also be remembered for something equally apposite; during these years physical and social scientists concluded that race was not "real," at least for purposes of understanding individual and group capabilities and behavior. Academia provided a systematic and emphatic debunking of the underlying arguments for "scientific racism," concluding that race is nothing more than an artificial marker with no relevance for determining the possibilities of individual behavior (Hall 2000). Race's "reality"—its deep-seated importance in American society in structuring inequality and difference—is the product of political, economic, and social forces, not biology or genetics.

Race continues to be widely used to stigmatize, harm, and place costs on people who are deemed "other." Race may be a sociopolitical construction, but our intellectual advances cannot prevent it from being all too real as a technique of power and political combat: as Barbara Fields (1982: 159) aptly remarks, "once acted upon, a delusion may be as murderous as a fact." The problem before us at the beginning of the twenty-first century, then, is to better understand the mechanisms and forces that lead individuals and groups to create and maintain a reality out of an otherwise artificial marker. In this chapter, I examine the confrontation between the National Association for the Advancement of Colored People (NAACP) and the labor movement in the middle of the twentieth century over racial inequality and discrimination in unions. I hope to provide at least the beginnings of an explanation for why racism and racial inequality were so difficult to remove from union workplaces despite a seeming alliance of progressives in both the civil rights and labor movement.[1] In particular, I argue that labor leaders viewed racism as tangential and incidental to the labor movement, and believed that African Americans could achieve equality in the movement without a direct confrontation with race. The NAACP was initially in agreement with labor's perspective, but quickly came to see the problem in unions as systemic, not sporadic. Once challenged, labor became more rigid, absolutely unwilling to see the fundamental place of race in dividing the movement; in turn, the NAACP would drift further away from confronting issues of class. The end result was that both progressive movements actively participated in creating a political gulf that served to embolden their enemies and hasten their own demise.

In making this argument, I wish to make two additional points relevant for American political development (APD) scholars. First, and contrary to conventional understandings in political science that perceive racism as a virus rooted in individual prejudice and bigotry, I argue that race remains a stubbornly rigid marker of inequality in American society despite its inherent artificiality because it is rooted in real political and economic structures that reinforce its significance. Structures and institutions are the hallmarks of power—they provide a place for power to lie, provide it with advantageous rules and weapons, and create a separation and protection for those with power from those without. Power constructs reality with the weapons at its disposal, and race is both one of the many weapons and a byproduct of this construction. In this regard, I argue, race is no more artificial than numerous other ideologies and material markers; its importance is manifested from the mix of rules and institutions that shape society and inequality.[2]

Second, in claiming that race is a constructed political category that maintains relevance because it is intertwined with contestations over power, I both build on and critique current understandings within the American political development literature that emphasize institutional foundations of racial inequality. APD's particular attention to politics has provided advances in understanding how the political sphere—through institutions, rules, laws, and practices—serves as an engine in creating and maintaining racial inequality. Because of their attention to the role that institutions and politics play in identity construction, political representation and power, as well as their attention to the temporal dimensions by which ideas and ideologies fluctuate through different eras and regimes, APD scholars can provide a unique resource to uncover why race continues to structure so much of society's inequalities. This research illuminates that the confluence of institutions, power, and interests shape racial politics in ways that cannot simply be explained through ideology, prejudice, or even hegemony.

Initially, the APD field paid little attention to race; in part because—similar to many of the labor leaders explored in this chapter—much of the scholarship was oriented around an understanding of class divisions as being fundamental to American society.[3] In the canon of the APD literature, the critical issues are industrialization and the rise of capitalism, labor inequality and activism, and the creation of a welfare state that slowly came to provide "universal" benefits (see e.g. Skowronek 1982; Skocpol 1992; Bensel 2000). Race is critical to all of these features of state-building, but gets nary a mention in scholarship premised in Marxist and neo-Marxist assumptions that presume class to be "real" and race to be a distraction used by capitalists to divide working-class movements. Since the 1990s, APD scholarship that emphasizes the importance of race has exploded, as scholars have examined how state institutions, laws, and actors create and maintain racial hierarchies (King 1997; Reed 1997; Walton 1997; Lieberman 1998; Marx 1998; Brown 1999; Kryder 2000;

Skrentny 2002; Bohrman and Murakawa 2005; Katznelson 2005). Influenced in different ways by Max Weber and Michel Foucault, this research illuminates that the confluence of institutions, power, and interests shape racial politics in ways that cannot simply be explained through ideology, prejudice, or even hegemony. Institutions are central to power, and as both Weber and Foucault have detailed, such institutions come to embody certain ideas and practices that are rigid in maintaining hierarchies.

In so doing, the literature provides an alternative both to scholars who see racism as a fading individual prejudice (Sears et al. 2000), as well as notable race construction scholars who have struggled to explain race's rigidity in light of its inherent artificiality (Appiah 1996; Gilroy 2000). The work of Rogers Smith (1997), for example, emphasizes the rigidity of racial hierarchies; racial prejudice is not simply an irrational attitude that will disappear as it is exposed for its lack of links to reality, but is a carefully developed ideology that becomes intertwined with institutional practices and interests that buffer elite interests against more radical ideologies and movements. Expanding on this theme, numerous race and APD scholars argue that moments of opportunities for racial transformation are limited and governed by external shocks to the system, which institutional bulwarks and the strategic interests of elites concerned with maintaining state order quickly close (Piven and Cloward 1978; Marx 1998; Klinkner and Smith 1999).

Boundaries for racial progress are even further present in the recent work on "racial orders." The concept of racial orders, popular for decades outside of political science, most notably in Marxist and post-Marxist work on the relationship between labor markets and racial inequality, has illuminated further boundaries to civil rights movements (see e.g. Wilson 1978; Gilroy 1987; Omi and Winant 1994; Wacquant 2001). Claire Kim's (2000) work on racial triangulation is one example. On the one hand, she argues that race is constructed and determined through unequal contestation between three groups placed on sides of the hierarchal triangle. On the other hand, these groups—Asian, black, and white Americans —are locked in, their positions in the hierarchy bounded and limited by social and political constructions that resist change. The recent work of Desmond King and Rogers Smith argues for an alternative but compatible notion of racial orders, as they claim that anti-egalitarian ideologies have been built into and entrenched by institutions that resist democratic politics (King and Smith 2005).

There is a tendency in this work, however—and perhaps because it is in itself confronting those who sublimate race to class—to unnecessarily juxtapose race against issues of class, claiming that racial ideologies exist independently from class based inequities. In so doing, race and APD scholars are in danger of providing a fairly stripped notion of power which both vaults race to an apolitical place that is based on notions of hierarchy and intolerance that seemingly exist outside of politics, and removes issues of class from what is clearly an intersectional problem of inequality. Class, and the politics and institutions they form, further situate race relations and hierarchies. Both race and class are constituted by and constructed from broader power dynamics, and while both are analytically important in their own right, they are not easily separated concepts when it comes to understanding inequality and the continuing historical racial project (see Reed 2002).

The labor movement: race is a distraction to fundamental class divisions

APD scholars have often portrayed the labor movement as one of the primary engines of American state-building and democratic expansion (see, notably, Orren 1995: 379). But from its beginnings, the labor movement has seen itself in explicitly racialized terms, leading it to often work to exclude as much as incorporate new groups into workplace and political democracy. In its earliest years, racism in the labor movement, writes Gwendolyn Mink (1986: 71–2), "invigorated national union solidarity. It gave racial dress to union interest, endowing traditional job- and organization-consciousness unionism with a coincident race consciousness" (see also Roediger 1999). When the National Labor Relations Act (or Wagner Act) was passed in 1935, the number of African Americans in trade unions was estimated at between 50,000 and 100,000 workers (Marshall 1964; and Labor Research Association cited in "Second Report on Discrimination in Labor Unions" 1940, *Papers of the NAACP* (*"NAACP"* hereafter), respectively), less than 1 percent of the labor movement.[4] At least 22 national unions at the time had formal bars against membership by non-white workers, including many of the largest craft unions in the railroad industries and construction trades (Marshall 1965; Arnesen 2001). Others maintained strictly Jim Crow unions that denied equal membership, voting rights, and representation by the national union or had informal and often locally specific policies of segregation. The Carpenters' union, for instance, employed black workers only for projects in black neighborhoods and, even then, consistently prioritized its segregated white local unions over black union members in competitions for prized projects ("Memorandum to Mr. White" 1943, *NAACP*; "Union Integration" n.d., *NAACP*; McCray 1944: 203). The International Machinists' local in Seattle, Washington, contracted by Boeing Aircraft Company, had a ritual that required every member of the organization to take an oath upon initiation stating "I further promise that I will never propose for membership in this Association any other than a competent white candidate" (cited in "To Hon. Francis Biddle" 1941, *NAACP*; see also Roediger 1994: 37–45; Lichtenstein 2001: 35, 40–1, 72; Nelson 2001).

The Wagner Act's passage led to tremendous increases in the number of union workers, and African American workers certainly benefited at least in part from this dramatic change in federal law (see Korstad 2003). But despite the numbers of overall union members increasing dramatically in the 1930s and 40s—the labor movement encompassed a third of the national workforce by the end of the 1940s—the increases for African Americans were far more halting. The Wagner Act included provisions that allowed unions to create closed shops that could exclude on the basis of race and in the first decade after the Act's passage numerous unions effectively locked black workers entirely out of certain industries, especially in the railroads and construction trades of the AFL (see Bernstein 2001).

The formation of the Congress of Industrial Organizations (CIO) was similarly a mixed result for the black worker. On the one hand, its entrance into labor affairs provided more opportunities to African Americans, as the CIO reached into economic spheres left untouched by the hegemonic AFL and exhibited a far greater openness to organize African Americans in their campaigns.[5] CIO leaders Philip Murray and Walter Reuther had extensive links with civil rights causes, providing financial assistance to civil rights organizations, and serving as members of civil rights boards such as the NAACP and the Fair Employment Practices Commission (FEPC). They also asserted that all CIO unions have non-discriminatory provisions, and they set up internal fair employment committees to examine issues of discrimination and inequality.[6]

But even CIO unions had extensive race problems, with segregated locals as well as unofficial segregation and exclusion in many of their southern locals, and extensive racial discrimination throughout northern and Midwest factories.[7] In part this was because the CIO leadership often had little authority with local union practices, and were often rebuffed by members when they issued orders for civil rights. For example, after the Textile Workers' Union of the CIO in Virginia hired African American workers in accordance with its national policy of non-discrimination, nearly 3,000 white members went on strike in protest; to end the strike, the CIO and the employer agreed to discontinue the hiring of black workers ("Race Issue Too Tough" 1944, *NAACP*; "Details of Strike at the Riverside Division of the Dam River Cotton Mills" 1944, *NAACP*). The UAW faced similar problems in the early 1940s. Five hundred white workers of the UAW-CIO walked off the job at the Curtiss–Wright plant in Columbus Ohio when an African American was hired ("To Mr. R.J. Thomas" 1941, *NAACP*). Meanwhile, southern CIO unions were, as Alan Draper points out, not "just unions that simply happened to be located in the South, they were *southern* unions." Their progressivism, as such, tended to depend largely on whether African Americans constituted a majority of the local's membership (Draper 1994: 12; see Minchin 2005: 28, 53; see also Lewis 1990; Honey 1993; Minchin 2001). Extensive surveys by the International Lady Garment workers found broad-based support among white workers for racial segregation, "considerable support" for the Ku Klux Klan, and almost unanimous opposition to African Americans' entering "their" workplace.[8] And as Michelle Brattain argues, many southern white workers enthusiastically supported the CIO because they saw racial integration as so improbable that they were happy to participate in what they perceived as meaningless discussions of racial solidarity that would never seriously confront the color-line (2001: 130).

CIO leaders were also emblematic of how labor generally saw the race problem in the movement. As we will see further in this chapter, even among those who wished to create greater equality in the labor movement, the opinion of labor leaders was that race was a distraction from the greater question of gaining economic equality. Reuther, Murray, Harry Bridges of the ILWU, and others in both the CIO and AFL, saw race in "class-essentialist" terms and believed that any lingering racial inequality would be resolved by—as Reuther suggested—"the size of the pie" (cited in Nelson 2001: 201).[9] Reuther thought that only with more jobs could "the Negro hope to end his tragic search for justice," while Murray argued that the government needed to pass "a full employment program . . . *before* we can answer the question of what will happen" to achieve racial equality (cited in Lichtenstein 2001: 77). They perceived racism as an artificial distraction for the labor movement promoted largely by employers and supported by a few ignorant racist workers. As such, these progressive leaders were quite consistent in their support of the NAACP and civil rights, and simultaneously disinterested in internal union race problems because they did not perceive racism as a systematic problem in the union movement. To the degree that racism was deemed important, the issue was far secondary to the maintenance of the institutional components of union power such as protecting seniority and local union autonomy.

The NAACP: understanding racism as bigger than the individual

Recent scholarship on the NAACP has portrayed the Association's leadership as quite the opposite of the labor leaders described above; they are perceived as promoting an agenda that emphasized changing racial classifications law while ignoring broader questions of class and substantive economic equality. Judith Stein (1998), for instance, portrays Association leaders as too quick to use courtroom litigation and showing little concern for unions, economic justice, or the fallout from an extremely costly and divisive strategy against a key ally, the unions, in the fight for social democracy.[10] Manning Marable (1991: 32) accuses the Association of "serving as the 'left wing of McCarthyism'", while Risa Goluboff (2003: 1977) portrays NAACP lawyers as only being interested in certain types of cases, usually involving rather narrow forms of race classification, and ignoring the more substantive and class-specific complaints of their clients. Lawyers representing the Legal Defense and Educational Fund (LDF) in the 1940s, Goluboff argues, "marginalized, cabined, and outright repudiated class issues through the complaints they pursued and those they ignored. By the 1950s, when the anti-segregation strategy that eventually led to Brown coalesced, they had succeeded in writing class out of their story" (Goluboff 2003: 1979).

But the Association's involvement in the labor movement reflects something more complicated and nuanced. They did promote legal racial equality, but with an acute understanding of the costs, and only after a lengthy attempt to work with the labor movement to avoid such costs. It is only when grassroots efforts failed, largely because the labor movement refused to accept the existence of systemic racism within its ranks, that the NAACP went towards a more race-specific approach.

The Association began in the 1940s to get more directly involved in union civil rights after years of ambivalence towards black laborers and grassroots activism. This was both because they saw the newly formed CIO as a potential ally and more pragmatically because black union members offered the potential for large numbers of new recruits and money for the organization (Bates 1997: 340–77). Frustrated by their failure to persuade the government to make civil rights changes, as early as 1938, Charles Hamilton Houston suggested that the Association look to labor unions for more "muscle" in the political arena (Kluger 2004: 201). The CIO, in turn, saw the NAACP as a useful ally. Many of the situations in which the NAACP involved itself were battles between rival AFL and CIO (and sometimes leftist/communist) unions, and the NAACP was often helpful in swaying a group of election voters who could determine which union gained control of the workplace.

The autoworkers' strike at Ford's River Rouge, with an estimated 9,000 African American workers, was an important turning point for the NAACP.[11] The River Rouge strike involved competing CIO and AFL autoworkers' unions fighting against each other and against the Ford Corporation, which opposed unionization. Many black workers were caught in the middle, skeptical towards both unions because of labor's history of racial discrimination, and at the same time largely sympathetic towards Henry Ford, who had always been willing to hire black workers during an era when many employers discriminated. During the strike, violence broke out on numerous occasions, and the national media made much noise (and quite likely exaggerated wildly) about black workers participating as strikebreakers and rabble-rousers for Ford ("Memorandum to Messrs White and Wilkins from Mr. Jones" 1941, *NAACP*). Walter White and other NAACP members stepped in aggressively to appeal to black workers not to act as strikebreakers. White countered the news stories with his own press release supporting the UAW-CIO for its efforts at promoting racial diversity, and going personally to the River Rouge plant to attempt to convince black strikebreakers to leave the factory (he was only able to convince a few black workers to leave with him). His efforts—symbolic or otherwise—increased trust between the UAW-CIO and the NAACP. But although White stepped in on behalf of the CIO, he also recognized what he called "the toughest decision" the black auto workers would "ever had to make" in determining whether to strike or take the jobs offered by Ford: "Widespread discrimination by some employers . . . has driven the majority of Negro workers to the ragged edge of existence. Henry Ford has not only hired more Negroes than any other Detroit employer but has given some of them the chance to rise above the menial ranks . . . The attempt to use Negroes as a club over the heads of those who wish to organize themselves in unions in the Ford plants, however, is a dangerous move in times like these" ("Statement of Walter White" 1941, *NAACP*).

With the victory at River Rouge, the Association eagerly joined union organizing drives around the country that would swell the ranks of its own membership. In Winston-Salem, N.C., for instance, hundreds of rank-and-file members of the Food, Tobacco and Agricultural Workers Local 22 joined the local NAACP, transforming it from a membership of 11 in 1941 into a large and militant branch with 2,000 members by 1946 (Korstad 2003). When the Association intervened on behalf of black Boilermakers in San Francisco, the two groups merged, providing a huge boost in members to what had been an almost defunct local membership. By 1947, the NAACP was working arm in arm with the CIO to mobilize new members for both organizations (Goluboff 2005: 1426; "To Mr. Walter White from George L-P Weaver" 1947, *NAACP*).

The late 1940s was arguably the high point of union–civil rights relations (see Korstad and Lichtenstein 1988). The CIO actively organized its members to join the Association and lobbied the NLRB to refuse union certification to any local that either barred or segregated membership on the basis of race. In doing so, the CIO was willing to help fund the legal battle and allow the NAACP to participate in NLRB matters as *amici* in situations where otherwise the Association would be unable to participate, as only labor organizations are allowed as one of the parties ("Memorandum to Mr. Marshall from Marian Wynn Perry" 1948, *NAACP*). The CIO declared that it would oppose segregation of any kind in any of its union locals four years before the Supreme Court declared it unconstitutional and provided money for civil rights organizing and amicus briefs on the major civil rights cases of the day, both labor and non-labor related.

Herbert Hill and the NAACP's Labor Department

The CIO–NAACP alliance would eventually stumble on the massive racial divides in the labor movement that could not be remedied without attention to deeply embedded power structures. The story of Herbert Hill, the NAACP's labor director, is indicative both of the efforts of both organizations to make changes, and the significant barriers that each movement faced. Through much of the 1940s and 1950s, Hill was actively involved in union civil rights struggles. Even in the South where segregation was most fierce, Hill thought that unions were amenable to making reforms to open themselves up to more black workers. Although he recognized that "there is a tremendous anti-Negro sentiment among our white members" and that the KKK had influence within the union, he argued that black workers could potentially join these CIO unions, and if they did, he believed that the union could dominate the entire industry in Alabama ("Memorandum to Mr. Marshall from Marian Wynn Perry" 1948, *NAACP*, Series A, Reel 14).

The NAACP, he thought, could both help black workers in the CIO and be helped by them. Recognizing that "many rank and file Negro workers felt a deep sense of frustration that the (local) CIO Unions . . . have not fulfilled the national commitments," he nonetheless pointed out that "there are many, many thousands of Negro CIO members, in fact the number of Negroes in the CIO very greatly exceeds the number of Negroes who belong to the NAACP in the State of Alabama. . . . Only by identification with the CIO in trade union matters, and by working closely with the CIO leadership will the NAACP be in position to effectively criticize those racial practices that are opposed to the interest of the Negro worker from within the CIO" ("Memorandum to Mr. Marshall from Marian Wynn Perry" 1948, *NAACP*, Series A, Reel 14).[12] Just a few years later, Hill declared "the first significant breakthrough in the Jim Crow pattern within the Southern oil refining industry" when he helped broker a settlement that enabled thirty-two black workers into the previously all-white Oil, Chemical, and Atomic Workers International Union ("Herbert Hill to Warner Brown" 1956, *NAACP*; "Herbert Hill to Dr. E.D. Sprott" 1956, *NAACP*).

Outside of the CIO, Hill was more combative and faced more resistance. He remarked in 1949 about the New York state construction trades, "the leadership of the AF of L construction trades locals is undoubtedly the most backward, bigoted, and odious trade union leadership to be found anywhere in the world." However, Hill felt that only internal organizing against the AFL bureaucracy could spark change, and suggested a plan to expose the problem ("Memorandum to Roy Wilkins from Herbert Hill" 1949, *NAACP*). Hill wrote to other NAACP leaders suggesting that "thousands upon thousands" of black auto union workers could provide "much towards the future growth and development" of local NAACP branches in Michigan and that there should be "day to day functional contact between our local branches and the UAW local unions" ("Herbert Hill to Mr. Edward M. Turner" 1953, *NAACP*). Hill met with southern segregated Oil Workers in an attempt to reach a resolution to integrate racially segregated locals and was able to get an agreement from the Oil Workers International Union to combine two southern locals in Beaumont Texas ("Memorandum to Mr. A. Maceo from Herbert Hill" n.d., *NAACP*). He wrote to the Texas NAACP after meeting with these workers that "we have a fundamental responsibility to the many thousands of Negro industrial workers in Texas who, in one form or another, suffer the effects of racial discrimination in industrial employment. Thousands of these workers belong to labor unions . . . it is quite possible, in certain instances, to use the trade union as an instrument to eliminate racial discrimination in industrial employment. In addition to this—I believe that we can register significant successes in a sustained program to eliminate segregation within the trade union movement itself in Texas" ("To Maceo Smith, Executive Secretary, Texas NAACP State Conference from Herbert Hill" 1953, *NAACP*).[13] A year later, Hill also worked with local civil rights leaders to secure black members into the previously exclusionary Trowel Trades of Miami

Florida ("Howard W. Dixon to Herbert Hill" 1954, *NAACP*). In Johnstown, Pennsylvania, the NAACP tried to provide a job as a sewing operator in the ILGWU for Lou Agnes Holmes. In this case, after constant letters and appeals were ignored for more than a year in response to an effort to get the union and employer to hire back a sewing machine operator, Hill suggested "the most important technique in this specific instance is to work very closely with the Northeast Department of the ILWGU and the Local Union representative. . . . The ILGWU has a collective bargaining agreement with the . . . Company, and therefore it has the power, not only to enforce a non-discriminatory policy, but also to carry out a positive program of equal job opportunity and racial integration within the plant" ("Herbert Hill to Atty. Charles M. Waugh" 1954, *NAACP*; "Memorandum: Press Release Item for Henry Moon, from Herbert Hill" 1953, *NAACP*; "Mrs. Catherine Berret to Mr. David Dubinsky" 1953 *NAACP*; "Herbert Hill to Mrs. Catherine Berret" 1953, *NAACP*). Similarly, Hill told an African American worker contemplating legal action against the Theatrical Stage Employees and Motion Picture Operators that the "first step" for the worker was to try to join the union ("To Mr. Lester P. Bailey, Field Secretary, from Herbert Hill" 1955, *NAACP*).

During these years, however, Hill and the NAACP also found themselves in the middle, and sometimes on the wrong side, of local union battles that involved complex ideological and political rivalries that were not easily navigated—sometimes it just was not very clear who was "good" and "bad." In the case of Alabama mine workers, the NAACP attempted to take sides in a certification struggle that involved not only the employer opposing unionization, but multiple international unions fighting against each other to be elected representatives. The AFL had been particularly upset with the NAACP years earlier when the Association took the side of the CIO in the River Rouge strike. Having had to apologize profusely to various national and local unions for intervening in a situation where the Association did not have all the facts, or simply for intervening in a way that was less than tactful, White, Wilkins, Hill, and others consistently admonished those who improperly got in the middle of union rivalries ("Memorandum to Mr. Hill from Mr. White" 1953, *NAACP*; "Memorandum to Mr. Walter White from Herbert Hill" 1953, *NAACP*; "Alfred Baker Lewis to Mr. Walter White" 1953, *NAACP*). But this problem constantly haunted the Labor Department's efforts as, in a time of active raiding by CIO and AFL unions against each other, the Association continually found itself taking sides with limited knowledge of the local environment and often without trusted people to guide them. Hill pointed out to White in 1954, when the NAACP decided to litigate against the CIO Oilworkers' International union, that "there are three groups of unions operating in the oil refining and chemical industries," including the CIO, the AFL, and various craft and independent unions: "A suit against the CIO Oilworkers' Union alone, while permitting the other unions in this jurisdiction to continue their discriminatory policy, of course does not make sense, and in fact would seriously negate the intent of NAACP objectives" ("Memorandum to Walter White from Herbert Hill" 1954, *NAACP*).

The NAACP also struggled internally with the position of communist unions, many of which were leading the organization of black workers, particularly during this time period when it was under great pressure to rid its organization of suspected communist sympathizers. The NAACP's record on communism, as referenced by Manning Marable's quote early in this section, was not its finest hour as its leadership worked actively and at times exuberantly to expel suspected communists from its ranks.[14] In 1947, the Association joined with the CIO in officially opposing working with those groups that were linked to communism ("To State Presidents and Secretaries, and Executive Secretaries of NAACP Branches" 1947, *NAACP*). Herbert Hill was stridently anti-communist, and in the process, attacked a number of unions that had the support of large numbers of black workers and very good civil rights records. Just two years earlier he had written a publication for the NAACP entitled "The Communist Party—Enemy of Negro Equality," in which he argued "if the Communists gained influence among Negroes they would not hesitate for a moment to foment racial strife and dissension" ("Herbert Hill," Robert F. Wagner Archives). In one case, for instance, Hill intervened in a contested union fight on behalf of the CIO–Steelworkers, against the communist-controlled Mine, Mill, and Smelter Workers Union, a union that one leading race scholar has described as having a "policy of racial egalitarianism [that] remained unmatched" (Kelley 1990: 151). The union also had the active support of both the President and Vice President of the local NAACP and the local President of the Negro Voters League. Black voters were decisive in the NLRB election vote, and CIO leaders as well as some black CIO members were outraged at the local NAACP's lack of support, leading to a significant split between the NAACP and a number of southern CIO unions.

A final issue of contention was that the Association, despite some internal division, emphasized integration of labor unions even in some cases where the black segregated workers wished to maintain their segregated workforce. As Risa Goluboff (2005) has well shown, the Association had contentious debates about situations where black workers were doing better in short-term but segregated employment situations. In the Boilermakers cases of the 1940s, the Association eventually accepted efforts at segregated but equal auxiliary locals. But by the late 1950s, following the victory in *Brown v. Board of Education* (1954), the Association pushed more uncompromisingly towards desegregation, and in certain contexts pitted itself against both George Meany and members of some black local unions—most notably in the South, such as Local 1419 of the International Longshoremen's Association, which felt it was stronger and better able to represent black workers by remaining segregated (Nelson 2001: 132–40).[15]

"Time Has Now Arrived for Decisive Action"[16]

After meeting in July of 1956, the new AFL-CIO Civil Rights Committee authored an optimistic report that trumpeted examples of successful reform and began a "major research study" entitled the "Economic Causes and Consequences of Discrimination" that blamed continuing racism on anti-union members of the KKK. Again, union leaders perceived the movement's problems as confined to a few individual racists in the South. And the AFL-CIO was not incorrect to blame part of the problem on segregationists in the South. By seemingly all accounts, the rising civil rights movement and *Brown v. Board of Education* polarized southern white union members who demanded their facilities stay segregated and that the AFL-CIO stop supporting civil rights organizations. Many white union members in the region quit, disaffiliated from, or disbanded their locals (see Brattain 2001; Draper 1994; "To Mr. Herbert Hill from Russell R. Laslev" 1959, *NAACP*).[17] Other internal union memoranda warned that union civil rights problems were becoming a bigger point of contention with politicians, civil rights leaders, and between white and black membership. One memo found that the "relationship between white and colored workers has deteriorated to the point where now there is practically no communication between the two groups," and that the problem was only likely to escalate to a much broader scale ("Civil Rights Committee Report on Civil Liberties and Internal Security" 1956, "Report on the Civil Rights Committee to the Executive Council of the AFL-CIO" 1956, "To Walter P. Reuther from George L.-P. Weaver, Re: The President's Committee on Government Contracts" 1956, "Willard S. Townsend to Mr. James B. Carey, Secretary-Treasurer, Industrial Union Department, AFL-CIO" 1956, Walter P. Reuther Archives).

But the problems were much more extensive, including in the north in the building trades and in the more progressive CIO unions. In a memorandum from Hill to Clarence Mitchell in 1958, Hill listed three national AFL-CIO affiliated unions that excluded African Americans by constitutional provisions, seven that excluded by "tacit consent," and ten more that segregated its black workers into auxiliary locals ("Memorandum to Mr Mitchell from Mr. Hill" 1958, *NAACP*). Hill's tone towards labor leaders became more urgent and less accommodating of the slow pace of reform—he began to suggest repeatedly in his letters that the Association would go before the NLRB to move for decertification of "those unions whose contracts contain the separate line of progression on a racial basis," and noted that he would consider bringing litigation ("To Sid Lens, Director, Local 329 Building Service Employees Union, AFL-CIO from Herbert Hill" 1956, *NAACP*). He had clearly lost his patience with AFL-CIO leaders, particularly Boris Shishkin, the AFL-CIO Director of Civil Rights, who rarely responded to his requests for meetings and conversations: "Because I have not received any communication in response to my memorandum (regarding the widespread abuses in the union movement) I can only assume the lack of positive action" ("To Mr. Boris Shishkin from

Herbert Hill" 1958, *NAACP*). In December of 1958, the NAACP sent a memorandum written by Hill that detailed specific acts of racial discrimination within the AFL-CIO. Roy Wilkins, in the cover letter to Hill's memorandum, wrote to George Meany that the NAACP had found an "institutionalized pattern of racial discrimination and segregation in many affiliated unions." Hill's 11-page memorandum detailed specific incidences within the labor movement involving exclusion, segregation, unequal wages, benefits, and conditions, and discriminatory seniority systems. Hill demanded "a direct frontal attack against segregation and discrimination within trade unions conducted on a systematic basis by the AFL-CIO" ("Herbert Hill Memorandum to Boris Shishkin" 1958, *NAACP*).[18] More specifically, he demanded the elimination of all segregated locals, the elimination of separate racial seniority lines in union contracts, the prevention of exclusionary practices, and the creation of a liaison between unions and state and federal fair practices committees ("To Charles S. Zimmerman, Chairman, AFL-CIO Civil Rights Committee from Herbert Hill" 1959, *NAACP*). Wilkins told Meany a year later, that "we note that you previously set October 31, 1958 as an absolute deadline for an end to Negro exclusion on federal construction projects ("To George Meany from Roy Wilkins" 1960, *NAACP*)." A. Philip Randolph, in a subsequent memorandum to Meany a few years later, reiterated these concerns, while emphasizing further the issue of apprenticeship programs, referring to a National Urban League report that found the virtual exclusion of blacks in these training programs in all of the 32 cities examined ("Memorandum: Re Civil Rights in the AFL-CIO, to George Meany from A. Philip Randolph" 1961, *NAACP*). In short, the letters and memorandums by the NAACP warning the AFL-CIO of eventual action were both frequent and full of extended deadlines and additional chances for unions to make changes.

Instead of changing, however, the leadership in the AFL-CIO became furious and defensive and demanded an apology from the NAACP. Meany was at the center of this, sometimes by denying discrimination, as he told Wilkins, "I suggest that you direct your protest to the employers who continue to discriminate" ("To Roy Wilkins from George Meany" 1960, *NAACP*). He told Roy Wilkins that the NAACP's attacks on the union were gross distortions and "a source of comfort to the White Citizens Councils in the South" and compared black militants to KKK members ("To Mr. Roy Wilkins from George Meany" 1962, *NAACP*). At other times, he simply seemed like a man cornered, and lambasted Randolph, Hill, the NAACP, and anyone else who he thought threatened the AFL-CIO. When A. Philip Randolph led the formation of the National American Labor Council to demand increased efforts by national unions and the federal government to promote more equality in employment for black workers, claiming that "Negro workers have been the victims of a veritable conspiracy by trade unions, industry and government in that they have been systematically denied job opportunities by blocking their entrance into apprenticeship training programs for the building trades' skilled crafts," he was savagely attacked by Meany and temporarily kicked off the union's leadership board ("Address by A. Philip Randolph at Negro American Labor Council Workshop and Institute Metropolitan Baptist Church" 1961, Walter P. Reuther Archives).[19] Most infamously, Meany publicly scolded Randolph at the AFL-CIO convention, yelling: "Who in the hell appointed you as guardian of the Negro members in America?" (cited in Marshall 1964: 190).

Meany was by no means alone with these sentiments. The response of union leaders, whether from the progressive CIO unions or the more conservative building trades, was generally the same: they tried to deny the existence of internal racism as being anything more than incidental, to blame its existence on outside forces, or to attack the civil rights activists as racists, radicals, and anti-union. The Steelworkers "rarely, if ever, mentioned combating racism as an objective. Instead, they spoke in vague generalities about the need to 'create a better economic and social climate in which to live'" (Nelson 2001: 204). When asked about segregated unions in its southern locals in the early 1960s, the Steelworkers alternately issued complete denials or blamed it entirely on the employer ("To Mr. Herbert Hill from Hugo L. Black, Jr." 1959, *NAACP*; "From Ben Fischer, Director Arbitration Department to Emanuel Muravchick, National Director, JLC" 1963, Robert F. Wagner Archives). The UAW's Reuther was "defensive and maladroit" in response to attacks from civil rights activists within the union, while its Secretary-Treasurer Emil Mazey accused the NAACP of misplacing "its criticism of labor for actions which were obviously the sins of management" (Lichtenstein 1997: 376, 379; see also Boyle 1998; and Thompson 2001: chapters 3 and 5). When challenged by more radical elements within his union, particularly the Trade Union Leadership Council, Reuther attempted to find quiet African American moderates to play the role of appeasers (Lichtenstein 1997: 376–81).

None of these leaders were one-dimensional bigots in any sense. Even Meany actively endorsed the Civil Rights Act and other measures to improve racial equality, and he often listened to and participated with the NAACP in ways that few corporate executive were ever willing to do. Meany, Reuther, and other union leaders, moreover, tended to oppose any type of activism that might threaten their leadership or the broader position of union power; civil rights activists such as the TULC and Dodge Revolutionary Union Movement (DRUM), in the UAW, the National Council of Distributive Workers of America, and the Coalition of Black Trade Unionists were often asking not just for racial equality but for a more radical vision of labor economics (see Thompson 2001: chapter 3; Williams 2005; "Building Trades Discrimination," Robert F. Wagner Archives).

After years of debating, the NAACP began to use legal means to attack union discrimination. Its legal division warned Boris Shishkin that it was ready to take legal action against railway unions that segregated black workers, and its membership resolved in 1960 to litigate against closed-shop agreements ("To Mr. Boris Shishkin, from Amos T. Hall" 1959, *NAACP*). Two years later, it formally filed decertification papers with the NLRB, asking the Board to strip the discriminatory unions of their statutory protection ("NAACP in Legal Attack" 1962, *NAACP*). This same year, Herbert Hill publicly attacked the ILGWU and UAW for discrimination, unions that had long been seen as among the most racially progressive.[20] Unions were again livid with the NAACP and particularly with Herbert Hill—Walter Reuther threatened to resign from the NAACP Board while the ILGWU accused Hill of anti-Semitism (see "William H. Oliver to Walter P. Reuther, Subject: Preliminary Analysis of Allegations Made Against United Auto Workers" 1962, Fleishman "Is the ILGWU Biased" 1962, "Alfred Baker Lewis to Walter Reuther" 1962, Walter P. Reuther Archives). But internally, worried union leaders admitted that the charges had considerable merit.[21] Members of the Civil Rights Department of the AFL-CIO feared the cases "could present serious problems for the entire trade union movement, unless the offenders immediately line up *in practice* with the Civil Rights policy of the AFL-CIO" ("Walter Davis to Boris Shishkin" 1962, Walter P. Reuther Archives).

A 1962 memo from Jacob Clayman of the AFL-CIO's Industrial Union Department to UAW president Walter Reuther, in which he criticized the absence of a union civil rights policy, aptly reflects where national unions were on the eve of the Civil Rights Act: The union's Civil Rights Department "does not have a concise or even a reasonably clear civil rights inventory relating to our various AFL-CIO unions. For example, no one has the answer to . . . which local unions have a separate line of job progression; which local unions have segregated meetings; which local unions have denied membership because of race; which local unions have separate personal facilities, etc.?" ("Jacob Clayman to Walter P. Reuther" 1962, Walter P. Reuther Archives). Clayman hoped that "the anger (even righteous and justifiable [toward decertification petitions filed by the NAACP with the NLRB] . . .) does not blind us to the need for positive reaction from the labor movement" (ibid.). A. Philip Randolph, a year earlier, had expressed a similar sentiment to George Meany: "While any report on racial discrimination in labor union circles by [civil rights groups] is sharply, soundly, and properly condemned, no effort is made by the Civil Rights Department of the AFL-CIO to make its own survey on the problem of race bias in trade unions" ("Memorandum: Re Civil Rights in the AFL-CIO, to George Meany from A. Philip Randolph" 1961, *NAACP*).

What was clear by the mid-1960s was that national unions had significant race problems and had not done enough of substance to address them. Randolph told Meany that "not one single step has been made to desegregate and integrate Jim Crow unions that are a part of national and international unions affiliated with the AFL-CIO" (ibid.). The Kennedy administration was just discovering the depth and degree of the problem, particularly in the building trades, calling it "an extremely bad situation" ("Memorandum from W. Willard Wirtz to Lyndon Baines Johnson" 1963, "Memorandum from W. Willard Wirtz to Honorable Lee White, re: Civil Rights Meeting with Union Leaders on June 13, 1963" 1963, National Archives).[22] Roy Wilkins of the NAACP told George Meany that "a Negro worker needs the patience of Job, the hide of an elephant plus a crowbar to get into Mr. Meany's own union—the plumbers" (cited in Nelson 2001: 235). Their priority was maintaining union power, and even progressive union leaders such as Reuther had endorsed the inclusion of locals into their membership that had constitutions mandating segregation. At the AFL-CIO general counsel meetings, only Randolph opposed the affiliation of white-only union locals. As evidence and charges of far more systematic problems surfaced, union leaders stonewalled, denied, and attempted to deflect the accusations.[23]

By 1968, numerous building trade presidents and members were vocal supporters of George Wallace's presidential campaign, vowing active defiance to even symbolic reform efforts (Boyle 1998: 253–6; Brattain 2001: 245–60; Nelson 2001: 290; Thompson 2001: 116). Frustrated by the glacial pace of change in many unions' civil rights policies, moreover, African-American union members and civil rights activists were increasingly organizing more radical movements such as the formation in 1968 of DRUM in the Midwest, and nonunion affiliated locals of the NAACP, including the Congress of Racial Equality (CORE) in Philadelphia and the Western Addition Community Organization (WACO) in San Francisco, to challenge stagnant unions with strikes and picketing.[24]

Conclusion

Union leaders saw race not as a systemic or institutional problem but merely as a distraction led by a relatively few prejudiced individuals. When accused of racial prejudices, they reacted defensively, ignoring the institutional role in perpetuating existing racial inequality, especially regarding seniority systems and specific collective bargaining agreements. Alternatively, the NAACP was far more focused on the institutional forms of racism and aware of the ways that race and class were inextricably fused. While they participated in the polarization that would create unhealthy divisions between the two movements in the post–civil rights era, they also recognized the need for the labor movement in ways that union leaders failed to reciprocate. Unfortunately, such arguments that saw race as more of a structural problem lost out in the fighting and name-calling that would embroil these two movements. And as the two movements argued with each other, truly powerful opponents mobilized to take advantage. The post-civil rights era history would quickly become dominated by the successes of those who opposed both the civil rights and labor movements, and to this day, leaders of the beleaguered movements struggle to learn these lessons as they search for a way of countering the conservative tide.

The division over race in the labor movement in many ways mirrors debates within American political development and political science with regard to understanding the importance of race and class. The conventional view within the field has been to see power relations primarily in terms of class matters, with race viewed as "exceptional" and "provocative," but also largely "irrational" and a distraction from true material divisions. Race and APD scholarship has taken a dramatic step in placing race at the forefront of understanding power relations and must continue to do so if we are to have a more accurate understanding of American democracy. But our scholarship should not further parallel the divide discussed in this chapter by seeking its own form of juxtaposition between class and race. Race continues to matter in America, not because it exists independently from other forms of power, but because it is a central component of a larger institutional, economic, and social nexus. Our goal as we move forward in the twenty-first century should not be to replace one fundamental category with another but to unpack and identify more clearly how this nexus restricts movement towards a truly progressive and equal politics and society.

Notes

1 The chapter provides only a snippet of a much larger political debate that involved the two movements, as well as elected officials, bureaucrats, and judges over racism and discrimination in the labor movement. I flesh out the broader debate more thoroughly in *Black and Blue: African Americans, the Labor Movement, and the Decline of the Democratic Party* (2008).

2 This is an argument inspired by Paul Gilroy (1987), and Michael Omi and Howard Winant (1994).

3 Though see Walton (1972); Katznelson (1976); Mink (1986); and Rogin (1988).

4 In 1968, the EEOC became the first Federal agency to collect yearly statistics of labor unions on the basis of race. The Bureau of Labor Statistics did not track union membership by race until 1984.

5 For discussions of the positive and "unprecedented" efforts of the CIO in organizing black workers, see Korstad and Lichtenstein (1988: 786); Cohen (1991); Zieger (1995: 155); Stepan-Norris and Zeitlin (2003).

6 The UAW passed an anti-discrimination resolution in 1941. See "UAW-CIO Heads Tell Plants 'No More Discrimination'" 1941, *NAACP*. The AFL had rejected such a resolution in 1940 despite formal appeals by A. Philip Randolph and Milton Webster representing the all-black Brotherhood of Sleeping Car Porters. "A.F. of L. Places its Stamp of Approval on Discrimination," 1940, *NAACP*. More broadly regarding Reuther, see Lichtenstein (1997: 379); and Sugrue (1998: 100–3). Regarding McDonald, see Foner (1974: 323); Nelson (2001); Stein (1998).

7 Nelson (2001) provides extensive detail of the differences in Steelworker and Longshore worker unions.

8 These surveys are available at George W. Meany Archives, Department of Civil Rights Records, 1943–67, Box 1. For discussion of specific locals, see Brattain (2001: 226–7); Draper (1994: 39).

9 Also see Nelson's (2001: 98–128) description of Bridges.

10 Stein (1998) argues that the Steelworkers' Union, a union that was far ahead of American society on issues of racial equality, was severely weakened by divisive litigation brought about by narrow-minded civil rights activists who had little concern with the broader impact their lawsuits were having on the union during a time of national economic downturn and the revitalization of anti-labor, big business.

11 For discussion of the strike, see Meier and Rudwick (1979); Korstad and Lichtenstein (1988); and Williams (2005).

12 Hill was criticized by others in the NAACP who felt that the Association was being used by the CIO to fight a communist union that had the support of black workers. See, e.g. "Memorandum to Mr. Gloster B. Current, Director of Branches from Mrs. Ruby Hurley" 1953, *NAACP*, Series A, Reel 11.

13 More extensively on Hill's efforts with the oil unions, see Lee (n.d.).

14 Also see Carol Anderson (2003) and Martha Biondi (2003) who argue that the anti-communist ideology of the Association led it to purge those who attempted to more deeply engage the nexus of race and class inequality that affected so many African-American workers at the time. Also see Horne (1985).

15 The issue for the ILA would not be resolved for years to come. In *Bailey v. Ryan Stevedoring Co.* (1976) (528 F. 2d 551: 553), the Fifth Circuit combined two segregated Longshore workers' unions in Baton Rouge, Louisiana, on the ground that segregation was inherently unequal.

16 From "To George Meany from Roy Wilkins," 1960, *NAACP*.

17 Lasley told Hill that "50 per cent of our stock yard locals disaffiliated with our union because of our civil rights policy" ("To Mr. Herbert Hill from Russell R. Laslev," 1959, *NAACP*).

18 These conclusions were later issued in an NAACP report, "Racism within Organized Labor: A Report of Five Years of the AFL-CIO 1955–1960."

19 "Less than one percent of building construction apprentices are Negro. Even in New York, probably the most liberal state in America, in 1940, according to the New York." ("Address by A. Philip Randolph at Negro American Labor Council Workshop and Institute Metropolitan Baptist Church," 1961, Walter P. Reuther Archives).

20 For good accounts of both the progressive tendencies and the racial divisions within the ILGWU, see Bao (2001); and Bender (2004).

21 See "William H. Oliver to Walter P. Reuther, Subject: Preliminary Analysis of Allegations Made Against United Auto Workers" (1962, Walter P. Reuther Archives), in which, while he criticizes many of Herbert Hill's claims as false, admits that ultimately, the UAW plants under discussion are strongly unequal in terms of the numbers of black workers and the status of those workers vis-à-vis white workers in the plants. Moreover, "the contract language remains unchanged which constitutes a glaring inequity and could cause embarrassment to the Union as well as the Corporation."

22 By 1967, William Gould wrote in an EEOC memo that the "toughest [discrimination] cases are de facto segregation in northern plants [such as the UAW]" (Gould, "Employment Security, Seniority and Race: The Role of Title VII of the Civil Rights Act of 1964: A Report to the EEOC," National Archives). The same year, Roger Wilkins of the NAACP, in a speech to the AFL-CIO, listed examples of systemic union discrimination in building trades, airline clerks, steelworkers, and firefighters (Riesel 1967).

23 At the UAW, for instance, repeated memos from William H. Oliver of its Fair Practices Department to Reuther indicated extensive racial problems. See "Memorandum from William H. Oliver," 1959, 1962, Walter P. Reuther Archives.

24 On DRUM, see Thompson (2001); and Meier and Rudwick (1979). On CORE and NAACP locals challenging the building trades in Philadelphia during the early 1960s, see Sugrue (2004). On WACO which challenged the union at the Emporium Capwell clothing store in San Francisco, see Schiller (2004: 129).

Bibliography

Primary sources

Cases cited

Bailey v. Ryan Stevedoring Co. (1976) 528 F. 2d 551 (5th Cir)
Brown v. Board of Education (1954) 347 U.S. 483

Papers of the NAACP

"A.F. of L. Places its Stamp of Approval on Discrimination" (December 7, 1940) by L. Lewis, *Pittsburgh Courier*, in J.H. Bracey, Jr. and A. Meier (eds) *Papers of the NAACP: Part 13, The NAACP and Labor, 1940–1955* (microfilm, 1992), Series A, Reel 3.

"Alfred Baker Lewis to Mr. Walter White" (September 29, 1953) in J.H. Bracey, Jr. and A. Meier (eds) *Papers of the NAACP: Part 13, The NAACP and Labor, 1940–1955* (microfilm, 1992), Series A, Reel 17.

"Details of Strike at the Riverside Division of the Dam River Cotton Mills as related to C.K. Coleman (President of the Local NAACP) by Mrs. Mary Lumpkin on Saturday, June 24, 1944" (June 24, 1944) in J.H. Bracey, Jr. and A. Meier (eds) *Papers of the NAACP: Part 13, The NAACP and Labor, 1940–1955* (microfilm, 1992), Series A, Reel 4.

"Herbert Hill Memorandum to Boris Shishkin, Director Civil Rights Department, AFL-CIO" (December 4, 1958) in J.H. Bracey, Jr. and A. Meier (eds) *Papers of the NAACP: Part 13, The NAACP and Labor, 1940–1955* (microfilm, 1992), Supplement to Part 13, Reel 1.

"Herbert Hill to Atty. Charles M. Waugh, President, Muskegon NAACP Branch" (February 19, 1954) in J.H. Bracey, Jr. and A. Meier (eds) *Papers of the NAACP: Part 13, The NAACP and Labor, 1940–1955* (microfilm, 1992), Series A, Reel 19.

"Herbert Hill to Dr. E.D. Sprott" (March 21, 1956) in J.H. Bracey, Jr. and A. Meier (eds) *Papers of the NAACP: Part 13, The NAACP and Labor, 1940–1955* (microfilm, 1992), Supplement, Reel 12.

"Herbert Hill to Mrs. Catherine Berret" (April 24, 1953) in J.H. Bracey, Jr. and A. Meier (eds) *Papers of the NAACP: Part 13, The NAACP and Labor, 1940–1955* (microfilm, 1992), Series A, Reel 19.

"Herbert Hill to Mr. Edward M. Turner, President, Michigan State Conference NAACP" (May 7, 1953) in J.H. Bracey, Jr. and A. Meier (eds) *Papers of the NAACP: Part 13, The NAACP and Labor, 1940–1955* (microfilm, 1992), Series A, Reel 19.

"Herbert Hill to Warner Brown" (March 12, 1956) in J.H. Bracey, Jr. and A. Meier (eds) *Papers of the NAACP: Part 13, The NAACP and Labor, 1940–1955* (microfilm, 1992), Supplement, Reel 12.

"Howard W. Dixon to Herbert Hill" (August 21, 1954) in J.H. Bracey, Jr. and A. Meier (eds) *Papers of the NAACP: Part 13, The NAACP and Labor, 1940–1955* (microfilm, 1992), Series A, Reel 3.

"Memorandum: Press Release Item for Henry Moon, from Herbert Hill" (December 17, 1953) in J.H. Bracey, Jr. and A. Meier (eds) *Papers of the NAACP: Part 13, The NAACP and Labor, 1940–1955* (microfilm, 1992), Series A, Reel 19.

"Memorandum: Re Civil Rights in the AFL-CIO, to George Meany from A. Philip Randolph, Subject, Race Bias in Trade Unions Affiliated to the AFL-CIO" (June 14, 1961) in J.H. Bracey, Jr. and A. Meier (eds) *Papers of the NAACP: Part 13, The NAACP and Labor, 1940–1955* (microfilm, 1992), Supplement to Part 13, Reel 1.

"Memorandum to Mr. Hill from Mr. White" (November 11, 1953) in J.H. Bracey, Jr. and A. Meier (eds) *Papers of the NAACP: Part 13, The NAACP and Labor, 1940–1955* (microfilm, 1992), Series A, Reel 13.

"Memorandum to Mr. Marshall from Marian Wynn Perry, RE: Conference with Frank Donner of the CIO" (September 17, 1948) in J.H. Bracey, Jr. and A. Meier (eds) *Papers of the NAACP: Part 13, The NAACP and Labor, 1940–1955* (microfilm, 1992), Series A, Reel 14.

"Memorandum to Messrs White and Wilkins from Mr. Jones" (April 5, 1941) in J.H. Bracey, Jr. and A. Meier (eds) *Papers of the NAACP: Part 13, The NAACP and Labor, 1940–1955* (microfilm, 1992), Series A, Reel 3.

"Memorandum to Mr. A. Maceo Smith, from Herbert Hill: Subject, Report of Labor Relations Assistant's activities in Texas" (n.d.) in J.H. Bracey, Jr. and A. Meier (eds) *Papers of the NAACP: Part 13, The NAACP and Labor, 1940–1955* (microfilm, 1992), Series A, Reel 20.

"Memorandum to Mr. Gloster B. Current, Director of Branches from Mrs. Ruby Hurley, Regional Secretary, re: Herbert Hill's Report" (July 17, 1953)) in J.H. Bracey, Jr. and A. Meier (eds) *Papers of the NAACP: Part 13, The NAACP and Labor, 1940–1955* (microfilm, 1992), Series A, Reel 11.

"Memorandum to Mr. Mitchell from Herbert Hill" (May 13, 1958) in J.H. Bracey, Jr. and A. Meier (eds) *Papers of the NAACP: Part 13, The NAACP and Labor, 1940–1955* (microfilm, 1992), Supplement to Part 13, Reel 1.

"Memorandum to Mr. Walter White from Herbert Hill" (November 23, 1953) in J.H. Bracey, Jr. and A. Meier (eds) *Papers of the NAACP: Part 13, The NAACP and Labor, 1940–1955* (microfilm, 1992), Series A, Reel 13.

"Memorandum to Mr. White from Mr. Thomas, re: Program for Work in the Field of Labor" (May 5, 1943) in J.H. Bracey, Jr. and A. Meier (eds) *Papers of the NAACP: Part 13, The NAACP and Labor, 1940–1955* (microfilm, 1992), Series A, Reel 6.

"Memorandum: to Roy Wilkins from Herbert Hill" (April 1, 1949) in J.H. Bracey, Jr. and A. Meier (eds) *Papers of the NAACP: Part 13, The NAACP and Labor, 1940–1955* (microfilm, 1992), Series A, Reel 20.

"Memorandum to Walter White from Herbert Hill, Re: Securing of Plaintiffs and Preparation of Material for Litigation Attacking Union-Management Discrimination in the Oil Refining Industry" (September 3, 1954) in J.H. Bracey, Jr. and A. Meier (eds) *Papers of the NAACP: Part 13, The NAACP and Labor, 1940–1955* (microfilm, 1992), Series A, Reel 13.

"Mrs. Catherine Berret to Mr. David Dubinsky, Pres., I.L.G.W.U." (6 March 1953) in J.H. Bracey, Jr. and A. Meier (eds) *Papers of the NAACP: Part 13, The NAACP and Labor, 1940–1955* (microfilm, 1992), Series A, Reel 19.

"NAACP in Legal Attack" (October 16, 1962) in J.H. Bracey, Jr. and A. Meier (eds) *Papers of the NAACP: Part 13, The NAACP and Labor, 1940–1955* (microfilm, 1992), Supplement, Reel 11.

"Race Issue Too Tough, Union Sees No Settlement Prospect" (31 May 1944) Register, in J.H. Bracey, Jr. and A. Meier (eds) *Papers of the NAACP: Part 13, The NAACP and Labor, 1940–1955* (microfilm, 1992), Series A, Reel 4.

"Second Report on Discrimination in Labor Unions" (May 13, 1940) in J.H. Bracey,

Jr. and A. Meier (eds) *Papers of the NAACP: Part 13, The NAACP and Labor, 1940–1955* (microfilm, 1992), Series A, Reel 4.

"State of Walter White" (5 April 1941) in J.H. Bracey, Jr. and A. Meier (eds) *Papers of the NAACP: Part 13, The NAACP and Labor, 1940–1955* (microfilm, 1992), Series A, Reel 3.

"To A. Maceo Smith, Executive Secretary, Texas NAACP State Conference, from Herbert Hill" (February 2, 1953), in J.H. Bracey, Jr. and A. Meier (eds) *Papers of the NAACP: Part 13, The NAACP and Labor, 1940–1955* (microfilm, 1992), Series A, Reel 20.

"To Charles S. Zimmerman, Chairman, AFL-CIO Civil Rights Committee from Herbert Hill" (February 10, 1959) in J.H. Bracey, Jr. and A. Meier (eds) *Papers of the NAACP: Part 13, The NAACP and Labor, 1940–1955* (microfilm, 1992), Supplement to Part 13, Reel 1.

"To George Meany from Roy Wilkins" (25 May 1960) in J.H. Bracey, Jr. and A. Meier (eds) *Papers of the NAACP: Part 13, The NAACP and Labor, 1940–1955* (microfilm, 1992), Supplement to Part 13, Reel 1.

"To Hon. Francis Biddle from Walter White, Secretary, NAACP" (October 10, 1941) in J.H. Bracey, Jr. and A. Meier (eds) *Papers of the NAACP: Part 13, The NAACP and Labor, 1940–1955* (microfilm, 1992), Series A, Reel 14.

"To Mr. Boris Shishkin, from Amos T. Hall" (April 6, 1959) in J.H. Bracey, Jr. and A. Meier (eds) *Papers of the NAACP: Part 13, The NAACP and Labor, 1940–1955* (microfilm, 1992), Supplement to Part 13, Reel 1.

"To Mr. Boris Shishkin from Herbert Hill" (October 16, 1958) in J.H. Bracey, Jr. and A. Meier (eds) *Papers of the NAACP: Part 13, The NAACP and Labor, 1940–1955* (microfilm, 1992), Supplement to Part 13, Reel 1.

"To Mr. Herbert Hill from Hugo L. Black, Jr." (March 23, 1959) in J.H. Bracey, Jr. and A. Meier (eds) *Papers of the NAACP: Part 13, The NAACP and Labor, 1940–1955* (microfilm, 1992), Supplement to Part 13, Reel 1.

"To Mr. Herbert Hill from Russell R. Lasley, Vice President of United Packinghouse Workers of America" (January 16, 1959) in J.H. Bracey, Jr. and A. Meier (eds) *Papers of the NAACP: Part 13, The NAACP and Labor, 1940–1955* (microfilm, 1992), Supplement to Part 13, Reel 1.

"To Mr. Lester P. Bailey, Field Secretary, from Herbert Hill" (August 3, 1955) in J.H. Bracey, Jr. and A. Meier (eds) *Papers of the NAACP: Part 13, The NAACP and Labor, 1940–1955* (microfilm, 1992), Series A, Reel 11.

"To Mr. R. J. Thomas, President, UAW-CIO, from Walter White" (November 21, 1941) in J.H. Bracey, Jr. and A. Meier (eds) *Papers of the NAACP: Part 13, The NAACP and Labor, 1940–1955* (microfilm, 1992), Series A, Reel 11.

"To Mr. Roy Wilkins from George Meany" (20 November 1962) in J.H. Bracey, Jr. and A. Meier (eds) *Papers of the NAACP: Part 13, The NAACP and Labor, 1940–1955* (microfilm, 1992), Supplement to Part 13, Reel 1.

"To Mr. Walter White from George L-P Weaver, Director, Committee to Abolish Discrimination, CIO" (May 16, 1947) in J.H. Bracey, Jr. and A. Meier (eds) *Papers of the NAACP: Part 13, The NAACP and Labor, 1940–1955* (microfilm, 1992), Series A, Reel 14.

"To Roy Wilkins from George Meany" (26 May 1960) in J.H. Bracey, Jr. and A. Meier (eds) *Papers of the NAACP: Part 13, The NAACP and Labor, 1940–1955* (microfilm, 1992), Supplement to Part 13, Reel 1.

"To Sid Lens, Director, Local 329 Building Service Employees Union, AFL-CIO from

Herbert Hill" (14 February 1956) in J.H. Bracey, Jr. and A. Meier (eds) *Papers of the NAACP: Part 13, The NAACP and Labor, 1940–1955* (microfilm, 1992), Supplement to Part 13, Reel 1.

"To State Presidents and Secretaries, and Executive Secretaries of NAACP Branches, from Gloster B. Current, Director of Branches" (February 19, 1947), in J.H. Bracey, Jr. and A. Meier (eds) *Papers of the NAACP: Part 13, The NAACP and Labor, 1940–1955* (microfilm, 1992), Series A, Reel 14.

"UAW-CIO Heads Tell Plants 'No More Discrimination,'" (October 17, 1941) in J.H. Bracey, Jr. and A. Meier (eds) *Papers of the NAACP: Part 13, The NAACP and Labor, 1940–1955* (microfilm, 1992), Series A, Reel 3.

"Union Integration" (no date, probably summer 1955) in J.H. Bracey, Jr. and A. Meier (eds) *Papers of the NAACP: Part 13, The NAACP and Labor, 1940–1955* (microfilm, 1992), Series A, Reel 3.

National Archives

Gould, William "Employment Security, Seniority and Race: The Role of Title VII of the Civil Rights Act of 1964: A Report to the EEOC," Records of the EEOC, Record Group 403, Records of Chairman Stephen Shulman, 1966–68, Box 4, National Archives.

"Memorandum from W. Willard Wirtz to Lyndon Baines Johnson" (June 12, 1963); and "Memorandum from W. Willard Wirtz to Honorable Lee White, re: Civil Rights Meeting with Union Leaders on June 13, 1963" (June 12, 1963), General Records of the Department of Labor, Record Group 174, Records of the Special Assistant and Executive Assistant to the Secretary, John C. Donovan, 1961–64, Box 8, National Archives.

Robert F. Wagner Archives

"Building Trades Discrimination," Box 9, Folder 4, Papers of Cleveland Robinson, Robert F. Wagner Archives, New York University.

"From Ben Fischer, Director Arbitration Department to Emanuel Muravchick, National Director, JLC," December 11, 1963, Jewish Labor Council Papers, General Files, United Steelworkers of America, Robert F. Wagner Archives, New York University.

"Herbert Hill," Robert F. Wagner Archives, Jewish Leadership Council Papers, New York University.

Walter P. Reuther Archives

"Address by A. Philip Randolph at Negro American Labor Council Workshop and Institute Metropolitan Baptist Church" (February 17, 1961) Box 348, Folder 7, Walter P. Reuther Archives, Wayne State University.

"Alfred Baker Lewis to Walter Reuther" (October 19, 1962) Box 504, Folder 1, Walter P. Reuther Archives, Wayne State University.

"Civil Rights Committee Report on Civil Liberties and Internal Security" (August 29, 1956) Box 304, Folder 8, Walter P. Reuther Archives, Wayne State University.

Fleishman, H. "Is the ILGWU Biased" (November 5, 1962) Box 504, Folder 2, Walter P. Reuther Archives, Wayne State University.

"Jacob Clayman to Walter P. Reuther" (November 2, 1962) Box 504, Folder 4, Walter P. Reuther Archives, Wayne State University.
"Memorandum from William H. Oliver" (February 5, 1959) Box 503, Folder 27, Walter P. Reuther Archives, Wayne State University.
"Memorandum from William H. Oliver" (November 1, 1962) Box 504, Folder 3, Walter P. Reuther Archives, Wayne State University.
"Report of the Civil Rights Committee to the Executive Council of the AFL-CIO" (August 29, 1956) Box 312, Folder 5, Walter P. Reuther Archives, Wayne State University.
"To Walter P. Reuther from George L-P Weaver, Re: The President's Committee on Government Contracts" (December 7, 1956) Box 312, Folder 5, Walter P. Reuther Archives, Wayne State University.
"Walter Davis to Boris Shishkin" (August 22, 1962) Box 504, Folder 4, Walter P. Reuther Archives, Wayne State University.
"Willard S. Townsend to Mr. James B. Carey, Secretary-Treasurer, Industrial Union Department, AFL-CIO" (April 23, 1956) Box 304, Folder 5, Walter P. Reuther Archives, Wayne State University.
"William H. Oliver to Walter P. Reuther, Subject: Preliminary Analysis of Allegations Made Against United Auto Workers by the NAACP Labor Secretary Which Were Unfounded" (November 1, 1962) Box 504, Folder 3, Walter P. Reuther Archives, Wayne State University.

References and secondary sources

Anderson, C. (2003) *Eyes off the Prize: The United Nations and the African American Struggle for Human Rights, 1944–55*, New York: Cambridge University Press.
Appiah, K.A. (1996) "Race, Culture, Identity: Misunderstood Connections," in K.A. Appiah and A. Guttman (eds) *Color Conscious: The Political Morality of Race*, Princeton, NJ: Princeton University Press.
Arnesen, E. (2001) *Brotherhoods of Color, Black Railroad Workers and the Struggle for Equality*, London: Harvard University Press.
Bao, X. (2001) *Holding Up More than Half the Sky: Chinese Women Garment Workers in New York City, 1948–1952*, Urbana: University of Illinois Press.
Bates, B.T. (1997) "A New Crowd Challenges the Agenda of an Old Guard in the NAACP, 1933–1941," *American Historical Review*, 102: 340–77.
Bender, D.E. (2004) *Sweated Work, Weak Bodies: Anti-Sweatshop Campaigns and Languages of Labor*, New Brunswick, NJ: Rutgers University Press.
Bensel, R.F. (2000) *The Political Economy of American Industrialization, 1877–1900*, New York: Cambridge University Press.
Bernstein, D.E. (2001) *Only One Place of Redress: African Americans, Labor Regulations, and the Courts from Reconstruction to the New Deal*, Durham, NC: Duke University Press.
Biondi, M. (2003) *To Stand and Fight: The Struggle for Post War Civil Rights in New York City*, Cambridge: Harvard University Press.
Bohrman, R. and Murakawa, N. (2005) "Remaking Big Government: Immigration and Crime Control in the United States," in J. Sudbury (ed.) *Global Lockdown: Gender, Race, and the Rise of the Prison Industrial Complex*, New York: Routledge.
Boyle, K. (1998) *The UAW and the Heyday of American Liberalism 1945–1968*, Ithaca, NY: Cornell University Press.

Brattain, M. (2001) *The Politics of Whiteness: Race, Workers, and Culture in the Modern South*, Princeton, NJ: Princeton University Press.

Brown, M.K. (1999) *Race, Money, and the American Welfare State*, Ithaca, NY: Cornell University Press.

Cohen, L. (1991) *Making a New Deal: Industrial Workers in Chicago, 1919–1939*, New York: Cambridge Press.

Draper, A. (1994) *Conflict of Interests: Organized Labor and the Civil Rights Movement in the South, 1954–1968*, Ithaca, NY: ILR Press.

Fields, B.J. (1982) "Ideology and Race in American History," in J.M. Kousser and J.M. McPherson (eds) *Region, Race, and Reconstruction: Essays in Honor of C. Vann Woodward*, New York: Oxford University Press.

Foner, E. (1974) *Organized Labor and the Black Worker, 1619–1973*, New York: Praeger.

Frymer, P. (2008) *Black and Blue: African Americans, the Labor Movement, and the Decline of the Democratic Party*, Princeton, NJ: Princeton University Press.

Gilroy, P. (1987) *"There Ain't No Black in the Union Jack:" The Cultural Politics of Race and Nation*, Chicago: University of Chicago Press.

—— (2000) *Against Race: Imagining Political Culture Beyond the Color Line*, Cambridge: Belknap Press.

Goluboff, R.L. (2003) "'We Live in a Free House Such as It Is:' Class and the Creation of Modern Civil Rights," *University of Pennsylvania Law Review*, 151: 1977–2018.

—— (2005) "'Let Economic Equality Take Care of Itself:' The NAACP, Labor Litigation, and the Making of Civil Rights in the 1940s," *UCLA Law Review*, 52: 1393–1486.

Hall, S. (2000) "Old and New Identities, Old and New Ethnicities," in L. Black and J. Solomos (eds) *Theories of Race and Racism*, New York: Routledge.

Honey, M.K. (1993) *Southern Labor and Black Civil Rights: Organizing Memphis Workers*, Urbana: University of Illinois Press.

Horne, G. (1985) *Black and Red: W.E.B. Du Bois and the Afro-American Response to the Cold War, 1944–1963*, Albany: State University of New York Press.

Katznelson, I. (1976) *Black Men, White Cities: Race, Politics and Migration in the United States 1900–1930 and Britain 1948 to 1968*, Chicago: University of Chicago Press.

—— (2005) *When Affirmative Action Was White: An Untold History of Racial Inequality in America*, New York: Norton.

Kelley, R.D.G. (1990) *Hammer and Hoe: Alabama Communists During the Great Depression*, Chapel Hill: University of North Carolina Press.

Kim, C.J. (2000) *The Politics of Black-Korean Conflict in New York City*, New Haven, CT: Yale University Press.

King, D.S. (1997) *Separate and Unequal: Black Americans and the U.S. Federal Government*, New York: Oxford University Press.

—— and Smith, R.M. (2005) "Racial Orders in American Political Development," *American Political Science Review*, 99: 75–92.

Klinkner, P.A. and Smith, R.M. (1999) *The Unsteady March: The Rise and Decline of Racial Equality in America*, Chicago: University of Chicago Press.

Kluger, R. (2004) *Simple Justice: The History of Brown v. Board of Education and Black America's Struggle for Equality*, New York: Vintage.

Korstad, R.R. (2003) *Civil Rights Unionism: Tobacco Workers and the Struggle for*

Democracy in the Mid-Twentieth-Century South, Chapel Hill: University of North Carolina Press.

—— and Lichtenstein, N. (1988) "Opportunities Found and Lost: Labor, Radicals and the Early Civil Rights Movement," *Journal of American History*, 75: 786–811.

Kryder, D. (2000) *Divided Arsenal: Race and the American State During World War II*, New York: Cambridge University Press.

Lee, S. (n.d.) "Hotspots in a Cold War: The NAACP's Postwar Labor Constitutionalism, 1948–1964" (unpublished manuscript)

Lewis, E. (1990) *In Their Own Interests: Race, Class, and Power in Twentieth Century Norfolk, Virginia*, Berkeley: University of California Press.

Lichtenstein, N. (1997) *Walter Reuther: The Most Dangerous Man in Detroit*, Urbana: University of Illinois Press.

—— (2001) *State of the Union: A Century of American Labor*, Princeton, NJ: Princeton University Press.

Lieberman, R.C. (1998) *Shifting the Color Line: Race and the American Welfare State*, Cambridge, MA: Harvard University Press.

McCray, G.F. (1944) "The Labor Movement," in F. Murray (ed.) *The Negro Handbook: A Manual of Current Facts, Statistics, and General Information Concerning Negroes in the United States*, New York: Wendell Malliet.

Marable, M. (1991) *Race, Reform and Rebellion: The Second Reconstruction in Black America, 1945–1990*, Jackson: University of Mississippi Press.

Marshall, F.R. (1965) *The Negro and Organized Labor*, New York: Wiley.

—— (1964) "Unions and the Negro Community," *Industrial and Labor Relations Review*, 22: 179–202.

Marx, A.W. (1998) *Making Race and Nation: A Comparison of South Africa, the United States, and Brazil*, New York: Cambridge University Press.

Meier, A. and Rudwick, E.M. (1979) *Black Detroit and the Rise of the UAW*, New York: Oxford University Press.

Minchin, T.J. (2001) *The Color of Work: The Struggle for Civil Rights in the Southern Paper Industry*, Chapel Hill: University of North Carolina Press.

—— (2005) *Fighting Against the Odds: A History of Southern Labor Since World War II*, Gainesville: University of Florida Press.

Mink, G. (1986) *Old Labor and New Immigrants in American Political Development: Union, Party, and State, 1875–1920*, Ithaca, NY: Cornell University Press.

Nelson, B. (2001) *Divided We Stand: American Workers and the Struggle for Black Equality*, Princeton, NJ: Princeton University Press.

Omi, M. and Winant, H. (1994) *Racial Formation in the United States: From the 1960s to the 1980s*, New York: Routledge.

Orren, K. (1995) "The Primacy of Labor in American Constitutional Development," *American Political Science Review*, 89: 377–88.

Piven F.F. and Cloward, R.A. (1978) *Poor People's Movements: Why They Succeed, How They Fail*, New York: Vintage.

Reed, A.L. (1997) *W.E.B. Du Bois and American Political Thought: Fabianism and the Color Line*, New York: Oxford University Press.

—— (2002) "Unraveling the Relation of Race and Class in American Politics," *Political Power and Social Theory*, 15: 265–74.

Riesel, V. (1967) "NAACP Warns Labor Chief to Admit Black Workers or Government and Negroes Will Smash Down Union Doors," *Inside Labor*, December 13.

Roediger, D. (1994) *Toward the Abolition of Whiteness: Essays on Race, Politics, and Working Class History*, London: Verso.

—— (1999) *Wages of Whiteness: Race and the Making of the American Working Class*, London: Verso.

Rogin, M.P. (1988) *Ronald Reagan, the Movie: and Other Episodes of Political Demonology*, Berkeley: University of California Press.

Schiller, R.E. (2004) "The *Emporium Capwell* Case: Race, Labor Law, and the Crisis of Post-War Liberalism," *Berkeley Journal of Employment and Labor Law*, 25: 129–66.

Sears, D.O., Sidanius, J., and Bobo, L. (eds) (2000) *Racialized Politics: The Debate About Racism in America*, Chicago: University of Chicago Press.

Skocpol, T. (1992) *Protecting Soldiers and Mothers: The Political Origins of Social Policy in the United States*, Cambridge, MA: Harvard University Press.

Skowronek, S. (1982) *Building a New American State: The Expansion of National Administrative Capacities, 1877–1920*, New York: Cambridge University Press.

Skrentny, J.D. (2002) *The Minority Rights Revolution*, Cambridge, MA: Harvard University Press.

Smith, R.M. (1997) *Civic Ideals: Conflicting Visions of Citizenship in U.S. History*, New Haven, CT: Yale University Press.

Stein, J. (1998) *Running Steel, Running America: Race, Economic Policy, and the Decline of Liberalism*, Chapel Hill: University of North Carolina Press.

Stepan-Norris, J. and Zeitlin, M. (2003) *Left Out: Reds and American Industrial Unions*, New York: Cambridge University Press.

Sugrue, T.J. (1998) *The Origins of the Urban Crisis: Race and Inequality in Post-War Detroit*, Princeton, NJ: Princeton University Press.

—— (2004) "Affirmative Action from Below: Civil Rights, the Building Trades, and the Politics of Racial Equality in the Urban North, 1945–1969," *Journal of American History*, 91: 145–73.

Thompson, H.A. (2001) *Whose Detroit? Politics, Labor, and Race in a Modern American City*, Ithaca, NY: Cornell University Press.

Wacquant, L. (2001) "Deadly Symbiosis: When Ghetto and Prison Meet and Mesh," *Punishment and Society*, 3: 95–133.

Walton, H., Jr. (1972) *Black Political Parties: An Historical and Political Analysis*, New York: Free Press.

—— (1997) *African American Power and Politics: The Political Context Variable*, New York: Columbia University Press.

Williams, C. (2005) "The Racial Politics of Progressive Americanism: New Deal Liberalism and the Subordination of Black Workers in the UAW," *Studies in American Political Development*, 19: 75–97.

Wilson, W.J. (1978) *The Declining Significance of Race*, Chicago: University of Chicago Press.

Zieger, R.H. (1995) *The CIO, 1935–55*, Chapel Hill: University of North Carolina Press.

9 Legacies of slavery?

Race and historical causation in American political development

Robert C. Lieberman

The past is never dead. It's not even past.

William Faulkner, *Requiem for a Nun* (1951: 92)

"Southern conservatism," wrote Gunnar Myrdal in the 1940s, "is 'reactionary' in the literal sense of the word" (1944: 441). It has preserved an ideological allegiance not only to *status quo*, but to *status quo ante*. The region is still carrying the heritage of slavery. Myrdal's influential interpretation of race in American society and politics illustrates the power that the "legacy of slavery" idea holds in American life, both as a rhetorical device and as an analytical lens through which to view racial inequality in the United States. Even before the national history of the United States began, encounters among groups that were (or came to be) defined by racial difference centrally influenced the development of the nation's politics, society, and economy. European settlers arriving on North American shores beginning in the seventeenth century found a continent inhabited by aboriginal peoples. Within a dozen years of the first permanent European settlement, the first African slaves arrived in Virginia. Over the subsequent centuries, immigrants from Asia and Latin America joined Europeans in the United States. A society emerged in which "whiteness" conferred unique status, authority, and privilege. Punctuating and populating this race-based hierarchy was the forcible migration and enslavement of Africans and their descendants (Morgan 1975; Fields 1982; Holt 1995; Williams 2003).

Four centuries later, the imprint of slavery remains. Nearly a century and a half after the Civil War, the American racial and ethnic hierarchy is largely intact, with whites at the top and other groups arrayed in varying relations to whiteness either as subordinates or outsiders (Kim 1999; King 2005). Despite the civil rights revolution of the second half of the twentieth century, the incorporation of African Americans into American life remains uneven at best (Smith 1997; Hochschild 1999; Horton 2005). Although black Americans have progressed toward closing the socioeconomic and political gaps that have long separated them from whites, profound inequalities remain across a variety of realms—education, housing, income, wealth, employment, and political empowerment, to name but a few (Massey and Denton 1993; Oliver and Shapiro 1995; Jencks and Phillips 1998; Conley 1999; Harris et al. 2006; Katz and Stern 2006). Moreover, racial conflict and inequality, particularly involving African Americans, underscore many pressing debates in contemporary American politics—the imagery of poor black residents of New Orleans left behind in the wake of Hurricane Katrina, for instance, or the disagreements over the renewal of the Voting Rights Act (which was accomplished in 2006 only after strenuous debate) (Epstein et al. 2006; Lieberman 2006).

These apparent continuities between past domination and present inequality have given rise to commonplace arguments about the legacy of slavery, centered on the claim that the existence of race-based slavery in the increasingly distant past is a principal barrier to African-American achievement today. The imagery of slavery's legacy is deeply embedded in Western culture. The memory of slavery and redemption in Egypt is a central theme in Jewish tradition and liturgy, forming the core text and memory of the holiday of Passover. Recent biblical scholarship emphasizes the construction and situation of the exodus from slavery as a later emphasis in the liturgical canon, demonstrating that the story of the exodus was not widely accepted as a national or theological constitutive myth for Jews until around the time of the Babylonian exile, centuries after the events it supposedly depicts (Hoffman 1989). But in modern Jewish tradition, the trope of slavery as a timeless and transgenerational communal experience powerfully defines a historical, political, and theological tradition. In other traditions as well, the Exodus resonates as a narrative of political and spiritual liberation—notably in the African-American tradition, in which the rhetoric and imagery of the escape from bondage to the Promised Land resonate especially clearly (Walzer 1985).[1]

Similar rhetorical claims about an unmediated link between past and present appear in discussions of race in the contemporary United States as well. "As much as anything, being 'black' in America bears the mark of slavery," wrote political scientist Andrew Hacker (1992: 14) in the present tense 129 years after the Emancipation Proclamation. "And in our own time," he continued, "must it be admitted at the close of the twentieth century, that residues of slavery continue to exist? The answer is obviously yes." For Derrick Bell (1992), writing in the same year, the past was equally present in the present, although the legacy of slavery was as much one of triumph over desperate adversity as despair: "The fact of slavery refuses to fade, along with the deeply embedded personal attitudes and public policy assumptions that supported it for so long" (3). Nevertheless, "we must see this country's history of slavery, not as an insuperable racial barrier to blacks, but as a legacy of enlightenment from our enslaved forebears reminding us that if they survived the ultimate form of racism, we . . . can at least view racial oppression in its many contemporary forms without underestimating its critical importance and likely permanent status in this country" (12).

Claims about the legacy of slavery also come in material as well as metaphorical variants. In the wake of recent reparations paid by states to those they wronged—by the German government to survivors of the Holocaust, for example, or by the United States to its own citizens of Japanese descent who were interned during World War II—the call for reparations to descendants of slaves based on a notion of historical culpability and the legacy of past oppression has increased in recent years (Robinson 2000; Balfour 2003; Brooks 2004). As critics of reparations are quick to point out, however, reparations for slavery would benefit not the people who were themselves victims of state-sponsored racial oppression by a previous regime but their descendants, who may be systematically disadvantaged within their society but whose disadvantages may not, in fact, stem from the direct effects of past oppression. This policy debate directly invokes the question of slavery's legacy: to what degree and how is past state-imposed racial domination causally connected to present-day racial inequality?

Such claims and questions, moreover, about the long causal reach of histories of racial domination are not restricted to the United States. Parallel arguments about the legacy of colonialism in Europe are common (Balibar and Wallerstein 1991). These arguments focus particularly on the effects of institutions and practices of colonial rule on contemporary patterns of racial and ethnic inequality and policies to address these inequalities. In the case of Britain, for example, this argument usually connects historical structures of indirect colonial rule, which recognized native groups in the colonies and retained and co-opted native leadership, with present-day pluralism and multiculturalism. In the contrasting case of France, scholars see direct colonial rule, in which French administration replaced native elites, as the precursor to more assimilationist approaches to the modern challenges of ethnic and racial diversity (Katznelson 1976; Favell 1998; Joppke 1999).[2] These accounts similarly posit a causal connection between historical patterns of racial rule and contemporary political arrangements and outcomes. And in both their American and comparative variants, these arguments risk committing the same *post hoc ergo propter hoc* fallacy: if configurations of race relations and racial hierarchy resemble one another in the same country at two distinct historical moments, the earlier pattern must have caused the later one.

Past attempts to connect legacies of slavery (and other forms of racial rule) with present-day outcomes—both those that accept such legacies and those that deny them—have been generally unsuccessful at establishing convincing causal links between past and present. From the analytical gaps in these arguments, however, emerges an alternative argument about the legacies of slavery. This approach takes the problem of temporal causality more seriously and identifies both the conditions under which patterns of racial rule can be transmitted over time, even after emancipation or decolonization, and the mechanisms by which this might happen. I begin the remainder of this chapter by assessing past attempts to assert and refute the importance of the legacy of slavery in American politics, as well as parallel attempts to discern legacies of other forms of racial rule. Neither the legacies nor anti-legacies camp convincingly accounts for the causal mechanisms that might carry forward the legacies of slavery or colonialism to affect later political development. My alternative framework for assessing legacy (and anti-legacy) claims emphasizes how racial conflict can constitute political institutions and coalition-building processes. In developing this political argument, I adapt Desmond King's and Rogers Smith's (2005; reprinted as chapter 4 of this volume) racial-orders framework. A brief empirical sketch of the argument follows, suggesting how legacies of slavery, institutionalized through configurations of political institutions and coalitions, shaped the American welfare state, particularly in the structure of the Social Security Act of 1935. Alongside the American case, I briefly survey the parallel legacy of colonialism and its consequences for the emergent welfare states of Great Britain and France. I conclude by considering the importance of understanding causal mechanisms for arguments about historical restitution and transitional justice.

Legacies and mechanisms

Social scientists have offered a variety of arguments about the sources of racial inequality in the wake of slavery, but the touchstone for these arguments remains, sixty years after its publication, Gunnar Myrdal's *American Dilemma* (1944). Myrdal's interpretation of race's place in American life set the terms of the discussion for decades, offering a particularly influential version of the legacies argument. Myrdal's mechanism for the transmission of slavery's legacy is essentially psychological. Slavery, he argued, was supported by an elaborate political and social theory—"the most uncompromising conservative political philosophy which ever developed in Western civilization after the Enlightenment," he called it—in which black slavery was a necessary part of a hierarchical social order that held whites to be politically, if not socially and economically, equal to each other (441; see also Fitzhugh 1857; Hartz 1955; Morgan 1975). This hierarchical social theory, which deemed groups inherently unequal in social and political status, continued to shape American social beliefs and politics after the Civil War and Reconstruction (see Weber 1946). It persisted in the deep Southern commitment to white supremacy and black disenfranchisement, the iconography of the Lost Cause, and the traditional historiography of Reconstruction, which emphasized the atrocities and venality of the northern occupiers along with the innate incapacity of African Americans.[3] For Myrdal, these atavistic beliefs clashed with the universal American Creed of liberty and equality, producing the peculiar "American dilemma."

Thus for Myrdal the legacy of slavery resided in the hearts and minds of Americans and, above all, in the psychological dissonance produced by the conflict between egalitarian beliefs on the one hand and racial prejudice and racist practices on the other. This clash of beliefs afflicted both individual white Americans and the collectivity of American whites who believed both in the American Creed and in the subjugation of African Americans, a contradiction he believed would eventually be resolved in favor of liberty and equality (with a little push from social engineers—he was a Swede, after all). The psychological interpretation of legacies extends beyond the United States. E.J.B. Rose's

(1969: 3–6, 10–11) magisterial survey of British race relations, explicitly modeled on Myrdal's American study, identified a corresponding "British dilemma" in the tension between liberal ideals and racist practices arising out of colonial domination (although Rose was quite caustic about the apparent abandonment of the ideals in the late 1960s). Similarly, this tension between ideals and practices, particularly arising out of the history of colonization, is a common theme of French studies of racism (in keeping with the common French approach to race, which focuses on "racism" as a cast of mind rather than "race relations" as a problem of social relations) (Silverman 1992; Bleich 2003).

But while Myrdal's argument pinpoints the central dilemma of liberal, multiracial societies, it does not do justice to the multiple traditions that have contributed to definitions of national membership in all of these societies. As Rogers Smith (1997) has shown, Myrdal obscures the multiple political traditions that have contended for primacy in those struggles, particularly the tradition of "ascriptive Americanism," which seeks to define membership in the American community in exclusive racial, ethnic, and gendered terms. Rather than representing aberrant deviations from a dominant American Creed, racially exclusive beliefs and policies have long been part of the American political tradition, from slavery forward. Moreover, such essentialist definitions of national membership—in which national identity is constructed around shared characteristics that are believed to be fixed by birth or nature and deemed to be irreducibly necessary for national belonging—are hardly limited to the United States; they have played starring roles on the British and French stages as well (Rich 1991; Lebovics 1992; Birnbaum 1993; Kidd 1999).

Furthermore, the psychological approach generally ignores how politics, and particularly the organization of political power, perpetuates racial hierarchy. By interpreting political struggles over the definition of citizenship as symptom rather than cause, the Myrdalian approach obscures the role that politics as usual can play in keeping racial hierarchy alive. As Jennifer Hochschild (1984) shows in the American case, the commonplace tools of liberal democratic policymaking—incrementalism and popular control—actually impeded rather than advanced school desegregation, casting doubt both on Myrdal's analysis of the weight of the past and on his optimistic assessment of the possibilities of liberal democracy to shed that weight (see also Katznelson 1971, 1972).

Another interpretation of the legacy of slavery is sociological. This approach sees patterns of social relations such as family structure or marriage or child-rearing behavior, rather than internalized beliefs about racial inequality, as the principal mechanism by which the effects of slavery were carried forward through time. In his Labor Department report of 1965, Daniel Patrick Moynihan famously described what he saw as the deteriorating structure of the African-American family, leaving it mired in a "tangle of pathology" (U.S. Department of Labor 1965). Moynihan directly traced the roots of this sociological phenomenon to the particular conditions of slavery in the South, such as the nonrecognition of marriages between slaves and the prospects of family breakup by the sale of spouses and children. These practices under slavery, he argued, reproduced themselves after emancipation through the marriage and childbearing behavior of African Americans, and segregation reinforced these behavioral tendencies. The contours of late twentieth century black family structure thus constituted a direct legacy of slavery.[4] Emmanuel Todd (1991, 1994) takes a parallel approach to the legacies of colonialism in France, making a highly deterministic argument about the impact of family structures on the prospects for the assimilation of ethnic and racial minorities in France (see especially Todd 1994: 82–92).

In the immediate aftermath of the report, Moynihan's potted history of the black family came under withering scrutiny.[5] In particular, historian Herbert Gutman (1976) directly challenged Moynihan's thesis in the meticulous *Black Family in Slavery and Freedom*, arguing that slavery was not primarily culpable in shaping black family structure in the twentieth century. Similarly, scholars have criticized Todd's approach as fundamentally ahistorical, built on a static and essentialist view of French national identity that does not sufficiently consider how identity might itself change in the encounter with others (Noiriel 1996).[6] Moreover, these sociological arguments are too quick to take resemblances between slave or colonial social structures and contemporary ones as evidence of a direct, unbroken link, and hence a causal connection, between past and present. In so doing, they, like Myrdal's psychological interpretation, sidestep the role of other important social forces—economic change, political processes, and public policy, for example—in creating and reinforcing patterns of racial distinction and inequality (see, for example, Jackson 1985; Wilson 1987; Sugrue 1996). It is at least arguable, if not probable, that these forces have helped to construct and maintain minority family structure in these societies, rather than the other way around.

A third interpretation of the legacy of slavery is economic. In their major analysis of the economics of slavery, Robert Fogel and Stanley Engerman (1974) sought to revise the long-held view that slavery was, by the time of the Civil War, already a declining and economically moribund institution. They argued, instead, that slavery remained profitable and might plausibly have remained in place had the war, emancipation, and the Thirteenth Amendment to the Constitution not brought it to a decisive end. Abolition, they argued, critically and abruptly transformed the Southern economy in ways far more consequential for the subsequent status of African Americans than the residue of the peculiar institution itself. Fogel and Engerman's thesis provoked a frenzy of refutation and recrimination and they remain controversial (see Gutman 1975; Fogel 1989; Kolchin 1992). But their findings suggest the importance of enduring patterns in the political economy, such as the emergence of the system of debt peonage in the South and the separate low-wage labor market for African Americans, for understanding slavery's legacy for subsequent patterns of inequality (Wright 1986).

More recently, sociologist Dalton Conley (1999) has argued that the most important indicator of racial inequality is not income or employment or even education, but wealth. Conley shows, in fact, that discrepancies in family assets and inherited wealth account for much of the inequality between blacks and whites across a wide range of outcomes, including jobs, earnings, housing, and even family structure and related behavior such as premarital childbearing. Because family wealth is so closely linked to life chances and socioeconomic position, the heritability of wealth might be responsible for the transmission of the inequalities of slavery forward in time. In the immediate aftermath of the Civil War, the federal government possessed substantial amounts of land in the South that had been confiscated from white landholders in the course of the war. In January 1865, General William Tecumseh Sherman, who oversaw some of this land, issued his Special Field Order 15, which granted forty acres of land to newly freed black families on the coastal islands of Georgia (Oubre 1978; Foner 1988: 153–70). Sherman's army also distributed surplus mules, giving rise to the slogan, "forty acres and a mule," as an emblem of Reconstruction's potential to provide opportunity to nearly four million former slaves. Several months later, the federal government created the Bureau of Refugees, Freedmen, and Abandoned Lands (known as the Freedmen's Bureau), to take custody of this land and oversee its distribution to the freed slaves. This ambitious program of land reform did not happen for a number of reasons, but it is not far-fetched, for example, to imagine that if Reconstruction had achieved a more thoroughgoing redistribution of land in the South, the contemporary racial landscape in the United States would look very different.

The failure of land reform during Reconstruction, however, was primarily political, suggesting that attention to politics is necessary for understanding the legacies of slavery. More recently, historians have highlighted the role of politics and political struggles in shaping post-emancipation societies. These accounts of the transition from slavery to freedom have focused on issues of land redistribution, labor reform, and other aspects of economic reorganization, addressing particularly the role of former slaves themselves in mounting collective action to pursue the rights of citizenship (Fredrickson 1981, 1995; Foner 1988; Holt 1992; Marx 1998; Dubois 2004). Frederick Cooper et al. (2000), Thomas Holt (1992), and Rebecca Scott (2005) have documented post-emancipation struggles for citizenship in the United States, the Caribbean, and Africa, focusing particularly on labor participation and political activity, ranging from voting and political party activity to rebellion and revolution. These studies emphasize how political and economic conflicts in the immediate wake of emancipation shaped evolving categories of both citizenship and race and the terms on which former slaves were incorporated into post-emancipation societies, and they demonstrate how different political contexts profoundly shaped post-emancipation outcomes. This more explicitly political and historical approach, while not ignoring the attitudinal, sociological, and economic concerns of earlier studies, surpasses them in pointing to concrete political mechanisms and structures of power by which slavery leaves its mark when former slaves and transforming societies encounter each other.

Continuity or discontinuity?: legacies and intentionality

An alternative set of arguments minimizes the causal importance of legacies of slavery, colonialism, or other forms of racial rule. "Past and present one and the same?," scoff Stephan and Abigail Thernstrom (1997: 50–2). "An odd denial of historical change, it seems to us." They dismiss legacy arguments as resolutely as others embrace them, arguing instead that the rights revolution of the last half-century has obliterated all but the merest traces of the inequalities of slavery. Although the Thernstroms recognize that the effects of racial discrimination that carried over from the slavery era continued to shape racial inequality through much of the twentieth century, they argue that the events of the 1950s and 1960s—the end of school segregation, the dismantling of Jim Crow, the Civil Rights and Voting Rights Acts—effectively wiped away those historical effects. They essentially posit a historical rupture that separates, roughly speaking, pre-1954 from post-1965 race relations in the United States, as if those two eras overlapped not at all in their social, economic, or political milieus. But their account of a historical break falsely presumes that the end of one element of the pre-civil rights racial structure—explicit, state-sanctioned segregation—entailed the total destruction of the prevailing order, preparing the ground for construction of a new one. The Thernstroms' argument is an improvement, perhaps, on the ahistorical claims of Hacker and Bell, but they struggle to explain the stubborn persistence of racial conflict and inequality in certain realms of American society and politics (which they attribute to the perverse effects of affirmative action and other race-conscious policies that followed the putatively color-blind antidiscrimination approach of the Civil Rights Act) (Hochschild 1999; Brown et al. 2003).

The economist Thomas Sowell (1978, 1994) similarly proposes a historical chasm across which no causal effects of slavery could leap. For Sowell, the "legacy of slavery" is a rhetorical crutch on which African Americans (particularly those who live in impoverished and isolated inner cities) and their intellectual apologists lean to excuse all manner of violent, criminal, and otherwise antisocial behavior, such as dropping out of school and not working steadily. Although he denies repeatedly and strenuously that the "legacy of slavery" underpins contemporary inequality, he implicitly acknowledges the potential causal weight of history by contrasting former slaves and their descendants with both free blacks and West Indian immigrants, who are presumably equally subject to racism based on skin color but who have fared better in the political economy. He concedes that slavery placed African Americans at a social and economic disadvantage, leaving them uneducated and without the stable family and neighborhood structures that might have been conducive to economic progress. After emancipation, however, former slaves quickly acquired literacy and developed more stable family structures, severing them from any potential legacy of slavery and giving them, in effect, a clean historical slate. From the comparison he concludes that African Americans in the twentieth century developed a group culture inimical to education and economic achievement and that this latter-day self-imposed cultural deficiency accounts for poor economic performance.

Historian Winston James (2002), however, has shown the inaccuracy of Sowell's comparative claims, particularly about West Indians, because Sowell ignores important differences in the social and economic starting point of West Indian immigrants in the early twentieth century. William Julius Wilson (1996), moreover, has shown that the behavior of urban blacks is an adaptive response to changing structural conditions in postindustrial cities rather than a marker of cultural deviance. Most important, like the Thernstroms, Sowell selectively uses one or two indicators to argue that an entire political, social, and economic system came to an abrupt and complete end, thereby denying a wide range of plausible mechanisms of historical causality. Both Sowell and the Thernstroms offer variants of what Albert Hirschman (1991) has defined as the "perversity thesis," reactionary rhetoric that selectively emphasizes the negative unintended consequences of social action in order to claim that progressive reform efforts are inherently doomed to failure.

Erik Bleich (2005) convincingly refutes the claim about the links between forms of British and French colonialism and contemporary integration policies. Relying on arguments by Gary Freeman (1979) and Didier Lapeyronnie (1993), Bleich definitively exposes the flaws in the historical accounts at both ends of this story: British and French colonial practices each involved a mixture of direct and indirect rule, and British and French policymakers drew on a variety of sources and motives when devising integration policies in the twentieth century. In revealing these lacunae in the prevailing wisdom, however, Bleich also falls back on the same evidentiary standard for rejecting the hypothesis of historical influence: the absence of explicit evidence of intentionality. Taken together, these works hew to a fairly thin notion of historical causality, in which only a single causal hypothesis is effectively tested. When the evidence does not sustain the particular hypothesis, these authors then reject other specifications of a legacy argument that are motored by different mechanisms. Although they do not make the historical rupture case as explicitly as the Thernstroms or Sowell, their claims amount to the same thing: the absence of racial intentions, in effect, indicates that racial policymaking is on a new footing regardless of past arrangements.

Arguments about the role of race in the formation of the American welfare state provide the most prominent examples of this kind of causal synecdoche, using a single causal thread to stand in for a whole system of potential causal mechanisms. Many scholars have argued, for example, that race-laden political arrangements affected the Social Security Act of 1935, creating the institutional conditions for much of the subsequent racialization of the American welfare state. Others, however, suggest that these accounts conflate racial causes and consequences, arguing that because the participants in the Social Security debates of the New Deal did not explicitly express an intention to engineer the racial composition of social insurance and public assistance programs, we cannot conclude that race causally shaped the act. This case, discussed below, serves as a useful test for assessing competing arguments about the causal weight of slavery's legacy.

This assumption of radical historical discontinuity, which underlies anti-legacy arguments that rely on evidence of intentionality, indicates a larger fallacy that characterizes the historical rupture claims of anti-legacies argument. This approach tends to assume, at least implicitly, that political arrangements constitute highly coherent, internally consistent, stable, and self-reinforcing orders that succeed one another more or less without overlap, interrupted by moments of sweeping change (Ackerman 1991; Baumgartner and Jones 1993; Plotke 1996). But more recent theorizing about the temporal dimensions of politics and processes of political development has suggested that political change rarely, if ever, occurs this way. Rather, the political moments and outcomes are situated simultaneously in multiple institutional orders and ideological traditions, each with its own internal logic and pace (Lieberman 2002; Orren and Skowronek 2004). Thus change in one institutional or ideological domain is not necessarily linked to change in others and the complete transformation of political arrangements, in which an old order is thrown overboard and an entirely new one created, is unlikely. As Tocqueville (1955) pointed out, even the French Revolution did not accomplish such sweeping and complete change. Rather, elements of old patterns mingle with new ones. Consequently, cross-sectional analyses that draw short time horizons around both causes and outcomes and focus on contemporaneous factors, such as the presence or absence of racial intentions at the moment of a policy decision, tend to "discover" historical discontinuities because they ignore longer-term political processes (Pierson 2004: chapter 3). Thus even in a policymaking episode when racial intentions are not explicitly present, long-run power arrangements and ideological routines that systematically affect African Americans differently from whites (whether to their advantage or disadvantage) may be at work.

Alternative accounts of political change, however, emphasize mechanisms that do not depend on such radical discontinuity or punctuation. In her study of the evolution of vocational training policies in four countries, Kathleen Thelen (2004) highlights two specific alternative mechanisms of institutional change. One is "layering," in which new institutions do not replace old ones, but, rather are simply piled on top (see also Tulis 1987; Schickler 2001). Another is "conversion," in which existing institutions adapt to new circumstances by altering their goals or incorporating new actors. Building on Thelen's account, Jacob Hacker (2004: 246–9) adds a third mechanism, "drift," in which outcomes change gradually without corresponding institutional change, often because of changes in the underlying social or economic context. Other similar mechanisms include the displacement of an institution's initial aims with alternative goals that might alter or subvert its original purposes without eliminating the institution, or the gradual decline of an institution over time (Skowronek 2006). What these mechanisms share, and what makes them a useful touchstone for my analysis, is their account of what Wolfgang Streeck and Kathleen Thelen (2005) call "endogenous institutional change," major institutional change that comes about without formal reform. These mechanisms suggest that change and continuity can coexist, and that change in one component of an institutional "order" does not imply a complete break with the past. Thus, they suggest how legacies of past racial oppression might be carried forward even if some elements of the system of racial domination are not visibly present in the historical record at the moment in question.

Finding legacies: two hypotheses and the case of the American welfare state

The Social Security Act of 1935 and the formation of the American welfare state provide an exemplary case for examining these causal arguments and testing the claims of discontinuity inherent in anti-legacy arguments. A growing number of scholars claim that race politics profoundly shaped the structure of the Social Security Act, arguing that racially structured political institutions and power relations provided the political impetus for the exclusion of agricultural workers and domestic servants—accounting for a majority of the country's African-American work force—from Social Security and the radical decentralization of public assistance programs, all but inviting racial discrimination (Quadagno 1994; Lieberman 1998; Brown 1999; Poole 2006). Others, however, dispute this interpretation. Gareth Davies and Martha Derthick (1997) reject such arguments about the influence of past (and even contemporaneous) racial disadvantage on the grounds that the historical record provides no smoking gun—there is little evidence that the political actors consciously intended to discriminate when they took those decisions. They argue instead that the design of these policy instruments, which turned out to have racially exclusionary effects, arose instead from concerns about the administrative feasibility of collecting payroll taxes from farm workers and household employees. Daniel Béland (2005: 88–91, 96) dismisses the legacies argument on similar grounds, arguing that the political forces aligned with racial domination in the United States, particularly powerful Southerners in Congress, were not influential in shaping this particular aspect of the policy.

In a particularly tendentious version of this claim, historian Larry DeWitt (presumably inadvertently) reveals the fallacy of the intentionality argument and, by extension, of most anti-legacy arguments. "Rather than presuming racist motives without evidence," he writes, "it is more plausible, and more in keeping with the evidence of record, to believe that the members of Congress (of both parties and all regions) supported these exclusions simply because they saw *an opportunity to lessen the political risks to themselves*" (2004: 42, emphasis added).[7] DeWitt hits the nail on the head in pointing to the political opportunities available to policymakers. But he does not say what those political opportunities were, where they came from, or what risks policymakers averted by excluding farm workers and servants from coverage. Such opportunities and risks are a function of political and institutional contexts in which purposive and strategic political actors pursue their goals. Institutional contexts entail formal rules and organizations of governance as well as taken-for-granted understandings of the political world that frame the articulation of interests and influence political behavior (Thelen and Steinmo 1992; Hall and Taylor 1996; Immergut 1998). If these institutions systematically privilege one group over another, whether through the allocation of power or shared beliefs, then conscious intentions are not a necessary condition for political outcomes that reinforce or amplify inequality between groups. Instead, racial inequality might be built into political arrangements.

Anti-legacy arguments such as Davies and Derthick's and DeWitt's tend not to state explicit assumptions about the goals and motivations that underlie the behavior of policymakers, nor do they consider how institutional contexts shape the political opportunities available to policymakers to pursue those goals. When they do make implicit claims about policymakers' goals, they tend to capture only a small part of a full account and consequently overlook the nature of the political opportunities that strategic actors exploit and the political risks they face. DeWitt, for example, suggests fleetingly that members of Congress excluded agricultural and domestic employees from Social Security because they were reluctant to impose additional taxes on their constituents (2004: 42). This is certainly a reasonable assumption—no elected official wants to impose visible costs on his constituents, especially when the benefits associated with those costs are deferred far into the future. It does not, however, explain why they were willing in the first place to adopt the program, which created a system of individual taxation more extensive and intrusive than any before it (Arnold 1990). Another favorite, equally partial assumption of anti-legacy arguments is that policymakers were motivated by the demands of administrative efficiency in excluding farm and domestic workers, although little evidence suggests that efficiency has ever been an overriding criterion for policymakers in constructing government agencies, as Martha Derthick (1990) herself has shown in another context (see also Fiorina 1977; Moe 1989; Lewis 2003). Most important, these arguments tend to ignore the electoral setting of democratic policy, which coexists with other motivations but remains a paramount underlying goal (Mayhew 1974; but see also Fenno 1973; Mayhew 2000).

These interpretations of the question of race and Social Security suggest contrasting empirical implications that correspond to the competing hypotheses about historical continuity and discontinuity. First, consider racial intentions as a causal factor. Davies and Derthick, for example, show that explicit racial intentions did not dominate the debate about the structure of the Social Security Act. From this accurate empirical observation they infer that because the policy debate was silent on race, race could not have been a causal factor in the relevant policy decision. Instead, they see the racial inequality that indisputably followed from the act as merely the incidental consequence of other, race-neutral factors—such as the decision to exclude agricultural and domestic workers from Social Security to serve administrative efficiency. This conclusion, however, is erroneous. Silence about race does not mean that racial factors did not influence the distribution of power or the contours of decision-making. Conversely, express racial intentions alone are not sufficient to establish the causal importance of race in shaping outcomes; even explicitly acknowledged racial motives might merely accelerate or consolidate developments that occur for other reasons (Marx 1998; Lieberman 2003). Analytically, then, racial intentions are neither necessary nor sufficient to establish a causal relationship between past structures of racial inequality and subsequent outcomes. Thus it is unclear how to construct a testable hypothesis about the relationship between racial motives and racial outcomes. Empirically, in any event, racial motives are often too mixed and ambiguous to make a clear argument.

But as I have argued, arguments about racial intentions generally stand in for more comprehensive claims about historical discontinuities between past and present, and these claims are testable. At the limit, of course, it would be impossible to prove comprehensively a claim about a complete historical rupture in which no traces of past orders remain, which has in any case probably never occurred. But the question is not whether there are *any* remnants at all but whether there are any that might plausibly be causally connected to some present or future outcome. Constructing hypotheses about such plausible connections requires specifying some underlying theoretical framework for the event under consideration. In the case of the Social Security Act, because the event in question is a policy enactment, one would need a theory (or theories) of policymaking that mobilizes one or more causal factors to explain policy outcomes. The question then is whether those factors have changed significantly in ways that would be expected to induce a change in outcome. If all of these causal elements have undergone significant change, then one might reasonably infer that subsequent events are disconnected from historical legacies and arise from a new set of causes.

In racial terms, the question is whether the racial context underlying political action—the social relations, political arrangements, and power distributions structured according to racial categories—has changed. To define the racial context or setting of political activity, I draw on Desmond King and Rogers Smith's notion of racial orders, by which they mean political coalitions that bind together purposive, power-seeking actors and institutions in contexts in which "racial concepts, commitments, and aims" at least partially structure the political arrangements, norms, and taken-for-granted cultural understandings that "define the range of opportunities available to political actors" (chapter 4). King and Smith posit two contending and largely nonoverlapping racial orders—"white supremacist" and "transformative egalitarian"—that structure much of American political development. These racial orders, King and Smith show, provide political actors with overlapping material stakes in particular kinds of racial outcomes or particular ideological commitments around racial distinctions, with the result that much of American political development becomes explicable in racial terms.

An important question arises within the racial orders framework, however, which directly pertains to the question of continuity and the legacies of slavery.

When one racial order succeeds another, as when the "transformative egalitarian" order apparently triumphed in the 1960s, does the incoming order supplant the outgoing order completely, implying discontinuity in the polity's underlying racial framework for political action? Or, alternatively, do they interweave and overlap, implying at least the possibility of continuity in racial warrants for action, as suggested by the right's appropriation of color-blind liberalism and the legacy of *Brown v. Board of Education* in recent decades (Horton 2005: chapter 8; *Parents Involved v. Seattle* (2007) 551 U.S. __)? The historical discontinuity hypothesis is at bottom a claim about racial orders, or racial regimes: if a new racial order has supplanted an old one, changes in racial outcomes should result. If, conversely, racial outcomes persist under a new racial order, then we must look elsewhere—presumably either to intentions or happenstance—for the cause. In the case of Social Security, then, the historical discontinuity hypothesis would predict that the passage of Social Security, with its racially consequential provisions, coincided with or followed a substantial change in the American racial order.

But because racial orders interact and overlap with other kinds of institutional and ideological orders, their effects are often hidden. King and Smith show, for example, that racial orders had important, if unseen, consequences for significant events in American political development—the rise of bureaucratic autonomy, the institutional evolution of Congress, and modern immigration policy—that are conventionally understood in race-neutral terms (chapter 4). In other words, race need not be explicit to be a causal factor in all manner of outcomes because it might be built into political arrangements to shape actors' understanding of their own interests and the political opportunities that they are able to exploit in the service of those interests.

Racial orders, moreover, are not necessarily coherent and unified complexes of institutions, ideologies, and actors. Rather, they themselves are composed of parts that do not always necessarily hang together. These component parts of racial orders change at different paces, according to different logics. Consequently, as King and Smith show, the "transformative egalitarian" and "white supremacist" racial orders do not supplant one another in succession but rather coexist and contend with one another on ever-shifting political terrain. Only rarely and momentarily, if ever, does one of these overarching orders dominate politics unambiguously enough that the racial content and motivations of policymaking can be inferred in a straightforward way. At all other times, the racial content of policymaking remains hidden in complex and contradictory forces. Thus in exporting King and Smith's framework outside of the American context, I do not necessarily expect to find what they describe as full-blown racial orders—overarching and coherent agglomerations of actors, institutions, and ideas such as those they discern in the American context. Nevertheless, the framework allows an examination of how some, if not all, of the components of national politics are shaped by racial distinctions.

Legacies of slavery in the formation of the American welfare state

Empirical studies of welfare-state formation and growth have begun to substantiate the general claim that ethnic and racial heterogeneity inhibit the development of large and encompassing welfare states (Wilensky 1975: 50–69; Noble 1997; Alesina and Glaeser 2004; Cutler and Johnson 2004). These studies have generally not articulated precise causal mechanisms connecting racial or ethnic conflict and limited welfare states (Pontusson 2006). In the United States, the prevailing racial order of the early twentieth century produced political conditions that limited the possibilities for expansive universal social policy. Consequently, the imperative of white solidarity, which structured much of the American polity for roughly the first two-thirds of the twentieth century, helped to overcome class-based politics and was one of the central axes around which early social politics revolved.

The United States in 1935 adopted a fragmented, limited set of national welfare policies: national old-age pensions for a restricted set of industrial and commercial workers, decentralized public assistance programs for limited categories of poor people who were disconnected from the labor market, and a hybrid system of unemployment insurance. These policies severely limited minority access to the benefits and protections of the welfare state. Behind this pattern of welfare-state inclusion and exclusion lay national policymaking processes that revolved around persistent patterns of racial rule. Thus, key elements of the past racial order remained in place during the period of critical social reform. This racial order encompassed not only prevalent beliefs about the inferiority and subordinate status of African Americans but also key structural features of American politics, including federalism and regionalism, the party system, and the structure of policymaking institutions.

In the United States, the roots of this racial order lie in the aftermath of emancipation. The Thirteenth, Fourteenth, and Fifteenth Amendments to the Constitution made the newly freed slaves presumptive citizens, and during Reconstruction and even for a decade or more after, African Americans in the South exercised their voting rights under the protection of the national Republican Party. Beginning in the 1890s, however, Republicans found that they could win national elections without competing for Southern votes and they withdrew their support for black voting rights. Once this happened, Southern whites consolidated their power in the states by adopting new voting restrictions and segregation laws that ushered in a period of black disenfranchisement and white supremacy that lasted until the 1960s (Valelly 2004). These changes in Southern politics around the turn of the twentieth century made racial politics a crucial element of coalition building in national politics. Southern whites were heavily overrepresented in Congress and the Electoral College because African Americans were now counted fully in apportioning seats in the House of Representatives (a change from the three-fifths bonus for slave populations that the Southern states had enjoyed under the Constitution before the Civil War). The Solid South dominated the Democratic Party based on sheer numbers, seniority, and rules such as the two-thirds majority required to get the party's presidential nomination, while the Republicans were increasingly indifferent or even hostile to the politically voiceless claims of African Americans. During the first third of the twentieth century, then, racial politics shaped the operation of the most basic institutions of American politics—the separation of powers, federalism, the structure of representation, and the party system. Across a wide range of institutional forums, the possibilities for coalition building were stacked against African Americans.

With the coming of the New Deal, elements of this racial order began to change, suggesting a partial moment of historical discontinuity that might have severed future racial outcomes from past arrangements. New Deal relief policies benefited African Americans more than any federal policy since Reconstruction, both because black Americans were among the hardest hit by the Great Depression and because in some instances program administrators actively enforced racial fairness in relief operations (Sullivan 1996; Amenta 1998). Where they could vote, African Americans themselves began to shift away from their longstanding allegiance to the Republicans, the "party of Lincoln," and toward the Democrats, becoming part of the emergent Democratic coalition (Weiss 1983). Under the leadership of Charles Hamilton Houston, the National Association for the Advancement of Colored People's legal department began strategically to challenge segregation in the courts, which Franklin Roosevelt began to remake during his presidency (McMahon 2004). And under the Roosevelt administration, African Americans probably had more access to national political actors than they had had for generations. But as much as these changes were immediately significant and foreshadowed a greater transformation to come, the fundamental institutional characteristics of the pre-New Deal racial order—the interpenetration of race with the basic coalition-building processes of American policymaking—remained resolutely in place. This persistent racially ordered coalition underwrote racial exclusions across the range of the New Deal's most progressive and protective programs, including labor rights and standards, and race still structured policymaking within and between the parties and across all three branches of government (Carmines and Stimson 1989; Katznelson et al. 1993; Riley 1999; McMahon 2004; Farhang and Katznelson 2005).

This account of American welfare-state building is inconsistent with the discontinuity hypothesis, which holds that the Social Security Act represented a rupture in the racial order such that any racial consequences that followed from its passage were disconnected from the causal factors behind the act's passage. This is clearly not the case. Not only was the American welfare state layered on top of a preexisting and persistent racial order, the underlying racial order also shaped the political opportunities for building coalitions around the idea of solidaristic social reform—social polices that would bind citizens together on the basis of common national membership and shared social risk. In the United States, building such a coalition even for limited solidaristic reform required accommodating racial inequality as a persistent barrier to social solidarity. Institutional layering was thus necessary in the face of politically constructed and institutionally embedded racial difference. The adoption and implementation of the Social Security Act partially altered the American racial order in ways portending greater incorporation for minorities in some respects and greater isolation and inequality in others (Lieberman 1998), but the act was not independent of the racial order under whose auspices it arose.

Legacies of racial rule: a brief comparison

By briefly examining parallel cases of welfare-state development elsewhere, we can gently probe the broader applicability of the continuity argument as a way of advancing the political account of the legacies argument. The course of welfare-state building in Britain and France supports the continuity hypothesis in ways that similarly reveal the importance of racial orders in shaping policy developments around solidaristic social reform. Social policymaking in all three countries in the early twentieth century revolved around the same question: who was and was not entitled to full membership in society and on what terms? And in negotiating the dual challenge of appeasing or co-opting working-class political movements without capitulating to socialism, each also protected and extended systems of racial rule (whether in the form of colonial empires or a post-emancipation structure of white supremacy). The political task of social reform was to forge coalitions to construct solidarity across class lines without including suspect others in the benefits of social protection (Marshall 1964; Hobsbawm 1987: 102; Baldwin 1990). In each country, moreover, racial minorities—whether colonial subjects or descendents of slaves—were presumptive citizens, at least nominally entitled to the full array of civil, political, and social rights available to members of their societies (a stance that differentiated these countries from others that explicitly excluded nonwhites from social benefits in the early twentieth century, such as Australia, Canada, New Zealand, and South Africa) (U.S. Social Security Board 1937: 184).

The key question in Britain and France, as in the United States, is to what extent the underlying racial order and the imperatives of racial rule shaped the politics of social reform. Was welfare-state building similarly continuous with previous racial structures, or did it represent a rupture, such that subsequent patterns of racial inclusion or exclusion, equality or inequality, were disconnected from prior racially ordered politics? In each of the European cases, racial orders clearly patterned the politics of welfare-state building.

In Britain, as in the United States, white solidarity helped to overcome class-based political conflicts and was one of the central axes around which early social politics revolved. In a series of enactments before World War I, Britain constructed a much more centralized and inclusive welfare state than the United States: centralized national systems of old-age pensions, unemployment and sickness insurance, and labor exchanges designed to limit unemployment.

Despite initial attempts to limit the universality of these programs, they effectively and intentionally altered the centuries-old Poor Law basis of the British welfare state and began to replace localized relief with national social rights for all British citizens (as distinct from colonial subjects).

This development arose in a political context powerfully shaped by a prevailing racial order. British imperialism, which depended on a racialized understanding of the difference between British citizens at home and colonial subjects abroad, was at the center of British politics in the late nineteenth and early twentieth centuries (Mehta 1999). The British party system was in considerable flux in this period. The dominant but fragile Conservative Party united around support for imperialism but divided on social reform and trade policy. Opposition to the Conservatives was splintered between Liberals and the emerging Labour Party, who shared a commitment to social reform but were divided among themselves on support for imperialism, which was unpopular among Britain's middle and working classes. This unstable party alignment produced a policy stalemate for much of the 1890s and early 1900s, which was interrupted by the Boer War. The war was fought to protect and defend Britain's colonial domination over South Africa, but its unexpected length and ferocity exposed the need for social reform at home. A postwar governmental commission found that in the decade before the war, more than one-third of British army recruits had been deemed physically unfit for service; this finding led to a movement for "national efficiency" that included a program of social reform for the preservation of the "imperial race" (Report of the Inter-Departmental Committee on Physical Deterioration 1904: 95–97; Gilbert 1966: 59–101). In this context, imperialism and social reform came to be politically linked (Semmel 1960). But under the British system of party government, under which the dominant parliamentary party (or coalition) rarely gained unfettered control over policymaking and cross-party coalitions, this linkage was not easily translated into policy.

In France, by contrast, the welfare policies that emerged in the early twentieth century were neither administered nor financed by the national state. Rather, they extended older patterns of mutual societies organized around occupational, fraternal, religious, or other local attachments. French social policy thus mirrored neither the broadly inclusive system of solidaristic social citizenship of Britain nor the fragmented and structurally exclusionary American system. The early French welfare state was comparatively race-neutral. The racial structure of French politics similarly encompassed a commitment to imperialism, but French imperialism entailed a much more ambiguous relationship between citizens and subjects than its British variant (Conklin 1997; Wilder 2005). On the one hand, French colonial thought and practice was based on deeply rooted notions of racial difference and superiority, embodied in the idea of France's "civilizing mission" ("la mission civilisatrice") toward its subjects. On the other hand, French imperialism aligned with a broadly universal vision of "Greater France" that involved incorporating colonial subjects into the French nation. At the same time, this process of assimilation into "Frenchness" also focused inward on people who lived at the periphery (both geographically and culturally) of France itself, particularly through relatively coercive institutions such as the schools and the army (Weber 1976). This ambiguity interacted with the highly fragmented parliamentary politics and weak party structure of France's Third Republic to inhibit the formation of coalitions for solidaristic social reform. France is, in essence, a "negative case," in which the imperative of racial exclusion does not seem to have impelled the formation of a social reform coalition; but even in this case, the continuity between the old imperial racial order and the emerging politics of social reform contributes to an explanation of the shape of the French welfare state.

This brief comparative account of the general persistence of elements of preexisting racial orders in each case substantiates the continuity hypothesis and reveals a common set of layering processes at work in each. In the United States and Britain especially, race helped to overcome other axes of political conflict, particularly class, in the formation of social policy coalitions. In Britain in the years before World War I, social reform and imperial governance combined to support a coalition that created inclusive national welfare policies in order to unify Britons across class and against a racially defined threat from the outside. In the United States, the coalition behind the creation of the welfare state in the 1930s also protected racial rule, but within the boundaries of the United States proper so that the imperative of uniting whites behind a program of social reform produced a policy approach that was necessarily exclusionary and decentralizing rather than inclusive and national. In interwar France, by contrast, racial diversity was as much an opportunity as a threat for the prospects of nation building, and French social reform did not mobilize racial antagonisms to overcome class divisions in constructing welfare state policies. The result was the perpetuation of the Third Republic's preexisting corporatist pattern of social provision, based on civil society attachments, without a clear racial valence.

The presence of the past

This comparison reveals an important political mechanism by which legacies of slavery and other forms of racial rule can influence political outcomes over time. Legacies of slavery, colonialism, and other patterns of racial domination are not merely rhetorical devices or metaphorical constructs. Nor are they simply habits of mind, belief, or intention that can be easily observed and erased. They are, rather, political processes that exist, like the institutions of slavery and colonialism themselves, at the intersection of race, power, and state structure. In these cases, processes of politics and policymaking were racially structured— as reflected in such durable patterns of authority as party systems, legislatures, and federalism—and the resultant racial orders shaped policy outcomes, with far-reaching consequences. Legacies of slavery and colonialism, embedded in material political institutions such as these, shaped the development of the

American and British welfare state particularly through the layering of new policies over older patterns of race relations and racialized political arrangements. The particular ways that political arrangements embed racial rule can shape subsequent decisions even when the initial racial conditions that gave rise to those arrangements—such as slavery—have disappeared and when decision making does not appear on the surface to be about race at all. This need not always be true, as the case of French welfare state development shows. We must also investigate what kind of historical continuities do and do not constitute legacies that might have material causal weight in the future. My purpose here has been simply to demonstrate that racial legacies are plausible and common and that they have been important to American political development, and to suggest an analytical strategy for discerning their effects. Further work will specify more precisely under what conditions they are more (and less) likely to appear and operate.

But even once we have established how it is that histories of racial oppression can shape national destinies, hard questions remain. As time passes and the history of direct oppression recedes, where do legacies lie (Cowen 2006)? The analysis here suggests that we can never be rid of the residue of history, but this does not mean that we must always be in thrall to it. At what point do gradual changes in the racial order cumulate into something entirely new so that the present is effectively dissociated from the past? Just as we cannot assume that the past is dead, we should not presume that its ghosts always haunt present-day politics in the same way. Rather, we must find an analytical means to distinguish the real ghosts from the false ones, to find the mechanisms that account for the persistent presence of the past, in order to uncover its effects.

Understanding the mechanisms connecting past and present cannot, in the end, answer the urgent questions of justice or culpability that many societies face today: what moral or political obligations do present-day regimes face to redress the harms that followed from the actions of their predecessors? I have sought here to develop a causal argument about the connection between past and present, not to assess either moral claims about historical restitution or political arguments about their efficacy (see Barkan 2001; Elster 2006; Torpey 2006). But the moral and political judgments needed to answer such questions and to devise sensible and humane policies of transitional justice depend critically on such causal claims, so it seems worth the effort to get them right.

Notes

1   Imagery of "the promised land" was common in twentieth-century civil rights rhetoric. W.E.B. Du Bois invokes it repeatedly in *The Souls of Black Folk* (1903) and it punctuates Martin Luther King Jr.'s speech to the sanitation workers of Memphis the night before his assassination (April 3, 1968). The titles of several important historical works on the civil rights movement have also invoked imagery of the exodus: Nicholas Lemann's (1991) account of the postwar migration of African Americans, *The Promised Land*; and Taylor Branch's (1988, 1998, 2006) three-volume history, *Parting the Waters, Pillar of Fire*, and *At Canaan's Edge*.

2   For a summary of these arguments, see Bleich 2005. On parallels between slavery and colonialism as forms of rule, see Lieberman (2005: 28–31).
3   Myrdal (1944: 444–5) also emphasizes that this view of Reconstruction also served the north by rationalizing the compromise of 1876 that signaled the beginning of the end of Reconstruction. (See also Du Bois 1935: 711–27; Foner 1988: xix–xxiv).
4   Moynihan's appropriation of history here is highly dubious. He relies on Frank Tannenbaum's (1946) questionable argument about the differences between American and Brazilian slavery, although he does not cite Tannenbaum directly (and misstates the date of Tannenbaum's book in his one mention of Tannenbaum). Instead, he quotes extensively from Nathan Glazer's gloss on Tannenbaum (Elkins 1963: ix–xii). He also relies on Elkins's research but rather similarly cites Thomas Pettigrew's (1964: 13–14) one-paragraph summary of Elkins rather than Elkins himself. Consequently, Moynihan's historical argument is hard to take seriously, even though his statistical portrait of the deterioration of African-American family life is alarming. (See also Scott 1997: 150–5; Marx 1998: 48–64),
5   A number of critiques and defenses of Moynihan are compiled in Rainwater and Yancey (1967).
6   Noiriel targets LeBras and Todd (1981), but the critique applies equally to Todd's later work.
7   Daniel Béland (2005: 89) cites the passage approvingly. DeWitt mischaracterizes the arguments he criticizes, which rely less centrally on the direct racial intentions of policymakers than he asserts, although Mary Poole (2006) shows that explicit racial motives were more on display in the Social Security debate than previously thought.

Bibliography

Primary sources

King, Martin Luther (3 April 1968) speech delivered at Mason Temple (Church of God in Christ Headquarters), Memphis, Tennessee.
Parents Involved in Community Schools v. Seattle School District No. 1. (2007) 551 U.S.
———.
Report of the Inter-Departmental Committee on Physical Deterioration. 1904. Cd. 2175, pp. 95–97.
U.S. Department of Labor, Office of Policy Planning and Research (1965) *The Negro Family: The Case for National Action*, Washington: Government Printing Office.
U.S. Social Security Board (1937) *Social Security in America: The Factual Background of the Social Security Act as Summarized from Staff Reports to the Committee on Economic Security*, Social Security Publication No. 21, Washington: Government Printing Office.

References and secondary sources

Ackerman, B. (1991) *We the People: Foundations*, Cambridge, MA: Harvard University Press.
Alesina, A., and Glaeser, E.L. (2004) *Fighting Poverty in the U.S. and Europe: A World of Difference*, Oxford: Oxford University Press.

Amenta, E. (1998) *Bold Relief: Institutional Politics and the Origins of Modern American Social Policy*, Princeton, NJ: Princeton University Press.

Arnold, R.D. (1990) *The Logic of Congressional Action*, New Haven, CT: Yale University Press.

Baldwin, P. (1990) *The Politics of Social Solidarity: Class Bases of the European Welfare State, 1875–1975*, Cambridge: Cambridge University Press.

Balfour, L. (2003) "Unreconstructed Democracy: W. E. B. Du Bois and the Case for Reparations," *American Political Science Review*, 97: 33–44.

Balibar, E. and Wallerstein, I. (1991) *Race, Nation, Class: Ambiguous Identities*, London: Verso.

Barkan, E. (2001) *The Guilt of Nations: Restitution and Negotiating Historical Injustices*, Baltimore, MD: Johns Hopkins University Press.

Baumgartner, F.R., and Jones, B.D. (1993) *Agendas and Instability in American Politics*, Chicago: University of Chicago Press.

Béland, D. (2005) *Social Security: History and Politics from the New Deal to the Privatization Debate*, Lawrence: University Press of Kansas.

Bell, D. (1992) *Faces at the Bottom of the Well: The Permanence of Racism*, New York: Basic Books.

Birnbaum, P. (1993) *"La France aux Français": Histoires des haines nationionalistes*, Paris: Seuil.

Bleich, E. (2003) *Race Politics in Britain and France: Ideas and Policymaking since the 1960s*, Cambridge: Cambridge University Press.

—— (2005) "The Legacies of History?: Colonization and Immigrant Integration in Britain and France," *Theory and Society*, 34: 171–95.

Branch, T. (1988) *Parting the Waters: America in the King Years, 1954–1963*, New York: Simon and Schuster.

—— (1998) *Pillar of Fire: America in the King Years, 1963–65*, New York: Simon and Schuster.

—— (2006) *At Canaan's Edge: America in the King Years, 1965–68*, New York: Simon and Schuster.

Brooks, R. (2004) *Atonement and Forgiveness: A New Model for Black Reparations*, Berkeley: University of California Press.

Brown, M.K. (1999) *Race, Money, and the American Welfare State*, Ithaca, NY: Cornell University Press.

Brown, M.K., Carnoy, M., Currie, E., Duster, T., Oppenheimer, D.B., Schultz, M.M., and Wellman, D. (2003) *Whitewashing Race: The Myth of a Color-Blind Society*, Berkeley: University of California Press.

Carmines, E.G. and Stimson, J.A. (1989) *Issue Evolution: Race and the Transformation of American Politics*, Princeton, NJ: Princeton University Press.

Conklin, A.L. (1997) *A Mission to Civilize: The Republican Idea of Empire in France and West Africa, 1895–1930*, Stanford, CA: Stanford University Press.

Conley, D. (1999) *Being Black, Living in the Red: Race, Wealth, and Social Policy in America*, Berkeley: University of California Press.

Cooper, F., Holt, T.C., and Scott, R.J. (2000) *Beyond Slavery: Explorations of Race, Labor, and Citizenship in Postemancipation Societies*, Chapel Hill: University of North Carolina Press.

Cowen, T. (2006) "Restitution: How Far Back Should We Go?" in J. Elster (ed.) *Retribution and Reparation in the Transition to Democracy*, Cambridge: Cambridge University Press.

Cutler, D.M. and Johnson, R. (2004) "The Birth and Growth of the Social Insurance State: Explaining Old Age and Medical Insurance Across Countries," *Public Choice*, 120: 87–121.

Davies, G. and Derthick, M. (1997) "Race and Social Welfare Policy: The Social Security Act of 1997," *Political Science Quarterly*, 112: 217–35.

Derthick, M. (1990) *Agency Under Stress: The Social Security Administration in American Government*, Washington DC: Brookings Institution.

DeWitt, L. (2004) "It Was Not About Race: The Decision to Exclude Agricultural and Domestic Workers from the U.S. Social Security Act," typescript.

Dubois, L. (2004) *A Colony of Citizens: Revolution and Slave Emancipation in the French Caribbean, 1787–1804*, Chapel Hill: University of North Carolina Press.

Du Bois, W.E.B. (1903) *The Souls of Black Folk*, Chicago: A.C. McClurg & Co.

—— (1935) *Black Reconstruction in America, 1860–1880*, New York: Harcourt Brace.

Elkins, S.M. (1963) *Slavery: A Problem in American Institutional and Intellectual Life*, reprint, New York: Grossett and Dunlap.

Elster, J. (ed.) (2006) *Retribution and Reparation in the Transition to Democracy*, Cambridge: Cambridge University Press.

Epstein, D., Pildes, R.H., de la Garza, R.O., and O'Halloran, S. (eds) (2006) *The Future of the Voting Rights Act*, New York: Russell Sage Foundation.

Farhang, S. and Katznelson, I. (2005) "The Southern Imposition: Congress and Labor in the New Deal and Fair Deal," *Studies in American Political Development*, 19: 1–30.

Faulkner, W. (1951) *Requiem for a Nun*, New York: Random House.

Favell, A. (1998) *Philosophies of Integration: Immigration and the Idea of Citizenship in France and Britain*, New York: St. Martin's.

Fenno, R.F., Jr. (1973) *Congressmen in Committees*, Boston, MA: Little, Brown.

Fields, B.J. (1982) "Ideology and Race in American History," in J.M. Kousser and J.M. McPherson (eds) *Region, Race, and Reconstruction: Essays in Honor of C. Vann Woodward*, New York: Oxford University Press.

Fiorina, M. (1977) *Congress: Keystone of the Washington Establishment*, New Haven, CT: Yale University Press.

Fitzhugh, G. ([1857] 1960) *Cannibals All!, or, Slaves without Masters*, reprint, Cambridge, MA: Harvard University Press.

Fogel, R.W. (1989) *Without Consent or Contract: The Rise and Fall of American Slavery*, New York: W.W. Norton.

Fogel, R.W. and Engerman, S.L. (1974) *Time on the Cross: The Economics of American Negro Slavery*, Boston, MA: Little, Brown.

Foner, E. (1988) *Reconstruction: America's Unfinished Revolution*, New York: Harper & Row.

Fredrickson, G.M. (1981) *White Supremacy: A Comparative Study in American and South African History*, New York: Oxford University Press.

—— (1995) *Black Liberation: A Comparative History of Black Ideologies in the United States and South Africa*, New York: Oxford University Press.

Freeman, G.P. (1979) *Immigrant Labor and Racial Conflict in Industrial Societies: The French and British Experience*, Princeton, NJ: Princeton University Press.

Gilbert, Bentley B. (1966) *The Evolution of National Insurance in Great Britain: The Origins of the Welfare State*, London: Michael Joseph.

Gutman, H.G. (1975) *Slavery and the Numbers Game: A Critique of* Time on the Cross, Urbana: University of Illinois Press.

—— (1976) *The Black Family in Slavery and Freedom, 1750–1925*, New York: Pantheon.

Hacker, A. (1992) *Two Nations: Black and White, Separate, Hostile, Unequal*, New York: Charles Scribner's Sons.

Hacker, J.S. (2004) "Privatizing Risk Without Privatizing the Welfare State: The Hidden Politics of Social Policy Retrenchment in the United States," *American Political Science Review*, 98: 243–60.

Hall, P.A. and Taylor, R.C.R. (1996) "Political Science and the Three New Institutionalisms," *Political Studies*, 44: 936–57.

Harris, F.C., Sinclair-Chapman, V., and Mackenzie, B.D. (2006) *Countervailing Forces in African-American Civic Activism, 1973–1994*, Cambridge: Cambridge University Press.

Hartz, L. (1955) *The Liberal Tradition in America: An Interpretation of American Political Thought Since the Revolution*, New York: Harcourt Brace.

Hirschman, A.O. (1991) *The Rhetoric of Reaction: Perversity, Futility, Jeopardy*, Cambridge, MA: Harvard University Press.

Hobsbawm, E. J. (1987) *The Age of Empire, 1875–1914*, New York: Pantheon.

Hochschild, J.L. (1984) *The New American Dilemma: Liberal Democracy and School Desegregation*, New Haven, CT: Yale University Press.

—— (1999) "You Win Some, You Lose Some: Explaining the Pattern of Success and Failure in the Second Reconstruction," in M. Keller and R.S. Melnick (eds) *Taking Stock: American Government in the Twentieth Century*, Cambridge: Cambridge University Press.

Hoffman, Y. (1989) "A North Israelite Typological Myth and a Judaean Historical Tradition: The Exodus in Hosea and Amos," *Vetus Testamentum*, 39: 169–82.

Holt, T.C. (1992) *The Problem of Freedom: Race, Labor, and Politics in Jamaica, 1832–1938*, Baltimore, MD: Johns Hopkins University Press.

—— (1995) "Marking: Race, Race-Making, and the Writing of History," *American Historical Review*, 100: 1–20.

Horton, C.A. (2005) *Race and the Making of American Liberalism*, Oxford: Oxford University Press.

Immergut, E.M. (1998) "The Theoretical Core of the New Institutionalism," *Politics and Society*, 26: 5–34.

Jackson, K.T. (1985) *Crabgrass Frontier: The Suburbanization of the United States*, New York: Oxford University Press.

James, W. (2002) "Explaining Afro-Caribbean Social Mobility in the United States: Beyond the Sowell Thesis," *Comparative Studies in Society and History*, 44: 218–62.

Jencks, C. and Phillips, M. (eds) (1998) *The Black–White Test Score Gap*, Washington DC: Brookings Institution.

Joppke, C. (1999) *Immigration and the Nation-State: The United States, Germany, and Great Britain*, Oxford: Oxford University Press.

Katz, M.B. and Stern, M.J. (2006) *One Nation, Divisible: What America Was and What It Is Becoming*, New York: Russell Sage Foundation.

Katznelson, I. (1971) "Power in the Reformulation of Race Research," in P. Orleans and W.R. Ellis Jr. (eds) *Race, Change, and Urban Society*, Beverly Hills, CA: Sage Publications.

—— (1972) "Comparative Studies of Race and Ethnicity: Plural Analysis and Beyond," *Comparative Politics*, 5: 135–54.

—— (1976) *Black Men, White Cities: Race, Politics, and Migration in the United States, 1900–30, and Britain, 1948–68*, Chicago: University of Chicago Press.

Katznelson, I., Geiger, K., and Kryder, D. (1993) "Limiting Liberalism: The Southern Veto in Congress, 1933–1950," *Political Science Quarterly*, 108: 283–306.

Kidd, C. (1999) *British Identities before Nationalism: Ethnicity and Nationhood in the Atlantic World, 1600–1800*, Cambridge: Cambridge University Press.

Kim, C.J. (1999) "The Racial Triangulation of Asian-Americans," *Politics and Society*, 27: 105–38.

King, D. (2005). *The Liberty of Strangers: Making the American Nation*, Oxford: Oxford University Press.

King, D.S. and Smith, R.M. (2005) "Racial Orders in American Political Development," *American Political Science Review*, 99: 75–92.

Kolchin, P. (1992) "More *Time on the Cross?*: An Evaluation of Robert William Fogel's *Without Consent or Contract*," *Journal of Southern History*, 58: 491–502.

Lapeyronnie, D. (1993) *L'individu et les minorités: La France et la Grande Bretagne face à leurs immigrés*, Paris: Presses Universitaires de France.

Lebovics, H. (1992) *True France: The Wars over Cultural Identity*, Ithaca, NY: Cornell University Press.

LeBras, H. and Todd, E. (1981) *L'invention de la France: Atlas anthropologique et politique*, Paris: Livre de Poche.

Lemann, N. (1991) *The Promised Land: The Great Black Migration and How It Changed America*, New York: Alfred A. Knopf.

Lewis, D.E. (2003) *Presidents and the Politics of Agency Design: Political Institutions in the United States Government Bureaucracy, 1946–1997*, Stanford, CA: Stanford University Press.

Lieberman, E.S. (2003) *Race and Regionalism in the Politics of Taxation in Brazil and South Africa*, Cambridge: Cambridge University Press.

Lieberman, R.C. (1998) *Shifting the Color Line: Race and the American Welfare State*, Cambridge, MA: Harvard University Press.

—— (2002) "Ideas, Institutions, and Political Order: Explaining Political Change," *American Political Science Review*, 96: 697–712.

—— (2005) *Shaping Race Policy: The United States in Comparative Perspective*, Princeton, NJ: Princeton University Press.

—— (2006) "'The Storm Didn't Discriminate': Katrina and the Politics of Color Blindness," *Du Bois Review*, 3: 7–22.

Marshall, T.H. (1964) "Citizenship and Social Class," in *Class, Citizenship, and Social Development*, Garden City, NY: Doubleday.

Marx, A.W. (1998) *Making Race and Nation: A Comparison of the United States, South Africa, and Brazil*, Cambridge: Cambridge University Press.

Massey, D.S. and Denton, N.A. (1993) *American Apartheid: Segregation and the Making of the Underclass*, Cambridge, MA: Harvard University Press.

Mayhew, D.R. (1974) *Congress: The Electoral Connection*, New Haven, CT: Yale University Press.

—— (2000) *America's Congress: Actions in the Public Sphere, James Madison through Newt Gingrich*, New Haven, CT: Yale University Press.

McMahon, K.J. (2004) *Reconsidering Roosevelt on Race: How the Presidency Paved the Road to Brown*, Chicago: University of Chicago Press.

Mehta, U.S. (1999) *Liberalism and Empire: A Study in Nineteenth-Century British Liberal Thought*, Chicago: University of Chicago Press.

Moe, T.M. (1989) "The Politics of Bureaucratic Structure," in J.E. Chubb and P.E. Peterson (eds) *Can the Government Govern?*, Washington DC: Brookings Institution.

Morgan, E.S. (1975) *American Slavery, American Freedom: The Ordeal of Colonial Virginia*, New York: W.W. Norton.

Myrdal, G. (1944) *An American Dilemma: The Negro Problem and Modern Democracy*, New York: Harper & Brothers.

Noble, C. (1997) *Welfare as We Knew It: A Political History of the American Welfare State*, New York: Oxford University Press.

Noiriel, G. (1996) *The French Melting Pot: Immigration, Citizenship, and National Identity*, trans. G. de Laforcade, Minneapolis: University of Minnesota Press.

Oliver, M.L. and Shapiro, T.M. (1995) *Black Wealth, White Wealth: A New Perspective on Racial Inequality*, New York: Routledge.

Orren, K. and Skowronek, S. (2004) *The Search for American Political Development*, Cambridge: Cambridge University Press.

Oubre, C.F. (1978) *Forty Acres and A Mule: The Freedmen's Bureau and Black Land Ownership*, Baton Rouge: Louisiana State University Press.

Pettigrew, T. (1964) *A Profile of the Negro American*, Princeton, NJ: D. Van Nostrand and Co.

Pierson, P. (2004) *Politics in Time: History, Institutions, and Social Analysis*, Princeton, NJ: Princeton University Press.

Plotke, D. (1996) *Building a Democratic Political Order: Reshaping American Liberalism in the 1930s and 1940s*, Cambridge: Cambridge University Press.

Pontusson, J. (2006) "The American Welfare State in Comparative Perspective: Reflections on Alberto Alesina and Edward Glaeser, *Fighting Poverty in the U.S. and Europe*," *Perspectives on Politics*, 4: 315–26.

Poole, M. (2006) *The Segregated Origins of Social Security: African Americans and the Welfare State*, Chapel Hill: University of North Carolina Press.

Quadagno, J. (1994) *The Color of Welfare: How Racism Undermined the War on Poverty*, New York: Oxford University Press.

Rainwater, L. and Yancey, W.L. (1967) *The Moynihan Report and the Politics of Controversy*, Cambridge, MA: MIT Press.

Rich, P. (1991) *Race and Empire in British Politics*, 2nd edn, Cambridge: Cambridge University Press.

Riley, R.L. (1999) *The Presidency and the Politics of Racial Inequality: Nation-Keeping from 1831–1965*, New York: Columbia University Press.

Robinson, R. (2000) *The Debt: What America Owes to Blacks*, New York: Dutton.

Rose, E.J.B. (1969) *Colour and Citizenship: A Report on British Race Relations*, London: Oxford University Press.

Schickler, E. (2001) *Disjointed Pluralism: Institutional Innovation and the Development of the U.S. Congress*, Princeton, NJ: Princeton University Press.

Scott, D.M. (1997) *Contempt and Pity: Social Policy and the Image of the Damaged Black Psyche*, Chapel Hill: University of North Carolina Press.

Scott, R.J. (2005) *Degrees of Freedom: Louisiana and Cuba After Slavery*, Cambridge, MA: Harvard University Press.

Semmel, B. (1960) *Imperialism and Social Reform: English Social-Imperial Thought, 1895–1914*, London: George Allen and Unwin.

Silverman, M. (1992) *Deconstructing the Nation: Immigration, Racism, and Citizenship in Modern France*, London: Routledge.

Skowronek, S. (2006) "The Reassociation of Ideas and Purposes: Racism, Liberalism, and the American Political Tradition," *American Political Science Review*, 100: 385–401.

Smith, R.M. (1997) *Civic Ideals: Conflicting Visions of American Citizenship in U.S. History*, New Haven, CT: Yale University Press.

Sowell, T. (1978) "Three Black Histories," in Thomas Sowell (ed.) *Essays and Data on American Ethnic Groups*, Washington: Urban Institute.

—— (1994) *Race and Culture: A World View*, New York: Basic Books.

Streeck, W. and Thelen, K. (2005) "Introduction: Institutional Change in Advanced Political Economies," in W. Streek and K. Thelen (eds) *Beyond Continuity: Institutional Change in Advanced Political Economies*, Oxford: Oxford University Press.

Sugrue, T.J. (1996) *The Origins of the Urban Crisis: Race and Inequality in Postwar Detroit*, Princeton, NJ: Princeton University Press.

Sullivan, P. (1996) *Days of Hope and Rage: Race and Democracy in the New Deal Era*, Chapel Hill: University of North Carolina Press.

Tannenbaum, F. (1946) *Slave and Citizen: The Negro in the Americas*, New York: Alfred A. Knopf.

Thelen, K. (2004) *How Institutions Evolve: The Political Economy of Skills in Germany, Britain, the United States, and Japan*, Cambridge: Cambridge University Press.

Thelen, K. and Steinmo, S. (1992) "Historical Institutionalism in Comparative Politics," in S. Steinmo, K. Thelen, and F. Longstreth (eds) *Structuring Politics: Historical Institutionalism in Comparative Analysis*, Cambridge: Cambridge University Press.

Thernstrom, S. and Thernstrom, A. (1997) *America in Black and White: One Nation, Indivisible*, New York: Simon and Schuster.

de Tocqueville, A. (1955) *The Old Régime and the French Revolution*, trans. Stuart Gilbert, Garden City, NY: Doubleday.

Todd, E. (1991) *The Making of Modern France: Politics, Ideology, and Culture*, trans. Anthony and Betty Forster, Oxford: Basil Blackwell.

—— (1994) *Le destin des immigrées: Assimilation et ségrégation dans des démocraties occidentales*, Paris: Seuil.

Torpey, J. (2006) *Making Whole What Has Been Smashed: On Reparations Politics*, Cambridge, MA: Harvard University Press.

Tulis, J.K. (1987) *The Rhetorical Presidency*, Princeton, NJ: Princeton University Press.

Valelly, R.M. (2004) *The Two Reconstructions: The Struggle for Black Enfranchisement*, Chicago: University of Chicago Press.

Walzer, M. (1985) *Exodus and Revolution*, New York: Basic Books.

Weber, E. (1976) *Peasants Into Frenchmen: The Modernization of Rural France, 1870–1914*, Stanford, CA: Stanford University Press.

Weber, M. (1946) "Class, Status, Party," in *From Max Weber: Essays in Sociology*, trans. H.H. Gerth and C. W. Mills (ed.), New York: Oxford University Press.

Weiss, N.J. (1983) *Farewell to the Party of Lincoln: Black Politics in the Age of FDR*, Princeton, NJ: Princeton University Press.

Wilder, G. (2005) *The French Imperial Nation-State: Negritude and Colonial Humanism between the Two World Wars*, Chicago: University of Chicago Press.

Wilensky, H. (1975) *The Welfare State and Equality: Structural and Ideological Roots of Public Expenditures*, Berkeley: University of California Press.

Williams, L.F. (2003) *The Constraint of Race: Legacies of White Skin Privilege in America*, University Park: Pennsylvania State University Press.

Wilson, W.J. (1987) *The Truly Disadvantaged: The Inner City, the Underclass, and Public Policy*, Chicago: University of Chicago Press.

—— (1996) *When Work Disappears: The World of the New Urban Poor*, New York: Alfred A. Knopf.

Wright, G. (1986) *Old South, New South: Revolutions in the Southern Economy since the Civil War*, New York: Basic Books.

10 The origins of the carceral crisis: Racial order as "law and order" in postwar American politics

Naomi Murakawa

Tonight there is violence in our streets, corruption in our highest offices, aimlessness among our youth, anxiety among our elders and there is a virtual despair among the many who look beyond material success for the inner meaning of their lives . . . The growing menace in our country tonight, to personal safety, to life, to limb and property, in homes, in churches, on the playgrounds, and places of business, particularly in our great cities, is the mounting concern, or should be, of every thoughtful citizen in the United States. Security from domestic violence, no less than from foreign aggression, is the most elementary and fundamental purpose of any government, and a government that cannot fulfill that purpose is one that cannot long command the loyalty of its citizens. History shows us—demonstrates that nothing—nothing prepares the way for tyranny more than the failure of public officials to keep the streets from bullies and marauders.

> Barry Goldwater, accepting the nomination for president at the
> 28th Republican National Convention, July 16, 1964

At the height of the civil rights era, after President Lyndon Johnson signed the 1964 Civil Rights Act and while thousands of blacks registered to vote during the 1964 Freedom Summer, the Republican presidential candidate Barry Goldwater campaigned using a particular indictment of the struggle for black freedom: black civil rights, he suggested, are linked to crime. Throughout his campaign speeches, Goldwater traced rising crime rates to black civil disobedience, black demands for equality under the law, and black reliance on the welfare state. Goldwater conflated civil disobedience with "violence in our streets" and black activists with "bullies and marauders," and in so doing he contended—subtly but undeniably—that black freedom necessitates a strong "law and order" response.

In the years following Goldwater's defeat, political leaders declared victory over Jim Crow while simultaneously passing more mandatory minimums, funding more prison construction, and reinstating the death penalty, all with disproportionate impact on black Americans. Incarceration rates have increased more than five-fold since Goldwater warned of the "growing menace" to "personal safety" in 1964, and during this same period the black-to-white incarceration disparity has increased from roughly three-to-one to roughly seven-to-one. This combination of scale shift and disparity increase has brought seismic demographic ruptures for black Americans: nearly 10 percent of the black voting-age population is currently disenfranchised due to a felony conviction; there are more black men in jails and prisons than in colleges and universities; incarceration rates for black women are roughly six times those of their white counterparts; and nearly one million black children have a parent in jail or prison (Mumola 2000; Manza and Uggen 2006: 253; Western 2006: 15–16). If "political development" is considered a "durable shift" in the "exercise of control over persons or things that is designated and enforceable by the state" (Orren and Skowronek 2004: 123), then the modern growth of the carceral state—propelled in large part by the incarceration of black Americans—should be a prime area of study in American political development.

When and how did "law and order" become so conflated with racial order, so politically prominent, and so consequential to the development of the U.S. carceral state? Scholars mark the mid- and late 1960s as pivotal years for crime policy, with Goldwater identified as a kind of inaugural figure for the era of mass incarceration. Scholars emphasize different factors that made the 1960s ripe for "law and order" appeals, giving particular attention to the roles of crime, riots, public punitiveness, and racial backlash (for detailed literature review, see Gottschalk 2006: chapter 2).[1] Crime rates began rising in the early 1960s, urban riots accelerated through 1967 and 1968, and some scholars argue that consequently public opinion turned to favor longer prison sentences (Wilson 1975; Page and Shapiro 1992: 90–4; Marion 1994). Other scholars suggest that 1960s liberalism went too far too fast for white Americans, who became disillusioned with the excesses of the Great Society, black power, and black rioters. In this line of analysis, carceral state development is part of a broader racial backlash that retrenches black progress through race-coded appeals to welfare, school choice, and crime (Edsall and Edsall 1992; Beckett 1997; Flamm 2005). In the 1960s context of crime and racial tension, analysts credit Goldwater with "setting the scene for debate about crime" (Rosch 1985: 25), as Goldwater "constructed what would become the standard conservative formulation of law and order" (Flamm 2005: 33).[2]

This chapter represents an effort to retrace the trajectory of race-laden "law and order" political appeals. Conventional wisdom suggests that the 1960s ushered in a new era of racialized crime politics, but this chapter suggests that national leaders explicitly and routinely addressed black civil rights in criminological terms—and they did so nearly two decades before escalating crime rates, before widespread riots, and before the Goldwater presidential campaign of 1964. Since President Harry Truman's creation of the Committee for Civil Rights in 1946, opponents and supporters of black civil rights linked "the Negro problem" with "the crime problem." Specifically, civil rights opponents and southern Democrats in Congress argued that crime was a manifestation of black civil rights that had gone too far: civil rights breed crime, they claimed, by disrupting the naturally harmonious segregation of the races and by validating black discretion on selective law-obedience. Civil rights proponents and many northern Democrats responded that street crime was evidence that black civil rights had not gone far enough: unfulfilled civil rights agendas breed crime, they claimed, because racial inequality sustains black deprivation and engenders black distrust of laws. While seemingly opposite interpretations, both explanations attribute crime to black civil rights, and both interpretations identify blacks as default suspects in the crime problem (Murakawa 2005).

The postwar transformation of racial order into "law and order" is more than just a back-story to current scholarship. Historicizing "law and order" actually challenges notions that 1964 "set the scene for debate about crime;" in a sense, deeper racial antecedents emerge when "law and order" itself is studied in a long-term political sequence rather than in a cross-sectional moment of all factors contemporaneous with the 1964 presidential campaign. That is, a snapshot of the Goldwater moment can seem like a perfect storm for tough on crime appeals: many white voters disapproved of the pace of civil rights reform, southern Democrats were disenchanted with their party, and, most importantly, crime rates were actually rising and riots were actually accelerating in frequency and severity. Instead of a snapshot of 1964, this chapter retraces how concerns for racial order were articulated as "law and order" over the entire postwar period, even before the perfect-storm conditions of increased crime and accelerated riots.

Conventional wisdom holds that the U.S. faced an actual crime problem in the 1960s that was infused with racial politics. This chapter suggests the opposite. The U.S. did not confront a crime problem that was then racialized; it confronted a race problem that was then criminalized. The battle to preserve Jim Crow in the 1940s and 1950s segued into the battle against crime in the mid-1960s. Section I of this chapter identifies early "law and order" political rhetoric as developed through resistance to anti-lynching legislation, school and neighborhood integration, and civil rights legislation in the years 1946 through 1963. Section II traces how "law and order" claims from black civil rights debates were then transplanted into crime debates in the years 1964 through 1968.

Jim Crow's racial order maintains law and order, 1946–63

In the years immediately following World War II, at the same time that many whites came to believe that racism was an affront to American democracy (Myrdal 1944; Dudziak 1988), many whites also came to believe that racial integration was an affront to their safety. Even though crime rates were notably low and stable for more than a decade after the war, the frequency and meaning of interracial contact in "the street" was changing.[3] Whites in the urban North complained of dangerous public parks, public schools, and public transportation; whites in the South cautioned that black civil rights would make the South as chaotic as Chicago, Detroit, and New York. Postwar racial configurations—particularly the nexus of rising black activism, renewed federal attention to black civil rights, white violence against black veterans, and black urbanization alongside white suburbanization—led many white Americans to express racial anxiety in criminological terms.

In detailing the mobilization of "law and order" rhetoric from 1946 through 1963, this section sketches a timeline and a rhetorical trajectory for crime on the national agenda. During this period, "law and order" rhetoric is a subsidiary of the postwar struggle for black freedom, so major benchmarks proceed from President Truman's creation of the Committee on Civil Rights in 1946, to *Brown v. Board of Education* in 1954, to the Civil Rights Act of 1957, to the sit-ins in 1960, to the March on Washington in 1963. Southern Democrats in Congress, as well as many whites in the South and the urban North, defended Jim Crow by suggesting that segregation maintains law and order while integration breeds crime; that black civil rights protesters are criminals.

To Secure These Rights *through* Brown v. Board of Education: segregation maintains law and order; integration breeds crime

At the end of World War II, black veterans returning home to the South faced public beatings and lynchings sometimes involving local police, and subsequent black protest made "race . . . an issue the federal government was unable to ignore" (Dudziak 1988: 77). In September of 1946, the newly formed National Emergency Committee Against Mob Violence met with President Harry Truman to call for federal intervention against lynching. After the meeting, President Truman established the Committee on Civil Rights to study racial violence and discrimination. The Committee's 1947 report, *To Secure These Rights*, proposed federal antilynching protection, elimination of the poll tax, creation of a Fair Employment Protection Commission, and other legislation to strengthen federal civil rights.

Racial conflict—particularly white violence against black veterans—prompted the creation of Truman's Committee on Civil Rights, and southern Democrats protested by offering their own interpretations of federalism, race, violence, and lawlessness. In the 1948 presidential campaign, southern Democrats protested President Truman's civil rights advocacy by forming the States' Rights Party. Southern Democrats in Congress mobilized familiar arguments: federal civil rights legislation violates states' rights, duplicates protections already imparted to blacks, and threatens to destroy the salutary and natural social system of segregation (Caro 2002: 954–7). Southern Democrats also issued another, less commonly recognized set of arguments against civil rights legislation: segregation maintains law and order, while integration breeds crime.

Southern Democrats opposed Truman's plan by sketching a picture of crime and disorder in the "integrated" urban North, juxtaposed against lawful and orderly living in the segregated South. This argument was nothing new: antebellum defenders of slavery presented the image of a peaceful South, where whites were benevolent patriarchs who nurtured and disciplined blacks, maintaining a mutually beneficial racial order (Mendelberg 2001: 75). Following World War II, southern Democrats argued that race riots in Detroit, public-school disorders in New York, and crime in Washington, DC, were the inevitable injuries of integration. In contrast, they contended, "the social structure of the South is best for all concerned," yielding "less inter-racial crime and less racial friction than any section of the country" (Senator James Eastland (D-Mississippi), *Cong. Rec.* 1948: A2337; see also Representative William Norrell (D-Arkansas), *Cong. Rec.* 1948: A1571). Southern Democrats in Congress claimed to "understand the Negro;" antilynching laws were unnecessary because southern officers knew to be "more lenient on the Negro who violates the law" (Representative William Winstead (D-Mississippi), *Cong. Rec.* 1948: 1008).

Antilynching debates prompted an even more specific defense of segregation as order maintenance. Truman's Committee on Civil Rights proposed antilynching legislation wherein federal criminal law would allow imprisonment of lynch-mob participants and local police that failed to control them. Betraying their assumption that the lynching of a black man was a response to his actual raping of a white woman, southern Democrats suggested that the antilynching bill "ought to be called a bill to encourage rape" (Representative John Rankin (D-Mississippi), *Cong. Rec.* 1948: A4739). Southern Democrats suggested that Truman should show less concern for black men and more concern for "bringing about the conditions whereby the women of the Nation can walk without fear of attack and assault" (Representative Stephen Pace (D-Georgia), *Cong. Rec.* 1948: 1233). Of course, the political idea of the "black male rapist" has deep historical antecedents: opponents of Emancipation and Reconstruction frequently spoke of the hypersexual black male and his uncontrollable lust for white women (Oshinsky 1997: chapter 4). Following World War II, the political idea of the "black male rapist" held renewed currency because of challenges to Jim Crow, questions of whether white women would happily return home after their wartime jobs, and the lynchings of black veterans.

White citizens of the South similarly held that integration would simply make them easy prey for black criminals. Following the *Brown v. Board of Education* decision to overturn the "separate but equal" doctrine in 1954, southern segregationists formed the White Citizens' Council. Publications from the White Citizens' Councils stated that blacks possess genetically determined "criminal tendencies," and that "savages stalk corridors in northern 'blackboard jungles.'" The Mississippi Association of Citizens' Councils released a one-page flier entitled *Crime Report Reveals Menace of Integration*, which claimed to prove that blacks are innately more devious than whites (quoted in McMillen 1971: 186–7).

White citizens in the urban North also suspected that integration would increase black-on-white crime. Residential integration in Detroit, for example, prompted whites to form at least 192 neighborhood organizations between 1943 and 1965, with organizations variously called "protective associations" or "homeowners' associations" (Sugrue 2005: 211). Neighborhood associations sought to maintain residential segregation in the name of protecting homes from devaluation and protecting families from black-on-white crime. One neighborhood association poster recruited members through references to gangsters and crimes of immorality: "Home Owners Can You Afford to . . . Have your children exposed to gangster operated skid row saloons? Phornographic [sic] pictures and literature? Gamblers and prostitution? You Face These Issues Now!" In a sense, race-mixing did bring more crime in the streets, but of whites against blacks, not blacks against whites, as blacks who moved into formerly all-white neighborhoods faced vandalism, arson, assault, and harassment instigated by white Detroiters. White violence against blacks breaking residential barriers was organized and involved thousands of whites, and most incidents followed neighborhood association meetings (Sugrue 1996: 217–33).

Montgomery bus boycotts through the march on Washington: black protesters are insolent criminals; federal civil rights legislation encourages black lawlessness

As black civil rights gained momentum, southern states deployed their criminal justice apparatus to combat black protesters as if they were criminals. During the Montgomery bus boycotts, initiated in December 1955 by Rosa Parks's arrest for breaking a segregation ordinance, Montgomery's mayor declared what he called a "get tough" policy. Montgomery police ticketed and arrested blacks driving in car pools; they arrested blacks waiting for rides on charges of vagrancy or hitchhiking; they arrested Dr. Martin Luther King, Jr. for driving five miles an hour faster than the speed limit (Barkan 1984).

A year after the bus boycotts, the Democratic Congress passed, and President Dwight Eisenhower, signed the Civil Rights Act of 1957—the first law to redress racial inequality since the Civil Rights Act of 1875. The enacted legislation established a national Commission on Civil Rights and a civil rights division at the Justice Department. In vocalizing opposition to the Civil Rights Act of 1957 and its failed previous version in 1956, southern Democrats continued to argue that integration made whites vulnerable to black criminality. This line of argument is spelled out explicitly by Representative Elijah Forrester (D-Georgia):

> The truth is, that at the present time, where segregation has been abolished, such as public parks, restaurants, theaters, schools, and transportation, the Negro has virtually had the full use thereof. In the District of Columbia, the public parks have become of no utility whatever to the white race, for they enter at the risk of assaults upon their person or the robbery of their personal effects. This will be denied, but not successfully, for no matter how strenuously it is denied, it remains absolutely true. The District of Columbia, the guinea pig for the social

experiments, has now become a place that schoolchildren of this Nation cannot come into and walk the streets at night with safety. Unless the pendulum swings back before it is too late, I predict that in 10 years, the Nation's Capital will be unsafe for them in the daytime.

(*Cong. Rec.* 1956: 12946)

In this account, integration gives way to black domination of public places, which gives way to black assault and robbery of whites, which gives way to white retreat and an inability to safely walk the street. White fear of social equality between the races takes a decidedly spatial tone in these arguments, as does the phrase "crime in the streets." In 1865, southern whites complained that newly emancipated blacks shoved white people off the sidewalks. In the 1920s, southern opponents of antilynching bills warned that southern blacks would resume disrespectful street behavior if lynching became a criminal offense, and opponents stated that blacks shoving whites on the street was an everyday occurrence in the North (Rable 1985: 205).

Like White Citizens' Councils, many southern Democrats protested who the Civil Rights Act of 1957 offered "proof" of segregation's benefits by favorably comparing southern crime rates to northern crime rates. Representative Thomas Abernathy (D-Mississippi) reasoned that "race relations are much better in the South than in the North," and civil rights legislation will only "stir strife and discord among us" (*Cong. Rec.* 1956: 12939). Representative Abernathy highlighted crime control as a specific benefit of segregation, stating that "there is less crime among the Negroes of the South than among those in the North" (*Cong. Rec.* 1956: 12943; see also Representative Basil Whitener (D-North Carolina), *Cong. Rec.* 1957: 8658). In the same vein, Representative James Davis (D-Georgia) asserted that "racial violence between southern white people and southern Negroes is rare indeed;" in contrast, "racial animosity and racial violence is greater in your section than it is in mine" (*Cong. Rec.* 1956: 14154).

Few directly rebutted the charge that integration breeds crime. Senator Jacob Javits (R-New York), a supporter of the Civil Rights Act of 1957, characterized crime in the North and the South as the "penalty for a long number of years in which we have failed to bring up to parity the education, housing, and employment opportunities of the Negro members of all our communities" (*Cong. Rec.* 1959: 18384). Liberal Republicans and northern Democrats of later years would echo Senator Javits's logic: accepting the presumption of crime's black center, they would argue that black crime is a manifestation of structural, not volitional, failures (Scheingold 1984, 1991).

In addition to perpetuating the argument that integration breeds crime, southern Democrats also contended that the Civil Rights Act of 1957 would empower black organizations to defend black criminals under the guise of civil rights. Representative Basil Whitener (D-North Carolina) opposed the establishment of a Civil Rights Division of the Department of Justice on the grounds that it was simply an avenue for the exoneration of black criminals.

Representative Whitener stated that "there are many good law-abiding Negroes in this country," but "nevertheless the bulk of the crimes of violence are committed by Negroes." "Radical" organizations like the NAACP, "under the guise of protecting civil rights," run to "the assistance of Negro criminals and seeks to protect them from the punishment for the crimes they commit." In this line of thinking, the establishment of a Civil Rights Division would therefore "tie the hands of law-enforcement officers throughout the country, and would place law-abiding men, women, and children at the mercy of brutal, merciless, hardened criminals" (*Cong. Rec.* 1957: 8658).

In this argument, the Civil Rights Division is a special privilege for blacks, and as such it could become a vehicle for black organizations to suppress law enforcement and defend the worst of their race. This logic was not new to Congress: opponents of Reconstruction argued that efforts to redress racial inequality, such as the Fourteenth and Fifteenth Amendments and the Freedman's Bureau, were giving blacks undeserved and unfair privileges (Mendelberg 2001: 75). In this framework, efforts to redress racial inequality are nothing more than special privileges for blacks, and, in the case of a Civil Rights Division, such special privileges could lead to the dangerous exoneration of black criminals.

Integration-breeds-crime arguments were impotent in stopping the Civil Rights Act of 1957, but southern Democrats stuck to this logic in subsequent civil rights debates. The Civil Right Act of 1960, passed by a Democratic Congress and signed by President Eisenhower, established criminal penalties for obstructing voter registration and voting. The enacted legislation was a modest effort to secure black voting rights, and it proffered little in the way of "promoting integration" per se, but southern Democrats still countered with warnings that the new civil rights legislation would bring crime waves because of increased race-mixing. In opposing the bill in 1959, Senator Strom Thurmond (R-South Carolina) argued that "political demands for integration of the races" would bring a "wave of terror, crime, and juvenile delinquency." As proof for this claim, Senator Thurmond pointed to "crime after crime in integrated New York" and other "integrated sections of the country" (*Cong. Rec.* 1959: 18382, 18385). Senator James Eastland (D-Mississippi) argued that "law enforcement is breaking down because of racial integration," and he advised northern politicians to address "the rape, the murder, the muggings, the crime on the streets of northern cities, rather than point their finger at the South, which is the most peaceful section of the United States" (*Cong. Rec.* 1960: 3982). Senator William Fulbright (D-Arkansas) stated that southern cities have seen an upsurge in strife "that grew out of the Supreme Court decision," and in integrated northern cities like Washington, DC "one does not feel safe to walk on any street" (*Cong. Rec.* 1960: 3982). Southern Democrats were quick to cite mainstream news sources that validated their claims, including a *U.S. News & World Report* article that claimed "terror on the streets is a growing problem in big American cities." The reason: "Police say racial frictions are closely related to the upsurge in crime. Trouble brews, for example, when Negroes or Puerto Ricans move into neighborhoods once regarded as predominantly Irish or Italian" (*U.S. News & World Report,* September 14, 1959: 65).

Echoing their opposition to President Truman's antilynching proposal, Southern Democrats again suggested that black men raping white women was a consequence of the racial mixing encouraged by legislation like the Civil Rights Act of 1960. Senator Johnston (D-South Carolina) listed "three women, including a girl of 13 years of age," "the 60-year old wife of a Presbyterian minister," and "many other instances" of rape. According to Johnston, "a colored man instigated and is tied in with each of these cases;" the victim, presumably white, needs no racial specification (*Cong. Rec.* 1960, 106, pt. 3: 3983). Senator Eastland (D-Mississippi) stated that the culture and conditions of the integrated north mean that "a white woman is not safe on the streets of their cities or in their schools or within the walls of an apartment house" (*Cong. Rec.* 1960: 3984).

Southern Democrats were so insistent that civil rights generate crime that they proposed making the Civil Rights Commission responsible for collecting crime data. Following a recommendation from former President Herbert Hoover, in 1960 Senator Eastland (D-Mississippi) proposed a bill (H.R. 8315) requiring the recently established Civil Rights Commission to conduct a census of all criminal victimizations in the country. Specifically, this census would show "what races the offenders come from," with the intended effect of "stir[ring] the leaders of various racial groups to action" in disciplining their own. This task is rightly entrusted to the Civil Rights Commission, argued Senator Eastland, because the Commission serves no "useful purpose," and because there is no civil right more important than "the God-given right of all people to be secure in both their persons and property from the trespass of others."

Senator Eastland then asserted a central argument of this chapter: when national leaders attribute crime to black civil rights, then federal intervention in crime control logically follows. Senator Eastland explained: "If the multitude of bills proposing Federal legislation on so-called civil rights constitutes a legitimate exercise of power on the part of the Federal Government under the Constitution, certainly security of person should also be classified as one of the paramount Federal rights . . . If the Negro is entitled to equal social status, why does not he earn equality? Why is he responsible for most of the crimes in this country?" (*Cong. Rec.* 1960: 4020–2). In Senator Eastland's logic, if black civil rights are the legitimate exercise of federal power, then so too is control of black crime; if blacks assume full citizenship, then they must face full punishment for their crimes; if the federal government promotes black civil rights, then it must control the ensuing black criminological mess. Like Barry Goldwater, Senator Eastland issued a threatening prediction that black freedom would require harsher law and order. Senator Eastland and Barry Goldwater lost their immediate battles, but their rhetoric of racial order as "law and order" prevailed.

In the eyes of many segregationists, the rise of black civil disobedience in 1961 and 1962 only further reinforced the idea that black civil rights activists were disrespectful agitators and deliberate lawbreakers. The Woolworth's lunch counter sit-ins in February 1960 prompted student sit-ins in 54 cities in nine states, and Freedom Riders of 1961 penetrated the South to fight for full service in buses, terminal restaurants, and waiting rooms (McAdam 1982: chapter 7). At the state level, southern politicians deployed the criminal justice arsenal—criminal law, police, jail, and prison—against black activists engaged in nonviolent direct action and civil disobedience. State police arrested participants of all variety of sit-ins, marches, and demonstrations, and they also arrested known activists outside of any protest context (Barkan 1984). Arrests were made of grounds of criminal trespass, breach of the peace, and criminal mischief, to name just a few (Heyman 1965: 167–8).

In this context, southern Democrats opposed the civil rights bill in Congress with an argument that would persist with only mild variation over the coming decade: civil rights protest is lawbreaking, they argued, and therefore federal civil rights legislation rewards black lawlessness. In this calculus, black protest is a form of criminal extortion, and therefore civil rights legislation is misguided federal capitulation to extortion. Southern Democrats warned of the "growing tendency to force the passage of legislation" by "demonstrations, mob violence, and disrespect to peace officers," and now even "court orders and court decisions are being influenced by illegal demonstrations and surging mobs" (Representative William Jennings Bryan Dorn (D-South Carolina), *Cong. Rec.* 1963: 11804). Southern Democrats called black demonstrators "street mobs," and faulted them for making the streets unsafe, saying that "Negro demonstrators are flowing into the streets, rampaging as an unruly, unchecked mob" (Representative George Huddleston, Jr., D-Alabama, *Cong. Rec.* 1963, 109, pt. 9: A3740). Southern Democrats insisted that the "federal Government should never permit illegal demonstrations and marches upon this Capitol designed to coerce and force Congress to submit to mob rule and the law of the jungle" (Representative William Jennings Bryan Dorn (D-South Carolina), *Cong. Rec.* 1963: 11804).[4] In an article often quoted by southern Democrats, conservative columnist David Lawrence of *U.S. News & World Report* suggested that civil rights legislation represents "the coercion of our legislative or executive process by street mobs" (1963: 104).

In arguing that integration breeds crime, southern Democrats blended criminological street crime—robbery, assault, stranger rape—with black people simply being in the streets unregulated by Jim Crow—using parks, schools, buses, and other public spaces as if they had equal right to them. In arguing that civil rights reward black lawlessness, southern Democrats conflated predatory, stranger street crime with politically-motivated, group-organized lawbreaking in the form of civil disobedience against unjust laws and traditions. This early conflation of black freedom with black crime calls into question the assertion that Barry Goldwater "constructed what would become the standard conservative formulation of law and order;" instead, Barry Goldwater simply continued a dialogue put in play by southern Democrats nearly two decades earlier.

Reformulating the racial underpinnings of "law and order"

Early framings of "law and order" were born race-laden, with southern Democrats warning that "dangerous streets" follow from racial integration, black civil rights, and black activism. This section traces the evolution of street crime in congressional debates during the Johnson Administration, when crime hit the national agenda in its own right. The years from 1964 through 1968 deserve particular attention as years of critical firsts: the presidential election of 1964 was the first to feature crime as a central campaign issue; after 1964 national research commissions on crime and presidential messages on crime became commonplace for the first time; and from 1965 through 1968 Congress made its first forays into controlling everyday street crime, including the 1968 Omnibus and Safe Streets Act to begin distribution of vast federal monies to state law enforcement. These were foundational years for federal crime politics. For northern Democrats, this period of initial federal intervention marked a short but path-setting period of crime policy development, with pushes for equality-based and rehabilitative crime policy dovetailing with civil rights liberalization and the Great Society, all fortified with race-specific structural blame attribution. For Republicans and southern Democrats, pushes for law and order were fortified with race-specific volitional blame attribution set a decade ago. The black-rights-breed-crime argument had become more complex, more culturally than biologically grounded, but its essential logic remained, as if the same blame attribution had simply moved from congressional debates on civil rights to congressional debates on crime. While seeming to have opposite interpretations of the crime problem, both Democrats and Republicans issued race-specific blame attributions, connecting crime rates to the fate of black civil rights.

Three factors facilitated the categorization of crime as a matter of black equality during this foundational period. The first factor is that official statistics revealed an alarming increase in crime, and there was no consensus as to the cause; together, this meant that crime was a problem open to politically interested blame attribution. The total crime rate jumped 135 percent between 1964 and 1968, and in 1968 both violent and property crime rates were at their highest levels recorded to date by the FBI. There are many possible explanations for crime's sudden rise. One explanation is simply demographic: the enormous birth cohort of "baby-boomers" hit their teenage years in the mid-1960s, and generally the population aged 15 to 24 years commits 70 percent of all crimes. The baby-boom cohort as young adults elevated crime rates because of the sheer force of their numbers and the sheer age distinctiveness in predatory offending and victimization; conversely, crime's decline three decades later represents the youngest of the baby-boomer cohort ageing out of the most criminally active years (Blumstein 2000; Fox 2000). Another explanation is simply methodological: sudden improvements in data collection exaggerated crime's increase as characterized by the *Uniform Crime Reports*. Scholars in the 1960s noted that crime data collection rather than crime itself changed significantly, with crime reporting enhanced by new centralization of complaint handling, new record automation, new 911 emergency calling, and a generally higher percentage of police and sheriff's offices reporting their crimes to the FBI (Biderman 1966: 151; Cronin et al. 1981: 8). Demographic and methodological explanations hold merit, but political blame attribution entails matching explanation not to empirical validity but to electoral and ideological interests; and, with alarming official crime rates, political leaders were well-positioned to do exactly that.

The second factor facilitating the categorization of crime as a matter of black equality was urban riots from 1965 through 1968. In 1965, riots in Watts killed 34, injured more than 800, motivated almost 4,000 arrests, and damaged roughly $40 million worth of property. There were nearly 100 additional riots in 1966 and 1967, including riots in Detroit and Newark that matched the intensity of Watts. In 1968, the assassination of Dr. Martin Luther King, Jr. ignited riots in 175 cities. Riots eased the conflation of street crime with black frustration over equality. Few think of a riot as a traditional street crime, as a riot tends to be a time-bound group reaction to a public prompt. Despite dissimilarities, riots matched previously established markers of street crime: riots erupted on the streets, frightened people, and the rioters were predominantly black. Moreover, riots were not just incidentally black, but their triggers were specific to struggles for black equality, such as the assassination of a national black leader or police brutality against blacks. Police brutality against blacks sparked many of the urban riots, including the two major riots of 1967. In Newark, riots erupted after police beat and arrested a black taxi driver, and in Detroit, riots erupted after police raided a black "speakeasy." Public opinion on this matter divided sharply along racial lines, with more than two-thirds of black survey respondents identifying police brutality as the major contributor to riots, while only one in six white survey respondents held this opinion (*Congressional Quarterly Almanac* 1967: 796).

The third factor facilitating the categorization of crime as a matter of black equality is the rising principle of racial equality in the 1960s. By the mid-1960s, expressions of overt white superiority were largely frowned upon, treated as anachronistic and distasteful if not entirely untrue. Opinion polls reveal a profound transformation of white attitudes toward blacks from the 1940s through the 1960s. For example, when asked, "Do you think white students and black students should go to the same schools or separate schools," the portion of respondents answering "the same" was only 32 percent in 1942, but this portion jumped to 50 percent in 1956, 73 percent in 1968, and 90 percent in 1982 (Schuman et al. 1985). Perhaps some respondents silenced their "true beliefs" to voice "acceptable" answers to pollsters, but such behavior only underscores the influence of new social norms dictating the principle of racial equality. By the mid-1960s, black civil rights had won a fundamental ideological battle in defeating overt doctrines of white superiority, and the principle of racial equality had become a genuine part of American political culture (Skrentny 2002: 65).

The ascendant principle of racial equality profoundly influenced electoral incentives in crime control—and in complicated fashion. For northern Democrats, the rising popularity of civil rights, as well as the greater enfranchisement of black voters, black migration northward, and heightened black support for the Democratic Party, all brought potential electoral benefits in categorizing crime as another manifestation of racial inequality. In 1964 and during the Johnson Administration, the Democratic Party was rapidly establishing itself as the party of black civil rights. As well-documented by Carmines and Stimson (1989), the issue of civil rights pushed the parties to align along racial lines, and 1964 marked a critical turning point. Before 1964, most Americans did not distinguish the parties in terms of civil rights; after 1964, most Americans identified the Democratic Party as the champion of civil rights and the Republican Party as the opponent of civil rights. In the national election of 1964, Republican presidential candidate Barry Goldwater ran against the Civil Rights Act of 1964; his candidacy marked the beginning of black abandonment of the party of Lincoln, and since that election African American voters have consistently supported Democratic candidates in presidential elections at rates of over 80 percent (Huckfeldt and Kohfeld 1989: 14–15; Frymer 1999: 87).

For Republicans, the principle of racial equality, as well as black defection from the Republican Party and growing white resentment toward the racial liberalism of the Democratic Party, added up to a complicated calculus about how to frame crime for electoral gain. Statements issued a mere decade ago—references to blacks as "lawless jungle dwellers" and claims that "forced race-mixing breeds crime"—were too overtly white supremacist for the new racial zeitgeist. At the same time, however, growing white disenchantment preserved the electoral incentive to call crime a problem of excessive racial liberalism. To negotiate this delicate racial terrain, Republicans began to deploy negative racial code words and images to increase their base of primarily white voters and to win over resentful white Democrats (Edsall and Edsall 1992; Frymer 1999: 87; Mendelberg 2001).

These three factors—rising crime, riots, and the new social norm of racial equality—facilitated the categorization of crime as a matter of black equality. But facilitation is not determination; political leaders could have grappled with crime in a number of ways. They could have highlighted methodological shifts in crime measurement; they could have emphasized age specificity and demographic transformations; they could have decoupled race from crime, talking about street crime only in terms of the "real" street crime of robbery, theft, and assault. As I will discuss below, however, members of Congress intensified racial blame attributions, with northern Democrats endorsing structural explanations for black crime, and Republicans and southern Democrats embracing volitional explanations for black crime.

President Lyndon Johnson and the Democratic-controlled Congress faced rising crime rates, urban riots, and Republican criticisms that Democratic leniency toward crime and civil rights activism foments lawlessness. Despite these challenges, Democrats managed to hold true to their 1964 Democratic platform vow of combating crime by seeking to "eliminate its economic and social causes." From 1964 through 1967, the unified Democratic government passed crime legislation oriented toward equality, rehabilitation, and alternatives to incarceration. Democrats established legal counsel for poor federal defendants with the Criminal Justice Act of 1964; they established "halfway houses" for prisoner re-entry with the Prisoner Rehabilitation Act of 1965; they created civil commitment for drug addicts as an alternative to incarceration with the Narcotic Rehabilitation Act of 1966; they made bail procedures easier with the Bail Reform Act of 1966; they funded state after-school youth programs with the Juvenile Delinquency Prevention and Control Act of 1968; and they established serious gun restrictions with the Federal Gun Control Act of 1968. In short, in the four years before passage of the massive Omnibus Crime Control and Safe Streets Act of 1968, Democrats were remarkably successful in casting crime policy in rehabilitative, equality-oriented terms. During this same period, the Warren Court also bolstered the rights of criminal defendants, particularly poor criminal defendants. In 1963, the Supreme Court held in *Gideon v. Wainwright* that poor state defendants were entitled to state-provided legal counsel for all felony offenses. In 1964, the Supreme Court held in *Escobedo v. Illinois* that police must inform suspects of the right to remain silent and the right to consult an attorney before answering questions. In 1966, the Supreme Court reaffirmed rights of the accused with *Miranda v. Arizona*, which provided guidelines for carrying out *Escobedo*.

In total, the first major federal initiatives did not begin with a punitive bang. Instead, Johnson and the Democratic-controlled Congress opened the possibility of orienting federal crime control away from prison-centered policy. Central to this approach was the move to think of crime as the problem of a broad range of political institutions; crime was not just a failing of criminal justice administration, but it was also a failing of agencies of social welfare, employment, and housing. This reorienting of crime control developed alongside the federal government's heyday of civil rights liberalization. Pressure from the civil rights movement, Kennedy's death, and fears of American credibility in the communist world all pushed the Democratic-controlled government to pass significant civil rights legislation during the Johnson Administration, most notably the Civil Rights Act of 1964, the Voting Rights Act of 1965, and the Fair Housing Act of 1968 (Frymer 1999: 99).

While some scholars suggest that only Republicans racialized crime to win disgruntled white voters (Friedman 1993: 274–5), northern Democrats also proffered race-specific blame attributions. Race was central to Democratic structural blame attribution, as northern Democrats claimed that white racism and blocked economic opportunities generate crime. In explaining crime through the lens of black equality, northern Democrats incorporated crime policy in their broader ideological and electoral commitments to civil rights liberalization and the Great Society.

In contrast to Republicans and southern Democrats, northern Democrats argued that crime was an indication that civil rights had not gone far enough. For Johnson, crime reduction was inextricably linked to the promotion of civil rights and antipoverty programs. In criticizing Barry Goldwater, Johnson said that "there is something mighty wrong when a candidate for the highest office bemoans violence in the streets but votes against the War on Poverty, votes against the Civil Rights Act, and votes against major educational bills that come before him as a legislator" (Johnson 1964: 1371). For northern Democrats, the solution to crime was "compassion for those warped by the discrimination and bigotry of the past" (Representative James Ottara (D-California), *Cong. Rec.* 1967: 19960). In opposition to one of the more than 90 bills of the 90th Congress that criminalized "riot-inciting," Representative Emanuel Celler (D-New York) argued that such punitive measures were "futile" because they are "neither preventative nor curative," failing to address the root cause, which is "the discontent of the Negro, his disenchantment as to promises made but not fulfilled, the dreary, slow pace by which he achieves equality" (*Cong. Rec.* 1967: 19352). According to Celler, black leaders "ask for better housing" and "we offer them jail;" black leaders "ask for better facilities for education" and we "read them a riot act;" black leaders ask for more employment" and we give them jobs "in prison garb" (*Cong. Rec.* 1967, 131, pt. 15: 19352). Adherents to this view even sympathized with black criticisms of the police, characterizing the police as a "powerful instrument of the status quo" that has no "legitimacy in the ghetto" (Representative William Ryan (D-New York), *Cong. Rec.* 1967: 21102).

Race's centrality to the structural explanations was most clearly articulated in Johnson-supported research commissions on crime. Johnson's prominent national research commissions preached a new-fangled, social scientific approach to addressing the "root causes" of crime. National research commissions recommended wide-ranging policies for aggressive federal intervention in crime control, but they attributed crime to the same underlying cause: inequality and deprivation rooted in white racism. The National Advisory Commission on Civil Disorders—known as the Kerner Commission after its chair, Otto Kerner—generally fingered white racism as the underlying cause of riots. Identifying the problem as "segregation and poverty" that have created in the "racial ghetto a destructive environment totally unknown to most white Americans," the Kerner Commission advocated a solution of closing "the gap between promise and performance" (National Advisory Commission on Civil Disorders 1968). President Johnson's Commission on Law Enforcement and the Administration of Justice issued a similar punchline. The Commission's central claim was that "widespread crime implies a widespread failure by society as a whole," and it therefore advocated a crime reduction plan "to eliminate slums and ghettos, to improve education, to provide jobs." Even though crime was on the rise for all racial groups, northern Democrats kept their focus on black crime, thereby linking their agendas on crime, civil rights, and the Great Society.

Against this progressive moment of crime policy, southern Democrats intensified their race-specific opposition to equality-based crime control, and Republicans followed suit. Republicans and southern Democrats issued two main arguments against structurally oriented crime policies, all in terms specific to blacks. The first argument, carried over from earlier debates on civil rights legislation, is that civil rights reward black lawlessness: civil rights validate selective lawbreaking, raise expectations, and keep the federal government in a position of having to grant more rights for fear of greater crime and lawlessness. The second argument is that efforts to reduce structural inequality—civil rights, antipoverty programs, and the Great Society—are criminogenic: such efforts promote crime by eroding individual work ethics, rewarding laziness, and blurring the distinction between what is earned and what is taken. These arguments are worth describing in some detail, as Republicans would preserve these arguments through the turn of the millennium, maintaining their core logic while minimizing their racial roots.

The first argument, that civil rights reward black lawlessness, mutated little from its earlier form issued in debates over civil rights legislation in the late 1950s and early 1960s. In debates over the Omnibus Crime Control and Safe Streets Act of 1968 and its failed 1967 antecedent bill of the same name, southern Democrats described the dangers of selective law-obedience in terms specific to the dangers of black discretion and collective action. Civil rights leaders "have the arrogance to place themselves above standards of civilized society and to openly defy established principles of law and order" (Representative Roy Taylor, D-North Carolina, *Cong. Rec.* 1967, 113, pt.15: 19352). Similarly, Representative William Colmer (D-Mississippi) blamed "leaders of SNCC and other similar organizations" for "preaching 'black power' and inciting riots" (*Cong. Rec.* 1967: 19348). Representative Charles Bennett (D-Florida) indicted "individuals such as Stokeley Carmichael" who "play upon the fears and frustrations of an impressionable minority of Negro youths to vigorously encourage terrorism and violence" (*Cong. Rec.* 1967: 19351).

In addition to encouraging selective law-obedience, Republicans and southern Democrats argued that civil rights activism generates crime through the additional mechanism of the infinite escalation of rising expectations. In one particularly stark articulation of this causal claim, Representative O.C. Fisher (D-Texas) presented recent history this way:

America is plagued today with insurrections, murder, arson, looting, and violence on a scale such as might be expected to occur in darkest Africa . . . The simple undeniable fact is that the White House and the Congress, through three or four administrations, must bear a major portion of the blame for the demonstrations and riots which have rocked this nation . . . Congress enacted a major civil rights bill on May 6, 1960. The measure was ballyhooed at the time as the ultimate answer to what the politicians claimed was America's long-neglected obligation to the Negro race. What happened? Instead of satisfying the Negroes it served to whet their appetites . . . This business of passing special laws for Negroes—grand and glorious laws—amid drum beats and false utopian promises of the new life is nothing short of a cruel hoax.

(*Cong. Rec.* 1967: 21546)

Instead of this cruel hoax, Fisher argued that blacks would be better served by fostering "friendly relationships on the local level with prospective employers, by convincing them of one's honesty and good faith and willingness to work and produce" (21546). Here, crime, demonstrations, and riots all merge as products of excessive civil rights. Government overindulgence makes blacks misplace their efforts in battles to win political justice, distracting them from the more laudable, realistic efforts of proving honesty and loyalty to potential (assumedly white) employers.

Representative Watkins Abbitt (D-Virginia) traced the development of lawlessness as a lineage from civil rights leaders, to followers who want something for nothing, to government officials who coddle criminals:

In my opinion, much of the lawlessness we have in America today was brought about by the attitude of many of our national leaders, civil rights officials, and others who have encouraged lawlessness; have encouraged certain elements of our society that they have the right to take what they want and desire regardless of the effect upon others. Then certain elements of the judiciary moved in. These criminals were coddled, treated like innocent babes, and given to understand that they were immune from prosecution.

(*Cong. Rec.* 1967: 21197)

Since 1964, Republicans have followed southern Democrats in arguing that civil rights reward black lawlessness. The Republican platform of 1964 criticized the Kennedy Administration for "exploit[ing] interracial tensions [with] extravagant campaign promises," thereby "encouraging disorderly and lawless elements" (Republican Party Platform 1964). With the successful passage of civil rights legislation and structurally oriented crime policy, Republicans intensified this same racialized blame attribution. According to the Republican critique, the Johnson Administration had "inundated" Congress with "a never-ending stream of radical social legislation designed to promote educational and residential racial balance," and Johnson's effort to control crime after liberalizing civil rights was analogous to "locking the barn door after the horse had gotten out" (Representative Paul Fino, R-New York, *Cong. Rec.* 1967, 131, pt. 16: 21198). Johnson and northern Democrats preferred "social reform" rather than "preventing crime," and their "philosophy for dealing with our racial and urban problem have, in effect, appealed only to the weaknesses of man" rather than "individual responsibility" (Representative Don Clausen, R-California, *Cong. Rec.* 1967, 131, pt. 16: 21204).

Black selective law obedience, Republicans argued, has implications for larger trends in crime control, because "Martin Luther King, Stokeley Carmichael, and Rap Brown have developed a philosophy that the Negro is justified in taking to the streets to redress his grievances," and this has pressed misguided liberals to "push further and further toward lawlessness" (Representative John Ashbrook (R-Ohio), *Cong. Rec.* 1967: 19961). In this same vein, several Republicans submitted to the *Congressional Record* editorials from George S. Schuyler, described in the record as "a Negro conservative." Like so many white Republicans and Southern Democrats in Congress, Schuyler contended that "Negro leadership itself . . . must share much of the blame for the smoking cities, the vandalism and the armed attacks by some young Negroes on the forces of law and order." Lawbreaking could not be attributed to poverty, discrimination, and cultural deprivation, Schuyler argued, because violence began with "the campaign of agitation and incitement by Negro activists" (from Schuyler editorial submitted by William Steiger (R-Wisconsin), *Cong. Rec.* 1967: 23159; also see Schuyler editorials with the same thesis as submitted by John Saylor (R-Pennsylvania), *Cong. Rec.* 1967: 23159).

Representative John Ashbrook (R-Ohio) blamed crime on indulgent government officials, elite sociologists, and, not least of all, black civil rights leaders:

> A series of liberal court decisions hampering law enforcement, rewarding rioters rather than punishing them, sociological gobbledygook which gives a rationale for plunder and lawlessness, lax law enforcement by politically motivated public officials who are overly solicitous about the Negro vote, and a supine Congress which refuses to act have combined to make rioting a way of life for a small minority of city Negroes.
>
> (*Cong. Rec.* 1967: 19961)

The second argument against structurally oriented policies, issued by Republicans and southern Democrats alike, is that they are criminogenic. From this perspective, civil rights, antipoverty programs, and the Great Society generate crime by eroding the work ethic and fostering black laziness. Representative Clarence Miller (R-Ohio) declared that "we do not need new laws" or "more welfare and assistance programs" to reduce crime; instead, "we need to reevaluate the give-away programs that have lulled a downtrodden element into the belief that society owes them a living" (*Cong. Rec.* 1967: 20037). Representative John Saylor (R-Pennsylvania) predicted that riots would end when "arsonists and looters are treated as the criminals they are. The administration may be able to buy time through premiums and promises, but there will never come a time when those who profit from the uprisings will be entirely satisfied with their booty" (*Cong. Rec.* 1967: 23158). This argument is not necessarily black-specific, but Republicans generally made it so. Representative William Steiger (R-Wisconsin) deduced that blacks who riot must be welfare dependent, because the "Negro who has had to surmount unusual obstacles in his quest for better living would least of all want to surrender his possessions to total destruction" (*Cong. Rec.* 1967: 23158). Representative John Rarick (D-Louisiana) simply declared: "the boycotts, riots, and violence never would have occurred without the war on poverty" (*Cong. Rec.* 1967: 13394).

Just as the programmatic agenda of the Great Society faced indictment, the actual workers in antipoverty programs faced charges of "stirring up" blacks. Many in Congress believed that antipoverty workers, notably members of the Office of Economic Opportunity, incited riots. "In Newark . . . antipoverty workers fomented the race riots of last summer . . . poverty money was used to rent vehicles and sound equipment which were used to agitating during the riots" (Representative Harold Collier, R-Illinois, *Cong. Rec.* 1967: 36163). Many members of Congress noted in outrage that antipoverty workers in Newark, Memphis, Chicago, Pittsburgh, and Nashville were "black militants" and "young black power advocates" who encourage violence and "teach Negro children to hate whites" (*Cong. Rec.* 1967: 36163). In these blame attributions, the agents and programs of civil rights liberalization are at fault: over-zealous civil rights activists, over-generous programs for racial and social equality, and excessive black freedom manifest as normlessness thereby eroding respect for law.

Conclusion

While many scholars contend that national leaders began addressing "law and order" because of the sharp escalation of crime or white disillusionment with civil rights in the 1960s, this chapter identifies how "law and order" rhetoric developed in tandem with the struggle for black civil rights in the postwar period. In the years before significant crime escalation, opponents of civil rights liberalization protested in criminological terms, arguing that integration breeds crime and civil rights reward black lawlessness. The persistent opposition to civil rights in the name of impending criminological threat suggests that there was no sudden racial backlash through crime control; the "backlash" metaphor may be misleading to the extent that it implies discontinuity between a great stride forward and a sudden illiberal aftermath (Kryder and Micky 2007). This account ultimately resonates with Nikhil Singh's (2004: 8) analysis that "the notion of a backlash against the excesses of black radicalism willfully ignores historically entrenched opposition to even the most moderate civil rights reforms throughout the white South and much of the urban North across the entire post-World War II period."

The development of "law and order" explored in this chapter illuminates a crucial but poorly understood aspect of the U.S. carceral state: the alarming mass incarceration of black Americans is not just a matter of racial peaks in offending, racial profiling in policing, or racial animus in sentencing. In addition to these forces, the evolution of racial politics at large shapes the development of the carceral state. In the years following World War II, threats to Jim Crow's racial order prompted demands for "law and order," even when crime rates were low and stable. Race set the agenda for "law and order," and the consequences for rhetoric and policy are profound. With blame for crumbling "law and order" conflated with black freedom, the regulation of black people through a growing carceral state becomes a seemingly normal state response.

Notes

1 Explanations for the rise of the carceral state are too complex to review here; my major point is that varying accounts collectively identify the mid-1960s as foundational years for law and order politics. Marie Gottschalk (2006: 2) concludes that the half-dozen major explanations—escalating crime, an increasingly punitive public, the war on drugs, the prison-industrial complex, changes in American political culture, and changes in electoral configurations—all "concentrate on developments since the 1960s."

2 There are, of course, important exceptions to the dominant trend of dating carceral state development to the mid-1960s. Marie Gottschalk (2006) suggests that law and order themes permeate American political development, and her central argument addresses why carceral state development faced so little opposition from liberal interest groups; her work does not focus on the connections between racial order and law and order.

3 During the prosperous decade following World War II, from 1946 to 1956, the total crime rate averaged 1,480 crimes per 100,000 population. From 1957 to 1963, as southern Democrats grew more vociferous in harnessing "rising crime" to black civil rights, the total crime rate *fell* to an average of only 1,200 crimes per 100,000 population. Southern Democrats who lamented "rising crime" in the early 1960s did not exactly lie: crime rose slightly in each year from 1960 to 1963, but only after hitting a record low in 1959, and the crime rate in 1963 had not rebounded to the postwar average.

4 It was not uncommon for members of Congress to classify blacks as recent descendents of jungle dwellers when debating civil rights legislation. Speaking against the Civil Rights Bill of 1956, Representative William Colmer (D-Mississippi) declared that "it is impossible by legislative enactment or judicial decree to place overnight a race of people, who until a few generations ago were unenlightened human beings, running wild in the jungles of Africa, on an equal plane with another race of people who for thousands of years have enjoyed the benefits of civilization, education, culture, and Christianity" (*Cong. Rec.* 1956: 12917).

Bibliography

Primary sources

Cases cited

Brown v. Board of Education (1954) 347 U.S. 483.
Escobedo v. Illinois (1964) 378 U.S. 478.

Gideon v. Wainwright (1963) 372 U.S. 335.
Miranda v. Arizona (1966) 384 U.S. 436.

Reports

Committee on Civil Rights. (1947) *To Secure These Rights: The Report of the President's Committee on Civil Rights*, New York: Simon and Schuster.
National Advisory Commission on Civil Disorders. (1968) *Report of the National Advisory Commission on Civil Disorder*, New York: Bantam Books.

References and secondary sources

Barkan, S. (1984) "Legal Control of the Southern Civil Rights Movement," *American Sociological Review*, 49: 552–65.
Beckett, K. (1997) *Making Crime Pay: Law and Order in Contemporary American Politics*, New York: Oxford University Press.
Biderman, A.D. (1966) "Social Indicators and Goals," in R.A. Bauer (ed.) *Social Indicators*, Cambridge, MA: MIT Press.
Blumstein, A. and Wallman, J. (2000) *The Crime Drop in America*, Cambridge: Cambridge University Press.
Carmines, E.G. and Stimson, J.A. (1989) *Issue Evolution: Race and the Transformation of American Politics*, Princeton, NJ: Princeton University Press.
Caro, R.A. (2002) *The Years of Lyndon Johnson: Master of the Senate*, New York: Vintage Books.
Cronin, T., Cronin, T., and Milakovich, M. (1981) *U.S. v. Crime in the Streets*, Bloomington: Indiana University Press.
Dudziak, M.L. (1988) "Desegregation as a Cold War Imperative," *Stanford Law Review*, 41: 61–120.
Edsall, T.B. and Edsall, M.D. (1992) *Chain Reaction: The Impact of Race, Rights, and Taxes on American Politics*, New York: W.W. Norton & Co.
Flamm, M.W. (2005) *Law and Order: Street Crime, Civil Unrest, and the Crisis of Liberalism in the 1960s*, New York: Columbia University Press.
Fox, J.A. (2000) "Demographics and U.S. Homicide," in A. Blumenstein and J. Wallman, (eds) *The Crime Drop in America*, New York: Cambridge University Press.
Friedman, L.M. (1993) *Crime and Punishment in American History*, New York: Basic Books.
Frymer, P. (1999) *Uneasy Alliances: Race and Party Competition in America*, Princeton, NJ: Princeton University Press.
Gottschalk, M. (2006) *The Prison and the Gallows: The Politics of Mass Incarceration in America*, New York: Cambridge University Press.
Heyman, I.M. (1965) "Civil Rights 1964 Term: Responses to Direct Action," *Supreme Court Review*, 1965: 159–86.
Huckfeldt, R. and Kohfeld, C.W. (1989) *Race and the Decline of Class in American Politics*, Urbana: University of Illinois Press.
Johnson, L.B. (1964) Remarks on the City Hall Steps, Dayton, Ohio. *Public Papers of the President 1964*, Volume 2. Washington, D.C.: U.S. Government Printing Office.
Kryder, D. and Micky, R. (2007) "The Politics of Racial Backlash: Consequences of an

American Metaphor," paper presented at the annual meeting of the Western Political Science Association, Las Vegas.

Lawrence, D. (1963) "What's Become of 'Law and Order'?" *U.S. News and World Report*, 26 August: 104–XX.

McAdam, D. (1982) *Political Process and the Development of Black Insurgency*, Chicago: University of Chicago Press.

McMillen, N. (1971) *The Citizens' Council: Organized Resistance to the Second Reconstruction, 1954–1964*, Urbana: University of Illinois Press.

Manza, J. and Uggen, C. (2006) *Locked Out: Felon Disenfranchisement and American Democracy*, New York: Oxford University Press.

Marion, N. (1994) *A History of Federal Crime Control Initiatives, 1960–1993*, Westport, CT: Praeger Press.

Mendelberg, T. (2001) *The Race Card: Campaign Strategy, Implicit Messages, and the Norm of Equality*, Princeton, NJ: Princeton University Press.

Mumola, C.J. (2000) "Incarcerated Parents and Their Children," Washington, D.C.: Bureau of Justice Statistics.

Murakawa, N. (2005) "Electing to Punish: Congress, Race, and the American Criminal Justice State," unpublished thesis, Yale University.

Myrdal, G. (1944) *An American Dilemma: The Negro Problem and Modern Democracy*, New Brunswick, NJ: Transaction Publishers.

Orren, K. and Skowronek, S. (2004) *The Search for American Political Development*, New York: Cambridge University Press.

Oshinsky, D.M. (1997) *Worse Than Slavery: Parchman Farm and the Ordeal of Jim Crow Justice*, New York: Free Press.

Page, B. and Shapiro, R. (1992) *The Rational Public: Fifty Years of Trends in Americans' Policy Preferences*, Chicago: University of Chicago Press.

Rable, G. (1985) "The South and the Politics of Antilynching Legislation, 1920–1940," *Journal of Southern History*, 51: 201–20.

Republican Party Platform (1964) http://www.presidency.ucsb.edu/showplatforms. php?platindex=R1964, accessed January 18, 2008.

Rosch, J. (1985) "Crime as an Issue in American Politics," in E. Fairchild and V. Webb (eds) *The Politics of Crime and Criminal Justice*, Beverly Hills, CA: Sage Publications.

Scheingold, S. (1984) *The Politics of Law and Order: Street Crime and Public Policy*, New York: Longman.

—— (1991) *The Politics of Street Crime*, Philadelphia, PA: Temple University Press.

Schuman, H., Steeh, C. and Bobo, L. (1985) *Racial Attitudes in America: Trends and Interpretations*, Cambridge, MA: Harvard University Press.

Singh, N. (2004) *Black Is a Country: Race and the Unfinished Struggle for Democracy*, Cambridge, MA: Harvard University Press.

Skrentny, J. (2002) *The Minority Rights Revolution*, Cambridge, MA: Belknap Press.

Sugrue, T. (1996) "Segmented Work, Race-Conscious Workers: Structure, Agency, and Division in the CIO Era," *International Review of Social History*, 41: 389–406.

—— (2005) *The Origins of the Urban Crisis: Race and Inequality in Postwar Detroit*, Princeton, NJ: Princeton University Press.

Western, B. (2006) *Punishment and Inequality in America*, New York: Russell Sage Foundation.

Wilson, J.Q. (1975) *Thinking About Crime*, New York: Basic Books.

11 The modern presidency, social movements, and the administrative state: Lyndon Johnson and the civil rights movement*

Sidney M. Milkis

Introduction: presidential ambition and social movements

This chapter investigates the critical, uneasy alliance formed between Lyndon Johnson and the civil rights movement. More generally, it investigates the interplay between the presidency and social movements. Very little scholarship systematically addresses the relationship between the presidency and social movements, and that which does tends to emphasize the inherent conflict between a centralizing institution designed to conserve the constitutional order and grassroots associations dedicated to structural change.[1] For example, Elizabeth Sanders (2007) recently argued that contrary to progressive assumptions about the presidency as a force for reform and democratic expression, under most circumstances the institution either reacts slowly or resists the demands of insurgent groups. Similarly, Daniel Tichenor (2007) has shown that presidents resist the reform aspirations of social movements until their political interest dictates otherwise; even then, presidents seek to stand apart from or capture, rather than embrace, militant activists and their causes.

Sanders and Tichenor shed important light on the conservative nature of the executive office. As James Sterling Young (1995) has pointed out, the tension between presidents and reform rests in constitutional obligation, which, as stated explicitly in the oath of office, is "to preserve, protect, and defend the Constitution."[2]

Stephen Skowronek (1997) offers a more complex, paradoxical view of the executive office. Each incumbent swears *both* "to execute the office of President of the United States," presupposing their independent intervention in political affairs, *and* "to preserve protect and defend the Constitution of the United States," requiring the affirmation of the existing order of things. This sets up a strong executive, but one in the grips of a dilemma: it is "a governing institution that is inherently hostile to inherited governing arrangements" (1997: chapters 1–3).

Constrained by constitutional norms, the separation and division of powers, and a highly mobilized but decentralized party system, the disruptive potential of executive power was limited until the twentieth century. With the advent of the modern presidency, however, the White House was more likely to proclaim support for progressive change. At the same time, as Jeffrey Tulis (1987) points out, the modern presidency rested in reformers' dedication to direct popular leadership, which threatened to subject presidents to the vagaries of public opinion.

What is often overlooked in the study of the modern presidency is that its potential to advance reform requires an alliance with social movements. To be sure, modern executives have often shied away from too close a relationship with controversial social movements, lest they risk alienating other supporters. Nonetheless, the consolidation of the modern presidency during the New Deal realignment invested the executive with powers and public expectations that made the White House a vantage point for social and economic reform (Milkis 1993). Once the White House became the center of growing government commitments, its occupants were more likely to profess support for the same high ideals—environmental protection, equal rights for women and minorities, the rights of labor—that social movements championed (Miroff 1981: 14). This relationship was often symbiotic, as for example, the labor movement benefited from its position as a principal constituent of FDR's New Deal coalition (Milkis 1993: chapter 3).

The Progressive vision of the "modern presidency" reached its fullest expression in Lyndon Johnson's alliance with the civil rights movement. Until the Johnson presidency, the idea that the executive might act as a spearhead of social justice—to use Theodore Roosevelt's beguiling phrase, "the steward of the public welfare"—had proven more a dream than a reality. Anticipated but not fulfilled by TR's Bull Moose campaign in 1912, this vision, as Tichenor (2007) has revealed, was only partially and haltingly expressed in the relationship between Woodrow Wilson and the movement for women's suffrage and between Franklin Roosevelt and the labor movement. Only with Johnson was the full arsenal of modern presidential powers—political, administrative, and rhetorical—deployed on behalf of insurgent interests and demands. He put himself out front on civil rights, seeking from the start to lead the movement towards its goals, tap its energy, and manage its unfolding. Tying his presidency to this cause from the beginning, Johnson defied the structural logic that had traditionally kept insurgent movements and presidents at arm's length. In turn, Johnson's inability to sustain that vanguard role exposed more fully than any other example the unresolved constitutional tensions at the heart of the progressive vision.[3] Indeed, it may be said that the modern presidency imploded upon the unraveling of Johnson's relationship to the civil rights movement.

Johnson's predecessor, John F. Kennedy, seeking to nurture a fragile liberal consensus and riveted by the heightened tensions of the cold war, kept his distance from the civil rights movement; following the historic model, JFK only acted when highly incendiary and well publicized clashes between activists and the guardians of Jim Crow forced him to pursue reform as a matter of national necessity. Johnson was contemptuous of this course; his trumpeting of a Great Society signaled his intention to push the reformist side of the modern presidency to its limit.[4] The "liberating" potential Johnson and his aides spied in the modern presidency dovetailed with the political climate of the 1960s. The power and wealth of the United States, Johnson proclaimed, provided an unparalleled opportunity, indeed a duty, to build a political order in which "material progress" would be "only the foundation" for a "richer life of mind and spirit"—a "place where the city of man serve[d] not only the needs of the body and the demands of commerce but the desire for beauty and the hunger for community" ("The Great Society," 1964). To Johnson and his political allies, the civil rights revolution demonstrated not only the power and possibility of organized protest, but also the unsuspected fragility of resistance in America to liberating changes. In the relatively calm early days of LBJ's leadership, aides such as Bill Moyers and Richard Goodwin, and Johnson himself, envisioned such new social forces as potential agents of a new generation of reform. The way Johnson joined with civil rights leaders in pushing through the 1964 and 1965 civil rights legislation appeared to justify this vision (Goodwin 1988: 275).

Even as Johnson celebrated the civil rights movement, however, he sought to control it. Like FDR, he was a presidentialist: the thrust of his institutional approach was to strengthen the managerial tools of the presidency with a view to enhancing the programmatic ambition and energy of the executive branch. But he badly misjudged the difficulty of expanding the liberal coalition to movements that spurned White House direction. The struggle against forced segregation in the South during the 1960s showed that even with the emergence of an executive establishment, anchored by the modern presidency, the deeply rooted belief that ordinary citizens were responsible for posing hard challenges to existing political order persisted (Block 2007). The civil rights movement, a fissiparous mixture of interest-oriented organizations that sought traditional rights long denied African Americans and militants intent on recasting the very framework of political life, perfectly expressed this adversarial culture and the uneasy relationship it was bound to have with even a self-proclaimed ally in the White House.

Ironically, the liberating energy that LBJ and his political allies valued in the civil rights movement made a firm bond with its leaders impractical. By the middle of his second term, Johnson retreated from the notion that he was the leader of the civil rights movement; indeed, its growing militancy abetted the rise of antiwar activism that viewed Johnson as the hated symbol of the status quo. Just as surely as the early convergence of interests between civil rights activists and the White House sustained Johnson's presidency, so the sharp divergence of ambitions later on facilitated its precipitous collapse.

Although the Vietnam War contributed to this estrangement between LBJ and his former liberal allies, the movement that emerged to protest the war was a sign of more than a foreign policy controversy; the estrangement between Johnson and the new liberal activists he once sponsored signaled new political and social forces that fundamentally challenged the modern presidency.

By supporting programs such as the War on Poverty that transformed the culture and institutions of national administration, Johnson unwittingly bestowed legitimacy on this insurgency.

The doomed alliance between LBJ and the social movements of the 1960s represented a critical test of the Progressive Era conceit that the presidency is inherently disposed to ally itself with movements for reform and liberation. The modern presidency—the hub of the American administrative state—embodies a reform program that attempted to reconcile leadership and centralized administrative power—to invest grand ambition in national administration that would make the bureaucracy more accountable and innovative. The Great Society, more than any other period of American history, shows the success and limitations of this modern state-building project. It freed an outsized politician to invest his political fortunes in forces of liberation, only to weaken the potential for extraordinary leadership in the future. Johnson's effort to apply "leverage" over the civil rights movement and to make his own distinctive mark on the American reform tradition set loose forces that ultimately diminished his legacy, weakened the executive office, and exposed the limits of the modern presidency.

Lyndon Johnson and the politics of race

When Johnson assumed the presidency, he had substantial reasons for taking a strong civil rights stand. By this time, the Solid South was no more, as Eisenhower and Nixon had won substantial support below the Mason–Dixon line. The best hope for shoring up the national Democratic party lay in expanding the black vote. Black voters were suspicious of a southern president, as were many northern liberals who had become strongly committed to the civil rights cause after the demonstrations in Birmingham, Alabama, and the March on Washington in 1963. Johnson felt the need to prove himself to the growing civil rights movement by carrying out—indeed surpassing—the civil rights program of the Kennedy administration.

Equally important, Johnson wanted to make his own historic mark on the presidency and he viewed civil rights reform and an alliance with the leaders of the civil rights movement as critical to the success of the Great Society. Viewing the growing civil rights movement as an opportunity for the White House to take bolder action, Johnson was scornful of the Kennedy administration's cautious moves toward new federal intervention, even as it pushed unsuccessfully for a major civil rights bill in 1963 (Conkin 1986: 164). During his presidency, Johnson's immense ambition combined with deep conviction.[5] In May 1964 he gave two courageous speeches in Georgia, one before the state legislature where he declared unequivocally that the time had come for "justice among the races" ("Remarks at a Breakfast of the Georgia Legislature," 1964: vol. 1: 648). "Heed not," the President urged the southern lawmakers at a breakfast meeting in Atlanta, "those who seek to stir old hostilities and kindle old hatreds, who preach battle between neighbors and bitterness between

States" (vol. 1: 648). Johnson insisted that he would never feel that he had done justice to his "high office"—the national constitutional office—so long as those old hatreds continued to rend the country. This constitutional responsibility presupposed, as LBJ had preached to Kennedy, searing the American creed, and how racial discrimination tarnished it, into the national consciousness.[6] He would not fulfill his responsibility as President "until every section of the country is linked, in single purpose and joined devotion, to bring an end to injustice, to bring an end to poverty, and to bring an end to the threat of conflict among nations" (648). Johnson did not scold or preach; his tone was one of gentle persuasion rather than threat of coercion. The President sought to stir the conscience of his southern audience—to moderate their racial prejudice with an appeal to their "bias" for law and the Constitution: "In your search for justice, the Constitution of the United States must be your guide. Georgians helped write the Constitution. Georgians have fought and Georgians had died to protect that Constitution. . . . Because the Constitution requires it, because justice demands it, we must protect the constitutional rights of all of our citizens, regardless of race, religion, or the color of their skin" (649).

Johnson's campaign to take his civil rights fight into the deep South reverberated far beyond Georgia's borders. In going before the legislature of a southern state to make an unflinching statement on civil rights, he gained the hard won respect of northern liberals and civil rights leaders. It was "becoming of the President of the United States," a *Washington Post* editorial declared, that he should make such a "forthright statement" below the Mason–Dixon line (May 9, 1964: A8). Johnson's words were not novel; he and other Presidents had said as much before. "But said in this setting," the *Post* recognized, "the words have special impact, special meaning. They throw down the gauntlet of a challenge: they say to the South—in part because they are spoken by a President of the United States who is himself a Southerner—'Remember that you are Americans; remember that you belong to a Union, not a confederacy.'"

The reaction to Johnson's moral appeal was hardly less impressive in the South than it was in the North. To be sure, he did not overcome all resistance. At the breakfast meeting in Atlanta, which also included Governor Carl E. Sanders and Senator Herman Talmadge, the audience applauded the President on several occasions but not when he spoke of equal rights (Kilpatrick 1964). Similarly, when he thumped the podium at his second stop in Georgia, the town of Gainesville, and shouted that "the Constitution of the United States applies to every American of every race, of every religion, of every region in this beloved country," there was no applause from the large and otherwise enthusiastic audience. Nonetheless, as the *Richmond Times Dispatch* admitted, "despite his uncompromising civil rights stand, the President's public appeal made its impact" (May 9, 1964: 1, 11). No major Georgia official, save the unreconstructed states rights Senator Richard Russell, boycotted LBJ's visit. Moreover, although there were notes of disagreement among the huge crowds that greeted the president in Atlanta and Gainesville—white workers wearing coveralls held up a sign along the Atlanta motorcade that read "Kill the Bill"—

the overwhelming response to Johnson's visit was remarkably positive, an indication, LBJ insisted, that a "new South" was ready to turn the page of racial intolerance.

Johnson's remarkable and widely praised trip to Georgia strengthened his resolve to see civil rights legislation enacted that would dismantle legal barriers to black equality. Much is made, and rightfully so, of Johnson's skill in moving legislation through a recalcitrant Congress; what is often overlooked is how the fight for civil rights legislation saw Johnson's mastery of the legislative process joined to moral leadership. Martin Luther King, who had met LBJ during his tenure as Vice President and quickly sized him up as a valuable ally, recognized the importance of the president's early and earnest advocacy of civil rights:

> [Lyndon Johnson's] approach to civil rights was not identical with mine— nor had I expected it to be. Yet his careful practicality was nonetheless clearly no mask to conceal indifference. His emotional and intellectual involvement was genuine and devoid of adornment. . . . [I]t was Vice President Johnson I had in mind when I wrote in *The Nation* that the white South was splitting, and that progress could be furthered by driving a wedge between the rigid segregationists and the new white elements whose love of their land was stronger than the grip of old habits and customs.
>
> (1998: 243)

For a time, LBJ's "careful practicality" and moral leadership made him an indispensable ally of the civil rights movement. His greatest strength as majority leader of the Senate had been personal persuasion, a talent he now used to convince the Senate Republican leader, Everett Dirksen, to endorse the 1964 Civil Rights bill and enlist moderate Republicans in the cause. This support did not come without a price. Dirksen insisted on compromises that reduced the power of the Equal Employment Opportunity Commission and limited the authority of the Justice Department to bring suits against businesses to those situations in which a clear "pattern and practice" of discrimination existed.[7] These compromises responded to moderate Republicans' distaste for overlapping bureaucracies and excessive litigation, as well as their desire to protect northern and western businesses from intrusive federal agencies. Still the principal objective of the Civil Rights bill—eliminating entrenched segregation in the South—was preserved.

Dirksen's support of the Civil Rights bill also followed from the Senator's perception, confirmed by the president's successful southern tour, that public opinion's support for civil rights was building in the country. Investing the prestige of his office in a cause and a movement, Johnson persuaded Dirksen and most members of Congress that civil rights reform could no longer be resisted. As Dirksen put it, paraphrasing Victor Hugo's diary: "No army is stronger than an idea whose time has come" (cited in Hulsey 2000: 196).[8] The bipartisan alliance that Johnson and Dirksen formed sounded the death knell for the conservative coalition of southern Democrats and Republicans against civil rights. For the first time, the Senate voted cloture against a southern filibuster designed to thwart a civil rights bill and did so by a considerable margin of 71 to 29. Once the filibuster was killed, Congress passed the bill quickly, and Johnson signed it on July 2, 1964. Throughout the fight for this legislation, Johnson drew strength from and collaborated with civil rights leaders, even seeking their support for his decision not to delay signing the bill until Independence Day.[9]

Having gained credibility with civil rights leaders during the first critical year of his presidency, Johnson solidified an alliance with them during the dramatic prelude to the enactment of the 1965 voting rights legislation, which would enfranchise millions of African Americans. On January 15, 1965, Johnson put in a call to King, on the occasion of the civil rights leader's 36th birthday. LBJ urged the Reverend King and the grassroots organization he headed to put pressure on Congress by dramatizing "the worst conditions [of blacks being denied the vote] that you can run into . . . If you can take that one illustration and get it on the radio, get on the television, get it in the pulpits, get it in the meetings—every place you can—then pretty soon the fellow who didn't do anything but drive a tractor would say, 'Well, that is not right—that is not fair'" (Johnson Tapes, January 15, 1965).

In the days that followed, Johnson might have had second thoughts about this importunity, because King and civil rights activists would take direct action in Selma that aroused massive resistance from local police and state troopers, as well as national demonstrations in support of the marchers, some of which were directed at the president for not taking immediate action to avert the violence in Alabama. Nonetheless, when King sought his public endorsement of the Selma campaign, Johnson, rejecting the advice of White House aides who sought to shield him from public involvement in the crisis, acknowledged the civil rights demonstrators' cause and pledged to do something about it. "I should like to say that all Americans should be indignant when one American is denied the right to vote . . . all of us should be concerned with the efforts of our fellow Americans to register to vote in Alabama . . . I intend to see that the right [to vote] is secured for all our citizens" (cited in Kotz 2005: 267).[10]

The following month, as the crisis in Selma worsened, Johnson lived up to this promise. On March 15, 1965, for the first time in 19 years, a president appeared before a joint session of Congress to present a legislative message. Sensing that America was at a pivotal moment in its long and tortured history of slavery and discrimination, hoping to seize the opportunity presented by the brave civil rights demonstrators, Johnson spoke with unusual feeling about the voting rights act. "The real hero" of the struggle for voting rights, "was the American Negro. His actions and protests, his courage to risk safety and even to risk his life, have awakened the conscience of the nation. His demonstrations have been designed to call attention to injustice, designed to provoke change, designed to stir reform . . . And who among us can say that we would have made the same progress were it not for his persistent bravery and faith in

America" ("Special Message to Congress: The American Promise" 1965). Johnson's speech warned that the enactment of the voting rights bill was but one front in a larger war that must include not just federal laws to throw open the "gates of opportunity" but also affirmative action against ignorance, ill-health, and poverty that would enable individual men and women to "walk through those gates":

> What happened in Selma is part of a far larger movement which reaches into every section and State of America. It is the effort of American Negroes to secure for themselves the full blessings of American life.
>
> Their cause must be our cause too. Because it is not just Negroes, but really it is all of us, who must overcome the crippling legacy of bigotry and injustice.
>
> And we shall overcome.

Johnson thus adopted as his own rallying cry a line from an old hymn that had become the slogan of the civil rights movement. LBJ had not won over southern congressmen, most of who slumped in their seats as the joint session erupted in applause. Nonetheless, he had triumphed where FDR failed— without embroiling himself in an enervating purge campaign, as Roosevelt had in 1938, he joined civil rights activists to discredit southern resistance to liberal reform.[11] As Johnson embraced the ringing anthem of the civil rights movement, Dr. King, watching the speech on television in Montgomery, Alabama, was moved to tears. As he wrote of the historical address, "President Johnson made one of the most eloquent, unequivocal, and passionate pleas for human rights ever made by a President of the United States. He revealed an amazing understanding of the depth and dimension of the problem of racial justice . . . we had the support of the President in calling for immediate relief of the problems of the disinherited people of our nation" (King 1998: 288). More suspicious than King of the president, whom he had always dismissed as a "politician," John Lewis, president of the Student Nonviolent Coordinating Committee (SNCC), acknowledged that on this night LBJ was "a man who spoke from his heart, a statesman, a poet" (Lewis 1998: 340; see also Kotz 2005: 312).[12]

Johnson recognized that his alliance with the civil rights movement risked substantial Democratic losses in the South. The President's encouraging visit to Georgia gave him hope that he would be forgiven by white southerners; this was the very purpose of his appeal to conscience. But the elections of November 1966 revealed the South was not in a forgiving mood. Three segregationist Democrats—Lester Maddox in Georgia, James Johnson in Arkansas, and George P. Mahoney in Maryland—won their party's gubernatorial nomination. In Alabama, voters ratified a caretaker administration for Lurleen Wallace, since her husband, George, was not permitted to succeed himself. George Wallace, dubbed the "prime minister" of Alabama, had by 1966 emerged as a serious threat to consummate the North–South split in the Democratic party, either by entering the 1968 presidential primaries or running as a third party candidate. The 1966 gubernatorial race in California, where former movie star Ronald Reagan handily defeated the Democratic incumbent Edmund G. Brown, revealed that conservative insurgency was not limited to southern Democrats.[13]

The prospect of losing the White House in 1968 made certain members of the administration nervous, if not completely repentant, about Johnson having alienated southern Democrats. Nonetheless, the fear of "white backlash"—the new phrase for white resentment of black gains through political action—did not shake Johnson's determination to obtain civil rights progress through legislation and executive action. Johnson had no stomach for a "southern strategy" that retreated from civil rights. The defense of this cause above all was how he intended to make his mark on history, and Johnson's place in history meant more to him than serving another term as President or the standing of the Democratic party. Moreover, the civil rights movement had become far too powerful and the issues it raised too riveting for a return to relatively "safe" New Deal issues such as economic security and educational opportunity. Johnson believed that as long as the economy remained strong, the Democrats "could still squeeze through." "But whatever the consequences," White House aide, Harry McPherson has insisted, LBJ "was determined to make major advances in the area of civil rights" (McPherson, interview with author, July 30, 1985).

To Johnson's deep disappointment, however, the growing militancy of the civil rights movement gave further impetus to "white backlash." Tensions within the civil rights movement threatened to sever its critical but uneasy ties with the Johnson White House. Indeed, no sooner had Johnson invested his presidency in the cause of civil rights, than radical dissidents who scorned White House leadership gained greater influence over the movement. Johnson's voting rights sermon won little praise from militant civil rights activists in Alabama like James Foreman, the field secretary for SNCC. As far as radical SNCC dissidents were concerned, "the president's reference to our anthem was a 'tinkling, empty symbol,' Forman told one reporter. 'Johnson,' he later said to another writer, 'spoiled a good song that day'" (Lewis 1998: 340). As the schisms in the civil rights movement deepened along with the Administration's involvement in Vietnam, Johnson became the target, rather than the ally of civil rights activists.

Social protest and the limits of White House leverage

Toward the end of 1965, the energy and resources committed to the Great Society began to suffer, threatened by Johnson's preoccupation with the Vietnam War. From Franklin Roosevelt and subsequent presidents, LBJ inherited international commitments that pulled him away from the liberal activists to whom the early days of his presidency were dedicated.[14] African Americans were among the first to sense this change, and even moderate civil rights leaders, such as Martin Luther King, Jr., became visible participants in the anti-war movement. King saw the war not only as morally questionable but also as a growing commitment that would divert resources needed to address problems of poverty at home.

In late November, White House aide Hayes Redmon lamented these efforts of civil rights activists. "I am increasingly concerned over the involvement of civil rights groups with anti-war demonstrators," he wrote in a memo to Moyers. "The anti-Vietnam types are driving the middle class to the right. This is the key group that is slowly being won over to the civil rights cause. Negro leadership involvement with anti-Vietnam groups will set their programs back substantially" ("Memorandum, Hayes Redmon to Bill Moyers," 1965). King's opposition, especially, which he voiced publicly in September of 1965, angered Johnson and exposed the inherent conflict between the interests of the president and civil rights movement. Like Kennedy, Johnson deferred to FBI director Herbert Hoover's use of telephone wiretaps and hotel room microphones to discredit King on national security grounds; like Kennedy, he took seriously Hoover's ill-founded warning that Communists had infiltrated the civil rights movement.[15]

Johnson had tried to renew ties with King a few weeks earlier. In August, soon after race riots broke out in Watts, he called the civil rights leader to express his continued, indeed strengthened support for civil rights and to question him about rumors that he was opposed to the administration's actions in Vietnam (Johnson Tapes, August 20, 1965). Trying in vain to meet the demands of spiraling civil rights militancy, the president urged King to take seriously and help publicize a recent commencement address the President had given on June 4 at Howard University, with which Johnson sought to burnish his credibility as an ally of the civil rights movement, indeed lead it in advancing the cause of poor African Americans (Kotz 2005: 353). The Howard University address, LBJ told King, proclaiming that "freedom was not enough" and that the time had come to "seek . . . not just equality as a right and a theory but equality as a fact and as a result" ("Commencement Address at Howard University: 'To Fulfill These Rights,'" 1965: 636), demonstrated his administration's commitment to treat the most stubborn forces that sustained racial inequality (Johnson Tapes, August 20, 1965; Goodwin "Speech Draft" 1965). And yet, he complained, civil rights activists had in large part greeted it with a deafening silence. Johnson also urged the civil rights leader to support the administration on Vietnam, telling King: "I want peace as much as you do if not more so," because "I'm the fellow who had to wake up to 50 marines killed" (Johnson Tapes, August 20, 1965).

King acknowledged that Johnson's Howard University speech was "the best statement and analysis of the problem" he had seen and that "no president ever said it like that before" (Johnson Tapes, August 20, 1965). Indeed, he had saluted the president by wire soon after it was delivered "for your magnificent speech . . . [that] evinced amazing sensitivity" (Branch 2006: 234). Nonetheless, King and other civil rights leaders refused to acknowledge that the

Howard University Address, arguably the boldest presidential challenge to racial injustice in the country since Lincoln's Second Inaugural, established the White House as the principal agent of civil rights reform. King saw himself, and not the president, as the leader of the civil rights movement. Moreover, he feared that tying himself too closely to Johnson, in an atmosphere of mounting racial tension, would weaken his standing in the civil rights community. As David Carter (2001: 320) has written, "in this period of growing polarization it had become increasingly clear to civil rights leaders, and ultimately even to the President and his staff, that a White House blessing of a leader was tantamount to a curse."

In truth, King was the least of the administration's problems. Much more troublesome was the emergence of a new generation of black leaders dedicated to "black power," a militant, more threatening type of activism. As the civil rights movement trained its eye on the poverty-stricken ghettos of large northern cities, King lost influence to more militant leaders who were better attuned than he to the frustrations and rage of young urban blacks (Mann 1996: 480). People like Stokely Carmichael, newly elected head of SNCC, and other angry young civil rights leaders such as Floyd McKissick of the Committee of Racial Equality (CORE) were not only dissatisfied with the achievements of the Johnson administration's civil rights program, but also were contemptuous of its objective of racial integration. As Carmichael and Charles V. Hamilton, a political scientist who taught at Roosevelt University in Chicago, wrote in *Black Power*, a manifesto for the ascending militancy of the civil rights movement: "The goal of the black people must *not* be to assimilate into middle class America, for that class—as a whole—is without a viable conscience as regards humanity. The values of the middle class are based on material aggrandizement, not the expansion of humanity . . . The values of that class do *not* lead to the creation of an open society. That class *mouths* its preference for a free, competitive society, while at the same time forcefully and even viciously denying the black people as a group the opportunity to compete" (Carmichael and Hamilton 1967: 40, emphasis in original). "The underlying and fundamental notion," of Black Power, Carmichael wrote in his autobiography, "was that black folks needed to begin openly, and had the right and the duty, to define for ourselves, *in our own terms*, our real circumstances, possibilities, and interests relative to white America" (2003: 527, emphasis in original).

Ironically, Carmichael and Hamilton's (1967) critique of middle class America ostensibly conformed to the underlying premises of the Johnson's Great Society. As Johnson exhorted in his 1966 State of the Union message, "A great people flower not from wealth and power, but from a society which spurs them to the fullness of their genius . . . [S]lowly, painfully, on the edge of victory, has come the knowledge that shared prosperity is not enough. In the midst of abundance modern man walks oppressed by forces which menace and confine the quality of his life, and which individual abundance alone will not overcome" (Public Papers of L.B. Johnson 1966: I: 3). But the idea of liberation that the President trumpeted, when spoken by Black militants, aroused anger, not a sense of national renewal, in the smoldering ghettos of northern American cities. The growing militancy of black America erupted during the summer of 1966 as urban riots swept across the nation. In the wake of these developments, the moderately conservative middle class, as the White House feared, grew impatient with reform. The administration's string of brilliant triumphs in civil rights was snapped. Its 1966 Civil Rights bill, an open housing proposal, fell victim to a Senate filibuster. Johnson's leadership of the civil rights movement was a great asset to him in 1964; it had become something of a liability by the summer of 1966.

Since the emergence of the modern executive office in the Progressive Era, activist presidents had considered the White House to be a superior vantage point for guiding economic and social reform. As Bruce Miroff has pointed out, however, presidents with reform aspirations had sought to find a "symbolic point," where they appeared "to cooperate with a social movement for noble purposes" while retaining their "special commitment to law, order, and the general good" (Miroff 1981: 14). Even as he made unprecedented overtures to social activists during the first two years of his presidency, Johnson managed to maintain this "balance point" between the White House and the civil rights movement. For example, he effectively intervened in civil rights matters during the summer of 1964, the first of the long hot summers. Riots erupted in July of that year, soon after the Republican national convention nominated conservative Arizona Senator Barry Goldwater for President. As the rioting spread and civil rights demonstrations continued in 1964 after the passage of the Civil Rights Act, the administration feared that racial unrest would turn white voters against a president identified with the cause of African Americans. In July of that year, at LBJ's request, leaders of major civil rights organizations, including King, held a meeting in New York, where they called for a moratorium on black unrest.[16]

Johnson also actively intervened a month later in the struggle over the seating of the Mississippi delegation at the 1964 Democratic Convention. A Mississippi Freedom Democratic party (MFDP) challenged the "regular" delegation, on grounds that the state Democratic organization excluded blacks from membership. The conflict confronted Johnson and national Democratic party leaders with a dilemma, since they risked antagonizing the civil rights forces if they banned the Freedom party delegation and much or all of the South if they seated it. Johnson, with considerable help from Minnesota Senator Hubert D. Humphrey and the leader of the United Auto Workers, Walter Reuther, worked assiduously behind the scenes to achieve a compromise. The compromise plan included: the seating of the regular Mississippi delegation, provided its members signed a loyalty oath that pledged them to support the presidential ticket; the symbolic gesture of making MFDP delegates honored guests at the convention, with two of its members seated as special delegates at large; and a prohibition of racial discrimination in delegate selection at the 1968 convention.

Some civil rights leaders who scorned White House efforts to domesticate their movement resented Johnson's intervention in these two episodes. John Lewis of SNCC and James Farmer of CORE dissented from the moratorium on demonstrations, signaling their commitment to "direct action" as a critical method of civil rights progress. Moreover, SNCC and CORE bitterly criticized Johnson for his willingness to sacrifice the MFDP's moral cause on the altar of expediency. But most civil rights activists, including King, accepted the White House's leadership. King joined Whitney Young, the executive director of the National Urban League, Roy Wilkins, executive secretary of the National Association for the Advancement of Colored People, and A. Philip Randolph, chairman of the Negro American Labor Council, in signing the moratorium statement. Johnson's strong support for the Civil Rights Act, they believed, put a special premium not only on the election but also on the need to cultivate a climate in which racial progress could continue.

Similar considerations persuaded most civil rights leaders to swallow the MFDP compromise, albeit not without creating a great "sense of distress" in King and other moderate activists ("Memorandum, White to L.B. Johnson," 1964). The MFDP, through its lawyer, Joseph Rauh, accepted the compromise, which was adopted by the convention without notable objection ("Written communication from Sherwin Markman," 2004).[17] Not only were southern states threatening to walk out of the convention if the regular Mississippi delegation was purged, but Johnson and Democratic leaders also warned civil rights leaders that an unruly convention would cost the party the support of several border states and deprive Democrats of a chance to win an historic landslide—and a mandate for further reform.

These leaders recognized that LBJ's championing of fundamental reform of convention rules would have enormous long-term consequences for the Democratic party. Previously, state parties had sole authority to establish delegate selection procedures. Johnson's proposed solution to the MFDP controversy established the centralizing principle that henceforth the national party agencies would decide not only how many votes each state delegation got at the national convention but also enforce uniform rules on what kinds of persons could be selected. As the president told Reuther, "We don't want to cut off our nose to spite our face. If they [MFDP protesters] give us four years, I'll guarantee the Freedom delegation somebody representing views like that will be seated four years from now" (Johnson Tapes, August 9, 1964). Contrary to conventional wisdom, LBJ made it clear to all parties—civil rights reformers and regular southern delegates alike—that he did not propose this compromise merely as a short-term, stop-gap measure to ensure peace at the 1964 convention. Rather, he viewed the new nondiscrimination rule as a justified extension of the national party's power over state delegations that carried on discriminatory practices, a commitment to reform that was an important prelude to the 1965 Voting Rights Act and the banning of segregated delegations at the 1968 Democratic Convention ("Telephone conversation between L.B. Johnson, Hubert Humphrey, and Walter Reuther," Johnson Tapes, August 25, 1964).[18]

Although the MFDP compromise was accepted by the Democratic convention and most civil rights leaders, it left deep scars. In retrospect, many activists of the 1960s have viewed this episode as the turning point in the civil rights struggle, the moment which abetted the rise of Black Power activists and created an irreparable rift between the White House and the movement. The solution that Johnson and his aides engineered to the MFDP challenge, Carmichael and Hamilton claimed, "clearly said 'betrayal' and clearly symbolized the bankruptcy of the establishment" (1967: 93).

In the wake of the civil rights crisis of 1966, Johnson did not meet with civil rights leaders, yet he refused to sound a full retreat from civil rights reform. Instead, he followed Attorney General Nicholas Katzenbach's advice to send a number of his younger aides to various cities to meet with young black leaders. The Attorney General's suggestion was the origin of ghetto visits that White House aides made throughout 1967; a dozen or so visited troubled black areas in more than twenty cities, including Chicago, Philadelphia, New York, Detroit, Washington, DC, Los Angeles, and Oakland. On the one hand, the ghetto visits revealed the extent to which the modern presidency had assumed so many of the more important tasks once carried out by intermediary political associations like political parties. Rather than relying on local party leaders for information about their communities, Johnson asked his aides to live in various ghettos for a time, and then report directly to him about the state of black America. Local public officials and party leaders, even Chicago's powerful boss Richard Daley, were not told of the ghetto visits, lest they take umbrage at someone from the White House rooting about their home territories.

On the other hand, these visits marked the declining significance of the modern presidency as the leading agent of liberal reform—a symptom of its "extraordinary isolation."[19] This isolation was accentuated by the evolution of the civil rights movement, whose more militant leaders, representing an oppositional culture that tended to withdraw, rather than bestow legitimacy, on reigning institutions, gained ascendancy in urban ghettos. Johnson and other members of the White House were left to figure out why young urban blacks, as one aide put it, "were against just about every leader (Negro and white) . . . except [black power advocates like] Stokely Carmichael" ("Memorandum, Sherwin Markman for the President," 1967). The awkward presence of these Johnson aides—mostly white, mostly from small towns and cities in the Midwest and Southwest—spending a week, sometimes a weekend, in volatile ghetto environments such as Harlem and Watts was, as a leading participant put it, a "unique attempt by the President to discover what was happening in urban ghettos and why" ("Written communication from Sherwin Markman," 2004). Aides were not sent to organize or manipulate or steer, but solely to gain a sense of the ideas, frustrations, and attitudes at the basis of the riots.[20]

Given the growing emphasis that civil rights activists had begun placing on "liberation" and "community," the lengthy reports that White House aides prepared for the President unsurprisingly observed that growing black militancy appeared to vindicate the objectives of the Great Society. The volatile conditions in the ghetto did not stem from material deprivation alone, these reports argued; rather, as one White House aide put it, the most serious and common problem was that "the ghetto Negro lives in a world which is severed from ours" (Markman Memorandum, "Memorandum for the President,"1967). Sherwin Markman, who organized the White House ghetto visits, wrote in his summary report that the first essential key to understanding urban America was "alienation—of the ghetto Negro from the mainstream of American life, and of white America from the ghetto Negro." Although housing, education, and employment varied from city to city, the "disconnection" blacks felt from the rest of America was "not limited to one city or region, but [was] nation-wide in its pattern, and growing" (Markman Memorandum, "American Ghettos: Our Challenge and Response," 1967).

Markman sought to persuade LBJ that the severe alienation that afflicted urban America both explained and perhaps justified the black power movement. The "dramatic growth" of Black Power had become the "rally cry in the ghetto," he reported after a return visit to Chicago in February, 1968 ("Memorandum, Sherwin Markman to L.B. Johnson," 1968). "Power" should not be confused with violence, Markman insisted, even though "some advocates of the philosophy preach violence." After talking with intellectuals like Charles Hamilton, as well as militant black nationalists, Markman concluded that this vague concept most essentially meant "an increase in race consciousness and pride." In their early visits to urban areas, White House aides had discovered, as one report put it, that "perhaps the most significant symbol of the ghetto is the *absence of proud men*" ("Memorandum, Thomas E. Cronin to L.B. Johnson," 1967, emphasis in original).[21] Black power, Markman told LBJ, would bring "positive results" in filling that terrible void: "It is my judgment that the increased pride in race must inevitably lead to strong racial motivation for better social organization, better education, and better jobs" ("Memorandum, Sherwin Markman to L.B. Johnson," 1968).

By all accounts, Johnson was deeply moved by these reports. The President carried one of Markman's reports on the Chicago ghetto around with him and read it to members of the Cabinet, Congress, and the press, with the hope that it would persuade them to accept the White House's position on civil disorders ("Oral History of S.J. Markman," May 12, 1969: 28).[22] LBJ condemned the riots, declaring in a nationwide address of July 1967, "There is no American right to loot stores, or to burn buildings, or to fire rifles from the rooftops. That is a crime—and crime must be dealt with forcefully, and swiftly, and certainly—under law." At the same time, he insisted, "This is not a time for angry reaction. It is a time for action: starting with legislative action to improve the life in our cities. The strength and promise of the law are the surest remedies for tragedy in the streets" (Public Papers of L.B. Johnson 1968: 721, 723).

The ghetto reports apparently were pivotal in persuading Johnson to respond to the riots by intensifying his efforts to expand civil rights and the war on poverty programs. The administration continued to push for an open-housing bill, and in the aftermath of King's assassination, one was passed in 1968. That year, LBJ also submitted and Congress passed the most extensive and most expensive public housing legislation in American history. Finally, Johnson continued to support the War on Poverty's Office of Economic Opportunity, the White House office charged with administering poverty programs, even though its sponsorship of Community Action Programs (CAPs), requiring "the maximum feasible participation of residents of the areas and groups involved," was reportedly having a disruptive influence in many cities and was the target of bitter complaints from local party leaders.[23]

The President seethed privately about the "revolutionary" activity that some CAPs were fomenting. Nonetheless, encouraged by the ghetto reports of their valuable work in ameliorating the alienation of urban dwellers from American society and government, he never repudiated them publicly and continued to support federal funds for neighborhood organizations. The War on Poverty's Community Action Program was the Johnson administration's final, frail hope that it could benefit from the transformative energy of a movement over which it was rapidly losing influence.

The Johnson presidency and community action

Johnson's relationship with the War on Poverty helps explain how he both extended the reach of the modern presidency and built the skids for its diminishing influence. In part, the Johnson White House's delegation of administrative responsibility to these local citizen groups was intended to be an extension of the modern presidency. LBJ and his aides viewed state and local governments, and the party organizations that influenced them, as obstacles to good government, to the "enlightened" management of social policy. They conceived of CAPs as a local arm of the Office of Economic Opportunity, thus enabling the Johnson administration to bypass local governments and the entrenched, usually Democratic political machines.[24] Federal guidelines, in fact, stipulated that the community action program had to be conducted by a public or private nonprofit agency (or some combination thereof) other than a political party (Economic Opportunity Act 1964).

From this perspective, the CAP was evidence of the White House's ex cathedra effort to restore a sense of community. As Samuel Beer has pointed out, "the antipoverty program was not shaped by the demands of pressure groups and the poor—there were none—but by deliberations of [White House] task forces" (1990: 16).[25] At least in part, the communal concerns of the Johnson presidency were closely connected to administrative invention, a bold new initiative that embodied, in Nathan Glazer's words, "the profession-alization of reform in modern society" (cited in *The Administrative History of the OEO*: 18). In the hands of the Johnson administration, which relied to an unprecedented extent on presidential politics and governance, this invention never fulfilled its stated objective of popular participation. Especially after 1967, following the recommendations of the Heineman task force on government organization, Johnson tried to tighten White House management over the CAPs.[26] The following year, George Nicolau, stepping down after eighteen months of running the Harlem Community Action Agency (HARYOU-ACT), the largest in the nation, declared himself "a victim of that process which in the space of three short years created and has almost been overwhelmed by its own complexities and its own bureaucracy" (cited in Moynihan 1969: 139).

Nevertheless, although administrative centralization enervated the participatory aspirations of the War on Poverty, "participatory democracy" would became the clarion call of reformers who gained influence with the demise of Johnson's political fortunes. Seeking to make his own distinctive mark on the development of the American nation, Johnson's governing principles and programs posed fundamental challenges to New Deal liberalism. Most important, the Great Society did not embrace national administrative power as an instrument of social and economic power. Viewing the idealistic zeal of the civil rights movement as the potential source of a new political order, Johnson deliberately initiated and helped legitimize an assault on New Deal institutional forms.

The Johnson administration's expressed concern for "community" involvement, especially, revealed how "qualitative" liberalism was potentially in tension with the centralization of authority required by an extensive welfare state. Furthermore, the administrative innovation that gave rise to the War on Poverty was an attempt to respond to real problems that could not be readily addressed by executive administration. Moynihan argued that the Johnson administration blundered into the community action program and that the phrase mandating "maximum feasible participation" was a shallow rhetorical bow to the Jeffersonian tradition of local self-government. Yet, the ideas that informed the creation of the Community Action Program were not so distinctive from certain aspects of the New Deal, to more communal reform ideas and practices that Johnson understood well as a result of his experiences as the Texas director of the National Youth Administration (NYA), the New Deal agency created in 1935 to rescue young people from ignorance, unemployment, and enduring hardship ("National Resource Development Report" 1943: 394–5). The NYA, headed by the militant southern liberal, Aubrey Williams, was both more idealistic and less bureaucratic than most other New Deal agencies. Its programs were administered from state offices and under state relief administrators, who were encouraged to develop grassroots reforms that would provide meaningful work for young people and help keep them in school long enough to become self-sufficient.[27] The 1943 report of the National Resources Planning Board (NRPB), a planning agency that Roosevelt created in 1939 as part of the newly formed Executive Office of the President, singled out the NYA for avoiding bureaucratic inertia; it was one of the few New Deal agencies, the NRPB found, that did not "divorce the average citizen from participation in the problems involved in public-aid policy and administration" ("National Resource Development Report" 1943: 486).[28]

The cultural changes and social circumstances of the 1960s greatly aggravated the tension between enlightened administration and community control. After reading his White House aides' accounts of the conditions in the ghetto, Johnson developed a deeper appreciation of the limits of executive administration in fighting a war against racial discrimination and economic deprivation. More important, the riots and the White House aides' reports of them confirmed the Johnson administration's view that "community action" was a critical element of their program to establish a post–New Deal version of the welfare state. The architects of the Great Society were well aware of the political risks involved in delegating administrative responsibility to community action agencies; however, these risks were taken in the hope of revitalizing, indeed surpassing, the militant side of New Deal liberalism.

Johnson's surprising patience with the CAPs, his continuing, albeit certainly not unqualified, support of the War on Poverty, in the face of blistering criticism from Congress and local government officials, suggests that he did not disagree with this reform ambition.[29] He did not appreciate fully the tension between executive management and local self-determination. Nor did he sufficiently appreciate that the civil rights movement was a catalyst for an adversarial politics that was inherently suspicious of presidential leadership. The community action agencies took on the energy and aspirations of the civil rights movement and refocused it, thus giving a new generation of black leaders entrée into local and administrative politics. As a 1967 Senate investigation of the War on Poverty put it: "The Office of Opportunity policies and programs have produced . . . a sizeable cadre, for the first time in the Negro community, especially, of young energetic and striving leadership" ("Examination of the War on Poverty" 1967: 1238, 1241–2).[30] That "cadre of striving leaders" developed political bases that were not tied directly to the Democratic party or the White House (Andrews 1997: 800–19; Skrentny 2002; Kotz 2005).[31] Nonetheless, having invested his immense ambition in the Great Society, having staked his political fortunes in the social movements that it empowered, Johnson had little choice but to support the Office of Economic Opportunity and the community organizations it spawned, even as he grew increasingly aware of the fact that it aroused leadership and social forces that had come to view him "as part the white apparatus which created and fostered the perpetuation" of racial injustice ("Memorandum, Sherwin Markman for the President," 1967).[32]

Conclusion: Lyndon Johnson's legacy for the modern presidency and administrative state

The story of Lyndon Johnson's uneasy alliance with the civil rights movement argues for a theoretical framework that emphasizes neither the presidency nor social movements but, rather, the fascinating interplay between them. Against the general norm that presidents resist or respond reluctantly to the demands of insurgent groups, it shows how an ambitious president and social activists can form an alliance in the service of enduring reform. Although this fusion of presidential power to a movement for social justice was short-lived, the fragile partnership made possible the most dramatic civil rights legislation since the Reconstruction era. Without the work of Martin Luther King and other civil rights leaders in mobilizing demonstrations that elicited the violent reaction of segregationists and aroused strong sympathy in the country, no civil rights revolution would have been possible. At the same time, without Johnson's willingness to support, indeed, take advantage of the opportunity that civil rights direct action provided, the landmark laws of 1964 and 1965 might never have been enacted.

Thus, LBJ's alliance with the civil rights movement marks a critical test case of the view of Progressive and New Deal reformers that the modern executive office can be a principal agent of reform. Unlike Eisenhower, who treated racial strife in the South as a matter of domestic order, and Kennedy, who viewed civil rights as a legal issue, Johnson understood the inequality between black and white Americans as a ringing moral cause, one worthy of a deployment of the full powers of the modern presidency. Although the tension between Johnson and the civil rights movement is often characterized as a clash between practical politics and principle, Johnson, to be sure a ruthless, sometimes crude manipulator of power, was not consumed by power for its own sake. From the beginning of his presidency, Johnson was enthralled at the prospect of exploiting his mastery of politics to make a historic contribution to civil rights reform, to serve his enormous ambition by inspiring the nation to a higher purpose.

Yet this singularly determined fusion of executive power to a social movement eventually imploded. As early as 1965, it became clear that Johnson's effort to become a leader of the civil rights movement suffered from his attempt to manage all the other responsibilities that the modern presidency pulls in its train. Johnson's decision to expand America's involvement in Vietnam, in particular, stemmed in part from his firm belief that nothing could be accomplished unless certain received commitments were steadfastly affirmed; yet this unwittingly confirmed the view of civil rights activists, scarred by the compromise LBJ engineered to preempt the challenge of the Mississippi Freedom Democratic Party at the 1964 Democratic Convention, that the presidency could not be trusted with the mantle of leader of their cause.

Just as Johnson's ambition motivated him to a display a greater commitment to civil rights than his Democratic predecessors, so it seemed that LBJ's obsession with his place in history may have deprived him of the deft diplomacy required to extricate the country from a terrible situation in Vietnam (King 1998: 345). From the perspective of Civil Rights leaders, Johnson's unhealthy ambition and desire to centralize power in the White House drew him deeper into the war. As King wrote, "The Johnson administration seemed amazingly devoid of statesmanship, and when creative statesmanship wanes, irrational militarism increases. President Kennedy was a man who was big enough to admit when he was wrong—as he did after the Bay of Pigs incident. But Johnson seemed unable to make this kind of statesmanlike gesture in connection with Vietnam" (345).

Johnson was far from indifferent to this indictment of the administration's foreign policy; indeed, his commitment to bold domestic reform strongly influenced his decision to refrain from any full-scale mobilization of the Vietnam conflict. On the one hand, he feared that too much forbearance, let alone withdrawal, would allow the Right to use anticommunism to subvert domestic change, just as the "loss of China" had weakened liberalism on Truman's watch (McWilliams 2005: 222–3). On the other hand, the distractions of this limited war soaked up resources and exposed the President's attachment to received commitments to the social activists' charge that he was, after all, a trimmer.

At the end of the day, the Great Society revealed both the untapped potential for cooperation between the modern presidency and social movements and the inherent tensions between "high office" and insurgency that made such collaboration tempestuous. LBJ's abdication on March 31, 1968—his announcement that he would not seek or accept the nomination of his party for another term as president—marked a failure of his ambition to align himself and the powers of the modern executive with the carriers of a new politics— civil rights activists, consumer and environmental advocates, and those fighting for women's rights. The tasks of the modern presidency—the domestic and international responsibilities that constrained the "steward of the public welfare"—necessarily limited the extent to which Johnson could become a trusted leader of the social movements that arose during the 1960s. By 1968, Johnson, the self-fashioned agent of a political transformation as fundamental as any in history, had become a hated symbol of the status quo, forced into retirement lest he contribute further to the destruction of the liberal consensus. As he told Hubert Humphrey, in their private meeting of April 3, 1968: "I could not be the rallying force to unite the country and meet the problems confronted by the nation abroad and at home in the face of a contentious campaign and the negative attitudes towards [me] of the youth, Negroes, and academics" ("Memorandum of Conversation, Participants: The President; the Vice President; Charles Murphy; W.W. Rostow," 1968).

More enduringly, Johnson's travails contributed to the diminishment of the modern presidency. In part, this followed from Johnson's determination to achieve civil rights reform: race is an extremely contentious issue, and LBJ's effort to further progress in race relations was immensely controversial and politically dangerous. Equally important, the corrosion of the modern executive's authority followed from LBJ's attempt to wed civil rights reform and the Great Society; from his view, it was not enough to achieve just a better deal for those Americans who in Herbert Croly's capacious phrase did not partake of the "promise of American life." Johnson's ambition to push the country toward a Great Society made it impossible for him to find a "symbolic point," whereby his administration could form an alliance with the civil rights movement for a noble purpose and still uphold the modern executive office's obligation to domestic and international security (Miroff 1981: 14).

The Johnson administration, Wilson Carey McWilliams has written, "made real—and so far, almost the *only*—attempts to address the quality of life in America and to enlist public policy in the cause of beauty and community" (1985: 171–2, emphasis in original). Unlike the commitment to racial justice, however, this cause was an act of improvisation that was generated by the White House. The Executive Office of the President had been increasingly active in formulating and carrying out programs since the administration of Franklin Roosevelt. Under Johnson, however, political and policy responsibility was concentrated in the presidency to an unprecedented extent, so much so that "enlightened administration" gave way to a more personal, or "politicized," office, dominated by the White House Office and related policy staff (Dickenson 2005: 135–173). Major Great Society initiatives, such as the Community Action Program, were conceived in the White House, hastened through Congress by the extraordinary legislative skill of the president and his sophisticated legislative liaison team, and administered by new or refurbished executive agencies that had been designed to respond to the president's directives. The creation of the Great Society, then, marked the height of presidential government and a serious effort to advance "qualitative liberalism," but at the cost of weakening the institutional props of the modern executive. Much was still demanded of presidents; they remained at the center of citizens' ever-expanding expectations of government. Yet Johnson's personalization of the executive office and the antithetical social forces he unleashed fostered public cynicism about the merits of presidential policies, opposition to unilateral presidential power, and a greater inclination in the news media to challenge the wisdom and veracity of presidential statesmanship and proposals.

This was especially likely to happen given the Johnson administration's vision of a Great Society. The celebration of a "desire for beauty," "hunger for community," and "maximum feasible participation" called for efforts to limit the discretionary power of New Deal institutions. The Community Action Program, resulting from an effort to wed administrative invention and the rejection of centralized administration, perfectly captured the paradox of Lyndon Johnson's Great Society. There is a real sense in which this program, the signature innovation of the Great Society, marked a serious, if flawed, effort to routinize the intense emotion of the civil rights movement. To be sure, the Community Action Program initially gave Johnson credibility with social activists. Eventually, however, the attempt to give institutional form to insurgency indicted the modern pretension that the managerial capacities and administration mechanisms of executive leadership could serve as instruments of community control and social justice.

The difficulty of marrying executive administration and social insurgency bespoke the exalted turmoil of the 1960s. The intellectual historian William McLoughlin (1978: xiii) has argued that the social movements of the 1960s embodied the fourth great awakening in American history, an episode of spiritual rebirth that "begins in a crisis of beliefs and values and extends over a period of a generation or so, during which time a profound reorientation in beliefs and values takes place."[33] Viewing the 1960s as such a revelatory time helps put the estrangement between Johnson and the civil rights movement in perspective. "[Our] political leaders have never been the prophets of new light," McLoughlin argues; "they may implement it, but they do not originate it . . . Until a consensus is reached from the bottom up, it cannot be instituted from the top down. Presidential leadership follows, it does not create consensus" (213).

Ostensibly, Johnson's Great Society acknowledged the limits of the office he occupied to bring about a full-scale cultural transformation. "The success of his presidency and his programs," Johnson observed in explaining the objectives of the War on Poverty, could not be attained at the hand of "beneficent government" but instead required a new political activism: "A President can lead and teach, and explore, and set goals. He can have his eyes on the stars, with a vision that will flow therefrom, and he can have his feet on the ground, with a solid foundation that we need . . . But no leader can make a people more than they are, or make them more than they really want to be . . . These goals are going to demand your effort and your work and your sacrifice, and the best from every American" (Milkis 2005: 13). Operating at the high tide of the modern presidency, however, Johnson could not help but try to do the work for the people. Attempting to play a role for which the president was not scripted, seeking to control insurgent forces in a manner that his Great Society doctrine proscribed, Johnson drained the liberal administrative state of much of its governing authority.

Harry McPherson attempted to express the essence of the White House's effort to reconcile executive leadership and community control at the twilight of the Johnson presidency. Notes he prepared in November 1968 for a presidential address (never given) on intergovernmental relations disavowed the conservative view "that Washington was somehow wholly separate from (and an ominous threat to) the grassroots" ("Creative Federalism," n.d.). But the draft address also rejected "the liberal dogma that the Federal government has all the answers." And then, in a revelation of the full scope of the dilemma, McPherson expressed the concern that the newfound celebration of "participatory democracy" and recent denigration of "enlightened administration" had left the country without a national purpose; the Great Society, he lamented, had helped to bring to power issue oriented independents who failed to acknowledge a transcendent public interest. "Does this lack of a central core," a fellow White House assistant asked McPherson, "explain the emptiness we all sense . . . as Peer Gynt discovered when he peeled the onion" ("Memorandum, Fred Panzer to Harry McPherson," 1968).

In this sense, as Hugh Heclo has suggested, the movement politics of the 1960s might have departed from the pattern of previous awakenings in American history: "The long-standing national narrative of America's providential and benevolent moral mission in the world—a grounding component of earlier awakenings—became widely regarded by activists [in the 1960s] as little more than a conceit masking the country's failures and hypocrisy" (1996: 45). Because the social movements of the 1960s grew out of an unprecedented clash between America's oppositional culture and the modern executive establishment, which presumed to embody its aspirations, Lyndon Johnson became the focus of activists' sense of national betrayal.

LBJ paid dearly for the alienation of the social movements from the White House; just as surely, the civil rights movement and the other social protest movements it inspired paid a price for their rejection of presidential leadership. The 1960s unleashed new forces and new expectations that could not be quelled by the election of Richard Nixon. Indeed, it was the 1970s rather than the 1960s when affirmative action and many other civil rights measures became a real presence in American society. And yet, even as they continued to look to the national government to solve the problems thrown up by an industrial, and post-industrial order, the public interest groups that emerged during the 1970s, which evolved from the social movements of the 1960s, denigrated presidential leadership and administrative agencies, without which expansive government responsibility would become impractical.[34] Teaching Americans both to expect more from the government and to trust it less, the Great Society was the fulcrum on which decline of liberalism and the rise of conservatism tilted.[35]

Just as Ibsen's Peer Gynt discovered the limits of his search for the "true self," so Lyndon Johnson and the architects of the Great Society discovered the limits of reform in American politics. But these shortcomings were not simply attributable to the limits of leadership exposed by Johnson's immense ambition. The Great Society marked a bold effort to rediscover a sense of citizenship and community amid the recognition that the expansion of national administrative power was inevitable. That the Great Society taught us both to embrace and to distrust this "uneasy state" might be diagnosed as an unhealthy political schizophrenia. But perhaps we should credit Lyndon Johnson and the architects of the Great Society for recognizing that the uneasy state born of the 1960s—and the conflict it engendered between our need for government and our deep suspicion of it—had its source in our oldest and most profound need: our need to govern ourselves (Karl 1983: 238–9).

Notes

* The author thanks Greta Fowler Miller for her research support and editorial suggestions.
1 For an important exception, see Miroff (1981). This chapter owes much to Miroff's insights into social movements and the study of the presidency.
2 See also Marc Landy and Sidney M. Milkis (2000) which argues that all presidents who have been agents of major political realignments have been "conservative revolutionaries." Russell Riley (1999) argues that those presidents credited with championing racial equality, such as John Kennedy and Lyndon Johnson, often felt compelled to restrain, and at times suppress crusades for political and social reform.
3 Again, on the critical relationship between FDR and Labor, see Milkis (1993, chapter 3).

4 For a discussion of Johnson's leadership that highlights the relationship between the New Deal and the Great Society, see Milkis (2005).

5 Louis Martin, editor and publisher of the black newspaper, *Michigan Chronicle*, and an important official of the Democratic National Committee during the Johnson years, where he served as an effective liaison between the White House and the African American community, saw LBJ's southern background as the key to understanding the president's strong civil rights record: "Now my feeling about Johnson . . . is that since [he] was a southerner, he would normally, being a good politician, lean over backwards to prove that he was not a racist. Further, there's something in the folklore of Negro life that a reconstructed southerner is really far more liberal than a liberal Yankee . . . Johnson did many things that Kennedy would never have done" ("Oral History of Louis Martin," 1969). Pointing to the fragile yet indispensable link between civil rights reformers and the Johnson White House, Martin admitted that he "exploited this part of folklore," just as LBJ exploited his African-American advisors and civil rights leaders to make a distinctive mark on American history.

6 As Johnson's aide Bill Moyers wrote in fending off the cautionary importuning of other White House staffers, "This is a political year, but the President is not just thinking of the next election—*he is thinking of the next generation*. . . . He believes there is a danger that the *primacy of politics* this year will prevent the Nation from looking at the longer pull—hence *his deliberate decision to cast the spotlight on certain issues which ought to be imbedded in the Nation's consciousness*" ("Memorandum, Bill Moyers to George Reedy," 1964, emphasis in original).

7 The Equal Employment Opportunity Commission, charged with preventing racial and sexual discriminatory practices in employment, was stripped of its authority to file suit in the courts. The Commission could recommend, but only the Justice Department had the power to initiate a suit. The Justice Department, in turn, could file suits only under conditions where obvious discriminatory practices, which characterized Jim Crow laws in the South, prevailed. On Dirsken's relationship with Johnson and the role that the Republican Senate leader played in enacting civil rights legislation, see Hulsey (2000: 183–204).

8 Johnson's power over Congress had become so great by the summer of 1964 that he was able to pressure Republican Minority leader, Charles Halleck, to support a rule that enabled Congress to act on the president's poverty legislation. See the telephone conversation between Lyndon Johnson and Charles Halleck (White House Tapes, June 22, 1964).

9 See, for example, Johnson telephone conversation with Roy Wilkins, head of the National Association for the Advancement of Colored People (White House Tapes, July 2, 1964). Johnson was concerned that Republican legislators were heading off to the GOP convention and might not be able to participate in the signing ceremony, thus risking the bipartisan support LBJ had worked so hard to achieve. Wilkins expressed his support for LBJ's desire to sign the bill on July 2nd, emphasizing particularly the need to cultivate bipartisanship as "an overwhelming political reason" to act quickly.

10 As Kotz (2005) notes, King was elated with the President's expressed support for the marchers' cause.

11 In 1963, Johnson mentioned FDR's 1938 purge campaign to Kennedy aide, Theodore Sorenson. Johnson recalled that FDR had attempted a failed "purge" in the 1938 primary campaigns, trying to replace conservative southern and border state Democrats with 100 percent New Dealers who were committed to economic reform. In a telephone conversation with Ted Sorenson, Johnson explained that he believed that the president's moral commitment to civil rights should not be expressed in an effort to purge southern Democrats, but, rather, through an appeal to their consciences: "I think the President could do this in North Carolina or some

place. I'd invite the congressmen and senators to be on the platform . . . I'd have him talk about the contributions that they had made and then I'd say, 'Now, we have a problem here. No Nation—a hundred years ago in the Lincoln-Douglas debate, Lincoln said, No Nation can long endure half slave and half free. Now no world can long endure half slave and half free and we've got to do something about it in our own country'" (George Reedy Office Files, June 3, 1963).

12 Johnson showed a less poetic, more practical side to Lewis in asking for the civil rights movement's help in implementing the Voting Rights Act. Inviting the civil rights leader to meet with him privately in the Oval Office prior to signing the legislation, LBJ told him earnestly, "'Now John you've got to go back and get all those folks registered. You've got to go back and get those boys by the *balls*. Just like a bull gets on top of a cow. You've got to get them by the balls and you've got to *squeeze*, squeeze 'em till they *hurt*.' I'd heard that Lyndon Johnson enjoyed talking in graphic, down-home terms," Lewis later acknowledged, "but I wasn't quite prepared for all those bulls and balls" (Lewis 1998: 346, emphasis in original).

13 The openly segregationist campaigns in Arkansas and Maryland did not succeed, as pro-civil rights majorities formed behind the moderate Republican candidacies of Winthrop Rockefeller, Nelson's brother, and Spiro Agnew, a big Nelson supporter, respectively (see Hope 1966).

14 Johnson's enormous ambition, invested in the bold commitment to create a Great Society, could hardly be indifferent to world affairs. "History has a peculiar ability to forget what a president does at home and judges him on the size of his impact on the world beyond his shores," Bill Moyers wrote in a memo to Johnson in June 1965. This "irony of judgment would determine Johnson's place in history." "Some president, some day will come along and pass programs topping the Great Society—the country will have greater needs than today and he will have more GNP to use in solving them," Moyers's memo concluded. "But no president is likely again to have the chance to redeem Southeast Asia from Red China—or keep the Communists out the Caribbean—or save the U.N." ("Memorandum, Bill Moyers to LBJ," 1965).

15 As Kotz notes (2005: 236), both Kennedy and Johnson "failed to recognize a significant historical reality. The Communist Party's fifty-year campaign to recruit African Americans to its cause had been a colossal failure."

16 Because LBJ's efforts were *sub rosa*, direct evidence of his efforts to influence the civil rights leadership is lacking, but leaders of the major organizations convened on July 29 and issued statements that conformed to LBJ's immediate political objectives (see *New York Times*, July 30, 1964: 12; Miroff 1981: 10–11).

17 Written communication from Sherwin Markman, a Johnson White House aide, who was heavily involved in resolving the MFDC controversy.

18 LBJ was kept apprised of the Democratic National Committee's implementation of the 1964 Convention's call for greater participation; given the tight reins the White House kept on the committee, these activities certainly would not have gone on without the president's approval (see "Memorandum, Marvin Watson to L.B. Johnson," 1967). As became clear at the 1968 convention, the rule was no paper tiger. Having found no evidence that the Mississippi Democratic party had "complied with either the spirit or the letter" of the convention call prohibiting racial discrimination, the Credentials Committee voted overwhelmingly to bar the 1968 Mississippi regular delegation from its seats. A biracial delegation, including many members of the 1964 Mississippi Freedom party, was seated in its place (Milkis 1993: 210–16).

19 The term *extraordinary isolation* is Woodrow Wilson's (1908: 69).

20 For a primary account of the ghetto visits, see "Interview of S.J. Markman" (May 21, 1969).

21 White House Fellow, Thomas E. Cronin, who visited Baltimore, spoke of the "*absence of proud men.*"

22 See also "Notes of a Meeting with Peter Lisigor, of the *Chicago Daily News*" (1967); "Tom Johnson's Notes of Meetings, Meetings with Correspondents" (1968); and "Memorandum, Tom Johnson to L.B. Johnson" (1967).

23 In June 1965, James Rowe, who ran Johnson's 1964 campaign, informed the president that the Office of Economic Opportunity was "giving instructions and grants to local private groups for the purpose of training the Negro poor on how to conduct sit-ins and protest meetings against government agencies, federal, state and local." Johnson passed this memo on to Bill Moyers, with a pointed note: "For God's sake get on top of this and stop it at once" ("Memorandum, J. Rowe to L.B. Johnson," 1965). Shriver "started a damn revolution," LBJ complained to Richard Daley a few months later (Johnson Tapes, December 24, 1965).

24 The OEO was conceived as the president's managerial arm that could "cut across departmental lines to facilitate coordination." As its director, Sargent Shriver testified before a House committee, placing the OEO in the White House bestowed "an authority which the President wants because he wants to be a focal point with respect to this aspect of the domestic effort" (cited in *The Administrative History of the OEO*: 35–6). This line of reasoning invoked the administrative science of the Brownlow Committee report, the blueprint for the creation of the Executive Office of the President during Franklin Roosevelt's second term (on the Brownlow Committee report and the role it played during the Roosevelt years, see Milkis 1993: chapters 5–6).

25 Beer notes that the research based theories of two Columbia University sociologists, Richard Cloward and Lloyd Ohlin, had an especially important influence on the presidential task forces that shaped the antipoverty program. For Cloward's thoughts on the origins and development of the community action during the Great Society, see the essay by Fox Piven and Richard Cloward (2005) and *The Administrative History of OEO* (chapter 1).

26 The Heineman group was the second task force to report on government organization during the Johnson presidency; the first, chaired by Don K. Price, issued its study in 1964. Its recommendations appear in two lengthy memoranda: "Memorandum, Task Force on Government Organization to J.B. Johnson" (1966) and "A Final Report By the President's Task Force on Government Organization" (1967: 18–20).

27 On Johnson and the National Youth Administration, see Caro (1981, chapter 19); Conkin (1986: 74–9); and Dallek (1991: 123–44).

28 The NYA also stood apart from most other New Deal agencies in its commitment to equal opportunities for blacks. The national office urged state directors to enlist blacks on the state advisory boards. Johnson feared that this mandate would wreck his carefully orchestrated effort to win a broad base of support in Texas. He argued that the "racial question" in Texas "could not be upset over night," that the "attempt to mix Negroes and whites on a common board in this state" would "be shockingly against precedence." Without attacking the ramparts of Jim Crow directly, however, Johnson made a serious effort to surmount the political hazard of race. He appointed a "separate and distinct State Negro Advisory Board." And against the usual practice in the South, he developed programs to treat blacks equally even when separate. For example, Johnson included all black colleges in student aid programs; indeed, although blacks did not receive grants in proportion to their numbers in Texas, a higher percentage of black college students qualified for and gained aid (24 percent) than did whites (13 percent) ("Special Report on Negro Activities of the National Youth Administration of Texas," 1936; see also Conkin (1986: 78–9).

29 Johnson voiced such a view in his memoirs. "I heard bitter complaints from the mayors of several cities," he wrote. "Some funds were used to finance questionable activities. Some were badly mismanaged. That was all part of the risk. We created new bureaus and consolidated old ones. We altered priorities. We learned from our mistakes. But as I used to tell our critics, 'We have to pull the drowning man out of the water and talk about it later'" (Johnson 1971: 81).

30 For this quote and many of the ideas expressed in the discussion of the Community Action Program, I am indebted to Morone (1998: chapter 6).

31 Katz (2005) emphasizes how the Great Society and War on Poverty enhanced the role of public and quasi-public (privately controlled but government funded) employment of African Americans, both increasing their influence on public policy and contributing to advances in economic security. Skrentny (2002) comments on how the Great Society increased the influence of social movements on regulatory policy.

32 He had learned from reading Alexis de Tocqueville, he remarked on another occasion, that the leaders of revolutions often become their victims. By 1967, Johnson viewed himself as the early leader, and ultimate victim, of the civil rights revolution (Kotz 2005: 395).

33 The other three awakenings in American history occurred during the Revolution, Jacksonian democracy, and the Progressive Era.

34 On the connection between the Great Society and the reform politics of the 1970s, see Melnick (2005).

35 A full examination of the Great Society would have to explore how it changed not only liberalism but conservatism as well. By the end of the 1960s, Democrats and Republicans, conservatives and liberals, had all become, as Hugh Heclo puts it, "policy minded," and so they have remained committed to finding public solutions to economic and social problems (2005). Moreover, this commitment to government activism has been allied to a distrust of centralized power that has encouraged aggressive oversight of executive administration and insurgent assaults on the "Washington establishment." Rather than pursuing solutions to the nation's problems with New Deal style executive-centered and pragmatic policy measures, contemporary political activists engage in ideological and institutional confrontation that defies consensus and diminishes public trust in government.

Bibliography

Primary sources

Acts

Economic Opportunity Act of 1964, Title 2, Part A, Section 202 (a).

Executive papers

Public Papers of the Presidents: Lyndon B. Johnson, 1967 (1968) 2 volumes, Washington, D.C.: Printing Office.
The Administrative History of the OEO, Special Files, Johnson Library.

Interviews

McPherson, H. (1985) interviewed by Sidney Milkis, July 30, 1985.

Oral History of S.J. Markman (May 21, 1969) interviewed by D.P. McSweeney, Tape 1, 24–36, Johnson Library.

Oral History of L. Martin (May 14, 1969) interviewed by D.G. McComb, Tape 1, 22, Johnson Library.

Johnson Tapes

"Telephone conversation between L.B. Johnson and Charles Halleck" (June 22, 1964) Johnson Tapes.

"Telephone conversation between L.B. Johnson, Hubert Humphrey, and Walter Reuther" (August 25, 1964) Johnson Tapes.

"Telephone conversation between L.B. Johnson and Martin Luther King, Jr." (January 15, 1965) Johnson Tapes.

"Telephone conversation between L.B. Johnson and Martin Luther King, Jr." (August 20, 1965) Johnson Tapes.

"Telephone conversation between L.B. Johnson and Richard Daley" (December 24, 1965) Johnson Tapes.

"Telephone conversation between L.B. Johnson and Roy Wilkins" (July 2, 1964) Johnson Tapes.

"Telephone conversation between L.B. Johnson and Ted Sorenson" (June 3, 1963) George Reedy Office Files, Johnson Library.

"Telephone conversation between L.B. Johnson and Walter Reuther" (August 9, 1964) Johnson Tapes.

Memoranda and White House Files

Markman, S.J. "American Ghettos: Our Challenge and Response" (April 5, 1967) White House Central File: We9, Johnson Library.

"Memorandum, Bill Moyers to George Reedy" (May 21, 1964) White House Central Files—SP, Johnson Library.

"Memorandum, Bill Moyers to L.B.J." (June 21, 1965) Office Files of Bill Moyers, Johnson Library.

"Memorandum, Fred Panzer to Harry McPherson" (February 21, 1968) White House Central File, EX-SP.

"Memorandum, Hayes Redmon to Bill Moyers" (November 27, November 30, 1965) Office Files of Bill Moyers, Johnson Library.

"Memorandum, J. Rowe to L.B. Johnson" (June 29, 1965) White House Central File: Aides, Moyers, Johnson Library.

"Memorandum, Marvin Watson to L.B. Johnson" (April 19, 1967) Marvin Watson Files, Johnson Library.

"Memorandum of Conversation, Participants: The President; the Vice President; Charles Murphy; W.W. Rostow" (April 5, 1968) *White House Famous Names*, Box 6, Folder: Robert F. Kennedy, 1968 Campaign, Johnson Library.

"Memorandum, Sherwin Markman for the President" (February 1, 1967) White House Central File: We9, Johnson Library.

"Memorandum, Sherwin Markman to L.B. Johnson" (February 17, 1968) White House Central File: We9, Johnson Library.

"Memorandum, Task Force on Government Organization to L.B. Johnson" (December 15, 1966) White House Central File, Box 43, Folder: Heineman Task Force, Johnson Library.

"Memorandum. Thomas E. Cronin to L.B. Johnson" (May 11, 1967) White House Central File: We9, Johnson Library.

"Memorandum, Tom Johnson to L.B. Johnson, and attached notes for meeting with labor leaders" (August 10, 1967), Tom Johnson's Notes of Meetings, Box 1, Folder: August 9, 1967.

"Memorandum, Lee C. White to L.B. Johnson" (August 13, 1964) White House Central Files, Ex & Gen PL, Johnson Library.

"Notes of a Meeting with Peter Lisigor, of the Chicago Daily News" (August 4, 1967), Tom Johnson's Notes of Meetings, box, Folder: July 1967–May 1968.

"Tom Johnson's Notes of Meetings, Meeting with Correspondents" (May 1968), Tom Johnson's Notes of Meetings, Box 1, Folder: July 1967–May 1968.

"Written communication from Sherwin Markman to Author" (January 13, 2004).

Reports

"A Final Report By the President's Task Force on Government Organization" (June 15, 1967) *Outside Task Forces*, Johnson Library.

"Examination of the War on Poverty, prepared for the Subcommittee on Employment, Manpower and Poverty of the Committee on Labor and Public Welfare, United States Senate" (1967), vol. V, Washington, D.C.: Government Printing Office.

"National Resources Development Report of 1943, Part II: Security, Work, and Relief Policies" (1943) Washington, D.C.: Government Printing Office.

"Special Report on Negro Activities of the National Youth Administration of Texas" (March 16, 1936) NYA, Box 9, Johnson Library.

Speeches

Johnson, L.B. "Commencement Address at Howard University: 'To Fulfill These Rights,'" (June 4, 1965) *Public Papers of the Presidents: Lyndon B. Johnson, 1965*, 2: 635–40.

Johnson, L.B. "The Great Society" (May 22, 1964) Commencement Address at Ann Arbor, Michigan, Online. Available: <www.lbjlib.utexas.edu>

Johnson, L.B. "Remarks at a Breakfast of the Georgia Legislature" (May 8, 1964), *Public Papers of the Presidents: Lyndon B. Johnson, 1963–1964*, I: 645–651.

Johnson, L.B. "Special Message to Congress: The American Promise" (March 15, 1965) Online. Available: <www.lbjlib.utexas.edu>

Speech notes

Goodwin, R. (1965) "Speech Draft," White House Central File: SP 3–93, Box, 172, Johnson Library.

McPherson, Harry (n.d.) "Creative Federalism," Speech Notes, Aides: McPherson, Box 55.

References and secondary sources

Andrews, K.T. (1997) "The Impact of Social Movements on the Political Process: The Civil Rights Movement and Black Electoral Politics in Mississippi," *American Sociological Review*, 62: 800–19.

Beer, S. (1990) "In Search of a Public Philosophy," in A. King (ed.) *The New American Political System*, Washington, D.C.: AEI Press.

Block, J. (2007) "Agency and Popular Activism in American Political Culture," in S. Skowronek and M. Glassman (eds) *Formative Acts: American Politics in the Making*, Philadelphia: University of Pennsylvania Press.

Branch, T. (2006) *The Canaan's Edge: America in the King Years, 1965–68*, New York: Simon and Schuster.

Carmichael, S., with M.T. Ekwueme (2003) *Ready for Revolution: The Life and Struggles of Stokely Carmichael*, New York: Scribner.

Carmichael, S. and Hamilton, C.V. (1967) *Black Power: The Politics of Liberation in America*, New York: Vintage Books.

Caro, R.A. (1981) *The Years of Lyndon Johnson: The Path to Power*, New York: Vintage Books.

Carter, D.C. (2001) "Two Nations: Social Insurgency and National Civil Rights Policymaking in the Johnson Administration, 1965–1968," unpublished thesis, Duke University.

Conkin, P.K. (1986) *Big Daddy From the Pedernales: Lyndon B. Johnson*, Boston: Twayne Publishers.

Dallek, R. (1991) *Lone Star Rising: Lyndon Johnson and His Times, 1908–1960*, New York: Oxford University Press.

Dickenson, M. (2005) "The Executive Office of the Presidency: The Paradox of Politicization," in J.D. Aberbach and M. Peterson (eds) *The Executive Branch*, New York: Oxford University Press.

Fox Piven, F. and Cloward, R. (forthcoming) "The Politics of the Great Society," in S.M. Milkis and J. Mileur (eds) *The Great Society and the High Tide of Liberalism*, Amherst: University of Massachusetts Press.

Goodwin, R. (1988) *Remembering America: A Voice From the Sixties*, Boston: Little, Brown.

Heclo, H. (1996) "The Sixties False Dawn: Awakenings, Movements, and Postmodern Policy-Making," in B. Balogh (ed.) *Integrating the Sixties*, University Park: Pennsylvania State University Press.

—— (forthcoming) "Sixties Civics," in S.M. Milkis and J. Mileur (eds) *The Great Society and the High Tide of Liberalism*, Amherst: University of Massachusetts Press.

Hope, P. (1966) "New Faces Mark Victory of Republicans," *Washington Star*, 9 November, Located in Records of the Democratic National Committee, Box 75, Johnson Library.

Hulsey, B.C. (2000) *Everett C. Dirksen and His Presidents: How a Senate Giant Shaped American Politics*, Lawrence: University Press of Kansas.

Johnson, L.B. (1971) *The Vantage Point: Perspectives of the Presidency, 1963–1969*, Austin: Holt, Rinehart and Winston.

Karl, B. (1983) *The Uneasy State: The United States from 1915–1945*, Chicago: University of Chicago Press.

Katz, M.B. (2005) "The New African American Inequality," *Journal of American History*, 92: 75–108.

Kilpatrick, C. (1964) "Forget Past, LBJ Tells Deep South," *Washington Post*, May 9: A1, A4.

King, Jr., M.L. (1998) *The Autobiography of Martin Luther King, Jr.*, C. Carson (ed.), New York: Warner Books, Inc.

Kotz, N. (2005) *Judgment Days: Lyndon Baines Johnson, Martin Luther King, Jr., and the Laws That Changed America*, Boston, MA: Houghton-Mifflin.

Landy, M. and Milkis, S.M. (2000) *Presidential Greatness*, Lawrence: University Press of Kansas.

Lewis, J. (1998) with M. D'Orso, *Walking with the Wind*, New York: Simon and Schuster.

McLoughlin, W.G. (1978) *Revivals, Awakenings, and Reform*, Chicago: University of Illinois Press.

McWilliams, W.C. (1985) "Lyndon B. Johnson: The Last of the Great Presidents," in M. Landy (ed.) *Modern Presidents and the Presidency*, Lexington, MA: D.C. Heath.

—— (2005) "Great Societies and Great Empires," in S.M. Milkis and J. Mileur (eds) *The Great Society and the High Tide of Liberalism*, Amherst: University of Massachusetts Press.

Mann, R. (1996) *The Walls of Jericho: Lyndon Johnson, Hubert Humphrey, Richard Russell, and the Struggle for Civil Rights*, New York: Harcourt, Brace.

Melnick, R.S. (2005) "From Tax and Spend to Mandate and Sue: Liberalism after the Great Society," in S.M. Milkis and J. Mileur (eds) *The Great Society and the High Tide of Liberalism*, Amherst: University of Massachusetts Press.

Milkis, S.M. (1993) *The President and the Parties: The Transformation of the American Party System Since the New Deal*, Oxford: Oxford University Press.

—— (2005) "Lyndon Johnson, the Great Society, and the Twilight of the Modern Presidency," in S.M. Milkis and J. Mileur (eds) *The Great Society and the High Tide of Liberalism*, Amherst: University of Massachusetts Press.

Miroff, B. (1981) "Presidential Leverage over Social Movements: the Johnson White House and Civil Rights," *Journal of Politics*, 43: 1–23.

Morone, J.A. (1998) *The Democratic Wish: Popular Participation and the Limits of American Government*, revised edn by J.A. Morone, New Haven, CT: Yale University Press.

Moynihan, D.P. (1969) *Maximum Feasible Misunderstanding*, New York: Free Press.

Riley, R.L. (1999) *The Presidency and the Politics of Racial Equality*, New York: Columbia University Press.

Sanders, E. (2007) "Presidents and Social Movements: A Logic and Preliminary Results," in S. Skowronek and M. Glassman (eds) *Formative Acts: American Politics in the Making*, Philadelphia: University of Pennsylvania Press.

Skowronek, S. (1997) *The Politics Presidents Make: Leadership from John Adams to Bill Clinton*, Cambridge, MA: Harvard University Press.

Skrentny, J.D. (2002) *The Minority Rights Revolution*, Cambridge: Harvard University Press.

Tichenor, D. (2007) "Leadership, Citizen Movements, and Politics Rivalries Make," in S. Skowronek and M. Glassman (eds) *Formative Acts: American Politics in the Making*, Philadelphia: University of Pennsylvania Press.

Tulis, J. (1987) *The Rhetorical Presidency*, Princeton, NJ: Princeton University Press.

Wilson, W. (1908) *Constitutional Government in the United States*, New York: Columbia University Press.

Young, J.S. (1995) "Power and Purpose in *The Politics Presidents Make*," *Polity*, 28: 509–16.

12 The triumph of racial liberalism, the demise of racial justice

Daniel Martinez-HoSang

This chapter examines one of the dominant analytic constructs in studies of U.S. racial politics in the post-World War II era: the assertion that public debates over race and racism are best understood as a conflict between the enduring ideologies of "racial liberalism" and "racial conservatism."[1] In these frameworks, "racial conservatism" implies an endorsement of racial inequality and an aversion to anti-discrimination remedies which undermine "white rights." Racial liberalism, on the other hand, rejects ascriptive hierarchies, and embraces the norms of "equal opportunity" and a "level playing field." I explore the uses and limitations of these frameworks through an examination of two statewide California ballot initiatives over school desegregation and busing in the 1970s. I highlight the processes and practices by which competing political actors seek to articulate frameworks of meaning in order to naturalize and thereby justify particular policy solutions. This approach regards ideological formation as a contingent and localized process, in which specific political practices and institutional arrangements interact with the broader historical norms and themes usually labeled as "ideology." I utilize this framework to investigate how California's deeply separate and unequal system of public education was defended and renewed through a discursive framework that incorporated, rather than rejected, the leading tenets of racial liberalism.[2] Ultimately this chapter argues for a conceptualization of race within American political development (APD) that takes seriously the critical renovations and renewals in political debates over meaning of race and racism across time. That is, we must investigate why and how particular frameworks of racial meaning operated and what relations of power they enabled and naturalized.

In the first section I discuss the prevailing patterns of inequality within California public schools in the early postwar era, and the ways civil rights advocates and their allies attempted to dismantle these conditions. I then examine the political movements that arose to oppose these efforts, and the logics of white rights and freedom of association on which they were based. After discussing the limitations of those efforts, I explore the ways desegregation opponents articulated a new framework which recast "white rights" through an assertion of "racial innocence"—the disavowal of racist intent as the principle determinant of a "colorblind" and (and implicitly non-racist) ethos. Central to these claims of racial innocence was the incorporation of an emerging critique of prevailing desegregation remedies on the part of black and Chicano activists. I conclude with some brief reflections on the legacy of these California debates for the dynamics and trajectory of national racial politics since the 1980s.

Floyd Wakefield and the "white rights" defense of school segregation

In the early 1960s, the NAACP, the American Civil Liberties Union (ACLU), and other civil rights groups set out to dismantle the unmistakable patterns of racial segregation and inequality in California public schools. These efforts, including lawsuits filed against nearly every large school district in the state, legislative lobbying, and some local parent organizing, were not unprecedented. Well before World War II, African American, Chinese, and Japanese American parents and students successfully contested local and statewide statutes providing for their segregation. In 1946, the segregation of Mexican American students succumbed to a legal challenge by a group of parents in Orange County (*Mendez v. Westminster School Dist. of Orange County* 1946). A year later, Governor Earl Warren repealed all legislation permitting the segregation of racial minorities in public schools.

While few California school districts officially segregated students by race when the Supreme Court delivered its *Brown* decision in 1954, racial segregation and inequality continued to be the rule, rather than the exception, in many districts. The cases making their way through the state courts in the 1960s often revealed that decisions to set attendance zones, locate new school sites, and arrange feeder patterns between elementary, middle, and high schools were often based on maintaining and enforcing patterns of racial segregation. In Los Angeles, for example, funding formulas for campus maintenance were based on the square footage of school facilities, systematically favoring the sprawling, newly constructed campuses in the San Fernando Valley serving white students over the ageing, more compact buildings in older parts of the city populated by students of color. When overlaid on patterns of rigid residential segregation—made possible by state-sanctioned racially restrictive housing covenants and discriminatory lending policies (Self 2003)—these practices maintained rigid inequalities within the state's celebrated public education system (Caughey and Caughey 1966).

In 1963 the state Supreme Court ruled that where residential segregation existed, it was "not enough for a school board to refrain from affirmative discriminatory conduct. The harmful influence on the children will be reflected and intensified in the classroom if school attendance is determined on a geographic basis without corrective measures." The state court offered an expansive interpretation of the state Equal Protection Clause in determining that "right to an equal opportunity for education and the harmful consequences of segregation require that school boards take steps, insofar as reasonably feasible, to alleviate racial imbalance in schools regardless of its cause" (*Jackson v. Pasadena School District* (1963: 879)). The decision essentially made the distinction between *de jure* and *de facto* discrimination irrelevant, foregrounding the principle of equal educational opportunity and giving local desegregation advocates a potent tool in their negotiations with school boards.

The desegregation mandates facing nearly every large district in the state during this time demonstrates the progress realized by civil rights groups like the NAACP, the ACLU, and many local activists and policy makers that embraced nominal desegregation plans. And while every desegregation proposal met active grassroots opposition among parents and policymakers intent on preserving established schools, this opposition consistently failed to stem the tide of such policies.

To understand the barriers which early opponents of desegregation faced, we can examine the activism and efforts of Republican Assemblyman Floyd Wakefield of the Los Angeles suburb of South Gate. South Gate became a flashpoint during initial efforts to desegregate the Los Angeles Unified School District, which included schools in this overwhelmingly white, working-class city of 57,000 residents. Civil rights groups including the NAACP and the United Civil Rights Committee seized on South Gate High School as a particularly egregious example of the school board's racial gerrymandering of attendance boundaries: The attendance areas for South Gate High and nearby Jordan High School in Watts were regularly adjusted as black families in Watts moved closer to the South Gate border. South Gate High remained nearly 100 percent white and was kept in far better condition, while Jordan High was almost entirely black and badly in need of repair (Nicolaides 2002).

In addition to their demands for political representation and additional resources, civil rights groups insisted that attendance boundaries be redrawn to desegregate both South Gate and Jordon High Schools, a policy that would have required minimal district-provided busing, since the schools were less than a mile apart (Caughey and Caughey 1966). The ACLU also filed a lawsuit in 1963 to compel this change. *Crawford v. Los Angeles School Board* was eventually expanded to include the entire Los Angeles school district and all black and Mexican-American students; it would be nearly two decades before the case was resolved (*Crawford v. Los Angeles School Board* 1976, 1981; Caughey and Caughey 1973; Haro 1977; Landis 1984).

Floyd Wakefield, a local business owner, arose to the forefront of the grassroots effort within South Gate to repel the proposed changes. Born in 1919, Wakefield came of age during a time when South Gate's civic leaders proudly boasted of the city's rigid enforcement of racially restrictive covenants—the 1940 Census counted only two African Americans among a population of nearly 40,000, even as nearby Watts and Compton attracted a growing black population (Nicolaides 2002).

As fervently as civil rights groups organized marches, sit-ins, press conferences, and hunger strikes at the school board during late 1963 and early 1964, Wakefield and his supporters counter-mobilized with their own rallies, petitions, and other collective actions. While they disavowed any racist intentions, they nonetheless posed their interests and concerns in direct opposition to the "integrationists." To Wakefield, the struggle was between those who "believed in integration and swapping kids [and those who] didn't" (Nicolaides 2002). Their political vocabulary was defined by straightforward calls for local control and (white) parents' rights, and they made little effort to conceal their contempt for civil rights proponents. Wakefield thus drew from the same thinly veiled discourse of "white rights" animating much of the opposition to desegregation in the South, and to open housing laws in many neighborhoods in the North (Hirsch 1995; Kruse 2005).

Wakefield's leadership against school and housing desegregation in South Gate launched his political career as "the unequivocal voice of South Gate's 'silent majority'"(Nicolaides 2002). In 1966, he won a seat in the state Assembly, even though he ran as a Republican in a largely Democratic district. As an Assemblyman, Wakefield continued to take uncompromising stands against all desegregation policies, even as many of his fellow Republicans, including Governor Ronald Reagan, endorsed modest administrative directives urging local school districts to set desegregation goals. Reagan and other Republicans hoped that such legislation would provide local districts with an administrative framework to address racial imbalance without becoming subject to more far reaching court orders ("Wakefield Requests Veto on Race Bill," *Los Angeles Times*, December 12, 1971: SE2).

From Wakefield's perspective, however, such considerations were irrelevant; all efforts at "forced integration" were equally untenable. In 1970 and 1971, he proposed legislation that would effectively prohibit local districts from desegregating their schools. But the courts, which actively embraced the argument of civil rights groups that the Equal Protection Clause of the state constitution required an affirmative commitment to desegregate, stymied Wakefield each time. As the courts endorsed broad desegregation proposals for the Los Angeles and San Francisco school districts, Wakefield decided to take his case directly to voters.

In early 1972, Wakefield drafted and circulated a ballot initiative to add a provision to the state Education Code declaring "No public school student shall, because of his race, creed, or color, be assigned to or be required to attend a particular school." Proposition 21, or the "Wakefield Amendment" as it came to be known, also repealed a recently passed mandate for school districts to correct racial and ethnic imbalances within student enrollment ("Wakefield Requests Veto on Race Bill" 1971).

A fundraising appeal that Wakefield sent to his supporters two weeks before the election revealed the ways the Assemblyman sought to construct Proposition 21 as an unambiguous defense of white rights. Asserting that the busing agenda pursued by "liberals" was being masked by "press suppression" and the "pro-busing news-media," Wakefield solicited donations in order to buy television time for a campaign ad; his appeal included a photo storyboard for a commercial he hoped to begin airing immediately. The storyboard showed a terrified young white girl being forced to board a potentially dangerous bus as her mother stood by helplessly. The girl's forlorn and bewildered query, "Aren't we people too?" implicitly set the rights of white people—the "we"—against a racialized "other" receiving unwarranted advantages from, as the ad described, "that old government." The ad's concluding screen "Restore Freedom of Choice" was again explicitly racialized, for such a "freedom" was only available to white parents—minority students assigned to inferior and segregated schools had no such choice ("Dear Fellow Californian letter and storyboard" 1972).[3] The ad unmistakably cast busing as an abrogation of such white prerogatives, reciting a familiar defense of Jim Crow policies in the South. Thus the ad, and Wakefield's larger defense of segregated schools, defended a set of racially specific white rights as natural and inalienable.

Wakefield continually emphasized the racialized dimensions of his critique before the public. He referred to the modest desegregation mandate backed by Reagan and other Republicans as the "forced integration law," announcing that the "Courts have said we are not going to tolerate segregated (by law) schools. Now we're turning around and saying we're not going to tolerate integrating them by law either" ("2 Groups Promise Court Challenge to Busing Proposition," *Los Angeles Times*, November 9, 1972: A20). The brief ballot argument and rebuttal in favor of Proposition 21 used the phrase "forced integration" nine times, making Wakefield's politics clear: Segregation was natural and a matter of choice, while integration was artificial and required coercion (California Secretary of State 1972).

Proposition 21 passed with 63 percent of the vote during the November 1972 election. To be sure, the wide margin of passage reflected a larger national ambivalence towards busing. In March 1972, 74 percent of Florida voters supported a straw-ballot resolution in support of a constitutional amendment prohibiting "forced busing." Soon after, President Nixon called for a national moratorium on busing for desegregation and Congress adopted legislation declaring that such busing must be a remedy of last resort. The busing controversy loomed as a major issue in the 1972 presidential contest, and dominated local politics in cities such as Detroit, Boston, and Charlotte (Lassiter 2005).[4]

The Wakefield Amendment, however, in spite of its large margin of victory, failed to command any similar attention in California. His campaign collected only 329,675 signatures, barely enough to qualify the measure for the ballot, and only a handful of Republican clubs and conservative school board members endorsed the measure. Coverage of other ballot propositions, including a death penalty and coastal protection initiative, garnered far greater media attention "Proposition 21: Is it Anti-Busing or Anti-Integration?" *Los Angeles Times*, September 26, 1972: OC1; "County Board Supports Bible Version for Texts," *Los Angeles Times*, October 26, 1972: OC A11). The Proposition 21 campaign raised a modest $45,000 for the entire effort, including money donated from Wakefield's own campaign fund, securing only a handful of small contributors ("Proposition 21: Is it Anti-Busing or Anti-Integration?" *Los Angeles Times*,

September 26, 1972: OC1; "Campaign filing statement from California State Archives" 1972).

In addition, local attempts to block the implementation of court-ordered busing programs that similarly appealed to "white rights" claims also failed. Contrary to the claims made by desegregation foes, white parents and students did not uniformly oppose or flee from mandatory desegregation policies. Their actions and assessments were often contradictory, and we must balance the tension between examining the pro-segregationist expressions of many white parents seriously without treating them as historically inevitable. On the one hand, because local school districts often funneled the most resources—the newest buildings, the most experienced teachers, and the most comprehensive curricular offerings—to the schools serving white students, it is unsurprising that many parents would infer that maintaining a white dominant student body and teaching staff was critical to "protecting" the quality of their schools. In many cases, they eagerly pursued and embraced the relative opportunities and privileges afforded to them by segregated school systems. On the other hand, the doomsday admonitions that white parents would never tolerate desegregated schools also proved spurious. When the Berkeley and Riverside school districts voluntarily inaugurated a district-wide busing program in the late 1960s, and when districts such as San Francisco, Pasadena, Santa Barbara, and other cities instituted court ordered programs in the 1970s, the highly vocal opposition they faced typically gave way to rapid adjustment and acceptance among the majority of parents and students. Attempts to organize anti-busing boycotts failed consistently (Wollenberg 1976; Hendrick 1977). Even in Los Angeles, where busing programs faced more than a decade of relentless stigmatization and political and legal delay, the awkwardly crafted busing program that was eventually implemented for a few years in the late 1970s unfolded peacefully.[5]

Wakefield's triumph on election day was short-lived. Within two years, the state Supreme Court found the operative portion of Proposition 21, which prohibited student assignment based on race, color, or creed, to be in violation of the state and federal constitution. Associate Justice Raymond Sullivan asserted that Proposition 21 involved the "state in racial discrimination" and that the measure could not abrogate "the school district's constitutional duty not to segregate" (*Santa Barbara School District v. Superior Court* (1975)). Citing a recent U.S. Supreme Court decision from a case in North Carolina, Sullivan further asserted that "to forbid all assignments made on the basis of race would deprive school authorities of the one tool absolutely essential to fulfillment of their constitutional obligation to eliminate dual school systems" ("State High Court Rules Ban on School Busing Unconstitutional," *Los Angeles Times*, January 16, 1975: A3; *Swann v. Charlotte-Mecklenburg Board of Education* (1971)).[6]

Proposition 21 certainly delayed the implementation of new desegregation programs during the two years it was in effect, as local desegregation foes sought to use the measure's passage to repeal or limit such plans. In addition, the number of students attending racially segregated schools in the mid-1970s continued to grow, largely the result of increased white migration to the suburbs. But ultimately, Wakefield's goal of eliminating California's desegregation policies failed. His defense of the prevailing patterns of segregation as a matter of freedom of choice could not withstand judicial review; in attacking equal protection guarantees Wakefield attempted to challenge desegregation policies at the point of their greatest legal and political strength. In addition, as a political discourse, demands for white rights did not offer any solution or response to the growing crisis facing highly segregated black and Mexican American schools. Finally, by marking itself as opposed to "forced integration," white rights claims ran against a growing public consensus, shaped largely by the work of the southern civil rights movement but reflected in opinion polls nationally, that segregated schools were anathema to a pluralist democracy.[7] While most voters were far from enthusiastic about supporting large-scale busing and student reassignment initiatives, they were also opposed to explicitly defending a dual-education system. Wakefield's version of "racial conservatism," as it developed and operated in this period and setting, failed to put an end to the use of busing for desegregation.

Developing new challenges to school desegregation

Floyd Wakefield's defeat did not mark the end of the desegregation controversy. Instead, Wakefield's strident opposition to "forced integration" gave way to a more subtle and sophisticated defense of white political authority, centered in the burgeoning white suburbs north of Los Angeles. In the following section, I examine the practices and strategies embraced by a particular set of political actors that culminated, through an uneven process, in the articulation of a new critique of busing for desegregation, including: (1) A new emphasis on the remedy of busing rather than the ideal of integration; (2) A transformation of the arguments about equal protection law; (3) The forging of a multiracial coalition against busing; and (4) The adoption of new tactics to reach voters and shape the public debate.

From "forced integration" to "quality education for all"

As the state court overturned Proposition 21 in early 1975, the Los Angeles school district also came close to exhausting its legal challenges to the 12-year-old *Crawford v. Los Angeles* litigation, and was preparing to implement one of the country's largest desegregation programs, relying heavily on busing to traverse the district's expansive geography. Local opposition to this plan arose most forcefully in the rapidly growing San Fernando Valley. Valley residents had benefited enormously from a decade-long school construction boom begun in the 1950s—financed by a series of voter approved taxes and bond measures—that delivered spacious, modern campuses to the region, far more desirable than the older, often decaying schools in the urban core populated by minority students. More often then not, the most experienced teachers also gravitated to these suburban areas, and local schools in places such as Encino, Van Nuys, and Northridge became the prized possessions of their communities. Within a cultural milieu that repeatedly contrasted the safety and security of white middle-class suburbs in comparison to a menacing and racialized urbanity, the residents' attachment to their schools and neighborhoods was also heavily racialized (Cohen 2003; Avila 2004).

But the attack on school desegregation plans in the Valley beginning in the late 1970s sounded fundamentally different than Wakefield's white rights claims. Many of the Valley activists who fought desegregation frequently declared their opposition to "deliberate segregation," particularly in the South. But activists such as Roberta Weintraub and Bobbi Fiedler, two housewives who founded the grassroots anti-busing organization BUSTOP, asserted that Los Angeles schools were free of such intentional actions, and that desegregation plans must be limited to voluntary programs that preserved the rights of parents to keep their children in their current schools, however racially imbalanced they might be. BUSTOP recited apocalyptic scenarios of a mammoth busing order that would destroy their local schools, arousing enormous support from anxious Valley parents. In a growing number of rallies, press conferences, and school board meetings, BUSTOP members emphasized the threat long bus rides posed to their children's education and safety, rarely asserting their "right" to choose a segregated school. By attacking desegregation remedies, rather than the principle of "forced integration," BUSTOP effectively recast the defense of white prerogative and privilege on new terms.[8]

Such direct attacks on busing exploited the continued reluctance of liberal desegregation advocates to make a forceful and uncompromising stand in favor of the value the principle of racial equity and the value of an integrated education in general, and the necessity of busing in particular. This ambivalence was brought into sharp relief several years earlier during the public debate over Proposition 21. The American Civil Liberties Union (ACLU) of Southern California, which organized the public education campaign to defeat the ballot measure, refused to challenge Wakefield's contention that busing was an unlawful abrogation of parental rights. Treating the electorate's apprehension towards busing as an insurmountable "fact" rather than a contentious point of political struggle, they argued instead that Wakefield's measure would do little to stem the tide of court-ordered busing. They even tried harnessing anti-busing sentiments to their own cause, suggesting that if Proposition 21 was adopted, it might trigger litigation resulting in even more busing (California Secretary of State 1972). In addition, the ACLU and other Proposition 21 opponents made no mention of the hundreds of thousands of minority students toiling in segregated classrooms, nor asserted a moral claim for desegregation. By the late 1970s, groups such as BUSTOP, by shifting the debate from the obligations of integration to the contradictions of busing, exploited this ambivalence with great success.

Attacking the Equal Protection Clause

A second critical innovation embraced by desegregation opponents in the late 1970s concerned the legal claims used to argue that the prevailing patterns of racial isolation did not violate state and federal equal protection guarantees. Since the early 1960s, the Equal Protection Clauses in the state and federal constitutions had been the central legal principle driving most local desegregation orders. State courts in particular held that *de facto* discrimination still violated such protections. Wakefield's Proposition 21 was also invalidated on these grounds.

This legal conundrum was solved by State Senator Alan Robbins, a young Democrat representing the Van Nuys and North Hollywood area. Robbins was elected to the Senate in 1973 with liberal credentials: he supported the Equal Rights Amendment, the United Farmworkers, and defended California's fair housing laws. Deeply ambitious, Robbins soon challenged incumbent Los Angeles mayor Tom Bradley in the 1977 election as a champion of the Valley's interests. The popular Bradley crushed Robbins in the primary, but the campaign alerted Robbins to the enormous appeal of the busing issue, and the growing attention commanded by BUSTOP. Robbins soon got to work on an anti-desegregation constitutional amendment that would address the equal protection arguments. Robbins' training as a lawyer and a previous stint as a staff member of a commission that helped consolidate California's massive 75,000-word state constitution provided him unusual expertise in the area. Robbins took notice that the U.S. Supreme Court had recently turned away from enforcing the Fourteenth Amendment's equal protection guarantees in desegregation cases where intentional discrimination could not be proven. If this standard were imposed on the state courts, Robbins reasoned, then most school districts in California, which had abandoned formally discriminatory policies by 1950, would be exempt from desegregation orders.

Robbins' proposed constitutional amendment added a lengthy 176-word exemption to California's nearly 100-year-old Equal Protection Clause. It held that "with respect to the use of pupil school assignment or pupil transportation" the state Constitution could not be interpreted to impose "obligations or responsibilities which exceed those imposed by the Equal Protection Clause of the Fourteenth Amendment to the United States Constitution." In other words, as long as the U.S. Supreme Court interpreted the federal Equal Protection Clause as only prohibiting *de jure* school segregation, California courts would have to do the same. A lesser provision of the amendment affirmed the right of school districts to pursue voluntary desegregation programs at their discretion, an exception that Wakefield never proffered. The Robbins amendment thus addressed a legal bind that had stymied opponents of desegregation in California for fifteen years. His legislation prevented state courts from vigorously applying the state's equal protection guarantees. At the same time, by affirming the Fourteenth Amendment standard, the initiative also seemed immune from challenges on these grounds.

The multiracial attack on busing

In building support for his constitutional amendment, Robbins also pursued a political strategy markedly different from Wakefield. Like many of the BUSTOP activists, Robbins declared himself an unswerving supporter of integration; it was busing alone that Robbins claimed to oppose. To bolster his anti-racist credentials, Robbins sought the support of several leading African American and Chicano political leaders, a tactic Wakefield never would have embraced. For at least a decade, black and Chicano communities had expressed growing ambivalence towards desegregation plans that focused almost exclusively on rectifying rigidly determined racial imbalances. Such plans often left other questions of equity involving teacher and personnel hiring, "ability tracking," inadequate resources, parental involvement, curriculum, and language policy unaddressed. Many of these issues animated the largest student-led protest in the history of California public education—the Chicano student "blowouts" involving 22,000 students centered in East Los Angeles in the spring of 1968. The students' complaints—a curriculum which ignored Mexican American history and steered students away from college and towards vocational training, the paucity of Mexican American teachers, the continued use of corporal punishment, overcrowded campuses—reflected many of the same desires for justice and opportunity pursued by desegregation advocates. But the Chicano students made little mention of desegregation as a political imperative; their priority was the immediate improvement of conditions in East Los Angeles schools (Lopez 2003). The desegregation remedies proposed by the courts and civil rights lawyers in Los Angeles and elsewhere made little commitment to address these issues or the forms of cultural domination that fueled the walkouts.

Floyd Wakefield's antagonism towards all state-sponsored desegregation actions did not parse such distinctions in the political strategies of civil rights groups and student activists; the thunder of his exhortations to defend white rights left him tone deaf to other criticisms of desegregation. Robbins, by contrast, was alert to the growing criticism of prevailing desegregation plans within many minority communities, and courted prominent African-American, Chicano, and Asian-American figures to take visible, active roles in support of his proposed constitutional amendment. Robbins recruited State Senator Alex Garcia, a well-known East Los Angeles Democrat who had opposed Proposition 21 five years earlier, to be the principal co-sponsor of his legislation. Garcia contended that mandatory busing and student reassignment would undermine the tenuous status of newly established bilingual education programs. At Robbins' request, Garcia circulated a letter to colleagues urging support of the legislation:

> Compulsory busing in most California cities would mean the virtual end of bilingual education as we know it today. Where will you find sufficient bilingual instructors if you spread the Chicano students all over the school

district? . . . Please don't force us to try it 'for our own good': Thank you, but no thanks.

("Alex Garcia letter," 1977)

Garcia was joined by several other well-known Chicano activists, including John Serrano, an East Los Angeles social worker who served as the lead plaintiff in a landmark lawsuit to equalize funding for education between poor and wealthy districts. Serrano became one of the leading backers of the Robbins Amendment over the next two years.[9]

While Serrano and Garcia claimed to be representing a uniform position among Chicanos towards busing and desegregation, their comments pointed more to subjects of contentious debate than a fully formed consensus. To be sure, Chicano education activists in Los Angeles and elsewhere were wary of desegregation proposals that threatened the future of emerging bilingual education programs. Asian-American and Mexican-American advocates had only recently won the funding and legal mandate for bilingual education in the late 1960s and early 1970s, and a lack of qualified bilingual teachers raised issues about how such programs could be staffed if the students who needed them were reassigned across a large school district. No one wanted a return to the days when Mexican American students were punished for speaking Spanish on school grounds, even during recess.[10]

In addition, the 1968 Chicano "blowouts" heightened attention towards issues of cultural domination within public education. Indeed, many supporters of the Los Angeles desegregation plan, such as ACLU leader and UCLA professor John Caughey, spoke openly of identifying and distinguishing "unassimilated" Mexican Americans who would be prioritized in reassignment plans (Caughey and Caughey 1973). Such comments resonated uneasily with a long history of "Americanization" programs in the state rooted in assumptions of Mexican "cultural" pathology (Sanchez 1993). Chicano members of a community advisory committee set up to advise the Los Angeles school board on its desegregation plan sounded its trepidation towards "an integration policy that is totally assimilationist in nature—one that does not respect the rights and needs of the culturally different" (Haro 1977: 17). They argued repeatedly that student reassignment and desegregation were necessary but not sufficient: they demanded parity in resources, culturally relevant instruction and curriculum, and attention to racial discrimination in teacher staffing and hiring (Haro 1977).

On the other hand, many established Mexican-American civil rights organizations felt that support for bilingual education did not require opposition to desegregation. In testifying against the Robbins bill at a Sacramento hearing in January 1978, Peter Roos, speaking on behalf of the League of United Latin American Citizens (LULAC), the Mexican American Political Association (MAPA), the Mexican American Legal Defense and Education Fund (MALDEF), National La Raza Lawyers, and the Association of Mexican American Educators asserted: "[T]he concept that bilingual education and desegregation are incompatible precedes from the false premise that desegregation cannot be sensitive to the unique educational needs of those children integrated" ("Statement by Peter Roos in opposition to SCA 48" 1978; "A Summary of the Position and Policy statement of the Chicano Subcommittee of the Citizens' Advisory Committee on Student Integration"). Vahac Mardirosian, director of the Hispanic Urban Education Center, argued that Mexican and Mexican-American parents had to be made aware of the underlying reasons for school desegregation. He noted that "if parents are convinced that sending their children twenty-five to thirty miles will result in exactly the same education that child had when he was in the school next door, logically there really isn't a good reason for that parent to want to cooperate with a desegregation program." But, he added, "if parents understand that this process of desegregation ultimately will result in a better future for their children . . . most . . . would be willing to live with the additional anxiety" (Haro 1977: 24).

While many African-American leaders, including state legislators Maxine Waters, Diane Watson, and Yvonne Braithwaite Burke, were strong advocates of mandatory desegregation, Robbins found enough backing to boost his claim that opposition to busing was not a "white rights" issue but represented a multiracial consensus. Soon after introducing his proposed constitutional amendment, he secured the endorsement of Rev. William Jackson of the Beth-Ezel Baptist Church in Watts. Jackson did not necessarily represent or influence a large bloc of African American voters, but when he campaigned on behalf of the Robbins initiative he spoke as a black community representative, claiming widespread support. At an early 1978 press conference he explained: "I am here representing all those Black people who are terribly distraught about busing . . . We know what is best for our people" ("Press Release," 1978).

In making these claims, Jackson placed himself squarely within the civil rights tradition. He asked an Assembly committee holding a hearing on the bill: "How brutal can we be to impose this action (compulsory busing) on little children? We'd rather have $100 million spent on books and teaching aids than $100 million spent on busing." Similarly, another black parent recruited by Robbins to testify before the Assembly committee described the "humiliation and psychological damage done to the child" by busing, reciting the central themes of the famous evidence offered in the *Brown* case about the deleterious effects of segregation on the psychological development of black children ("Assembly Unit Kill Robbins' Antibusing Bill," *Los Angeles Times*, January 20, 1978: B3).

While desegregation plans were a legitimate source of the debate within black and Chicano communities, Robbins' own anti-racist commitments should be viewed with more suspicion. While he carefully developed his ties to black and Chicano leaders, he was unafraid of addressing and cultivating the reactionary populist sensibilities of white voters. That is, Robbins modified and adapted, rather then abandoned Floyd Wakefield's appeals to "white rights." These actions are made clear in a strategy memo developed by consultants hired by Robbins for a direct mail effort to raise money for his anti-busing amendment in the summer of 1978. The memo suggested targeting mailings to particular middle-class white communities across the state and referencing the nearby "undesirable areas" that included large black and Mexican American populations to which white children might be bused ("Anti-Busing List Order," 1977). In personal fundraising appeals to his Valley supporters, Robbins continued to associate busing with the dangers which lurked beyond their suburban enclaves, suggesting "Children in strange, unfamiliar neighborhoods are much more prone to violence than they would be in their own neighborhood, close to the safety of their own home, family and friends" ("Dear Opponent of Forced Busing letter," n.d).

Evidence such as this reveals the tenuous basis on which anti-busing campaigns sought to include black, Chicano, and Asian-American spokespersons. While their participation was made possible by a deep-seated apprehension towards prevailing desegregation proposals, their inclusion was mainly sought to legitimate assertions of white racial innocence. Fiedler later said that in preparing BUSTOP's legal challenge to the Los Angeles desegregation order, her group "focus[ed] heavily on minority children, because we knew that the charge of racism would be made the minute that we started trying to go to court" (Interview with Bobbi Fiedler 1988).

The intent of this approach was not lost upon Robbins' opponents. NAACP leader Virna Canson testified at a state Assembly hearing on the Robbins Amendment that: "One of the strategies of our opposition is to seek to project individual black spokesmen, exploit their individual points of view, and trade it off as a massive departure of NAACP from our historic goal of full integration." Canson, one of the few desegregation advocates to defend and champion the moral duty to desegregate, explained:

> The proponents of segregation have taken great comfort in a simplistic campaign phrase "A black child does not need to sit beside a white child to learn." Education in isolation is not an effective way to end this dismal record . . . Children may learn some things isolated from each other, but the larger goals of education cannot be achieved in isolation. Not only does a black child need to sit beside a white child, or a white teacher needs to work in a class room with non-whites to learn, but a white child desperately needs to sit beside a black child to learn and be prepared to be a citizen of this colored world.
>
> ("Testimony before the assembly judiciary committee in opposition to anti-integration measures," 1979)

But Robbins' putative incorporation of anti-racist themes and tactics was effective. Calls among busing opponents for the protection of "majority rights" quickly waned in favor of arguments that represented the interests of "all children." The *Los Angeles Herald Examiner* editorialized that the anti-busing movement "is not (and should not) be racist in either intent or effect. The goal of the movement is not to deny minority students a quality education, but to deny the state the power to wreck neighborhoods and lives" ("Quarrels with the courts," January 12, 1979: 11). Robbins affirmatively embraced "integration carried out in an orderly fashion" as a desirable goal, but asserted that "[c]ompulsory busing, where it has been mandated by the courts against the will of local residents, has caused not only racial tension, but actual racial strife, an unfortunate ingredient that we ought not to weave into the social fabric of our society" (Robbins 1977). Robbins' claim that the remedy—school desegregation—was the cause, rather than the solution to "racial strife" recited a theme that was familiar in postwar debates about anti-racism. Yet when sounded with populist, pluralist accents, it seemed more like a pragmatic assessment rather than a racist disavowal.

The privatization and professionalization of anti-desegregation activism

The final innovation pursued by Alan Robbins and his supporters concerned the tactics and strategies they employed to build a constituency for their campaign. In early 1978, an Assembly committee supportive of desegregation policies defeated a bill that would have placed Robbins' proposed constitutional amendment on the ballot. In response, Robbins began a signature-gathering effort to qualify the amendment by petition, hiring BUSTOP's Weintraub to coordinate the effort. In spite of Robbins' assurances that anti-busing sentiments guaranteed the measure would easily qualify, the campaign fell far short of collecting the required number of signatures. Indeed, several other grassroots efforts to qualify an anti-busing initiative for the ballot in the Valley and Orange County also failed. Local groups which organized to oppose the Los Angeles desegregation plan, including BUSTOP, were often paralyzed by internal strife, poor fundraising, and waning participation ("Antibusing Initiative Misses 1st Deadline," *Los Angeles Times*, May 6, 1978: A25).[11]

In the wake of these defeats, and the struggles they faced in sustaining grassroots organizations, Robbins and other desegregation opponents increasingly turned their attention towards direct mail as the primary means to address and recruit supporters. Robbins turned over much of his "grassroots organizing" to professional campaign consultants. Butcher-Forde, the self-proclaimed "Darth Vader of direct mail," was an Orange County-based consultancy that managed much of the direct mail campaign for Proposition 13, the blockbuster 1978 initiative that rolled back property taxes. Butcher-Forde took on the Robbins' initiative as a client. The coveted lists of voters and campaign donors Butcher-Forde developed through the anti-tax campaign provided an ideal audience for the Robbins' anti-busing effort. While the return from these fundraising appeals was never lucrative—the campaign raised approximately $250,000 between mid-1978 and late 1979, a reported 50 percent of which was kept by Butcher-Forde—it allowed Robbins to send out well over a million pieces of anti-busing campaign literature across the state during this period.[12]

BUSTOP also launched a continuous stream of appeals to carefully targeted voters across Southern California, and yielded more than $550,000 in tax-free contributions in the late 1970s. These appeals were usually signed by Fiedler or Weintraub, who had both won election to the Los Angeles school board, and often tied the anti-busing campaign to the anti-tax fervor sweeping the state in the wake of Proposition 13. A typical letter began: "Are you willing to pay *higher property taxes* to finance the forced busing of over *100,000* Los Angeles schoolchildren?" They included "Official Reply Ballots" and other "surveys" that allowed voters to register their anti-busing sentiments. Following Robbins, the BUSTOP mailers counseled the use of "constructive proposals for voluntary, *not* mandatory, integration" ("Bobbi Fiedler fund-raising letter," 1977).

While political campaigns had relied on direct mail for decades in California, it was through the busing and tax controversies that these efforts reached unprecedented levels of sophistication, scale, and impact.[13]

The anti-busing and anti-tax movements were not "grassroots" political projects in the mold of the labor, civic, and electoral formations that dominated California politics through the mid-1960s. Alan Robbins, and anti property-tax advocates Howard Jarvis and Paul Gann reached their constituency predominantly through direct mail and media coverage; when they did organize "rallies" and public meetings, it was more for the benefit of radio, television and newspaper journalists than to sustain ongoing grassroots organizations. This shift, what might be called the *privatization* of political activism, because it was built on individualized rather than collective actions, was embraced far more quickly by anti-tax and anti-busing leaders than by their opponents.

The professionalization and privatization of the anti-busing effort had one other important effect. The consultants employed by BUSTOP and Robbins also advised or directed dozens of campaigns for individual candidates in Southern California. By encouraging their clients to run in these campaigns as "anti-busing" candidates, they accelerated the use of busing as a publicity-grabbing campaign issue. This development not only forced other candidates to claim ever more extreme anti-busing positions, it ensured that an anti-busing message would be continually carried to millions of voters in the months leading to the vote on Robbins' measure ("Making Do In An Overcrowded School," *Los Angeles Times*, October 16, 1978: A3, A16).

Thus, even though Robbins and BUSTOP failed to sustain ongoing grassroots organizations, their strategic and continuous use of targeted mail appeals and their ability to make busing a central issue within many electoral contests paid enormous benefits. They persistently primed the electorate with a singular characterization of "busing" as an expensive, half-baked bureaucratic scheme that failed all children and accelerated the decline of public education. On one side within this discourse stood a handful of deep-pocket ACLU and NAACP attorneys, insular politicians, self-aggrandizing judges, and their academic advisors who found great pleasure in raising taxes to advance their own "social experiments." On the other side stood the vast majority of "innocent" taxpayers, parents, and children of all racial and ethnic backgrounds who would be forced to shoulder the burden of this preposterous scheme. They were a silent majority perhaps, but not in the revanchist mode of George Wallace, for they professed to value the education of all children. Robbins used the slogan "We Love All Kids" to promote his anti-desegregation measure (see Figure 12.1). For civil rights advocates, what began as an effort to challenge racial hierarchy and expand educational resources and opportunity had become effectively tarnished by their opponents as a disastrous folly of bureaucratic elites emptied of any anti-racist ethics.

The pressure applied directly to elected officials and candidates finally broke the ranks of the Democratic leaders who had previously refused to place Robbins' amendment on the ballot. In early 1979, Robbins allied with anti-tax activists to compel Governor Jerry Brown and the Legislature to call an unprecedented special election in November so that voters could consider the Robbins Amendment and an anti-tax proposition sponsored by Paul Gann, one of the main architect's of Proposition 13.

Robbins' Proposition 1, and Gann's Proposition 4, formed a formidable combination, and the campaigns collaborated in a number of local sites. There was little doubt that Robbins and his allies had succeeded in making any public defense or endorsement of "busing" an act of political suicide. A poll conducted in August found that while less than one in three respondents were aware of Proposition 1, nearly 80 percent registered their opposition towards "busing designed to achieve racial balance" (California Poll Study 7903, August 20–7, 1979).[14]

As the November election approached, it was clear that the ACLU, NAACP, and other desegregation advocates were far outmatched. While Robbins and his allies had spent several years and millions of dollars cultivating a political base for their anti-busing campaign, desegregation proponents focused almost entirely on litigation—they had no meaningful popular base to address.

Desperate for an argument that might convince voters to reject the Robbins initiative, the opposing campaign, again coordinated primarily by the ACLU, began suggesting to voters that passage of the Robbins' measure would actually lead to more court-ordered busing, because its implementation would invite greater judicial scrutiny. That desegregation advocates had to essentially

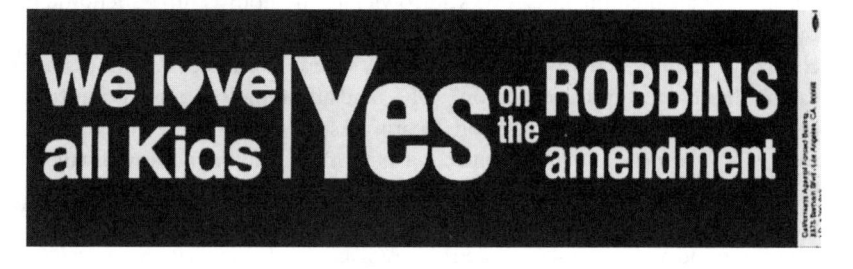

Figure 12.1 "We Love All Kids" bumper sticker

concede to their opponents that mandatory desegregation and busing were unpopular and undesirable and spoke to their broader inability to advance any affirmative argument for the benefits of a desegregated or integrated education. While the ACLU and the NAACP made reference to the need to improve funding, repair dilapidated buildings, or reduce class size, they largely failed to link their desegregation proposals to such broader imperatives and needs.[15]

And because the overwhelming attention of the courts, desegregation opponents, and the media was placed on issues of busing and student reassignment alone, they were effectively painted as being obsessed with busing at the expense of any other concerns. Thus while Robbins, Jackson, and Serrano suggested that the end of "forced busing" would bring new resources to teachers, classrooms and buildings, and bilingual education programs, their opponents could only counter that while busing may be undesirable, it was inevitable. In addition, the accusations that Proposition 1 represented a "'blatant attempt' to maintain the long legacy of racial segregation in California's schools" were severely undercut by Jackson and Serrano's insistence that the measure sought "equal, quality education" for all students (California Secretary of State 1979).

Proposition 1 marched to a landslide victory on election day, passing statewide by a 68 to 32 margin, 12 points higher than the margin of victory for Proposition 21, and received majorities in all 58 counties. Los Angeles County passed the measure by 74 percent. In the City of Los Angeles, the West San Fernando Valley communities that formed the nucleus of the anti-busing movement voted nine to one in favor of Proposition 1, with a 43 percent turnout rate. In the three South Los Angeles city council districts represented by African Americans, the measure was defeated by a 2 to 1 margin, but turnout lagged at 25 percent. It passed by almost 70 percent in the generally liberal Westside, and was approved by smaller majorities in the heavily Latino Eastside district ("Most of L.A. Voted Heavily for Prop. 1," *Los Angeles Times*, November 9, 1979: B3; "Prop 1 May Face Early Court Test," *Los Angeles Times*, November 8, 1979: B3).

In spite of the overwhelming passage of Proposition 1, anti-busing activists still waited anxiously to see whether Robbins' novel legal formulation would survive judicial review. In December 1980 the California Court of Appeals upheld the constitutionality of the measure, ruling "we do not believe a state constitutional amendment can be said to violate the Fourteenth Amendment by specifically embracing it" (654). The court also determined that the electorate had not acted with discriminatory intent in adopting the measure, calling the charge "pure speculation" (655) and affirming Robbins' contention of colorblind racial innocence. At one hearing Associate Justice Lynn Compton told ACLU attorney Fred Okrand "I just think you're being very unfair in imputing sinister motives to the people who adopted Proposition 1" ("Prop 1 Called Biased Against Minorities," *Los Angeles Times*, December 9, 1980: B24). The three judge panel also rejected the ACLU's assertion that the markedly inferior conditions in predominantly black and Mexican American schools demonstrated a pattern of intentional discrimination. The court held that "the two problems (unequal facilities and discrimination) frequently parallel one another but they are distinct and different problems" (*Crawford v. Los Angeles Board of Education* (1981: 647, 504); "Prop 1, Upheld: Bars L.A. Busing," *Los Angeles Times*, December 20, 1980: A1; "Foes of Busing Hail Los Angeles Victory," *New York Times*, March 13, 1981: A12; Ettinger 2003).

In June 1982, the U.S. Supreme Court affirmed the appellate court's decision by an 8 to 1 vote; Justice Thurgood Marshall offered the lone dissent. Writing for the majority, Justice Powell asserted that "It would be paradoxical to conclude that by adopting the Equal Protection Clause of the Fourteenth Amendment, the voters of the State thereby had violated it" (*Crawford v. Los Angeles Board of Education* 1982: 535). The measure "neither says nor implies that persons are to be treated differently on account of their race" (537). Moreover, because school boards could be ordered to relieve segregation in other ways that did not require mandatory busing, the initiative could not be construed as favoring segregation. In his dissent, Marshall noted that "Proposition I has placed an enormous barrier between minority children and the effective enjoyment of their constitutional rights, a barrier that is not placed in the path of those who seek to vindicate other rights granted by state law . . . The fact that California attempts to cloak its discrimination in the mantle of the Fourteenth Amendment does not alter this result" (559).

The Supreme Court's ruling was a death knell for mandatory desegregation programs across the state. Local school boards were still free to craft their own voluntary programs. But without the threat of a court order, these programs were largely feeble. Fiedler, Weintraub, and their allies on the school board dismantled Los Angeles' three-year-old desegregation program in the middle of the school year. Critics noted it was the first time in U.S. history that a court ruling resulted in the reassignment of minority students from desegregated schools to segregated ones ("Prop 1 Upheld," *Los Angeles Times*, December 20, 1980: A1). Pasadena, San Diego, and San Francisco soon scaled back or eliminated their own programs. In San Mateo, a local school district successfully used Proposition 1 to reject an intradistrict desegregation plan that would have required minimal busing. While these changes reflected a number of forces, especially the declining enrollment of white students in nearly all urban school districts, it was Proposition 1 that provided a populist, even anti-racist imprimatur to the movement to halt systematic desegregation of California schools.

In Los Angeles, after their court victory, Robbins and other anti-busing activists vowed to make full use of "voluntary measures" to achieve desegregation, including magnet schools and voluntary busing programs that provided students transportation to attend schools outside of their neighborhood. In reality most of these voluntary efforts were "one-way" programs, requiring students of color from Central, East, and South Los Angeles to be bused from their neighborhood schools to attend better resourced schools in West Los Angeles and in the Valley. By 1985, the district was busing 57,000 students

each day—more than at the height of the mandatory desegregation program—
for voluntary programs and to relieve overcrowding ("For L.A. Schools,
Double Jeopardy: Segregation, Overcrowding," *Los Angeles Times*, October
27, 1985: OC A7). Ironically, some students in South Gate High School,
which by the early 1980s was predominantly Latino, were forced to ride a bus
35 miles each way to the Valley community of Tujunga in order to relieve
overcrowding ("School Busing Furor Erupts in South Gate," *Los Angeles Times*,
June 28, 1981: SE1). The end of mandatory desegregation meant that the
burden of busing had fallen almost exclusively on students of color. One East
Los Angeles high school teacher demanded: "Where is Bustop now? Where are
all the anti-busing activists who assured us that the issue was not racism or
integration but busing itself? If busing was wrong for children from the San
Fernando Valley, then if follows that busing should be wrong for children from
the inner city" ("School Busing Takes a U-Turn," *Los Angeles Times*, December
13, 1981: H5).

Nor could Robbins offer much support to those politicians and activists he
had recruited to join the Proposition 1 campaign in the name of preserving
bilingual education programs. The attacks on bilingual education and language
rights began almost immediately after the busing debate subsided. By the mid-
1990s, when ballot initiatives were launched seeking to bar undocumented
immigrants from public schools and to ban bilingual education entirely,
Robbins was already out of politics. In November 1991, he pled guilty to
federal racketeering charges after accepting bribes from insurance companies
while serving as chair of the Senate Insurance Committee. He served two years
in prison.

Conclusion

Floyd Wakefield attempted to preserve California's deeply segregated system
of public education through a thinly veiled discourse of white rights and
freedom of choice, the touchstones of a political discourse often described as
"racial conservatism." To Wakefield, racial segregation was a natural, defensible
phenomenon that was beyond the pale of state interference. While the
electorate adopted his 1972 ballot measure prohibiting any race-based student
assignments, the initiative failed to pass judicial review, or earn the support of
a broad based constituency. School desegregation in California was not halted
by the autonomous forces of racial conservatism alone.

Alan Robbins, by contrast, challenged school desegregation on much
different grounds. He declared himself a faithful champion of integration, but
argued that mandatory busing programs did more harm to this cause than
good. He carefully recruited several leading African American and Mexican
American public figures to support his initiative, exploiting their ambivalence
towards prevailing desegregation measures. At the same time, he used a
sophisticated direct mail operation to constantly remind white voters of the
racialized dangers which lurked outside of their neighborhood. In valorizing

"voluntary" as opposed to "forced" integration, he too figured segregation as natural and treated the right of white students to remain in segregated settings (if they choose to do so) as inalienable.

When the Reagan administration moved to roll back court-ordered school desegregation programs nationally in the 1980s, it was Alan Robbins, rather than Floyd Wakefield, who helped provide the blueprint. The administration relied on the Supreme Court's Proposition 1 ruling to argue that school districts should be relieved from desegregation orders even if racial imbalance still existed, provided it could be demonstrated that the school board or electorate did not intentionally discriminate ("End Busing, Justice Dept. Asks Court," *Los Angeles Times*, December 7 1984: B1). Indeed the assaults on affirmative action and other anti-discrimination policies in the 1990s were fueled by similar claims of racial innocence.

"Racial conservatism" and "racial liberalism" may have some heuristic utility as broad descriptors of policy preferences. But in examining the ways political discourses function in embedded settings—through specific practices and institutional arrangements—these categories can obscure more than they reveal. Alan Robbins and other foes of desegregation made their claims almost entirely in the logics of racial liberalism and anti-racism, claiming that opposition to busing represented a principled pro-civil rights position.

Theoretical frameworks which attempt to draw a bright line between racial conservatives and racial liberals—or implicitly, between racists and anti-racists—and assign responsibility for the endurance of racial inequality to the former, cannot account for the transformations witnessed in California during this time. If the norms of racial liberalism have proven so accommodating to political forces seeking to reproduce racial hierarchy, then frameworks which seek to isolate those "traditions" or "orders" which sustain racism and place them outside the boundaries of liberalism are of limited value. Instead, we must ask why liberalism itself—as an active, evolving and embedded discursive formation —might reproduce such hierarchies through its own terms, logics, and conditions.

Notes

1 This construct of racial liberalism versus racial conservatism operates across multiple disciplines, including historical sociology (Rieder 1987), history (Hirsch 1995; Durr 2003) and much of the work on race and public opinion (Kinder and Sanders 1996). I take Gary Gerstle's (2002) formulation of "civic nationalism" versus "racial nationalism" and Smith and King's (2005) notions of competing racial orders as derived from the same conceptual assumptions.

2 This approach is influenced heavily by work in cultural studies and American Studies including Hall (1988), Singh (1998), Lipsitz (2001) and Duggan (2003).

3 Campaign filing reports suggest the campaign never purchased any television advertising time.

4 Florida voters also adopted by a greater percentage—79 percent—a resolution to guarantee "quality education" and "equal opportunity" for all children and prohibit a return to dual-school systems ("Retreat from Integration," 1972). The

Nixon and Congressional measures were largely symbolic as they did not delay the implementation of any local desegregation actions.

5 See among many examples: "Parents Meet to Work for, against Busing," *Los Angeles Times*, August 21, 1980: WS1, 9.

6 In *Swann*, the U.S. Supreme Court upheld a district-wide busing plan that was enacted primarily in response to racially segregated housing patterns rather than explicit race-based assignments, in order to achieve compliance with the *Brown* I mandate (Lassiter 2005).

7 A 1970 UCLA poll found that 75 percent of Los Angeles County residents favored desegregation, yet 69 percent opposed busing to achieve this goal (Wollenberg 1976).

8 This shift in strategies used to discredit school segregation was occurring in other cities as well. See, for example, Lassiter (2005).

9 These cases were *Serrano v. Priest* (1971) (*Serrano I*); *Serrano v. Priest* (1976) (*Serrano II*); *Serrano v. Priest* (1977) (*Serrano III*).

10 For a discussion of the "conflicting avenues of redress" pursued by advocates of desegregation and bilingual education see Brilliant (2003). The federal Bilingual Education Act, which established a legislative mandate and funding for these programs, was passed in 1968 and amended in 1974 (Crawford 2000).

11 On the failures of anti-busing groups in Orange County, see Frye (1981).

12 On Butcher-Forde and the rise of the initiative industry in the late 1970s see Schrag (1998) and Magelby (1984).

13 Butcher Forde collected at least $100,000 in fees from Californians Against Forced Busing, and was permitted to keep the names of and addresses of all donors as well as all of the materials they created ("Agreement between Bucher Forde Consulting and Californians Against Forced Busing").

14 1,104 cases, representative cross-section of California voters.

15 A group of progressive, predominantly white educators in Los Angeles called the Integration Project did set out to build the case among white voters in particular that a fully integrated school district, bolstered by reductions in class size, building improvements, and adequate training could provide quality education for all students ("An Integration Plan").

Bibliography

Primary sources

Cases cited

Brown v. Board of Education (1954) 347 U.S. 483.

Crawford v. Los Angeles Board of Education (1976) 17 Cal.3d 280.

Crawford v. Los Angeles Board of Education (1981) 113 Cal. App. 3d 633, 170 Cal. Rptr. 495.

Crawford v. Los Angeles Board of Education (1982) 458 U.S. 527.

Jackson v. Pasadena School District (1963) 59 Cal. 2nd 876.

Mendez v. Westminster School Dist. of Orange County, 64 F.Supp. 544 (D.C.Cal. 1946).

Santa Barbara School District v. Superior Court (1975) 13 Cal. 3d 315, 530 P.2d 605.

Serrano v. Priest (1971) 5 Cal.3d 584 (*Serrano I*).

Serrano v. Priest (1976) 18 Cal.3d 728 (*Serrano II*).

Serrano v. Priest (1977) 20 Cal.3d 25 (*Serrano III*).
Swann v. Charlotte-Mecklenburg Board of Education (1971) 402 U.S. 1.

Archives

"A Summary of the Position and Policy statement of the Chicano Subcommittee of the Citizens' Advisory Committee on Student Integration" (1978) in Folder 10, Box 5, Dorothy Doyle Collection, Southern California Library for Social Studies and Research.

"Agreement between Bucher Forde Consulting and Californians Against Forced Busing" (n.d.) in Folder: "Californians Against Forced Busing," Box 6, Series 1, Alan Robbins Collection, California State University, Northridge.

"Alex Garcia letter" (30 November 1977) in Folder "Busing," Series 1, Box 2, Alan Robbins Collection, California State University, Northridge.

"An Integration Plan" (1977) in Folder 3, Box 5, Dorothy Doyle Collection, Southern California Library for Social Studies and Research.

"Anti-Busing List Order" (1977) in Folder: "Support SCA 46, 1977," Box 3, Series 1, Alan Robbins Papers, California State University, Northridge.

"Bobbi Fiedler fundraising letter" (1977) in Folder 17, Box 1, Dorothy Doyle Collection, Southern California Library for Social Studies and Research.

"Campaign filing statement" (1972) in Folder "1972, Proposition 21" from California State Archives, Sacramento.

"Dear Fellow Californian letter and storyboard" (October 26, 1972) in Folder "Proposition 21 (1972)," Campaign Literature Collection, UCLA.

"Dear Opponent of Forced Busing letter by Alan Robbins" (n.d.) in Folder 9, Box 38, NAACP Papers, Bancroft Library, University of California, Berkeley.

"Press release" (January 4, 1978) in Folder "Busing Press Releases," Box 2, Series 1, Alan Robbins Papers, California State University, Northridge.

"Statement by Peter Roos in opposition to SCA 48" (January 19, 1978) in Folder "Committee Testimony," Box 5, Series 1, Alan Robbins Papers, California State University, Northridge.

"Testimony before the assembly judiciary committee in opposition to anti-integration measures" (March 14, 1979) in Folder 49, Box 37, NAACP Papers, Bancroft Library, University of California, Berkeley.

Other primary sources

Interview with Bobbi Fiedler (1988) conducted by Richard McMillian, transcribed by Farah Ortega, 17 November, Department of History and Urban Archives Library, California State University, Northridge.

References and secondary sources

Avila, E. (2004) *Popular Culture in the Age of White Flight: Fear and Fantasy in Suburban Los Angeles*, Berkeley: University of California Press.

Brilliant, M. (2003) "Color Lines: Civil Rights Struggles on America's Racial Frontier, 1945–75," unpublished thesis, Stanford University.

California Secretary of State (1972) "Ballot Pamphlet for 1972 General Election."

—— (1979) "Ballot Arguments for Proposition 1."

Caughey, J., and Caughey, L. (1966) *School Segregation on Our Doorstep: The Los Angeles Story*, Los Angeles, CA: Quail Books.

—— (1973) *To Kill a Child's Spirit: The Tragedy of School Segregation in Los Angeles*, Itsca: F.E. Peacock.

Cohen, L. (2003) *A Consumer's Republic: The Politics of Mass Consumption in Postwar America*, New York: Vintage.

Crawford, J. (2000) *At War With Diversity: U.S. Language Policy in an Age of Anxiety*, Tonawada: Multilingual Matters.

Duggan, L. (2003) *The Twilight of Equality? Neoliberalism, Cultural Politics and the Attack on Democracy*, Boston, MA: Beacon Press.

Durr, K. (2003) *Behind the Backlash: White Working-Class Politics in Baltimore, 1940–1980*, Chapel Hill, NC: UNC Press.

Ettinger, D. (2003) "The Quest to Desegregate Los Angeles Schools," *Los Angeles Lawyer*, March: 55–67.

Frye, B.E. (1981) "Quarrels with the Courts: A Comparative Study on Three Anti-Busing Community Groups Formed in Response to Mandatory Busing," unpublished MA thesis, School of Education, University of Southern California, Los Angeles.

Gerstle, G. (2002) *American Crucible: Race and Nation in the Twentieth Century*, Princeton, NJ: Princeton University Press.

Hall, S. (1988) *The Hard Road to Renewal: Thatcherism and the Crisis of the Left*, London: Verso.

Haro, C.M. (1977) *Mexicano/Chicano Concerns and School Desegregation in Los Angeles*, Los Angeles, CA: Chicano Studies Center Publications, UCLA.

Hendrick, I. (1977) *The Education of Non-Whites in California, 1849–1970*, San Francisco, CA: R&E Research Associates.

Hirsch, A. (1995) "Massive Resistance in the Urban North: Trumball Park, Chicago, 1953–1966," *Journal of American History*, 85:522–50.

Kinder, D.R. and Sanders, L. (1996) *Divided By Color*, Chicago: University of Chicago Press.

King, D. and Smith, R. (2005) "Racial Orders in American Political Development," *American Political Science Review*, 99:75–92.

Kruse, K. (2005) *White Flight: Atlanta and the Making of Modern Conservatism*, Princeton, NJ: Princeton University Press.

Landis, J.T. (1984) "The Crawford Desegregation Suit in Los Angeles 1977–1981," unpublished thesis, Education, UCLA.

Lassiter, M. (2005) *The Silent Majority: Suburban Politics in the Sunbelt South*, Princeton, NJ: Princeton University Press.

Lipsitz, G. (2001) *American Studies in a Moment of Danger*, Minneapolis: University of Minnesota Press.

Lopez, I.H. (2003) *Racism on Trial: The Chicano Fight for Justice*, Cambridge, MA: Belknap Press.

Magelby, D. (1984) *Direct Legislation: Voting on Ballot Propositions in the United States*, Baltimore, MD: Johns Hopkins Press.

Nicolaides, B.M. (2002) *My Blue Heaven: Life and Politics in the Working-Class Suburbs of Los Angeles, 1920–1965*, Chicago: University of Chicago Press.

Rieder, J. (1987) *Canarsie: The Jews and Italians of Brooklyn Against Liberalism*, Cambridge, MA: Harvard University Press.

Robbins, A. (1977) "Guest Editorial," *Los Angeles Times*, October 28: 14.

Sanchez, G. (1993) *Becoming Mexican American: Ethnicity, Culture and Identity in Chicano Los Angeles, 1900–1945*, London: Oxford University Press.

Schrag, P. (1998) *Paradise Lost: California's Experience, America's Future*, New York: New Press.

Self, R.O. (2003) *American Babylon: Race and the Struggle for Postwar Oakland*, Princeton, NJ: Princeton University Press.

Singh, N. (1998) "Culture/Wars: Recoding Empire in an Age of Democracy," *American Quarterly*, 50: 471–522.

Wollenberg, C. (1976) *All Deliberate Speed: Segregation and Exclusion in California Schools, 1855–1975*, Berkeley: University of California Press.

13 Reconciling fractures: the intersection of race and religion in United States political development

Nancy D. Wadsworth

Wherever race appears in American political history, religion is never far away. The history of religion in the United States is very much a story about race, and the corollary is also true: race in American political development has been centrally, not peripherally, related to religion. As in other frontier outposts of liberal capitalist expansionism, American categories of race and religion were constructed in relationship to one another—indeed, have fundamentally co-constituted each other. Together they have shaped the politics of labor, nation building, organizing, and citizenship (Fredrickson 2002). Also as belief systems, sources of identity, power structures, and bases for community, religion and race have overlapped and often been deeply enmeshed.

The rise of new cross-racial political alliances in recent years should motivate scholars to understand more about the relationship between race and religion in the U.S. For example, citizens have drawn from shared theological perspectives to build conservative-leaning, multiracial coalitions around marriage, family policy, Faith-Based Initiatives, and school vouchers (Wadsworth 2007). Such coalitions have influenced local, state, and national legislation, but they also stand to influence the membership and agendas of political parties, as well as policy agendas in the longer term. Most interestingly, they create new community identities and political discourses that transgress boundaries that used to divide these groups deeply. Religion-based, cross-racial alliances, particularly on the political right, are rare in American history. I will argue that these emergent coalitions reflect a significant political development that only makes sense when examined through the confluence of racial and religious history.

If scholars in the subfield of American political development (APD) are to comprehend the long-term influence of race on U.S. politics and political institutions, we cannot afford to relegate religion to the margins or, worse, leave it out of our inquiries. To do so is to misread the histories of *both* race and religion, as well as other important dimensions of power and identity (gender, class, sexuality, region, etc.) that often intersect with the two. While political scientists have contributed to both fields, largely separately, we have only recently begun to take their intersection seriously (Harris 1999; Ownby 2002; Williams 2003; Wilson 2005).

My use of the term intersectionality refers to three dimensions of intimate crossover between race and religion. First, as I elaborate, the *foundational* categories of race and religion in the U.S. context were forged in relation to one another. The racial stratification that prevailed here was supported by religion, as a system that gave race meaning, as an institutional structure that implemented it, and through people who believed in or resisted the racial system. So, second, race and religion intersect *sociologically*, as represented by the complex demographic history of American religious traditions that have been distinctly racialized. The denominational and sociological configurations of American religion developed *through* racial divisions, not despite them. American faith communities have in this sense perpetually been fractured by race—often through people's racial identifications, but also through their orientation to racial politics (so that, for example, abolitionism could unify white and black Baptists where race might have otherwise divided them). Thus, third, as with other categories like gender and class, race and religion function intersectionally at the level of *personal identity*, which puts people into different relationships to power at different moments. Sometimes religious identity reinforces racial difference; sometimes, as in the case of new multiracial alliances, it overcomes it, but for many Americans these aspects of identity are deeply intertwined.

In this chapter I identify limitations in two APD methodological frameworks for understanding the race–religion nexus, and propose a unified theoretical apparatus that allows us to recognize and interpret political developments at the intersection of religion and race. To illustrate the need for an intersectional framework, I first identify the sorts of gaps produced by studying race and religion through mostly segregated literatures in political science. I then suggest that Karen Orren and Stephen Skowronek's (2004) approach in *The Search for American Political Development* is insufficient for understanding race–religion intersections in APD, both because it emphasizes political institutions at the expense of cultural mechanisms, and because it tends to focus on one category (religion or race) while minimizing the *simultaneous influence* of the other. Desmond King and Rogers Smith's racial orders framework in APD (chapter 4 of this book) also acknowledges the influence of religious ideologies, identities, and institutions on American racial dynamics. However, this approach offers little insight into how religion functions as a powerful meaning-making system within—and indeed, how religion operates to drive—racial orders. Nor can it explain how or why religious groups align with particular racial orders and how cultural or political mechanisms inspire realignments of religious actors across racial orders over time. Thus, existing APD frameworks capture some aspects of race *or* religion across American history, but cannot explain developments like the rise of new cross-racial religious alliances in American politics.

To remedy these problems, I open by combining elements of King and Smith's framework with a slightly modified version of historian Paul Harvey's (2005) categorization of the three major racial traditions in American

Protestantism. This allows me to construct an intersectional model that captures what I call *religious racial orders*. I employ this framework to review broadly how profoundly related the two categories have been over the course of American political history, particularly within mainstream evangelical Protestantism.[1]

I then employ the religious racial orders framework to interpret efforts by conservative evangelical Christians at the turn of this century to face their racial history, address racial problems in their churches and religious institutions, and build a multiracial church movement—shifts which helped to create the conditions for the rise of strategic, cross-racial political alliances. I read this case of new evangelical racial initiatives as a political development that was not generated by and may never manifest through governing institutions *per se* since cultural mechanisms have primarily driven and articulated it. Yet this shift reflects important changes in American racial history and religious institutional development that influence American politics on the ground through new religiously based strategic alliances and political demands. This case reveals how APD scholarship might better recognize the complex relationship among religious traditions, racial projects, and political orders, and also promotes rethinking the lines we draw between political institutions and culture in our attempts to understand American political development.

Forgetting the crossroads

Though both race and religion in American politics have fascinated political scientists, we tend to overlook the many points of intercrossing between them. The literature in the discipline on racial power and structures of resistance has contributed to our understanding of American politics. But most studies tend toward one of three oversights when it comes to religion: they either ignore it, acknowledge it as part of the background but miss its political relevance, or examine religion through the functioning of organizational resources (e.g. church networks, leadership structures) while minimizing its significance as a belief system, set of practices, and power formations—all of which enable religion to found political ideology, activism, and institutional development.[2] Even groundbreaking studies of the modern civil rights movement sometimes missed the heart of religious activism by examining only the "bones" of structural resources and not taking religious ideas particularly seriously (McAdam 1982; Morris 1984).[3] Other disciplines that focus more on culture, as well as interdisciplines like American and religious studies, have performed better on these counts. I am not suggesting that *all* studies of race politics in the U.S. need to incorporate religion, or vice versa. However, particularly in APD, which considers historical factors and cultural influences on racial politics and identities, the risk is that by siphoning religion out of the picture, we allow a complicating—and politically pertinent—factor to disappear from view.

Political science scholarship on religion mirrors the intersectional gap in studies of race politics. Curiously, we "see" race in some studies of religious politics and overlook it in others. The small, growing literature on the religious views of racial minorities engages race, as race is central to its subject (Harris 1999; Ownby 2002; Yi 2002). But the flood of scholarship tracking the rise and ongoing influence of the modern religious right, for example, has barely examined race (scholars often eschew racial analysis in considering movements where whites, the racially unmarked category, are the main players).[4] The field is ripe for studies exploring the influence of white collective identity on the relationship between the religious right's emergence and the larger civil rights movement backlash in American conservatism. Scholars tracking American religious politics must also attend to theological and historical dimensions of the religiously based social conservatism of many Americans of color, which, as we will see, provides grounds for powerful new collective identities and cross-racial political alliances.[5]

Part of the challenge to building a more intersectional political science (and this applies to other intersections) is that much of the discipline still proceeds as if the realms of politics *per se* (e.g., voting, organizing, and exercising institutional power) and culture (where religion has been assumed to belong) can be neatly disentangled for analysis. Too, if some of us secular academics have hoped that religion could be safely restricted to the non-political realm, we may be disturbed to recognize the very blurred national separation of church and state (Segers and Jelen 1998; Gordon 2002; Mazur 2004) and the even muddier boundary between religion and politics as practices (Kramnick and Moore 1997; Smith 1998; Morone 2003). But the recent national elections, in which religious values informed many individual votes if not electoral outcomes (Green 2004), as well as policymaking that often explicitly invokes religious values, from Faith-Based Initiatives to American foreign policy decisions, are instructive: *religion matters* at least as much as race in the American context (West 1993; West and Glaude 2003). The intersectional challenge is equally pronounced in the APD subfield, where scholars analyzing major shifts in political orders have largely privileged one category (e.g., economics, labor, the state, and only more recently race) over others, tending to shunt aside "softer" cultural categories like religion.[6] Generally indexes in studies of both race and religion in APD reflect a lack of intersectional thinking, as race studies often have few references to religion in their indexes and vice versa.

We seem to be looking at one category or the other, when they are more often than not intertwined. When examining race in American politics, scholars of politics must remember that racial categories themselves have been historically constituted and enacted through religious beliefs and practices; that racial injustice—but also resistance to it—has frequently been articulated through religion; and that religious values and institutions inform racial politics across multiple dimensions.

Race–religion intersectionality in APD

Orren and Skowronek's *The Search for American Political Development* challenges APD scholars to develop methods that capture the dynamic relationships
among cultural patterns, historical circumstances, political strategies, and
institutions over time (2004: 4). In their view, the subfield of APD investigates
how *political orders*, defined as "durable shifts in governing authority," are
"designated and enforced through institutions" (123–4). Institutions embody
"built-in-mandates for controlling behavior at large and through time" (17–8).
APD scholarship ideally traces long-term shifts in power among and across
major political institutions, from, say, state bureaucracy to the courts to the
presidency, thereby capturing the relationship between multiple institutional
orders, which sometimes overlap or conflict under shifting political conditions.
Their definition centers institutions (though, they claim, not exclusively)
because relations of authority in government can be empirically tracked.[7]

Institutionally oriented APD studies have invaluably contributed to our
understanding of major political shifts in American history (Skowronek 1982;
Skocpol et al. 1985; Hattam 1993; Bensel 2000; Novkov 2001; Sterett 2003;
Skowronek et al. 2006). And with respect to the topic of this study, the modern
religious right's influence, institutions are relevant. Religious activists engage
politically through courts, political parties, other interest groups, presidents,
states, and legislatures. If, as scholars have noted, the rise of the New Right has
contributed to a shift in political orders since the 1960s (Himmelstein 1990;
Edsall and Edsall 1992; Winant 2004), and conservative evangelicals have
particularly influenced that ascendance through grassroots mobilization and
changes in party alignments, then we should attend to new racial projects
within conservative evangelicalism that reflect institutional changes.

We cannot separate institutions from the development of racial politics
in American history. However, a predominantly institutional focus is problematic for examining traditions of race relations *within* American religion,
as well as religious relations among American racial communities. Because
race and religion often play out in cultural arenas first, as they weave into
political spaces,[8] their interwoven relationship is only partially and incompletely
institutionalized, and their direct influence on formally political institutions can
be difficult to trace. Institutions within communities (e.g. denominational
organizations) also influence larger political institutions like parties, and vice
versa (Ammerman 1990). Race and religion may directly affect the former,
and indirectly affect the latter. Focusing primarily on the formal institutional
shifts toward which conventional APD points cannot always capture changes
created within religious racial traditions that may culminate in new racial and
religious discourses and new political developments. Tracking changes in
"cultural patterns," then, is at least as important, if not more so, than strictly
institutional analysis.

Orren and Skowronek use church–state relations as a site to illustrate their
approach. They read church–state relations as a story of the competition and

sometimes cooperation among the three political orders they identify: religion, free exercise, and political parties (143–55). According to their model, for the first century of U.S. history, the order of religion (comprised of houses of worship, denominations, interdenominational bodies, and voluntary movements) dominated much public sphere activity, exercising significant control even over nonmembers through its vast networks and influence.[9] This order was periodically checked by the free exercise order, which attempted to use governmental institutions to protect citizens *from* state-sanctioned religion, employing constitutional provisions and statutes regulating religion's political reach, while still partially sanctioning the notion of the United States as a (Protestant) religious country. The political party order was an interest-based, disciplined mechanism outside of government that selected leaders to represent local interests. Political parties functioned historically as an "in between" order, working "to connect . . . religious citizens and groups, to the institutions of government" but also serving as a buffer or filter between religious citizens and the state (144). For about 150 years, the free exercise and party orders existed in intercurrence; despite periodic clashes between religious and party interests, the two did not fundamentally threaten each other.

In the 1960s, however, the Supreme Court broke ranks with Congress and exerted authority over matters relating to religion, empowering the free exercise order. New independence replaced the institutional convergence between Congress and the Court in the realm of church–state relations, triggering a shift in orders (151). The political development question became whether the Court could maintain its dominance in the face of resistance from religious interests. Orren and Skowronek argue that the political party order responded along partisan lines to the Court's favoring of the free exercise order over religion, with Democrats clustering in the free exercise camp. This channeled the backlash energy of religious conservatives, especially Southerners, by the late 1970s, and the parties thus went from being "the shock absorbers for America's religious crusades" to institutions that take sides in the religious liberal-versus-conservative debate (153). Republicans and their religious allies' continued ability to challenge the free exercise order in church–state relations will depend, the authors maintain, on whether they can successfully confront the Court and other institutions on issues like abortion and homosexuality (154).

Orren and Skowronek's interpretation recognizes that religion has long functioned institutionally in the U.S. and that it has galvanized important political movements in the nation's history. The analysis, however, only superficially addresses the impact of race on this religious history.[10] Yet given that the political party order often reflected the order of religion—before, during, and even after the Civil War, and differently across region—why isn't the political development story of church–state relations simultaneously a story about race? The analytical construct the "order of religion" obfuscates the massive conflicts—many of which have concerned race—that have developed *within* this order. If but *one* order of religion has existed (which is debatable), it has never been a cohesive entity. Instead, it has been a contested, heterogeneous phenomenon encompassing a wide variety of often hostile traditions. A non-comprehensive list of the traditions relevant to race relations inside the world of Protestant evangelicals would include: the missionary tradition; the Great Awakenings; religious paternalism; mainline churches; white evangelical denominationalism; pre- and post-millennialism; African-American (and now other racial and ethnic) denominationalism; charismatic movements; revivalism; religious protest movements; and traditions of moral orthodoxy, such as Puritanism. Orren and Skowronek overlook how these various traditions achieved *different* relationships to political power and institutional authority at different moments in time through and beyond the order of parties, and miss how race often galvanized or divided them.

Attempting to capture such a dynamic and interactive set of forces under the notion of one religious order limits scholars' ability to see the deep dialogue between race and religion, a dialogue *simultaneously*, not separately, relevant to battles around power in American history. If we conceive of church–state relations without acknowledging the existence of competing religious orders, we risk both erasing the existence and influence of the religious traditions of people of color and overlooking the political significance of white supremacy in American religious political history. We also allow a false perception that by the late twentieth century, religion was primarily channeling debates about religious expression and morality—not particularly about race—into the political sphere.

Over a 300-year period, the American religious landscape has been anything but race-free. Rather, American religion has involved multiple racial projects simultaneously: white supremacy first and foremost, but also racial liberation, egalitarianism, and all the diverse expressions of denial, resistance, agitation, and forestalling in between.

Religious racial traditions in the United States

An intersectional approach centers what I call *religious racial traditions*. A religious racial tradition is a collection of beliefs, narratives, practices, and strategies applied to racial issues in American political culture by religious actors, groups, and institutions. Through religious racial traditions people employ a theological perspective as a lens through which they interpret and respond to some aspect of race relations. Even citizens who are not especially religious may be deeply informed by a religious racial tradition, as it becomes an inherited, taken-for-granted set of ideas and practices influencing their daily lives. The hybrid theoretical framework I propose to analyze how religious racial orders have influenced American political development draws from approaches to both racial and religious traditions in the U.S.

Rogers Smith and Desmond King's racial orders framework explores the critical function of race in American political development (see chapter 4 of this book). The Smith-King thesis counters Hartz in claiming that racial injustices were not merely anomalies in American history; rather, "the nation has been pervasively constituted by systems of racial hierarchy since its inception" (chapter 4, this book; c.f., Hartz 1955; Smith 1993). They identify two main racial institutional orders that have battled for dominance across U.S. history: (1) the "white supremacist" order and its more covert (less blatantly racist) modern variants, and (2) the "transformative egalitarian" order, which has sought through various and often-conflicted methods to create political equality across race. The racial orders framework thus links governing institutions to social movements (chapter 4).

Smith and King explicitly acknowledge that religious ideas, actors, movements, and institutions are often part of the coalitions that make up both racial orders (chapter 4). However, they barely elaborate how, where, or why religion gets involved in racial politics. Religious actors, institutions, or resources thus appear to be simply harnessed as coalition members to one of the two orders— as if the fundamental mechanisms that power the orders derive from some other (non-religious) source. This minimal engagement with religious forces misses their fundamental relevance, not just in terms of religious forces' institutional complicity with a racial order, but also with regard to their function in *constructing* the meaning systems, cultural environments, and actions that make racism, or resistance to it, meaningful.

Religious historian Paul Harvey's work in *Freedom's Coming* (2005) is worth incorporating into any APD framework that seeks to recognize the complex relationship between race and religion. Drawing on both the cultural dimensions of Southern mainstream and evangelical Protestantism and the political dynamics with which it has perpetually been entangled, Harvey identifies three major traditions defining the crossover between race and religion in the South. I modify these slightly to capture religious racial traditions that I suggest are applicable as ideal types more broadly to the nation.

Harvey's terms are "theological racism," "racial interchange," and "Christian interracialism." In the primarily black/white context of the American South, theological racism describes

> the conscious use of religious doctrine and practice to create and enforce social hierarchies that privileged southerners of European descent, who were legally classified and socially privileged as white, while degrading southerners of African descent, who were legally categorized and stigmatized as black.
>
> (2)

Applied more broadly, theological racism is essentially the American Protestant expression of Smith and King's white supremacist order: religion harnessed in service to racial hierarchy.

Harvey's "racial interchange" tradition refers to "the exchange of southern religious cultures between white and black believers in expressive culture, seen especially in music, in the formation of new religious traditions, and in lived experience" (3). In other words, sometimes religious folks spend time together in religious cultural settings, influencing each other's worship styles, theology, and practices. Through such exchanges, the culturally imposed boundaries between the races sometimes soften, though usually only temporarily, but these moments of crossover can generate new conversations about race (and religion) as time passes.

Finally, Harvey's third intersectional concept, "Christian interracialism," or what I will call the *religious racial justice tradition*, describes how Christians, white and of color, exert "self-consciously political efforts to undermine the system of southern [or, as we'll read it, national] racial hierarchy" (3). The religious racial justice tradition corresponds with Smith and King's trans-formative egalitarian order. Religious actors in this tradition employ theology and material resources to fight some aspect(s) of racist policy. However, as with transformative egalitarian efforts, these actors are not necessarily ideologically anti-racist; sometimes they fight policies (say, slavery or Indian removal) without challenging, or even while endorsing, the racial attitudes supporting them (76). Figure 13.1 illustrates how Smith and King's racial orders frame-work maps onto Harvey's religious traditions schema.

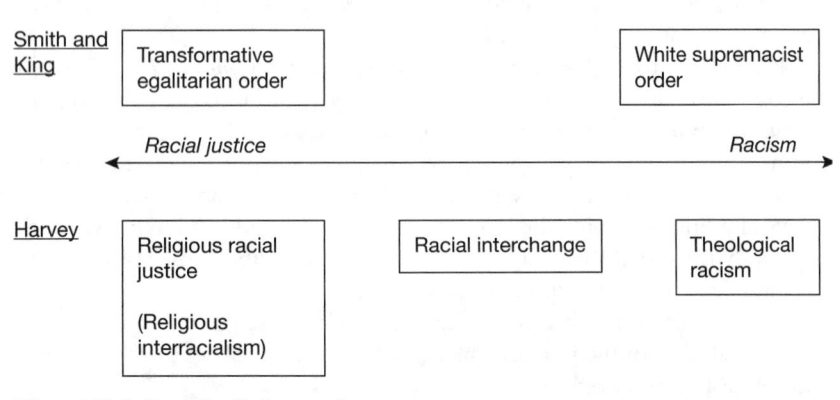

Figure 13.1 Racial-religious orders

I will now sketch how combining these factors through the *religious racial traditions* framework can paint a more appropriately complex portrait of religious and racial political history in the U.S. I then suggest how this inter-weaving of religion in American racial orders enables a better analysis of the recent rise of new cross-racial religious alliances.

Religious racial traditions

Theological racism

On the most damaging end of the racial spectrum, *theological racism* expresses the "deep-rooted, interlocking system of power" of white supremacy through religious traditions (Harvey 2005: 2). Using theological interpretation, imagined community, everyday speech, folklore, tracts, church services, and so forth, whites—not just Southerners and not just Christians—blended various aspects of religion with the often unstable and constantly revised white supremacist project (c.f., Schweiger and Matthews 2004; Dailey 2004).

Most fundamentally, through theological racism, the religious order in part actively constructed the racial categories that allowed white supremacy to function. Fueling racist beliefs before science emerged as a dominant rationale, religious views enabled Europeans to justify their hierarchic relationship over the "dark" and therefore "sinful" others they encountered (Fredrickson 2002). With its binary associations of sin/salvation, flesh/spirit, soiled/pure, and black/white, Christianity's dichotomous symbology mapped onto skin color and religious difference to justify the early oppression, and later extermination, of Jews in what Fredrickson identifies as the earliest expressions of racism in the West.[11] This new framework of inferiority-through-immutability extended easily to justify the persecution of other groups subjected to European expansion.

In the U.S. colonial era, whites consistently conflated Christianity with civilization and Anglo-Saxon identity in the project of nation-building. The combination of race and religion fundamentally, not incidentally, constructed the meaningful concepts of whiteness and savagism and the policies executed through them (Jordan 1974; Pearce 1967). Puritan teleology in the colonies justified universal land reform, representative government, rights of conscience, and notions of civic virtue, all perceived as necessary for whites to fulfill scriptural commandments (Pearce 1967: 128). Racialized national identity, anchored in a particular religious worldview with Manifest Destiny at its heart, led to the associated justifications for the slave trade, black servitude, the formal, codified political exclusion of nonwhites, and of course Indian genocide and removal (Horsman 1981; Tinker 1993; Morone 2003). Despite debates over and eventual elimination of religious qualification laws, American citizenship (indeed, Americanness) became firmly paired with whiteness and Christianity —though Jews and selective other ethnics could eventually be annexed as white (DuBois 1903; King 1963; Roediger 1991; Jacobsen 1998; Smith and Emerson 2000). Through religious paternalism designed to "save" those deemed as existing on the lower rungs of a Divinely ordained order (the so-called "sill class"), whites virtually extinguished African Muslim as well as Native American tribal religious traditions by forcefully imposing Christianity (Boles 1988; Marty 1990; Tinker 1993).

Even across two Great Awakenings in the nineteenth century, which transformed the power structures of Protestant Christianity and created more egalitarian religious practices, theological racism justified slavery and other forms of racial persecution and violence through the "Curse of Ham" and other mythologies (Goldenberg 2005). American Jews also found religious justification for white supremacist structures (Rosen 2000). The Jacksonian and subsequent administrations enlisted churches to execute state-sanctioned missionary projects designed to pacify and control Indians (Deloria and Cadwalader 1984; Tinker 1993). In the run up to the Civil War, all the largest

Protestant denominations—Baptists, Methodists, and Pentecostals—fractured over slavery and/or its extension into the Western frontier, with theological arguments wielded by both sides (Boles 1988; MacRobert 1988; Lincoln 1999; Morone 2003). The Southern Baptist Convention emerged specifically to defend southern slave culture. Theological racism buttressed the southern "Lost Cause" after the war, supported segregation, and fortified racially separatist denominations (Ammerman 1990). It also helped to defend colonization schemes, political inequality for non-whites, and nativism in the north.

Theological racism persisted in the twentieth century, supporting nativist and anti-immigrant policies, voting rights restrictions, religious and racial discriminations against Indian tribes, and ongoing denominational segregation. It lived on through Klan-sponsored violence in the South, the tacit (and sometimes overt) support of white churches for Jim Crow, and many Christians' general inaction on issues of racial equality. It continues presently through extremist movements like Christian Identity as well as more mainstream theological perspectives that deny or justify the existence of racial hierarchies (Barkun 1994).

Religious racial justice

The religion-based movements that resisted theological racism and fought white supremacy were pivotal in Smith and King's transformative egalitarian order.

The religious racial justice tradition included the tiny minority of American colonial Protestants who challenged the dominant white supremacist theology and Quakers who drew on scripture to offer counter-narratives to theological racism, though both groups were largely politically impotent with regard to racist policy (Pearce 1967). The segment of the black Christian community that survived, resisted, and directly challenged white supremacy critically influenced the cross-racial social justice movements of the eighteenth and nineteenth centuries and helped pave the way for the modern civil rights movement.[12] Early black reform organizations drew on biblically influenced "vocabularies of Exodus" that helped them envision and fight for freedom (Glaude 2000; Howard-Pitney 2005). After the denominational fractures of the late antebellum era, all-black denominations became a base upon which African Americans could build "a corporate identity and a political culture" and craft resistance strategies (Glaude 2000: 57). Facing a different set of circumstances, Native Americans also built traditions of political theology and revived indigenous religious practices to organize resistance to the federal government (Tinker 2004).

Scholars recognize the important function of religious activism in American abolitionist movements, but may know less about the role of evangelicals in the party politics that preceded the war. Divisions between radical and moderate evangelical abolitionists influenced the Second Party System of the 1830s and 1840s as well as the election of 1860 (Carwardine 1993: 132). The more orthodox wing of evangelicalism gave the abolition movement its ballast through the American Anti-Slavery Association and eventually the Liberty Party, while other evangelicals wedded to slavery and the Democratic party sneered. Grassroots white evangelicals in the north like Charles Finney supplied abolitionists with theological frameworks and revivalist impulses, though some evangelicals abandoned the cause when they saw it as interfering with their mission (Smith and Emerson 2000: 33). By the election of 1860, northern evangelicals were pushing three issues before the Republican Party—slavery, Catholicism, and political corruption—and influenced Republicans to define themselves as the party of Christian witness (Carwardine 1993: 302). Mainstream Christians repudiated radical abolitionists' methods and doctrine to advocate individualist rather than systemic adjustments; these moderates endorsed voluntary manumission of slaves by their masters and assisted settlement in West Africa through the American Colonization Society. These dynamics fit with Orren and Skowronek's notion of the political party order as the filter between the orders of religion and free exercise.

After the schisms of the Civil War and white northern evangelicals' short-lived support for Reconstruction, white evangelicals abandoned significant cross-racial social justice efforts until the social gospel era at the turn of the century (Luker 1991). In this era, mostly moderate mainline and liberal Protestants entered interracial grassroots movements seeking to provide a "better" racial environment in the wake of the upheavals caused by white backlash against black northern migration. Typically paternalist, the movement had fairly limited goals that, while sometimes productive, often echoed state interests in control and racial subordination (e.g., promoting the end of lynching; portraying blacks more positively; advocating better facilities for blacks but still in a segregated context).

The religious racial justice tradition did not regain significant steam until the civil rights movement. Although lack of space prohibits a full discussion of the role of religion in the movement, I would remind readers that in the context of the religious racial justice tradition, Martin Luther King, Jr.'s Southern Christian Leadership Council was not incidentally Christian; rather, it was fundamentally driven by a vision of racial justice that drew from the well of theological godfathers like Rauschenbusch and employed liberation theology more successfully than any other movement in American history. Johnny Williams (2003) demonstrates that "religion's historical/cultural legacy contributed to the development of an African-American protest tradition" through the civil rights movement much more deeply than scholars of the era have typically acknowledged (xix).

Placing these American religious communities comfortably alongside communities supporting theological racism under the "order of religion" in Orren and Skowronek's church–state relations framework seems inappropriate. Certainly the political parties channeled competing perspectives on race within religious communities. But how could traditions drawing on theological racism comfortably share power with traditions challenging it under one religious order?

Racial interchange

While most religious racial politics in the U.S. has revolved around the two poles just sketched, American religious traditions have also incorporated intermittent, somewhat rare periods of cross-racial exchange. These can and, in the context of new cross-racial religion-based alliances, do historically found reconsiderations of race relations inside and beyond religious communities, which can occur once the political conditions and attitudes that constricted these exchanges begin to shift.

Paul Harvey deftly traces how traditions of racial interchange have punctuated southern religious racial history in moments when religious cultural expression drew biracial audiences, despite the constantly circumscribed context of racial apartheid and terror (1997; 2005: chapter 3). Religious music, charismatic preachers, and revivals often brought blacks and whites into shared spaces they might not otherwise inhabit. Although racial interchange typically occurred in the "more private spaces of religious experience" rather than in institutional settings, these exchanges eventually informed public life and in some cases provided avenues to racial justice movements (2005: 110).

For the sake of space, I'll mention one development in the racial interchange tradition that illustrates new multiracial religious alliances: the racial story of the Pentecostal movement. Pentecostalism is an American-born charismatic worship tradition that emphasizes, among other things, "acts of the Holy Spirit" like speaking in tongues. It is currently one of the fastest-growing segments of Christianity in the world (Pew Forum on Religion and Public Life 2006). Pentacostalism matters for contemporary cross-racial religious coalitions because most Pentecostals are theologically traditionalist and, thus, conservative on moral issues like abortion and homosexuality (ibid., see "Social and Moral Issues" chart). Many voices advocating recently for traditional heterosexual marriage, such as John Ashcroft and black urban pastor Eugene Rivers, come from Pentecostal churches. Pentecostals are a potentially powerful constituency in the culture wars.

Pentecostalism arose from an unusual racial interchange moment, when members of the mainly white American Holiness movement and black Christians broke from mainstream evangelical sects in the late 1880s. For a short period in the early 1900s, they combined to form what was likely the first voluntarily multiracial religious movement in American Protestantism (MacRobert 1988). In 1906, William Joseph Seymour, a talented black preacher from the South who had been mentored in Texas by white Holiness leader Charles Parham, founded what would become the world-famous Azusa Street Mission in Los Angeles. Azusa attracted a radically class- and race-mixed congregation, built an international missionary expansion, and even trained white preachers under blacks. But theological racism cut short these huge advances in religious race relations. By 1911 Seymour's former mentor Parham was publicly vilifying his successful church, condemning racial integration, and, with other racist pastors, urging whites to start their own Pentecostal communities or take over black churches and vote blacks out—which they largely did (Synan 1961). Pentecostal organizations became almost entirely segregated by race, departing substantially from their early integrationist efforts. Early Pentecostalism's rise and fall exemplifies a moment of racial interchange that could not survive the pressures of racism in a segregationist religious climate.

Breaking new ground in race and religion

Racialized denominational splits within American Pentecostalism predominated for almost a century. But in 1994, in what came to be known as "The Memphis Miracle," white Pentecostal clergy met for three days with black Pentecostal clergy in an attempt to repair race relations. Many Pentecostal leaders expressed regret that white racism derailed a movement that might have served throughout the twentieth century as a model Christian multiracial community. Amidst prayers, footwashing ceremonies, and professions of repentance, whites actually dissolved their umbrella organization and, with their African-American brethren, created a new interracial group, the Pentecostal/Charismatic Churches of North America (Grady 1994).

The orders of Orren and Skowronek's church–state relations model cannot capture events like Pentecostalism's ascent as an interracial movement (that began, of all places, in the apartheid South). This phenomenon also falls between the categories of Smith and King's racial orders framework. Through the religious racial traditions framework, however, we can recognize the following: American Pentecostalism emerged from the racial interchange tradition, but was wrecked early on by theological racism. By the 1990s, however, the religious racial justice tradition had influenced white Pentecostal culture enough—albeit not through a governmental institution or legal mandate—for some whites to rethink their past and finally partner equally with people of color to try to create a racially reconciled movement.

Given the history of denominational segregation along racial lines, Pentecostalism's reversal on race is a significant cultural shift informed by political changes that may someday in turn influence political configurations. Such shifts cannot effectively register on the radar of APD approaches that focus primarily on *governing* (state) institutions as the locus of change, but they sometimes presage state institutional changes while themselves representing significant transformations in ideology, power structures, and historical patterns. They should therefore be considered political developments and analyzed as such.

White evangelicals face race

For the final portion of this chapter I will sketch the three major moments of change that have occurred through the new cross-racial initiatives within conservative evangelical Christian communities and consider how the religious racial traditions framework can help us to interpret them.

First, in the early 1990s white evangelicals began responding to calls that Christians of color had been making since the civil rights movement to address the ongoing racial divisions inside communities that otherwise shared many theological commitments (Smith and Emerson 2000: chapter 3; Gilbreath 2006). This encounter led to a wave of "racial reconciliation" discourse, which essentially addressed the wounds of evangelicals' racially fractured past through discussion, writing, rituals, and recognitions of racism at individual and group levels (Wadsworth, forthcoming). As with Pentecostalism's "Memphis Miracle," reconciliation also involved formal inquiries into and apologies for racism within white denominational and parachurch organizations, and bolstered attempts to integrate evangelical communities that had long been segregated. Mainstream evangelical magazines like *Christianity Today* made thousands of subscribers around the country aware of such efforts through frequent reports.

The deepening of racial reconciliation discourse sparked a second phenomenon. Leaders in evangelical ministry began building on the efforts of earlier pioneers like Seymour and urban reformer John Perkins to create intentionally multiracial and/or multicultural churches. Working against the historical reality that "eleven o'clock Sunday morning is the most segregated hour in America" (*Christian History and Biography* 1995), these ministries drew on a combination of theology (most often traditionalist), diversity training, hard work, and faith to build congregations that represent the diversity of their surrounding community or what they envision as a "racially integrated Body of Christ" (Yancey 2003; Christerson et al. 2005; Emerson 2006). Multiracial evangelical churches have sprung up in urban, suburban, and even rural communities (Anderson 2004). Despite the challenges they report in accommodating diverse cultural orientations, participants in the multiracial church movement believe they are changing the face of evangelical Christianity. A multicultural ministry speaking circuit now exists and a veritable cottage industry of books on how to build multiracial churches and organizations has proliferated in recent years.

Third, perhaps influenced by the above developments, theologically conservative evangelicals from different racial communities are working in strategic alliances to defend policy perspectives that demand relatively short-term commitments and (so far) do not require participants to switch political party preferences. For example, in 2004, Latino, African-American, and other Christians of color teamed up with white evangelical "family values" activists in a number of battles to "safeguard" the institution of heterosexual marriage against perceived encroachments by same-sex marriage advocates. Such cross-racial coalitions expanded the ranks and profile of anti-same-sex marriage proponents in Ohio, Massachusetts, New York, Colorado, and other states (Wadsworth, 2008). Evangelicals organized across racial lines have also combined resources to advocate for government-sponsored Faith-Based Initiatives, fatherhood programs, and Charitable Choice or other school voucher policies (Bartowski and Regis 2003). While many of these strategic alliances address

GOP-friendly conservative issues, evangelicals are also teaming up in more unexpected ways—for example, around environmental policies and the treatment of undocumented immigrants (Moyers n.d.).

Religion-based racial change efforts have produced important gains, such as acknowledging the legacy of the white supremacist tradition in evangelical history; beginning to address racism as a systemic, not just individual issue; and attempting to create more racially integrated organizations. Still, most participants admit that American evangelicalism is not yet a racially integrated or justice-oriented community (Gilbreath 2006). Meanwhile, as some old racial barriers begin to break down, openings for short-term political cooperation around areas of shared concern emerge. Without addressing the socio-economic issues and other policy areas that most concern citizens of color, these alliances will not necessarily lead these evangelical voters to abandon the Democratic Party. Nor will cross-racial alliances lead white conservative evangelicals to adopt a more liberal political ideology and sever their 30-year attachment to the GOP. However, as the racial dynamics within American evangelicalism begin to shift and short-term coalition building becomes more feasible, attachments to parties and platforms cannot so easily be taken for granted by power-holders, enabling broader changes.

How can scholars account for how such shifts within evangelical culture were able to occur when they did? What factors would encourage Christians of color to participate in reconciliation discourse and strategic cross-racial coalitions after having been thwarted by white theological racism for so long?

Again, an institutional perspective cannot explain these important shifts at the intersection of race and religion. Certainly civil rights era legislation undercut *de jure* forms of racial discrimination, and created attendant political and cultural changes that influenced the daily lives of evangelicals nationally, not just in the South. For the most part, however, the prevailing institutional political orders did not have jurisdiction over the *de facto* power structures in the churches, denominations, and other religious organizations such as missionary societies that perpetuated the cultural elements of Jim Crow. In fact, with courts charged with protecting private religious beliefs under the first amendment, the government was constitutionally hand-tied from mandating changes in this area. So the legal gains of the civil rights movement could not impose racial egalitarianism inside evangelicalism. Indeed, white evangelicals did not begin publicly addressing racial problems inside their own communities in the immediate aftermath of the civil rights movement, waiting *decades*, not just years, later.

Did the order of political parties shift in some way in the early 1990s to allow for or encourage religious conservatives to finally address race directly? I doubt it, given that the New Right rose in the early 1980s with the critical support of the religious conservatives, partly through the veiled racism of trickle-down economics, tax revolts, and welfare critiques (Sears and Citrin 1982; Edsall and Edsall 1992). Transformative egalitarianism is hardly what the GOP was embracing. I am somewhat sympathetic to Howard Winant's (2004: 16) argument that (what I term) theological racism helped to support the New Right's "white racial project" through subtextual white supremacist backlash disguised as "color-blind" acceptance of non-whites' political participation. Research on Southern Baptists in the post-civil rights movement partly supports this (Ammerman 1990; Newman 2001). Some white evangelicals also fit into the neoconservative white racial project, which, according to Winant, "seeks to provide white advantages through denial of racial difference" (57). This bolsters the finding of some observers of evangelical reconciliation efforts that, while participants of color generally seek acknowledgement of and even confrontation across racial difference, many whites still resist recognizing systemic power structures by leaning on more "color-blind" understandings of race (Smith and Emerson 2000: chapters 3–5; Stricker 2001).[13] At any rate, the right was not creating openings through GOP politics for whites to account for racism and their racist history in the 1990s. Indeed, racism workshops, formal apologies, forgiveness rituals, and racial integration efforts in evangelical communities ran *against* the grain of both New Right and neoconservative racial discourse at the time.[14]

I'll offer another illustrative example. The Southern Baptist Convention is a denomination that, drawing on theological racism, defined itself in explicitly racial terms in the mid-nineteenth century (Newman 2001). By the 1990s the SBC had transformed internally (some called it a takeover), allowing political conservatives, largely aligned with the GOP platform, to dominate the denomination (Ammerman 1990). The Convention's 1995 decision to apologize for slavery and other forms of racism to which it had contributed was not a result of any state institutional pressure or mandate, although changes brought about through political events like *Brown v. Board of Education* (1954) and the Civil Rights Acts of the 1960s certainly influenced that decision over time. Nor did that apology or the discussions surrounding it create any identifiable institutional change outside the denomination's own structural apparatus. We could not, in other words, explain how the apology came about or how it could shift American politics more broadly through institutional analysis. Instead, we must examine, as Mark Newman (2001) has, the cultural dimensions through which it became possible and through which a shift in racial discourse will or will not become integrated in Southern Baptist culture, and over the long term perhaps influence southern political culture. Likewise, any exploration of the new conservative evangelical race discourse through an APD framework must address cultural developments that subtly inform institutional shifts.

The broader point is that we cannot account for new racial initiatives in evangelicalism without incorporating some understanding of evangelical culture and history. None of the three branches of American government created new evangelical race initiatives (although religious conservatives' increased influence in all three since the 1980s is certainly relevant to the surge of new strategic cross-racial alliances). Nor did a major shift in the political party apparatus occur, wherein the parties suddenly began addressing race differently than they had since the civil rights movement. The relationship between the religious and free exercise orders did not transform so fundamentally in the 1990s as to instigate a cascade of progressive race-related developments in conservative American evangelical communities. Although both parties were taking religion more seriously by that decade, given the influence of conservative evangelicals in American politics, nothing had fundamentally shifted vis-à-vis the parties' ideological platforms on race or their coalition members. Moreover, most Americans of color (evangelical or not) still remained putatively wedded to the Democratic Party (Frymer 1999), while the Republican Party continued to be predominantly white.

Still, something important had shifted in the history of evangelical race relations. And the change was not just a subterranean cultural adjustment; it was a reversal of three hundred years of history, bearing the potential to challenge the power structures, denominational arrangements, grassroots environment, and even perhaps the political agendas of American evangelicalism. While recognizing that cross-racial initiatives in evangelical communities are still quite young and require a more comprehensive explanation, they can only be understood through a simultaneous recognition of both racial and religious developments. New evangelical racial initiatives are a byproduct of the confluence between American politics and culture. They emerge from interwoven influences, primarily the civil rights movement (which is also a development in religious history), Protestant denominational history (which is also a racial history), and contemporary evangelicalism's own unique cultural characteristics.

The civil rights movement relates to the emergence of racial reconciliation within evangelicalism because many (if not most) of the leaders that have propelled the movement were influenced by or themselves products of the civil rights era. Tom Skinner, a black evangelist protégé from Harlem, for example, was profoundly influenced by the Black Power wing of civil rights and used his rhetorical and organizational charisma passionately to confront white evangelical racism. In 1970, as a keynote speaker at an annual gathering of Christian college students from across the U.S., he shocked participants with a radical address titled, "The U.S. Racial Crisis and World Evangelicalism." In it he deconstructed the elements of white evangelical culture—including U.S. nationalism, fears of miscegenation, class politics, and whites' avoidance of the plight of the inner city— that supported the racist status quo (Gilbreath 2006: 67–70). Skinner died in 1994, but from this speech forward he left a legacy of racial justice efforts inside American evangelicalism. As evangelical journalist Edward Gilbreath documents, Skinner influenced many, if not most, of the leaders of racial reconciliation and multiracial ministry efforts.

The civil rights movement was also pivotal in shifting the American consensus toward racial egalitarianism (however incompletely achieved). As racism became less acceptable, generations of evangelicals also made attitudinal and institutional adjustments. Racism finally began to be articulated as a "sin" in white evangelical settings. And when anything is identified as a sin in a culture as theologically conservative as evangelicalism, avoiding addressing it becomes much more difficult. With the dawning recognition of this "sin," all but the most intransigent evangelical colleges eventually eliminated discriminatory admissions policies and, so, slowly began to produce racially diverse graduates. Racial progressives and moderates worked over a very long period, particularly in Baptist and Methodist denominations, to persuade their leaders to acknowledge past racial injustices and ongoing structural problems related to race (Newman 2001).

Leaders of parachurch organizations like InterVarsity Christian Fellowship eventually responded to critiques by racial justice advocates inside evangelicalism by beginning to integrate and address racial issues that concerned evangelicals. Later, the Christian men's organization Promise Keepers (PK), whose founder Bill McCartney pursued an early vision of multiracial organization, became probably the most influential parachurch group in the reconciliation movement. PK not only integrated its own staff and board but also built racial reconciliation into its core mission and trained participants to start reconciliation initiatives in their local church communities (Kehrein and Washington 1997). The evangelical music industry was challenged by artists of color to address cultural and racial biases embedded in its signing and promotion policies. Finally, other whites, who testified to being influenced by the civil rights movement, began either to partner with pastors of color to build "reconciliation churches" or to invest their energies in multiracial ministries.

All of these latter developments reflect generational changes that occurred in the aftermath of the civil rights movement. Today white evangelicals report drastically more progressive attitudes about racism than in the past (although as Smith and Emerson (2000) report, they still tend to rely on a theological "tool kit" that reads race as a problem of individual attitudes rather than systemic or institutionalized inequalities). But the civil rights movement alone did not create these shifts. Rather, such shifts could not occur until evangelicals began to engage with the long racial history inside their religious communities.

Conclusion

Even this cursory application of the religious racial traditions framework reveals that, consistently and foundationally, diverse religious traditions have intertwined with white supremacist and racial justice traditions. At the same time, competing racial projects have fractured, and united, religious communities in politically and culturally significant ways. The changes occurring in evangelical race relations today not only represent an important turnabout in American religious history, they also are beginning, and I believe will continue, to shape American politics more broadly. Short-term, religion-based, cross-racial alliances may lead to longer-term coalitions and even gradual—or given the right circumstances, dramatic—shifts in partisan attachments. Either way, as theologically conservative Christians begin to overcome the racial obstacles that have long divided them to embrace their religious commonalities, other configurations in American politics, like the civil rights community, the religious right, and religious progressives, stand to have their political assumptions disrupted.

We cannot sufficiently comprehend a phenomenon like this, a development in which racial and religious, cultural and institutional factors are implicated, without an intersectional analysis of American political development. Employing a racial orders framework combined with an understanding of racial traditions in American religion, I have shown how a hybrid religious racial traditions model can best help us interpret these important changes in U.S. history and politics. I look forward to participating in more research at this rich and complex arena of American political culture.

Notes

1 "Evangelical" is an umbrella term describing a cross-denominational spectrum of Protestant Christians whose beliefs emphasize a devotional Biblical study; an emphasis on personal conversion experience; missionary evangelism; and sometimes charismatic spiritual practices. I focus primarily on mainstream (as opposed to fringe sects of) evangelical Protestantism, both for the sake of space and because until the 1940s when Jews and Jehovah's Witnesses (a non-mainstream variant) became major players in church–state relations, it was, and probably remains, the most influential religious force on American political institutions (Kaplan 1989; Ivers 1995; Mazur 1999).

2 A few examples of studies of American racial politics that reflect these tendencies include Perry and Parent (1995), Walton (1994), Goldfield (1997), Gilliam (1975), Persons (2001), Sears et al. (2000), and Carmines and Sniderman (2001), but literally hundreds of studies could be added to this list. Studies of racial politics in the U.S. that do not look at religion have been, until about 2004, more the norm than the exception.

3 Johnny Williams (2003, chapter 1) reviews these kinds of oversights in greater detail.

4 A few examples of work on the religious right that largely omits race include Wuthnow (1988), Greenwalt (1988), Soper (1994), Himmelstein (1990), Snowball (1991), Diamond (1989 and 1995: chapters 7 and 10), Jelen (1991), and Wills (1990).

5 See, e.g., John Green's (2004) national surveys of religion and politics, which document the high rates of religiosity and conservative positions on "moral values" issues. Green's work and the Pew Forum for Religion in Public Life continue to be groundbreakers in this area.

6 As but one indication of this absence, the bibliographies listed on David Robertson's (2006) American Political Development website under the titles "religion" and "race" reveal scant crossover. Of 70 titles on the religion list, for instance, only 4 refer to race in the title and 3 of these consider religious organizational resources in the civil rights movement.

7 "Readers will find that our definition is heavily weighted toward political institutions. . . . A definition that references authority, in both its formal aspects and practical operations, provides a reliable empirical indicator of political development without closing off further debate about what factors might explain development as it occurs" (Orren and Skowronek 2004: xi).

8 We must continue asking the perpetual feminist question: where exactly does political space end?

9 Orren and Skowronek (2004: 146) note that "Leaving aside the controls churches exercise over their members . . . throughout the better part of their history, American clergy and churches have exercised all-but-complete control in diverse settings over nonmembers." Some examples they cite are orphanages, Indian reservations, and public schools.

10 In summarizing their church–state analysis, Orren and Skowronek (2004: 152) acknowledge a possible relationship *between* race and religion, recognizing that "race rather than religion might lay at the root" of the southern backlash that helped reinvigorate the order of religion in the 1970s. However, they ultimately conclude that despite the appeal of Christian political influence in the South, evangelicals' entry into politics was a phenomenon "independent" of race, spurred by Carter's rise in an election when most Southern Baptist ministers still identified as Democrats (152).

11 Jews' beliefs and blood, many Christians asserted, rendered them impossible to convert and therefore *permanently* inferior and second-class (c.f. Fredrickson 2002: chapter 1).

12 This is not to imply that Christianity in African-American communities did not sometimes serve as an obstacle to black liberation (Reed 1986).

13 This tends to be true for whites in general. See Steyn (2001) and Bush (2004).

14 Although Winant's (2004) framework illuminates some ideological attachments that impede conservative whites' ability to understand racial justice as a set of systemic objectives rather than individual prejudices, he identifies no "white racial project" that effectively captures the kind of cross-racial initiatives I have described.

Bibliography

Primary sources

Brown v. Board of Education of Topeka (1954) 347 U.S. 483.

Skinner, T. (1970) "The U.S. Racial Crisis and World Evangelicalism," delivered at *InterVarsity Christian Fellowship's* student mission convention *Urbana 70*. Online. Available: <http://www.urbana.org/_articles.cfm?RecordId=185> (accessed September 16, 2007).

References and secondary sources

Ammerman, N. (1990) *Baptist Battles: Social Change and Religious Conflict in the Southern Baptist Convention*, New Brunswick, NJ: Rutgers University Press.

Anderson, D.A. (2004) *Multicultural Ministry: Finding Your Church's Unique Rhythm*, Grand Rapids, MI: Willow Creek Association.

Barkun, M. (1994) *Religion and the Racist Right: The Origins of the Christian Identity Movement*, Chapel Hill: University of North Carolina Press.

Bartowski, J.P. and Regis, H.A. (2003) *Charitable Choices: Religion, Race, and Poverty in the Post-Welfare Era*, New York: New York University Press.

Bensel, R.F. (2000) *The Political Economy of American Industrialization, 1877–1900*, Cambridge: Cambridge University Press.

Boles, J.B. (ed.) (1988) *Masters & Slaves in the House of the Lord: Race and Religion in the American South 1740–1870*, Louisville: University Press of Kentucky.

Bush, M. (2004) *Breaking the Code of Good Intentions: Everyday Forms of Whiteness*, Lanham, MD: Rowman & Littlefield.

Carmines, E.G. and Sniderman, P.M. (2001) "The Future of Racial Politics: Beyond Fatalism," in W. Crotty (ed.) *The State of Democracy in America*, Washington, DC: Georgetown University Press.

Carwardine, R. (1993) *Evangelicals and Party Politics in Antebellum America*, New Haven, CT: Yale University Press.

Christerson, B., Emerson, M.O., and Edwards, K.L. (2005) *Against All Odds: The Struggle for Racial Integration in Religious Organizations*, New York: New York University Press.

Dailey, J. (2004) "Sex, Segregation, and the Sacred after Brown," *Journal of American History*, 91: 119–144.

Deloria, V., Jr. and Cadwalader, S.L. (eds) (1984) *The Aggressions of Civilization: Federal Indian Policy Since the 1880s*, Philadelphia, PA: Temple University Press.

Diamond, S. (1989) *Spiritual Warfare: The Politics of the Christian Right*, Boston, MA: South End Press.

—— (2000) *Not by Politics Alone: The Enduring Influence of the Christian Right*, New York: Guilford Press.

—— (1995) *Roads to Dominion: Right-wing Movements and Political Power in the United States*, New York: Guilford Press.

Du Bois, W.E.B. (1903) *The Souls of Black Folk*, Chicago: A.C. McClurg & Co.

Edsall, T.B. and Edsall, M. (1992) *Chain Reaction: The Impact of Race, Rights, and Taxes on American Politics*, New York: Norton.

Emerson, M.O. (2006) *People of the Dream: Multiracial Congregations in the United States*, Princeton, NJ: Princeton University Press.

Fredrickson, G.M. (2002) *Racism: A Short History*, Princeton, NJ: Princeton University Press.

Frymer, P. (1999) *Uneasy Alliances: Race and Party Competition in America*, Princeton, NJ: Princeton University Press.

Gilbreath, E. (2006) *Reconciliation Blues: A Black Evangelical's Inside View of White Christianity*, Downers Grove, IL: InterVarsity Press.

Gilliam, R.E., Jr. (1975) *Black Political Development: An Advocacy Analysis*, Port Washington, NY: Kennicat Press.

Glaude, E. (2000) *Exodus! Religion, Race, and Nation in Early Nineteenth-Century Black America*, Chicago: University of Chicago Press.

Goldenberg, D.M. (2005) *The Curse of Ham: Race and Slavery in Early Judaism, Christianity, and Islam (Jews, Christians, and Muslims from the Ancient to the Modern World)*, new edn, Princeton, NJ: Princeton University Press.

Goldfield, M. (1997) *The Color of Politics: Race and the Mainsprings of American Politics*, New York: New Press.

Gordon, S.B. (2002) *The Mormon Question: Polygamy and Constitutional Conflict in Nineteenth Century America*, Chapel Hill: University of North Carolina Press.

Grady, J.L. (1994) "Pentecostals renounce racism," *Christianity Today Magazine*, December 12: 58.

Green, J.C. (2004) "The American Religious Landscape and Politics, 2004," Pew Forum on Religion & Public Life. Online. Available: <http://www.pewforum.org> (accessed September 21, 2007).

Greenwalt, K. (1988) *Religious Convictions and Political Choice*, New York: Oxford University Press.

Harris, F. (1999) *Something Within: Religion in African-American Political Activism*, New York: Oxford University Press.

Hartz, L. (1955) *The Liberal Tradition in America*, New York: Harcourt Brace.

Harvey, P. (1997) *Redeeming the South: Religious Cultures and Racial Identities Among Southern Baptists, 1865–1925*, Chapel Hill: University of North Carolina Press.

—— (2005) *Freedom's Coming: Religious Culture and the Shaping of the South from the Civil War through the Civil Rights Era*, Chapel Hill: University of North Carolina Press.

Hattam, V. (1993) *Labor Visions and State Power: The Origins of Business Unionism in the United States*, Princeton, NJ: Princeton University Press.

Himmelstein, J.L. (1990) *To the Right: The Transformation of American Conservatism*, Berkeley and Los Angeles: University of California Press.

"History in the Making: Billy Graham Had a Dream" (1995) *Christian History & Biography*, 47, July 1. Online. Available <http://www.ctlibrary.com/4108> (accessed September 21, 2007).

Horsman, R. (1981) *Race and Manifest Destiny*, Cambridge: Harvard University Press.

Howard-Pitney, D. (2005) *The African American Jeremiad: Appeals for Justice in America*, Philadelphia, PA: Temple University Press, revised edn.

Ivers, G. (1995) *To Build a Wall: American Jews and the Separation of Church and State*, Charlottesville: University Press of Virginia.

Jacobson, M.F. (1998) *Whiteness of a Different Color: European Immigrants and the Alchemy of Race*, Cambridge, MA: Harvard University Press.

Jelen, T.G. (1991) *The Political Mobilization of Religious Belief*, New York: Praeger.

Jordan, W. (1974) *The White Man's Burden*, New York: Oxford University Press.

Kaplan, W. (1989) *State and Salvation: The Jehovah's Witnesses and Their Fight for Civil Rights*, Toronto: University of Toronto Press.

Kehrein, G. and Washington, R., with King, C.V. (1997) *Break Down the Walls Workbook: Experiencing Biblical Reconciliation and Unity*, Chicago: Moody Press.

King, D.S. and Smith. R. (2005) "Racial Orders in American Political Development," *American Political Science Review*, 99: 75–92.

King, M.L., Jr. ([1963] 1964) "Letter from the Birmingham City Jail," *Christian Century*, 80: 767–73.

Kramnick, I. and Moore, R.L. (1997) *The Godless Constitution: The Case Against Religious Correctness*, New York: W.W. Norton & Company.

Lincoln, C.E. (1999) *Race, Religion, and the Continuing American Dilemma*, New York: Hill and Wang.

Luker, R.E. (1991) *The Social Gospel in Black and White: American Racial Reform 1885–1912*, Chapel Hill: The University of North Carolina Press.

McAdam, D. (1982) *Political Process and the Development of Black Insurgency, 1930–1970*, Chicago: University of Chicago Press

MacRobert, I. (1988) *The Black Roots and White Racism of Early Pentecostalism in the USA*, New York: St. Martin's Press.

Marty, M. (ed.) (1990) *Religion & American Politics: From the Colonial Period to the 1980s*, New York: Oxford University Press.

Mazur, E.M. (1999) *The Americanization of Religious Minorities: Confronting the Constitutional Order*, Baltimore, MD: Johns Hopkins University Press.

Mazur, E.M. (2004) *The Americanization of Religious Minorities: Confronting the Constitutional Order*, new edn, Baltimore, MD: Johns Hopkins University Press.

Morone, J. (2003) *Hellfire Nation: The Politics of Sin in American History*, New Haven, CT: Yale University Press.

Morris, A. (1984) *The Origins of the Civil Rights Movement: Black Communities Organizing for Change*, New York: Free Press.

Moyers, B. (n.d.) "Is God Green?" PBS documentary. Online. Available: <http://www.pbs.org/moyers/moyersonamerica/green/index.html> (accessed September 21, 2007).

Newman, M. (2001) *Getting Right with God: Southern Baptists and Desegregation, 1945–1995*, Tuscaloosa: University of Alabama Press.

Novkov, J. (2001) *Constituting Workers, Protecting Women: Gender, Law, and Labor in the Progressive Era and New Deal Year*, Ann Arbor: University of Michigan Press.

Orren, K. and Skowronek, S. (2004) *The Search for American Political Development*, New York: Cambridge University Press.

Ownby, T. (ed.) (2002) *The Role of Ideas in the Civil Rights South*, Jackson: University Press of Mississippi.

Pearce, R. (1967) *Savagism and Civilization: A Study of the Indian and the American Mind*, Baltimore, MD: Johns Hopkins University Press.

Perry, H.L. and Parent, W. (eds) (1995) *Blacks and the American Political System*, Gainesville: University Press of Florida.

Persons, G.A. (ed.) (2001) *The Politics of the Black "Nation": A Twenty-Five-Year Retrospective (National Political Science Review)*, vol. 8, New York: Transaction.

Pew Forum on Religion and Public Life (2006) "Spirit and Power: A 10 Country Survey of Pentecostals." Online. Available: <http://pewforum.org/surveys/pentecostal/> (accessed September 21, 2007).

Reed, A. (1986) *The Jesse Jackson Phenomenon: The Crisis of Purpose in Afro-American Politics*, New Haven, CT: Yale University Press.

Robertson, David. (2006) *American Political Development: A Bibliography for Teaching and Research*. Online. Available: <http://www.umsl.edu/~poldrobe/sy431bib.html)> (accessed September 21, 2007).

Roediger, D. (1991) *The Wages of Whiteness*, New York: Verso Press.

Rosen, R. (2000) *The Jewish Confederates*, Columbia: University of South Carolina Press.

Schweiger, B.B. and Mathews, D.G. (eds) (2004) *Religion in the American South*, Chapel Hill: University of North Carolina Press.

Sears, D.O. and Citrin, J. (1982) *Tax Revolt: Something for Nothing in California*, Cambridge, MA: Harvard University Press.

Sears, D.O., Sidanius, J., and Bobo, L. (eds) (2000) *Racialized Politics: The Debate about Racism in America*, Chicago: University of Chicago Press.

Segers, M.C. and Jelen, T. (1998) *Wall of Separation? Debating the Public Role of Religion*, New York: Rowman & Littlefield.

Skocpol, T., Evans, P.B., and Rueschemeyer, D. (eds) (1985) *Bringing the State Back In*, Cambridge, New York: Cambridge University Press.

Skowronek, S. (1982) *Building a New American State: The Expansion of National Administrative Capacities 1877–1920*, New York: Cambridge University Press.

—— Shapiro, I. and Galvin, D. (eds) (2006) *Rethinking Political Institutions: The Art of the State*, New York: New York University Press.

Smith, C. (1998) *American Evangelicalism: Embattled and Thriving*, Chicago: University of Chicago Press.

Smith, C. and Emerson, M. (2000) *Divided by Faith: Evangelical Religion and the Problem of Race in America*, New York: Oxford University Press.

Smith, R. (1993) "Beyond Tocqueville, Myrdal, and Hartz: The Multiple Traditions in America," *American Political Science Review*, 87: 549–566.

Snowball, D. (1991) *Continuity and Change in the Rhetoric of the Moral Majority*, New York: Praeger.

Soper, C. (1994) *Evangelical Christianity in the United States and Great Britain: Religious Beliefs, Political Choices*, New York: New York University Press.

Sterett, S. (2003) *Public Pensions: Gender and Public Service in the States, 1850–1937*, Ithaca, NY: Cornell University Press.

Steyn, M. (2001) *"Whiteness Just Isn't What it Used to Be": White Identity in a Changing South Africa*, Albany: State University Press of New York.

Stricker, M. (2001) "A New Racial Ideology for the Christian Right? The Meaning(s) of Racial Reconciliation within the Promise Keepers Movement," unpublished thesis, Temple University.

Synan, V. (ed.) (1961) *The Holiness-Pentecostal Movement in the United States*, Grand Rapids, Michigan: William B. Eerdmans Publishing.

Tinker, G.E. (1993) *Missionary Conquest: The Gospel and Native American Cultural Genocide*, Minneapolis, MN: Augsburg Fortress Press.

—— (2004) *Spirit and Resistance: Political Theology and American Indian Liberation*, Minneapolis, MN: Augsburg Fortress Press.

Wadsworth, N. (2007) "New Traditional Marriage Alliances: The Challenge of Moral Multiracial Coalition," *Race/Ethnicity: Multidisciplinary Global Perspectives, Race and Coalition Issue*, Kirwan Institute: Ohio State University.

—— (2008) "Race-ing Faith and Fate: The Jeremiad in Multiracial 'Traditional Marriage' Alliances," *Race/Ethnicity: Multidisciplinary Global Contexts*, 1 (2).

—— (forthcoming) "Ambivalent Miracles: Evangelical Racial Reconciliation Efforts and American Political Culture," unpublished book title.

Walton, Jr. H. (1994) *Black Politics and Black Political Behavior: A Linkage Analysis*, Westport, CT: Praeger.

West, C. (1993) *Race Matters*, Boston, MA: Beacon Press.

West, C. and Glaude, Jr. E. (eds) (2003) *African American Religious Thought: An Anthology*, Louisville, KY: Westminster John Knox Press.

Williams, J.E. (2003) *African American Religion and the Civil Rights Movement in Arkansas*, Jackson: University Press of Mississippi.

Wills, G. (1990) *Under God: Religion and American Politics*, New York: Simon & Schuster.

Wilson, C. (2005) "Latino Congregations in the Inner City: Agents of Political Mobilization," paper presented at the American Political Science Association Conference, Washington, September 2005.

Winant, H. (2004) *The New Politics of Race: Globalism, Difference, Justice*, Minneapolis: University of Minnesota Press.

Wuthnow, R. (1988) *The Restructuring of American Religion*, Princeton, NJ: Princeton University Press.

Yancey, G. (2003) *One Body, One Spirit: Principles of Successful Multiracial Churches*, Downers Grove, IL: InterVarsity Press.

Yi, J. (2002) "God & Karate in the Southside," Ph.D. Dissertation, Political Science, University of Chicago.

Index